D0521173

MARVEL'S THE AVENGERS: AGE OF ULTRON PRELUDE. Contains material originally published in magazine form as MARVEL'S THE AVENGERS #1-2, AVENGERS: AGE OF ULTRON PRELUDE — THIS SCEPTER'D ISLE INFINITE COMIC 1, AVENGERS (1963) #57-58, AVENGERS (1998) #21-22 and AVENGERS (2010) #12.1. First printing 2015. ISBN# 978-0-7851-9355-5. Published by MARVEL WORLDWIDE, INC., a subsidiary of MARVEL ENTERTAINMENT, LLC. OFFICE OF PUBLICATION: 135 West 50th Street, New York, NY 10020. Copyright © 1968, 1999, 2011 and 2015 Marvel Characters, Inc. All rights reserved. All characters featured in this issue and the distinctive names and likenesses thereof, and all related indicia are trademarks of Marvel Characters, Inc. No similarity between any of the names, characters, persons, and/or institutions in this magazine with those of any living or dead person or institution is intended, and any such similarity which may exist is purely coincidental. **Printed in the U.S.A.** ALAN FINE, EVP - Office of the President, Marvel Worldwide, Inc. and EVP & CMO Marvel Characters B.V.: DAN BUCKLEY, Publisher & President - Print, Animation & Digital Divisions; JOE QUESADA, Chief Creative Officer; TOM BREVOORT, SVP of Publishing; DAVID BOGART, SVP of Operations & Procurement, Publishing; C.B. CEBULSKI, SVP of Creator & Content Development; DAVID GABRIEL, SVP Print, Sales & Marketing; JIM O'KEEFE, VP of Operations & Logistics; DAN CARR, Executive Director of Publishing Technology; SUSAN CRESPI, Editorial Operations Manager; ALEX MORALES, Publishing Operations Manager; STAN LEE, Chairman Emeritus. For information regarding advertising in Marvel Comics or on Marvel.com, please contact Niza Disla, Director of Marvel Partnerships, at ndisla@marvel.com. For Marvel subscription inquiries, please call 800-217-9158. **Manufactured between 1/9/2015 and 2/16/2015 by R.R. DONNELLEY, INC., SALEM, VA, USA.**

10 9 8 7 6 5 4 3 2 1

STRATEGIC HOMELAND INTERVENTION ENFORCEMENT

LOGISTICS DIVISION

MARVEL'S THE AVENGERS

STORY BY **ZAK PENN & JOSS WHEDON**

SCREENPLAY BY **JOSS WHEDON**

WRITER **WILL CORONA PILGRIM**   PENCILER, #1 & #2, PP. 1-3, 5-8, 10-11 **JOE BENNETT**   PENCILER, #2, PP. 4, 9, 12-20 **AGUSTIN PADILLA**

INKER, #1 & #2, PP. 1-3, 5-8, 10-11 **MÁRCIO LOERZER BENNETT**   INKER, #2, PP. 4, 9, 12-20 **AGUSTIN PADILLA**   COLORIST **JAY DAVID RAMOS**

LETTERER **VC'S CLAYTON COWLES**   ASSISTANT EDITOR **MARK BASSO**   EDITOR **BILL ROSEMANN**

MARVEL STUDIOS

SVP PRODUCTION & DEVELOPMENT **JEREMY LATCHAM**   PRESIDENT **KEVIN FEIGE**

THIS SCEPTER'D ISLE

WRITER **WILL CORONA PILGRIM**   STORYBORAD ARTISTS **GEOFFO & MAST**   PENCILER **WELLINTON ALVES**

INKER **MANNY CLARK**   COLORIST **JAY DAVID RAMOS**   LETTERER **VC'S CLAYTON COWLES**

PRODUCTION **ARLIN ORTIZ**   PROCUTION MANAGER **TIM SMITH 3**   CONSULTING EDITOR **EMILY SHAW**   EDITORS **BILL ROSEMANN & MARK BASSO**

LETTERER **VC'S CLAYTON COWLES**   ASSISTANT EDITOR **MARK BASSO**   EDITOR **BILL ROSEMANN**

AVENGERS CREATED BY STAN LEE & JACK KIRBY

COLLECTION EDITOR **JENNIFER GRÜNWALD**   ASSISTANT EDITOR **SARAH BRUNSTAD**   ASSOCIATE MANAGING EDITOR **ALEX STARBUCK**   EDITOR, SPECIAL PROJECTS **MARK D. BEAZLEY**

SENIOR EDITOR, SPECIAL PROJECTS **JEFF YOUNGQUIST**   SVP PRINT, SALES & MARKETING **DAVID GABRIEL**   EDITOR IN CHIEF **AXEL ALONSO**   CHIEF CREATIVE OFFICER **JOE QUESADA**   PUBLISHER **DAN BUCKLEY**   EXECUTIVE PRODUCER **ALAN FINE**

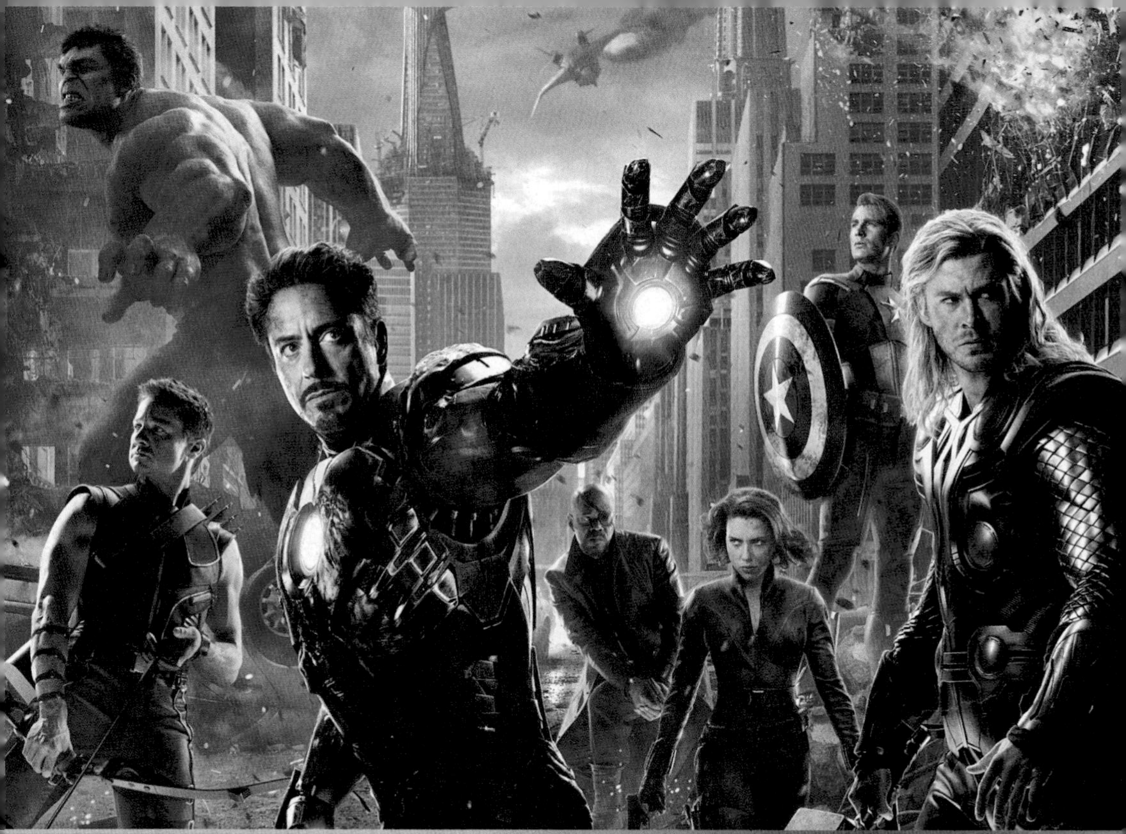

MARVEL'S THE AVENGERS

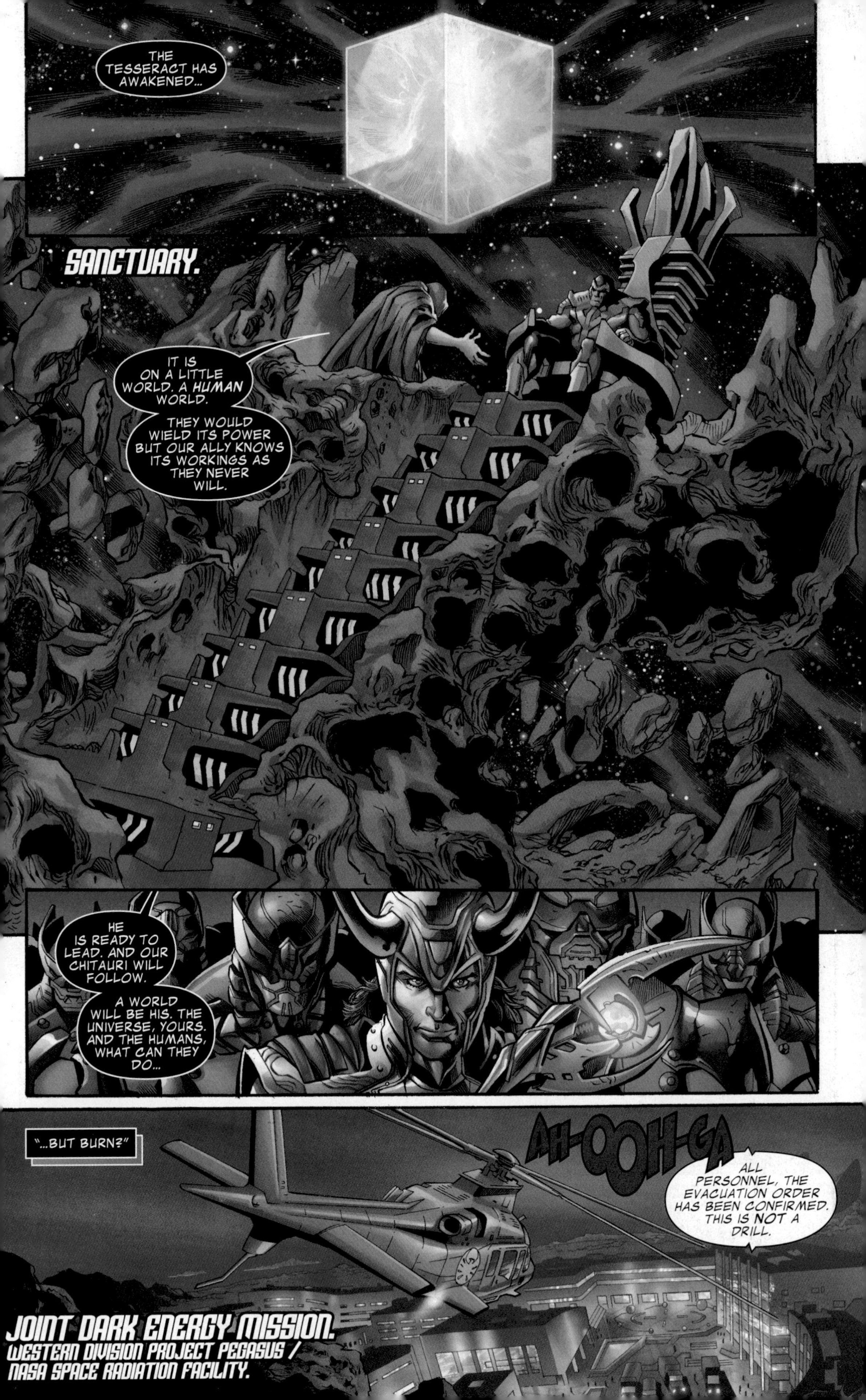

THE TESSERACT HAS AWAKENED...
SANCTUARY.
IT IS ON A LITTLE WORLD. A HUMAN WORLD.
THEY WOULD WIELD ITS POWER BUT OUR ALLY KNOWS ITS WORKINGS AS THEY NEVER WILL.
HE IS READY TO LEAD. AND OUR CHITAURI WILL FOLLOW.
A WORLD WILL BE HIS. THE UNIVERSE, YOURS. AND THE HUMANS, WHAT CAN THEY DO...
"...BUT BURN?"
AH-OOH-GA
ALL PERSONNEL, THE EVACUATION ORDER HAS BEEN CONFIRMED. THIS IS NOT A DRILL.
JOINT DARK ENERGY MISSION.
WESTERN DIVISION PROJECT PEGASUS / NASA SPACE RADIATION FACILITY.

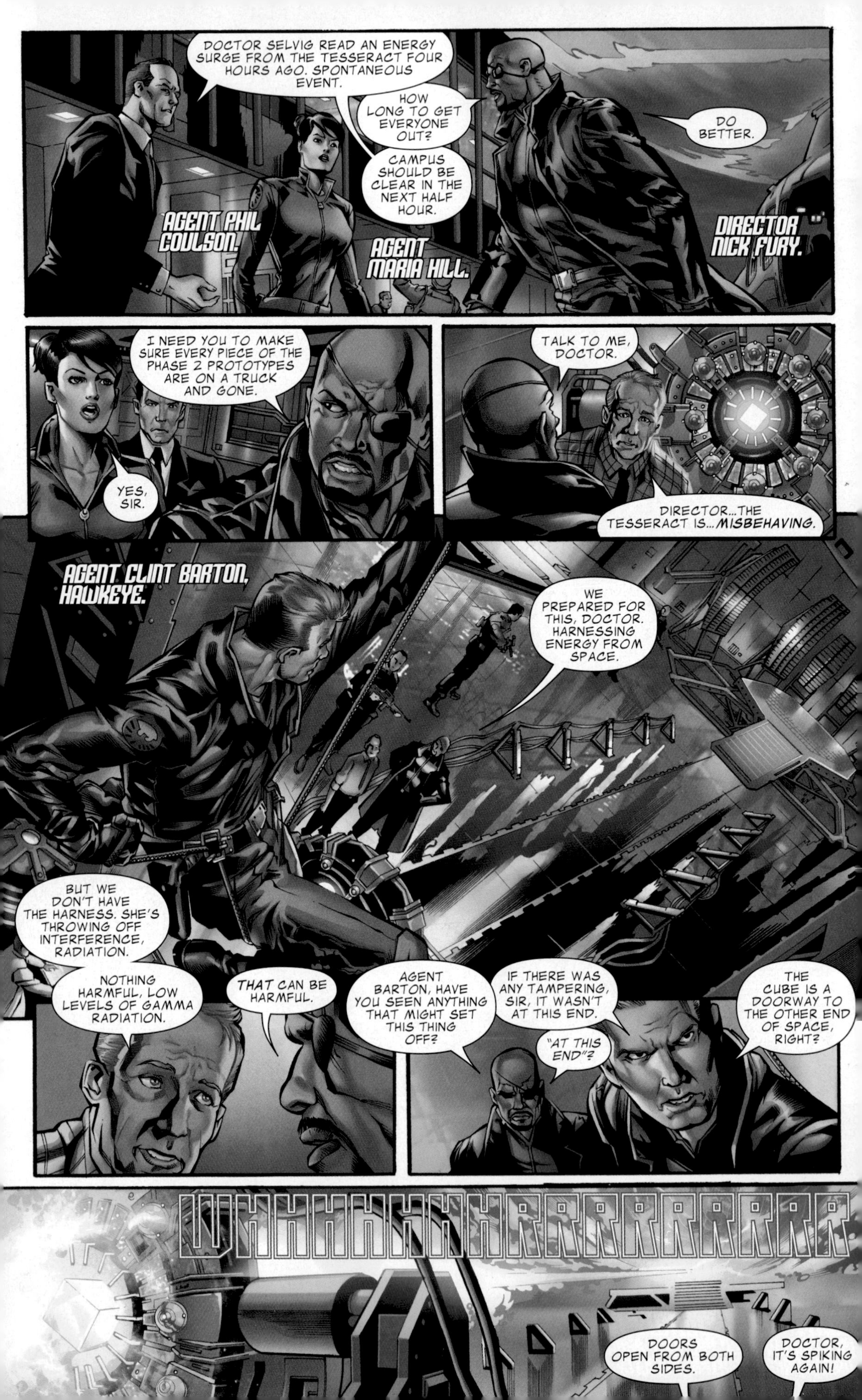
DOCTOR SELVIG READ AN ENERGY SURGE FROM THE TESSERACT FOUR HOURS AGO. SPONTANEOUS EVENT.
HOW LONG TO GET EVERYONE OUT?
CAMPUS SHOULD BE CLEAR IN THE NEXT HALF HOUR.
DO BETTER.
AGENT PHIL COULSON.
AGENT MARIA HILL.
DIRECTOR NICK FURY.
I NEED YOU TO MAKE SURE EVERY PIECE OF THE PHASE 2 PROTOTYPES ARE ON A TRUCK AND GONE.
YES, SIR.
TALK TO ME, DOCTOR.
DIRECTOR...THE TESSERACT IS...MISBEHAVING.
AGENT CLINT BARTON, HAWKEYE.
WE PREPARED FOR THIS, DOCTOR. HARNESSING ENERGY FROM SPACE.
BUT WE DON'T HAVE THE HARNESS. SHE'S THROWING OFF INTERFERENCE, RADIATION.
NOTHING HARMFUL, LOW LEVELS OF GAMMA RADIATION.
THAT CAN BE HARMFUL.
AGENT BARTON, HAVE YOU SEEN ANYTHING THAT MIGHT SET THIS THING OFF?
IF THERE WAS ANY TAMPERING, SIR, IT WASN'T AT THIS END.
"AT THIS END"?
THE CUBE IS A DOORWAY TO THE OTHER END OF SPACE, RIGHT?
WHHHHHHHHRRRRRRRRRR
DOORS OPEN FROM BOTH SIDES.
DOCTOR, IT'S SPIKING AGAIN!

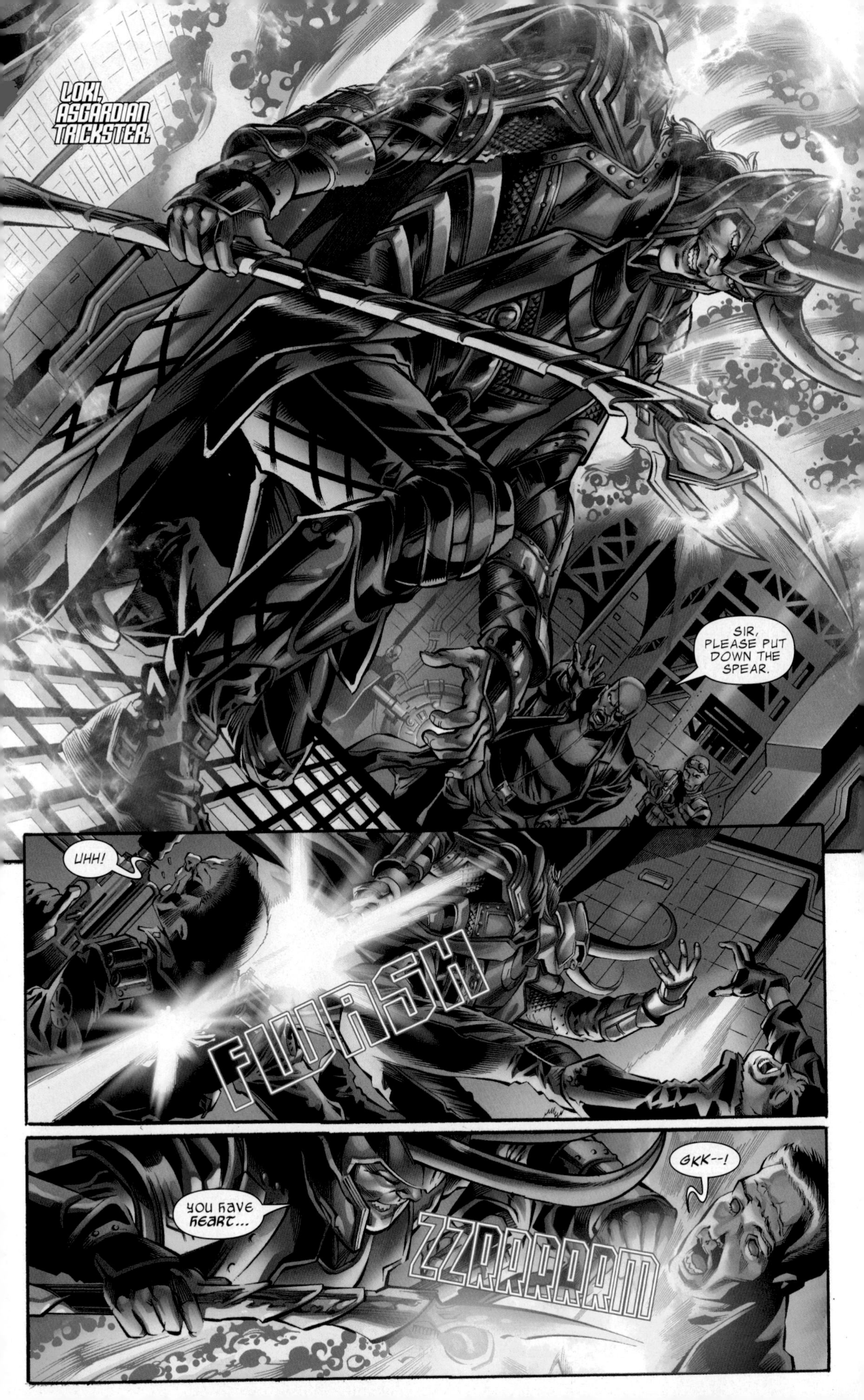
LOKI, ASGARDIAN TRICKSTER.
SIR, PLEASE PUT DOWN THE SPEAR.
UHH!
FWASH
YOU HAVE HEART...
GKK--!
ZZRRRRRAM

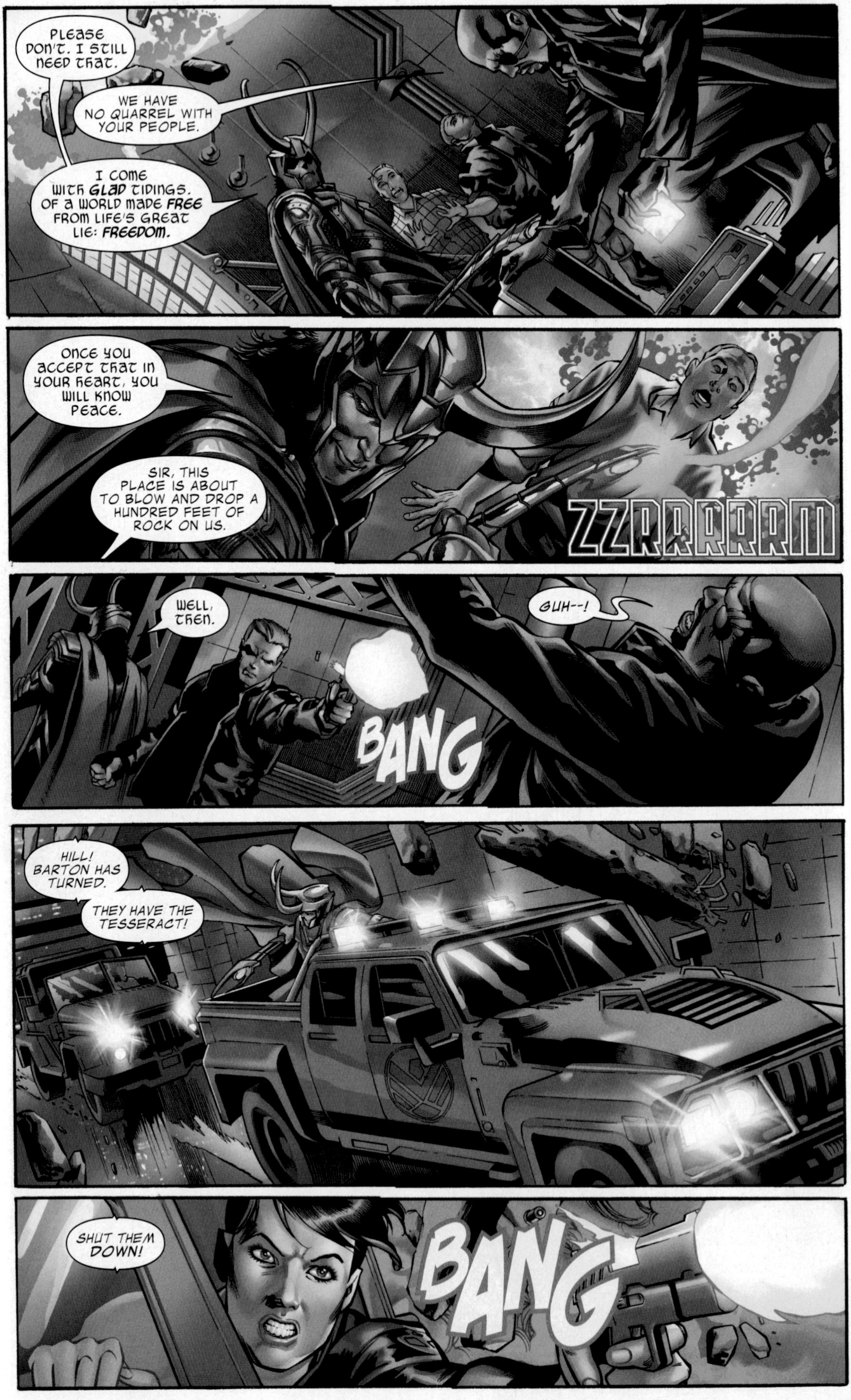
PLEASE DON'T. I STILL NEED THAT.
WE HAVE NO QUARREL WITH YOUR PEOPLE.
I COME WITH **GLAD** TIDINGS. OF A WORLD MADE **FREE** FROM LIFE'S GREAT LIE: **FREEDOM.**
ONCE YOU ACCEPT THAT IN YOUR HEART, YOU WILL KNOW PEACE.
SIR, THIS PLACE IS ABOUT TO BLOW AND DROP A HUNDRED FEET OF ROCK ON US.
ZZRRRRRM
WELL, THEN.
GUH--!
BANG
HILL! BARTON HAS TURNED.
THEY HAVE THE TESSERACT!
SHUT THEM **DOWN!**
BANG

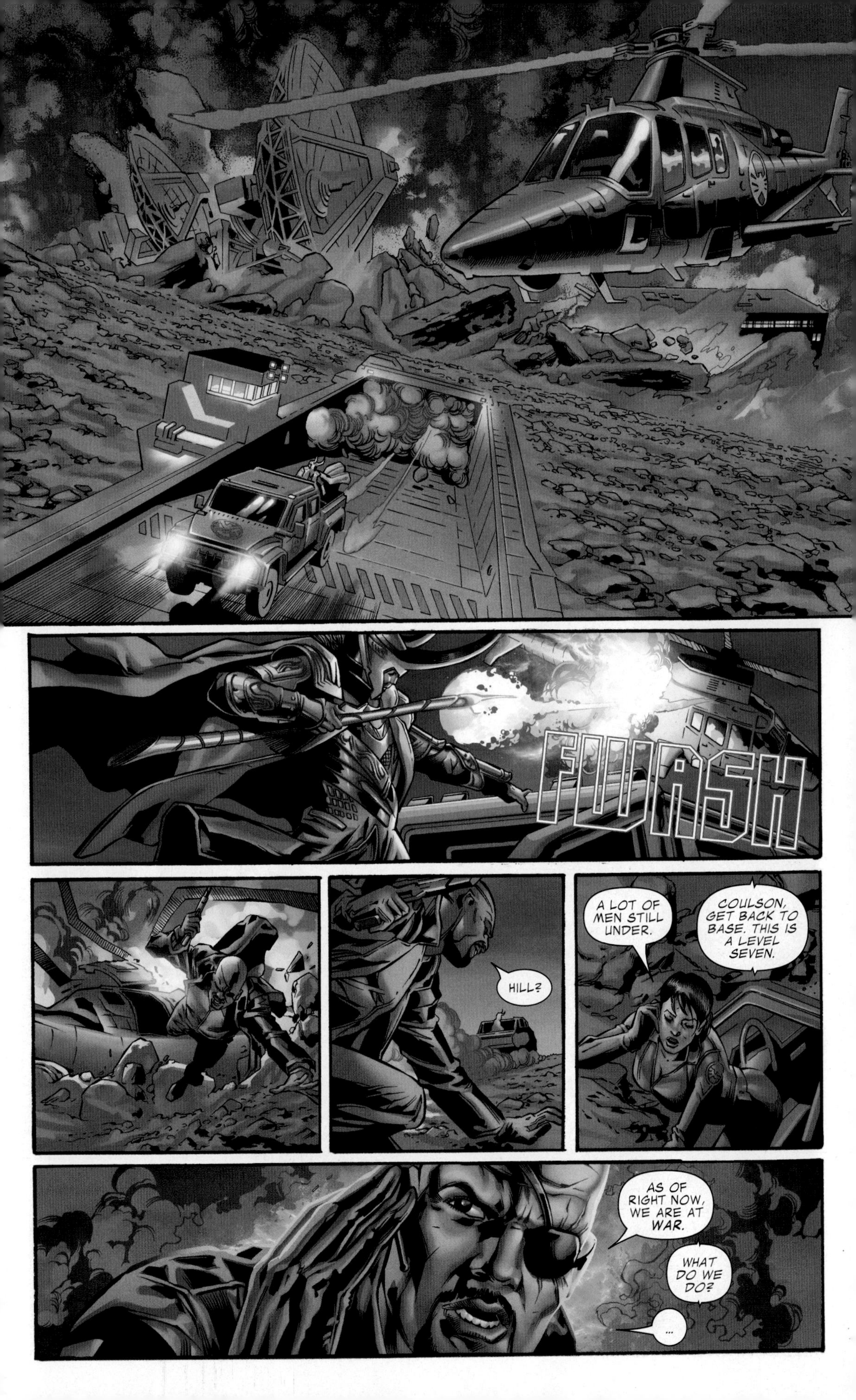
FWASH
HILL?
A LOT OF MEN STILL UNDER.
COULSON, GET BACK TO BASE. THIS IS A LEVEL SEVEN.
AS OF RIGHT NOW, WE ARE AT WAR.
WHAT DO WE DO?
...

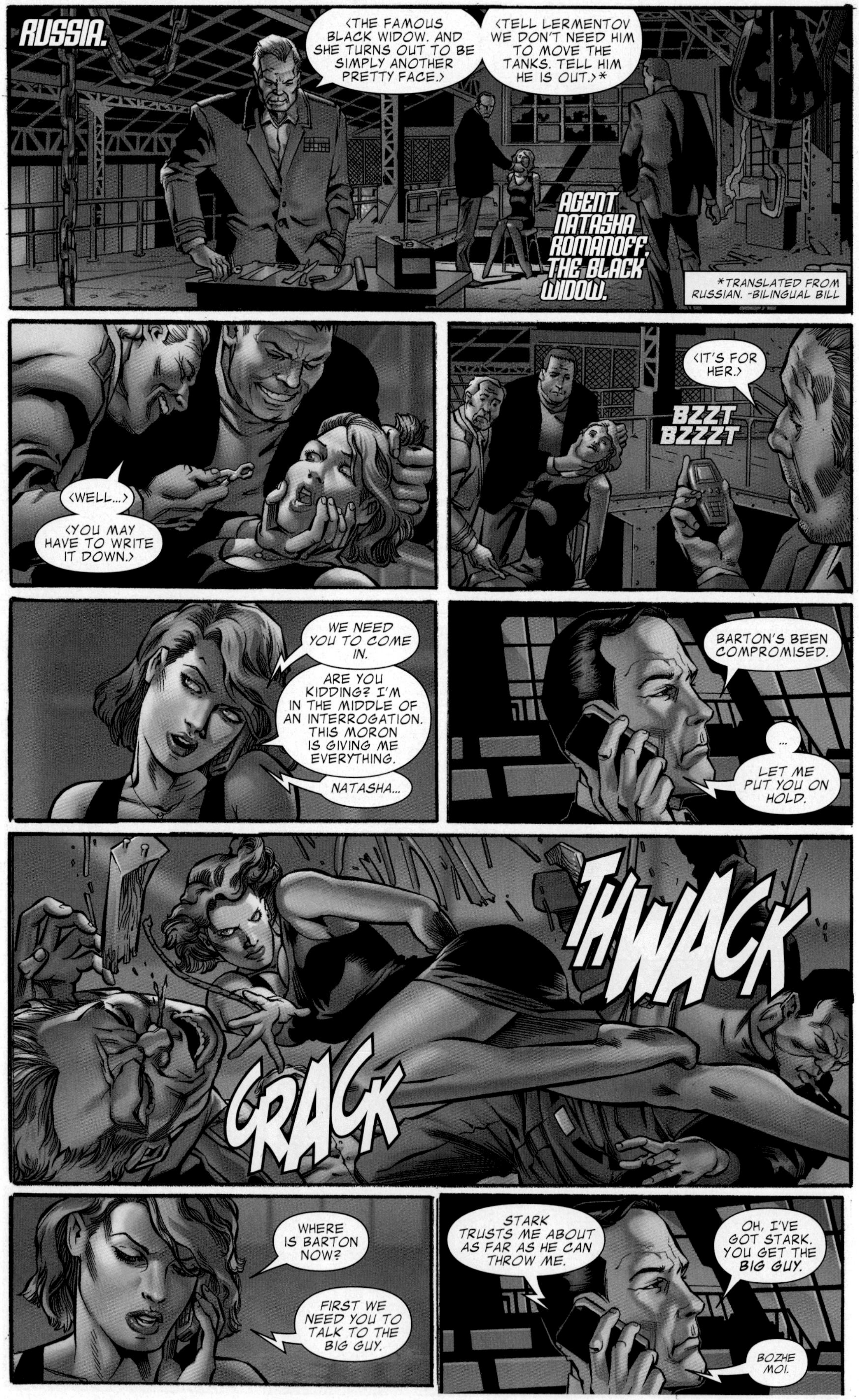
RUSSIA.
<THE FAMOUS BLACK WIDOW. AND SHE TURNS OUT TO BE SIMPLY ANOTHER PRETTY FACE.>
<TELL LERMENTOV WE DON'T NEED HIM TO MOVE THE TANKS. TELL HIM HE IS OUT.>*
AGENT NATASHA ROMANOFF, THE BLACK WIDOW.
*TRANSLATED FROM RUSSIAN. -BILINGUAL BILL
<WELL...>
<YOU MAY HAVE TO WRITE IT DOWN.>
<IT'S FOR HER.>
BZZT BZZZT
WE NEED YOU TO COME IN.
ARE YOU KIDDING? I'M IN THE MIDDLE OF AN INTERROGATION. THIS MORON IS GIVING ME EVERYTHING.
NATASHA...
BARTON'S BEEN COMPROMISED.
...
LET ME PUT YOU ON HOLD.
THWACK
CRACK
WHERE IS BARTON NOW?
FIRST WE NEED YOU TO TALK TO THE BIG GUY.
STARK TRUSTS ME ABOUT AS FAR AS HE CAN THROW ME.
OH, I'VE GOT STARK. YOU GET THE BIG GUY.
BOZHE MOI.

CALCUTTA.

HEY, KID! SLOW DOWN!

BRUCE BANNER, THE HULK.

YOU KNOW, FOR A MAN WHO'S SUPPOSED TO BE AVOIDING STRESS, YOU PICKED A HELL OF A PLACE TO SETTLE.

ARE YOU HERE TO KILL ME? BECAUSE THAT'S NOT GONNA WORK OUT FOR EVERYONE.

MY NAME IS NATASHA ROMANOFF AND I'M HERE ON BEHALF OF S.H.I.E.L.D.

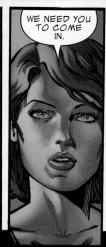

WE NEED YOU TO COME IN.

AND WHAT IF THE "OTHER GUY" SAYS NO?

YOU'VE BEEN MORE THAN A YEAR WITHOUT AN INCIDENT. YOU WANT TO BREAK THAT STREAK?

WELL, I DON'T EVERY TIME GET WHAT I WANT.

THE TESSERACT HAS THE POTENTIAL ENERGY TO WIPE OUT THE PLANET.

WHAT DOES FURY WANT ME TO DO, SWALLOW IT?

IT EMITS A GAMMA SIGNATURE THAT'S TOO WEAK FOR US TO TRACE. HE WANTS YOU TO FIND IT.

FURY DOESN'T WANT ME IN A CAGE?

NO ONE'S GONNA PUT YOU IN A--

STOP LYING TO ME!

CLICK-CLICK

I'M SORRY, THAT WAS MEAN.

STAND DOWN. WE'RE GOOD HERE.

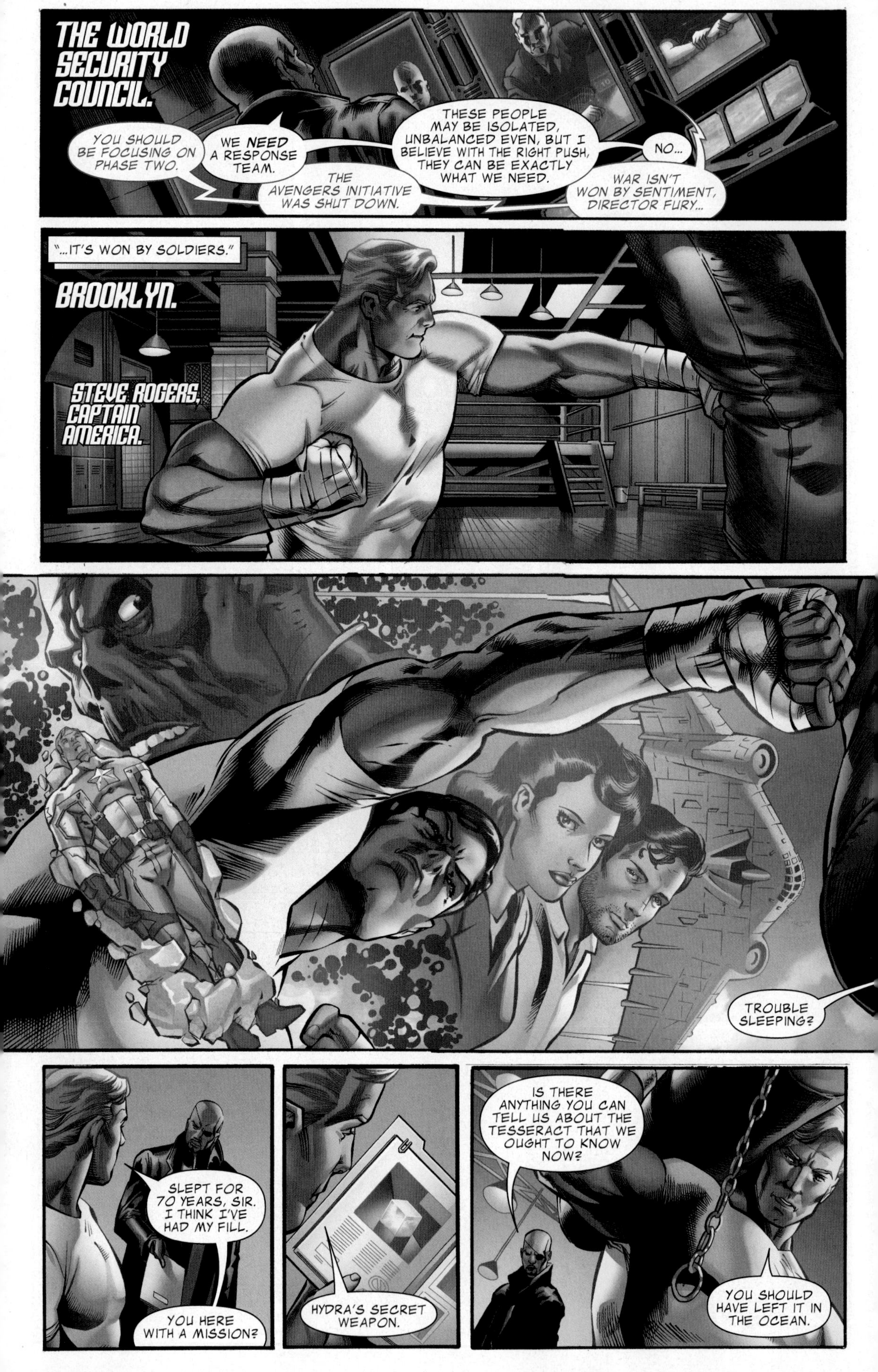
THE WORLD SECURITY COUNCIL.
YOU SHOULD BE FOCUSING ON PHASE TWO.
WE NEED A RESPONSE TEAM.
THE AVENGERS INITIATIVE WAS SHUT DOWN.
THESE PEOPLE MAY BE ISOLATED, UNBALANCED EVEN, BUT I BELIEVE WITH THE RIGHT PUSH, THEY CAN BE EXACTLY WHAT WE NEED.
NO...
WAR ISN'T WON BY SENTIMENT, DIRECTOR FURY...
"...IT'S WON BY SOLDIERS."
BROOKLYN.
STEVE ROGERS, CAPTAIN AMERICA.
TROUBLE SLEEPING?
SLEPT FOR 70 YEARS, SIR. I THINK I'VE HAD MY FILL.
YOU HERE WITH A MISSION?
HYDRA'S SECRET WEAPON.
IS THERE ANYTHING YOU CAN TELL US ABOUT THE TESSERACT THAT WE OUGHT TO KNOW NOW?
YOU SHOULD HAVE LEFT IT IN THE OCEAN.

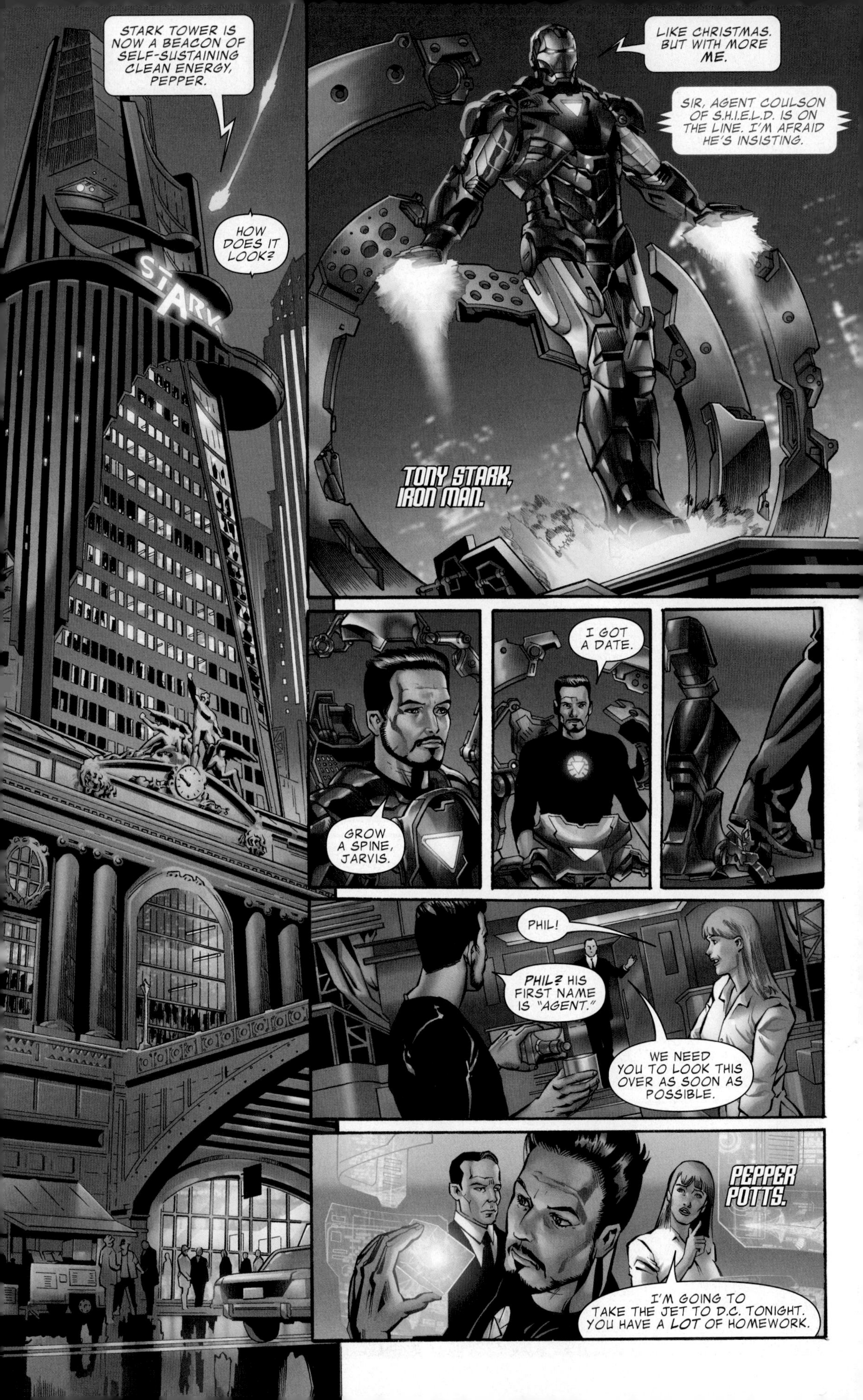
STARK TOWER IS NOW A BEACON OF SELF-SUSTAINING CLEAN ENERGY, PEPPER.
HOW DOES IT LOOK?
STARK
LIKE CHRISTMAS. BUT WITH MORE ME.
SIR, AGENT COULSON OF S.H.I.E.L.D. IS ON THE LINE. I'M AFRAID HE'S INSISTING.
TONY STARK, IRON MAN.
GROW A SPINE, JARVIS.
I GOT A DATE.
PHIL!
PHIL? HIS FIRST NAME IS "AGENT."
WE NEED YOU TO LOOK THIS OVER AS SOON AS POSSIBLE.
PEPPER POTTS.
I'M GOING TO TAKE THE JET TO D.C. TONIGHT. YOU HAVE A LOT OF HOMEWORK.

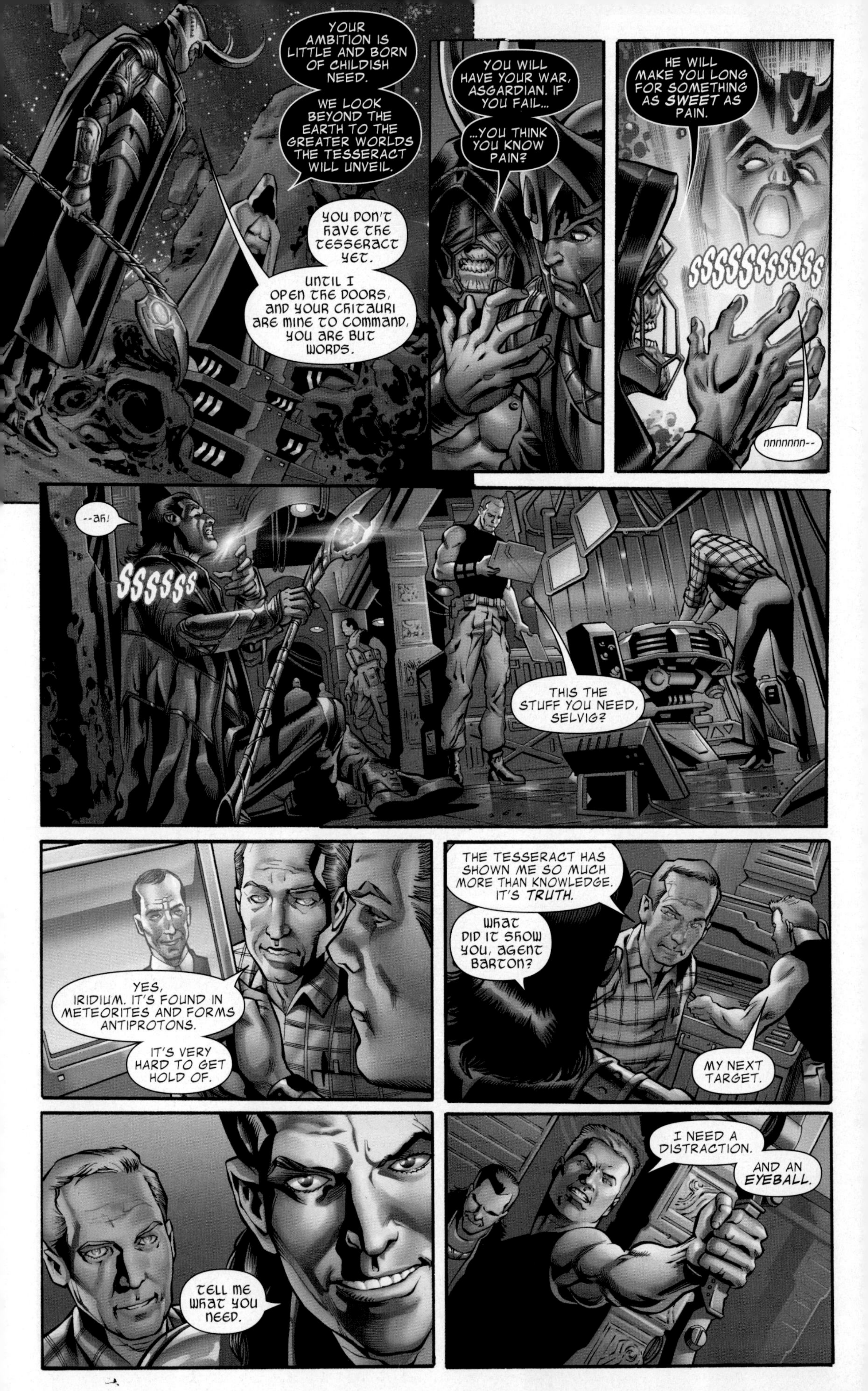
YOUR AMBITION IS LITTLE AND BORN OF CHILDISH NEED.
WE LOOK BEYOND THE EARTH TO THE GREATER WORLDS THE TESSERACT WILL UNVEIL.
YOU DON'T HAVE THE TESSERACT YET.
UNTIL I OPEN THE DOORS, AND YOUR CHITAURI ARE MINE TO COMMAND, YOU ARE BUT WORDS.
YOU WILL HAVE YOUR WAR, ASGARDIAN. IF YOU FAIL...
...YOU THINK YOU KNOW PAIN?
HE WILL MAKE YOU LONG FOR SOMETHING AS SWEET AS PAIN.
SSSSSSSSSSS
nnnnnnn--
--ah!
SSSSSS
THIS THE STUFF YOU NEED, SELVIG?
YES, IRIDIUM. IT'S FOUND IN METEORITES AND FORMS ANTIPROTONS.
IT'S VERY HARD TO GET HOLD OF.
THE TESSERACT HAS SHOWN ME SO MUCH MORE THAN KNOWLEDGE. IT'S TRUTH.
WHAT DID IT SHOW YOU, AGENT BARTON?
MY NEXT TARGET.
TELL ME WHAT YOU NEED.
I NEED A DISTRACTION.
AND AN EYEBALL.

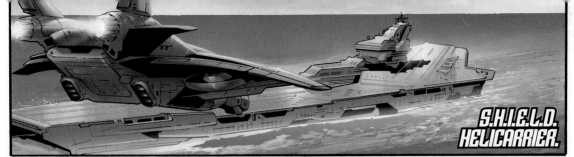

DR. BANNER. WORD IS YOU CAN FIND THE CUBE.

IS THAT THE *ONLY* WORD ON ME?

GENTLEMEN, YOU MIGHT WANT TO STEP INSIDE. IT'S GOING TO GET A LITTLE HARD TO BREATHE.

IS THIS A SUBMARINE?

NO, NO. THIS IS *MUCH* WORSE.

YOU HAVE TO NARROW YOUR FIELD OF SEARCH ON THE GAMMA SIGNATURE.

I'LL ROUGH OUT A TRACKING ALGORITHM, BASIC CLUSTER RECOGNITION. AT LEAST WE COULD RULE OUT A FEW PLACES.

WE'VE GOT A HIT ON THE FACE TRACE FOR LOKI.

CAPTAIN. YOU'RE UP.

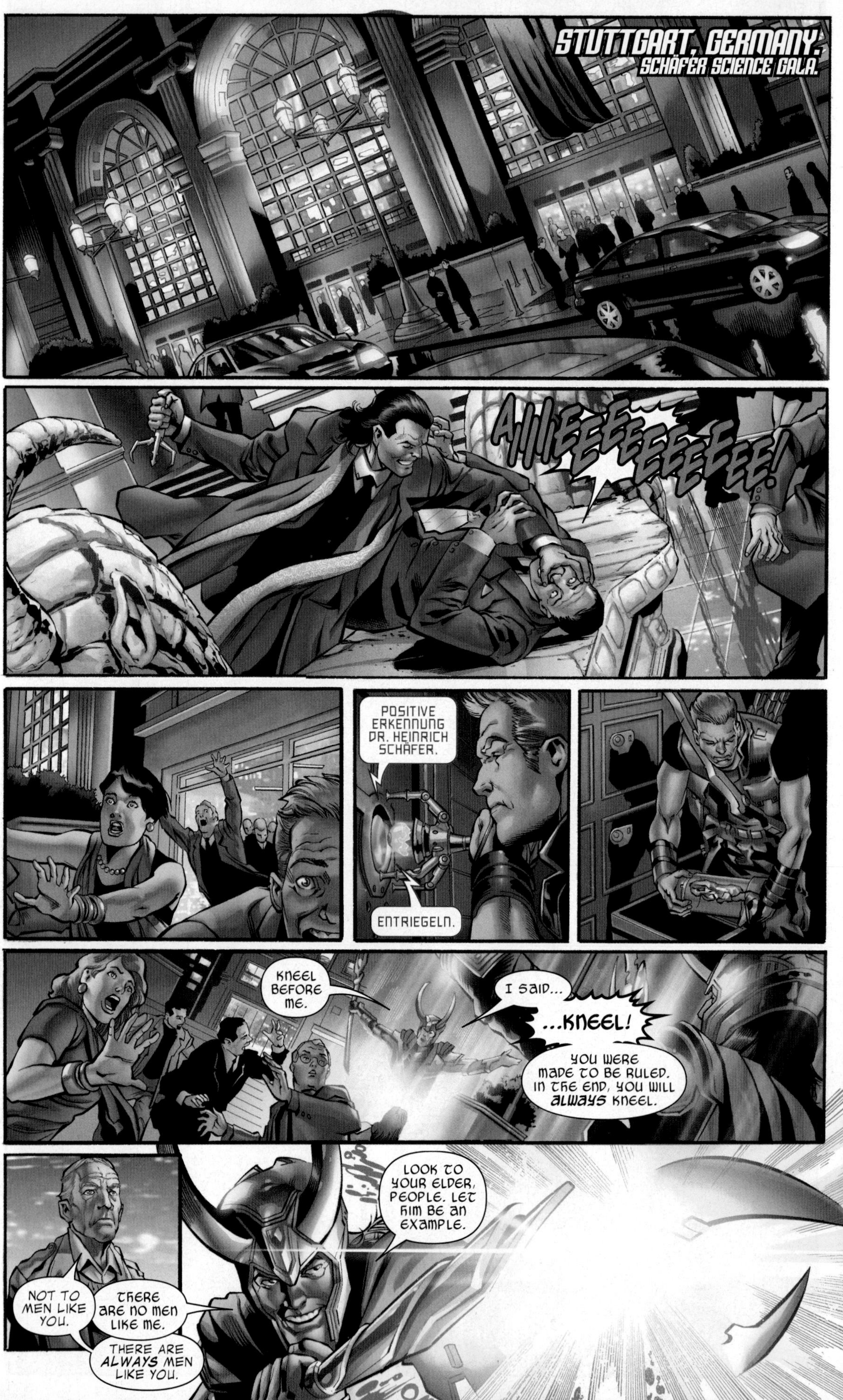
STUTTGART, GERMANY.
SCHÄFER SCIENCE GALA.
AIIIEEEEEEEEEEEE!
POSITIVE ERKENNUNG DR. HEINRICH SCHÄFER.
ENTRIEGELN.
KNEEL BEFORE ME.
I SAID...
...KNEEL!
YOU WERE MADE TO BE RULED. IN THE END, YOU WILL ALWAYS KNEEL.
LOOK TO YOUR ELDER, PEOPLE. LET HIM BE AN EXAMPLE.
NOT TO MEN LIKE YOU.
THERE ARE NO MEN LIKE ME.
THERE ARE ALWAYS MEN LIKE YOU.

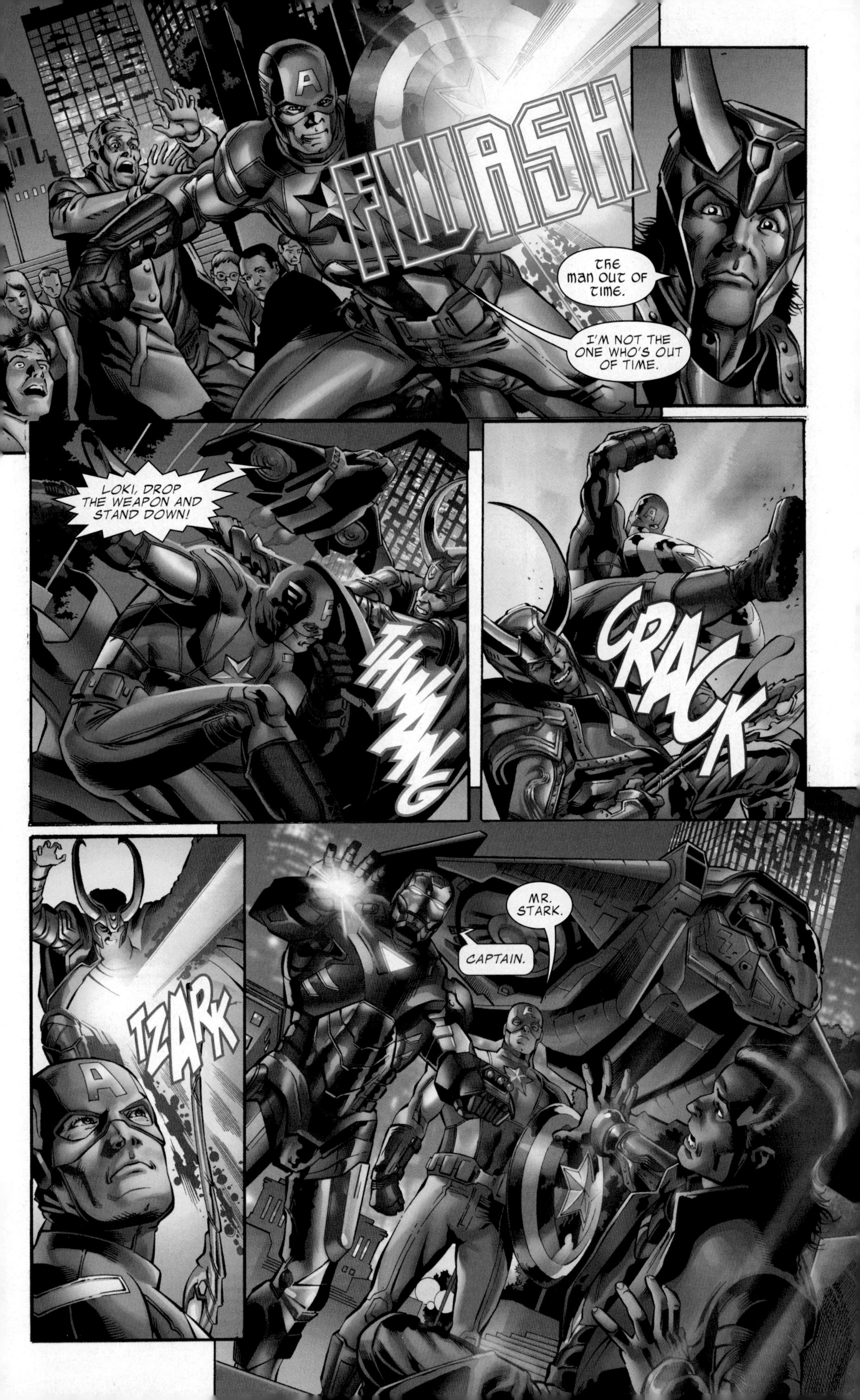
FWASH
THE MAN OUT OF TIME.
I'M NOT THE ONE WHO'S OUT OF TIME.
LOKI, DROP THE WEAPON AND STAND DOWN!
THWANG
CRACK
TZARK
MR. STARK.
CAPTAIN.

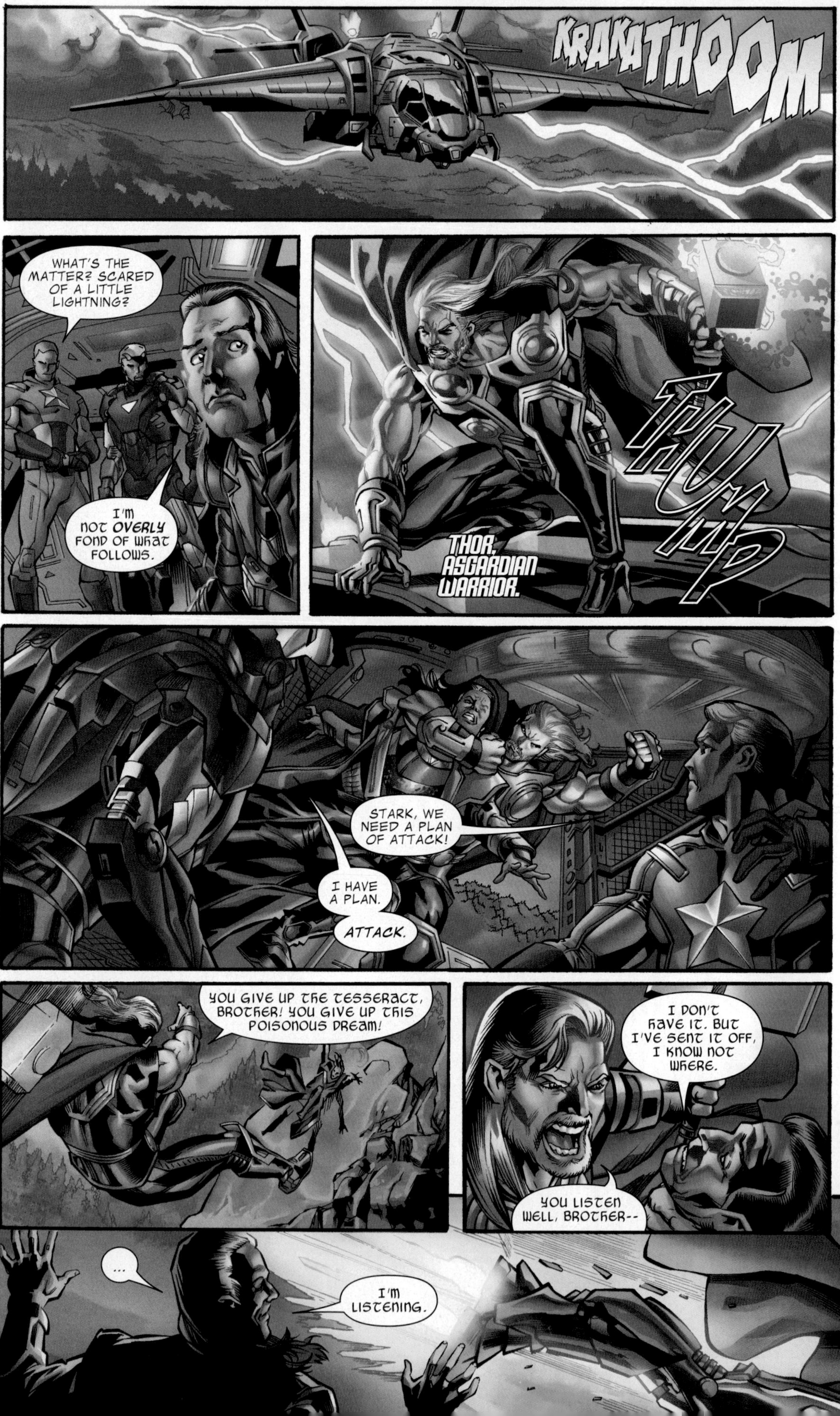
KRAKATHOOM
WHAT'S THE MATTER? SCARED OF A LITTLE LIGHTNING?
I'M NOT OVERLY FOND OF WHAT FOLLOWS.
THUMP
THOR, ASGARDIAN WARRIOR.
STARK, WE NEED A PLAN OF ATTACK!
I HAVE A PLAN.
ATTACK.
YOU GIVE UP THE TESSERACT, BROTHER! YOU GIVE UP THIS POISONOUS DREAM!
I DON'T HAVE IT. BUT I'VE SENT IT OFF, I KNOW NOT WHERE.
YOU LISTEN WELL, BROTHER--
...
I'M LISTENING.

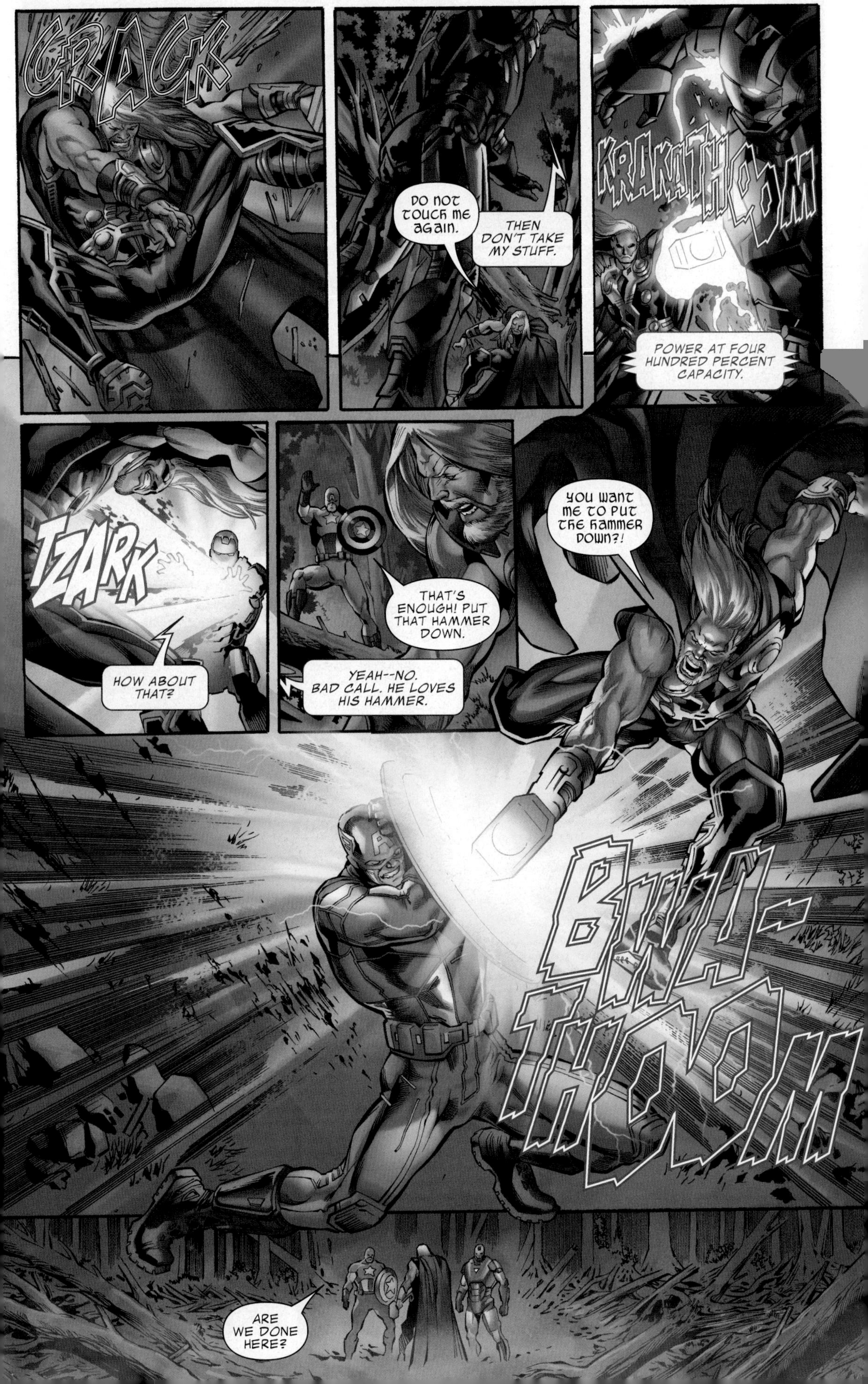
CRACK
DO NOT TOUCH ME AGAIN.
THEN DON'T TAKE MY STUFF.
KRAKATHOOM
POWER AT FOUR HUNDRED PERCENT CAPACITY.
TZARK
HOW ABOUT THAT?
THAT'S ENOUGH! PUT THAT HAMMER DOWN.
YEAH--NO. BAD CALL. HE LOVES HIS HAMMER.
YOU WANT ME TO PUT THE HAMMER DOWN?!
BWO-THOOM
ARE WE DONE HERE?

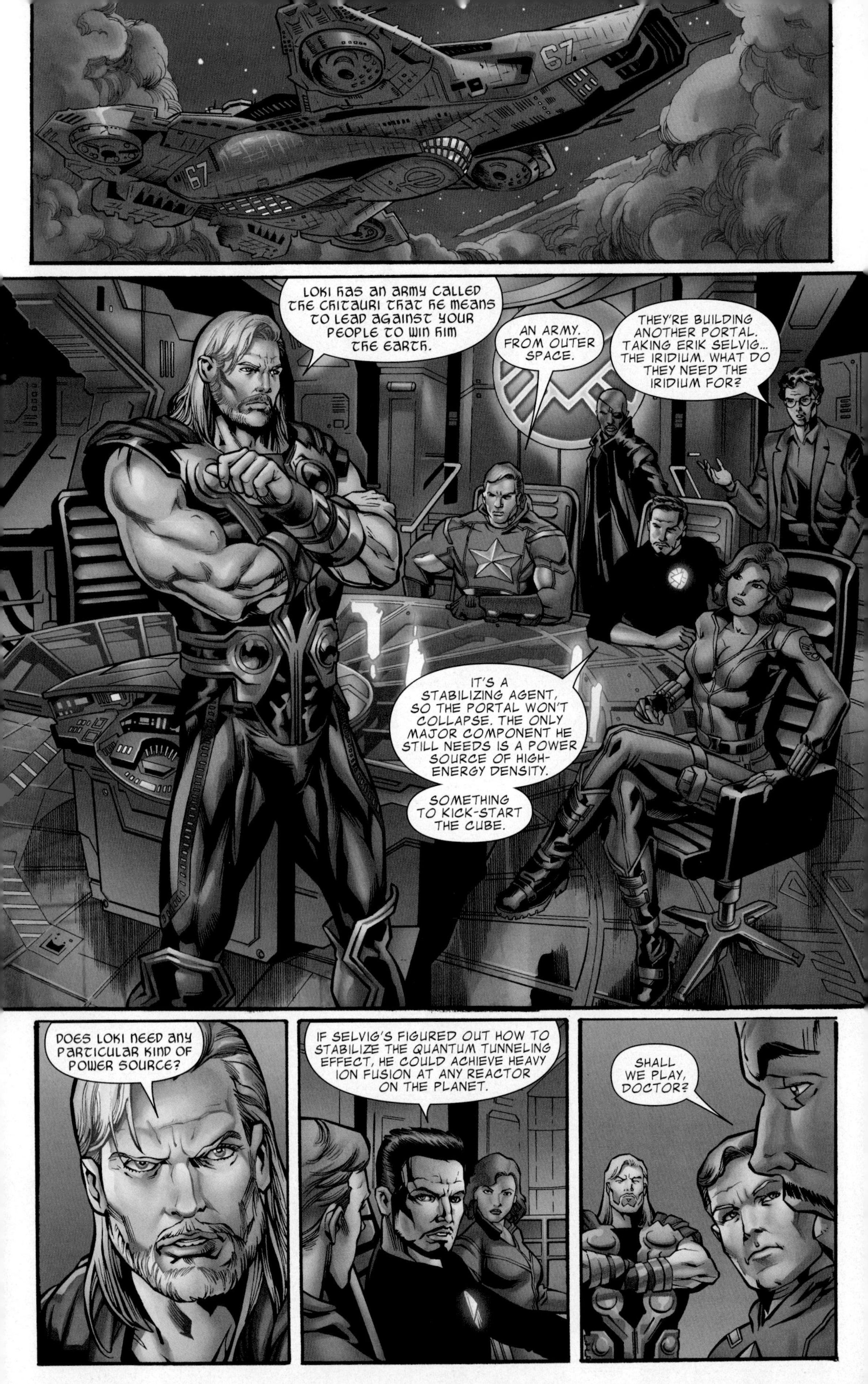
LOKI HAS AN ARMY CALLED THE CHITAURI THAT HE MEANS TO LEAD AGAINST YOUR PEOPLE TO WIN HIM THE EARTH.
AN ARMY. FROM OUTER SPACE.
THEY'RE BUILDING ANOTHER PORTAL. TAKING ERIK SELVIG... THE IRIDIUM. WHAT DO THEY NEED THE IRIDIUM FOR?
IT'S A STABILIZING AGENT, SO THE PORTAL WON'T COLLAPSE. THE ONLY MAJOR COMPONENT HE STILL NEEDS IS A POWER SOURCE OF HIGH-ENERGY DENSITY.
SOMETHING TO KICK-START THE CUBE.
DOES LOKI NEED ANY PARTICULAR KIND OF POWER SOURCE?
IF SELVIG'S FIGURED OUT HOW TO STABILIZE THE QUANTUM TUNNELING EFFECT, HE COULD ACHIEVE HEAVY ION FUSION AT ANY REACTOR ON THE PLANET.
SHALL WE PLAY, DOCTOR?

WHY DID FURY CALL US IN? WHY NOW? I CAN'T DO THE EQUATION UNLESS I HAVE ALL THE VARIABLES.

YOU THINK FURY'S HIDING SOMETHING?

I'M KIND OF THE ONLY NAME IN CLEAN ENERGY RIGHT NOW.

SO WHY DIDN'T S.H.I.E.L.D. BRING STARK IN ON THE TESSERACT PROJECT?

WHAT ARE THEY DOING IN THE ENERGY BUSINESS IN THE FIRST PLACE?

I THINK LOKI'S TRYING TO WIND US UP. THIS IS A MAN WHO MEANS TO START A WAR.

WE HAVE ORDERS AND WE SHOULD FOLLOW THEM.

OF THE PEOPLE IN THIS ROOM, WHICH ONE IS, A: WEARING A SPANGLY OUTFIT, AND B: NOT OF USE?

JUST FIND THE CUBE.

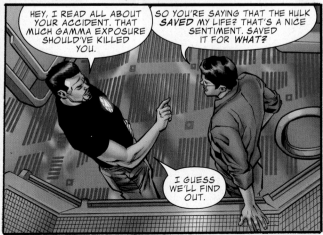

HEY, I READ ALL ABOUT YOUR ACCIDENT. THAT MUCH GAMMA EXPOSURE SHOULD'VE KILLED YOU.

SO YOU'RE SAYING THAT THE HULK SAVED MY LIFE? THAT'S A NICE SENTIMENT. SAVED IT FOR WHAT?

I GUESS WE'LL FIND OUT.

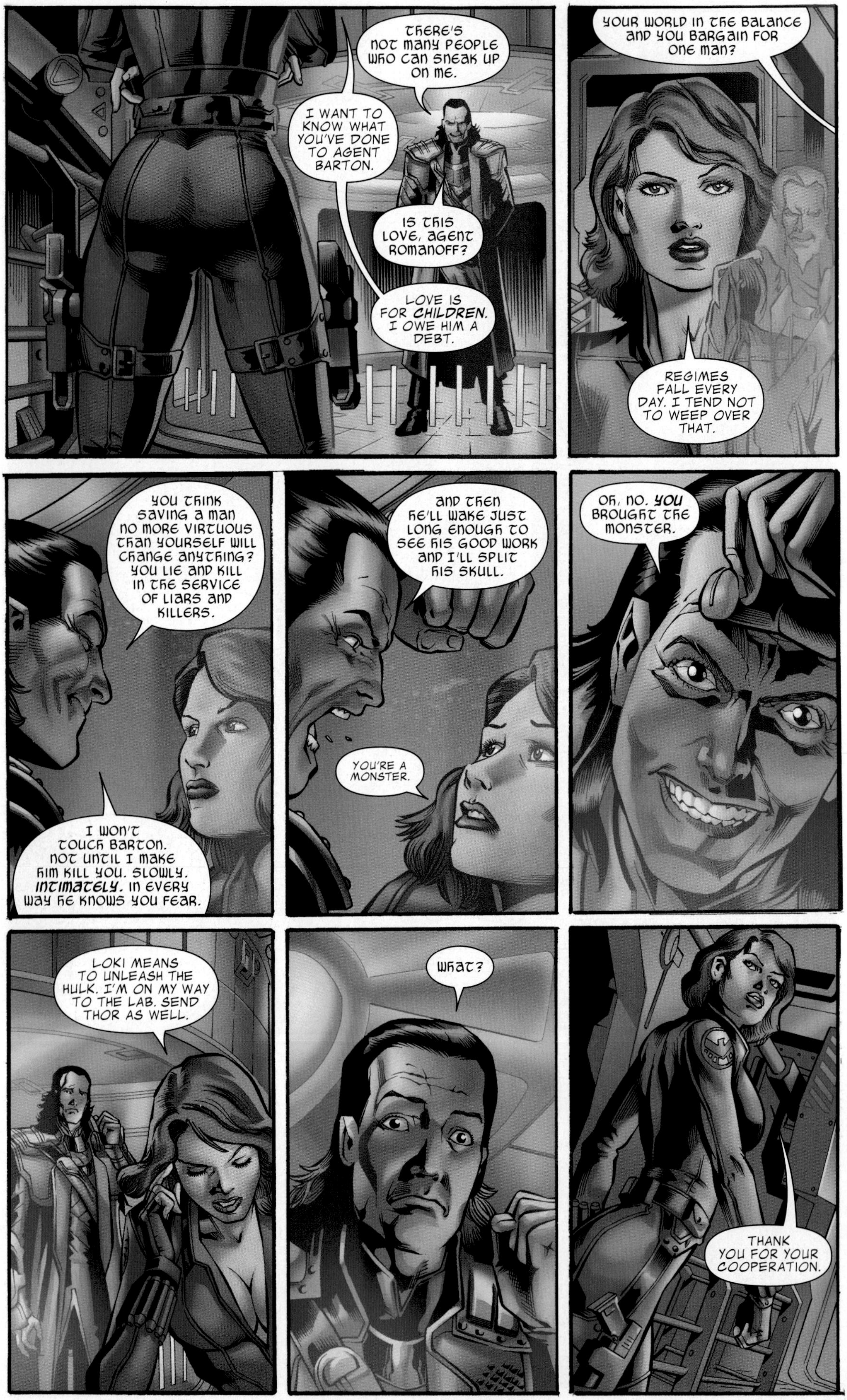
THERE'S NOT MANY PEOPLE WHO CAN SNEAK UP ON ME.
I WANT TO KNOW WHAT YOU'VE DONE TO AGENT BARTON.
IS THIS LOVE, AGENT ROMANOFF?
LOVE IS FOR CHILDREN. I OWE HIM A DEBT.
YOUR WORLD IN THE BALANCE AND YOU BARGAIN FOR ONE MAN?
REGIMES FALL EVERY DAY. I TEND NOT TO WEEP OVER THAT.
YOU THINK SAVING A MAN NO MORE VIRTUOUS THAN YOURSELF WILL CHANGE ANYTHING? YOU LIE AND KILL IN THE SERVICE OF LIARS AND KILLERS.
I WON'T TOUCH BARTON. NOT UNTIL I MAKE HIM KILL YOU. SLOWLY. INTIMATELY. IN EVERY WAY HE KNOWS YOU FEAR.
AND THEN HE'LL WAKE JUST LONG ENOUGH TO SEE HIS GOOD WORK AND I'LL SPLIT HIS SKULL.
YOU'RE A MONSTER.
OH, NO. YOU BROUGHT THE MONSTER.
LOKI MEANS TO UNLEASH THE HULK. I'M ON MY WAY TO THE LAB. SEND THOR AS WELL.
WHAT?
THANK YOU FOR YOUR COOPERATION.

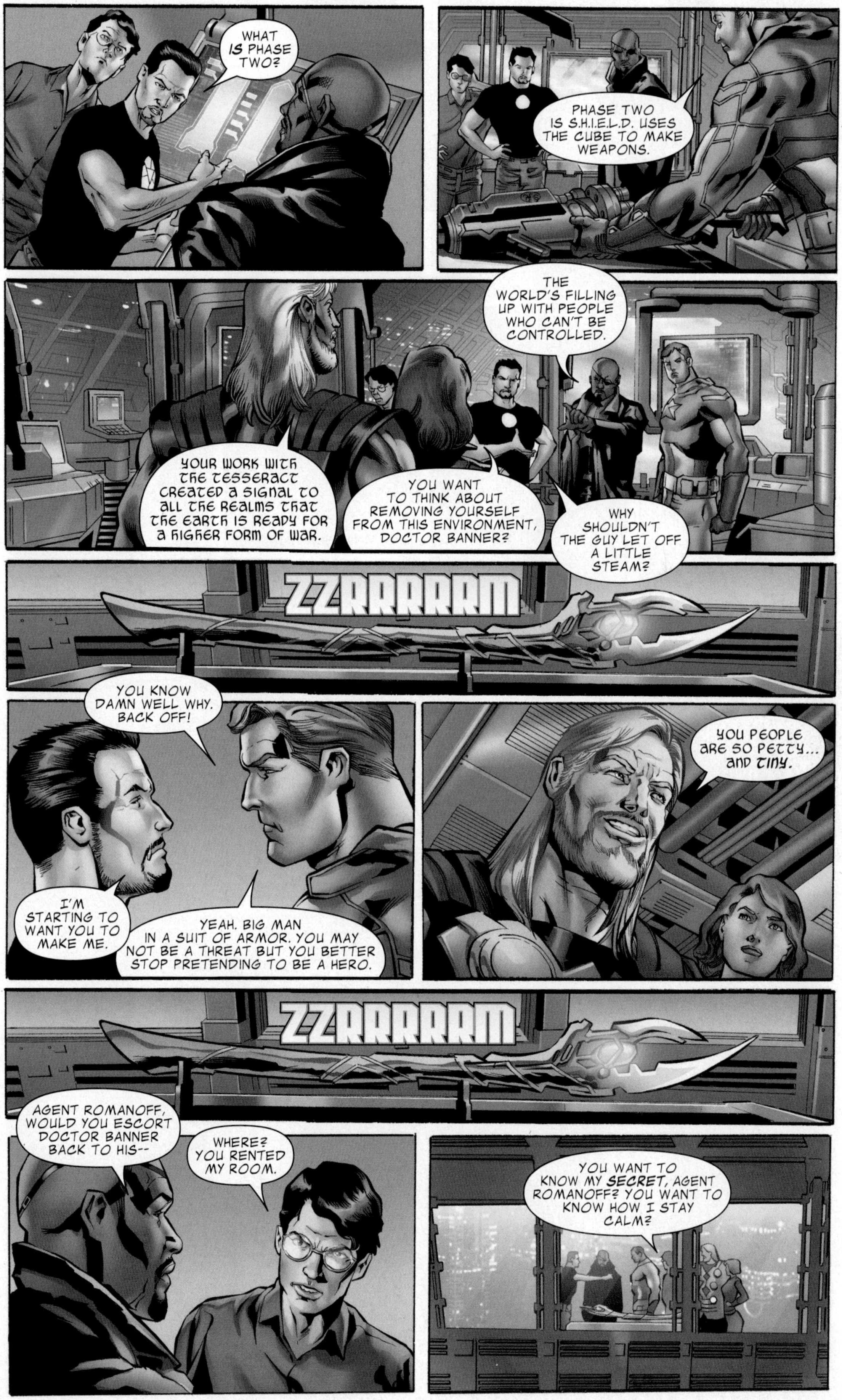
WHAT IS PHASE TWO?
PHASE TWO IS S.H.I.E.L.D. USES THE CUBE TO MAKE WEAPONS.
THE WORLD'S FILLING UP WITH PEOPLE WHO CAN'T BE CONTROLLED.
YOUR WORK WITH THE TESSERACT CREATED A SIGNAL TO ALL THE REALMS THAT THE EARTH IS READY FOR A HIGHER FORM OF WAR.
YOU WANT TO THINK ABOUT REMOVING YOURSELF FROM THIS ENVIRONMENT, DOCTOR BANNER?
WHY SHOULDN'T THE GUY LET OFF A LITTLE STEAM?
ZZRRRRRM
YOU KNOW DAMN WELL WHY. BACK OFF!
I'M STARTING TO WANT YOU TO MAKE ME.
YEAH. BIG MAN IN A SUIT OF ARMOR. YOU MAY NOT BE A THREAT BUT YOU BETTER STOP PRETENDING TO BE A HERO.
YOU PEOPLE ARE SO PETTY... AND TINY.
ZZRRRRRM
AGENT ROMANOFF, WOULD YOU ESCORT DOCTOR BANNER BACK TO HIS--
WHERE? YOU RENTED MY ROOM.
YOU WANT TO KNOW MY SECRET, AGENT ROMANOFF? YOU WANT TO KNOW HOW I STAY CALM?

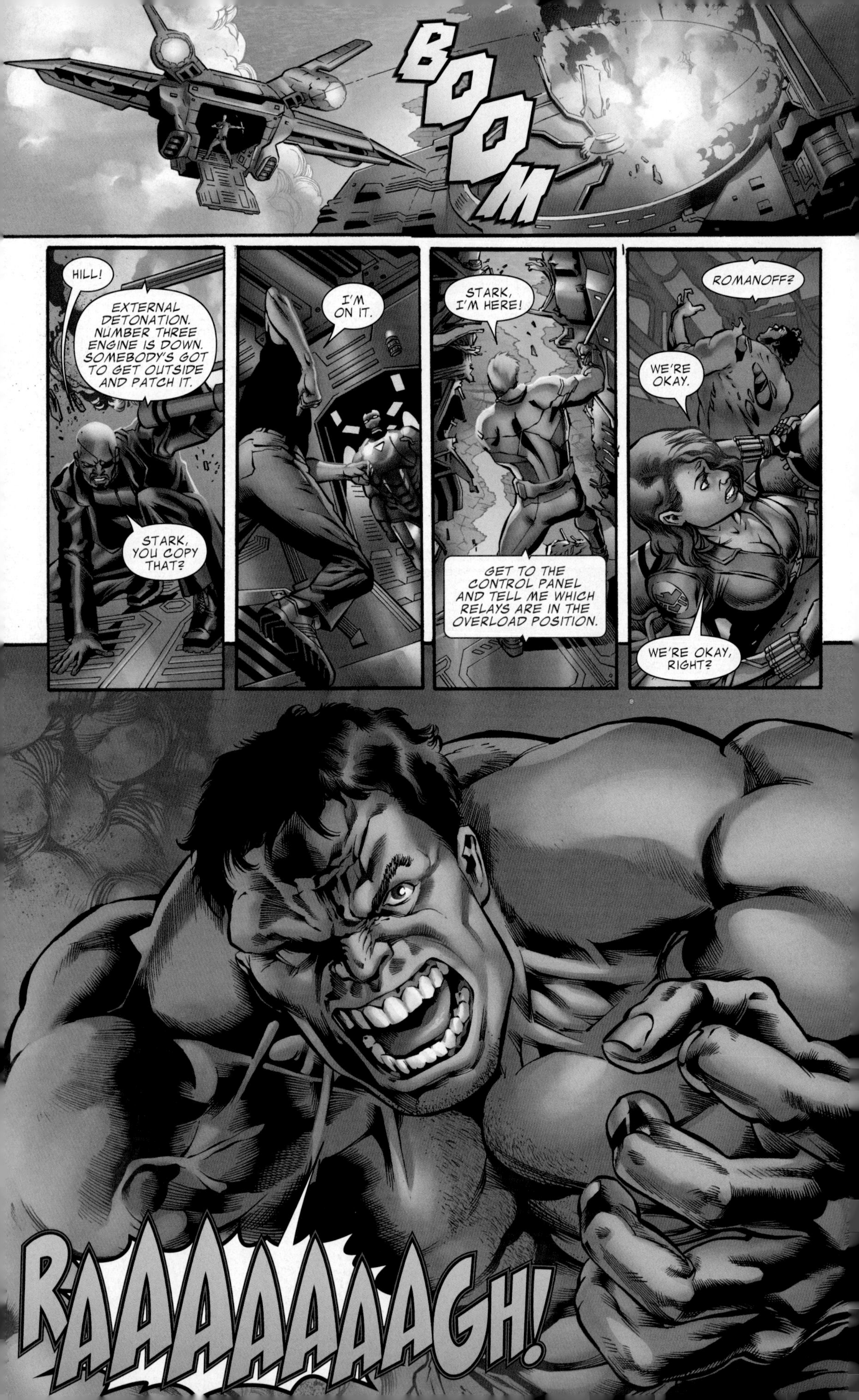
BOOM
HILL!
EXTERNAL DETONATION. NUMBER THREE ENGINE IS DOWN. SOMEBODY'S GOT TO GET OUTSIDE AND PATCH IT.
STARK, YOU COPY THAT?
I'M ON IT.
STARK, I'M HERE!
GET TO THE CONTROL PANEL AND TELL ME WHICH RELAYS ARE IN THE OVERLOAD POSITION.
ROMANOFF?
WE'RE OKAY.
WE'RE OKAY, RIGHT?
RAAAAAAAAGH!

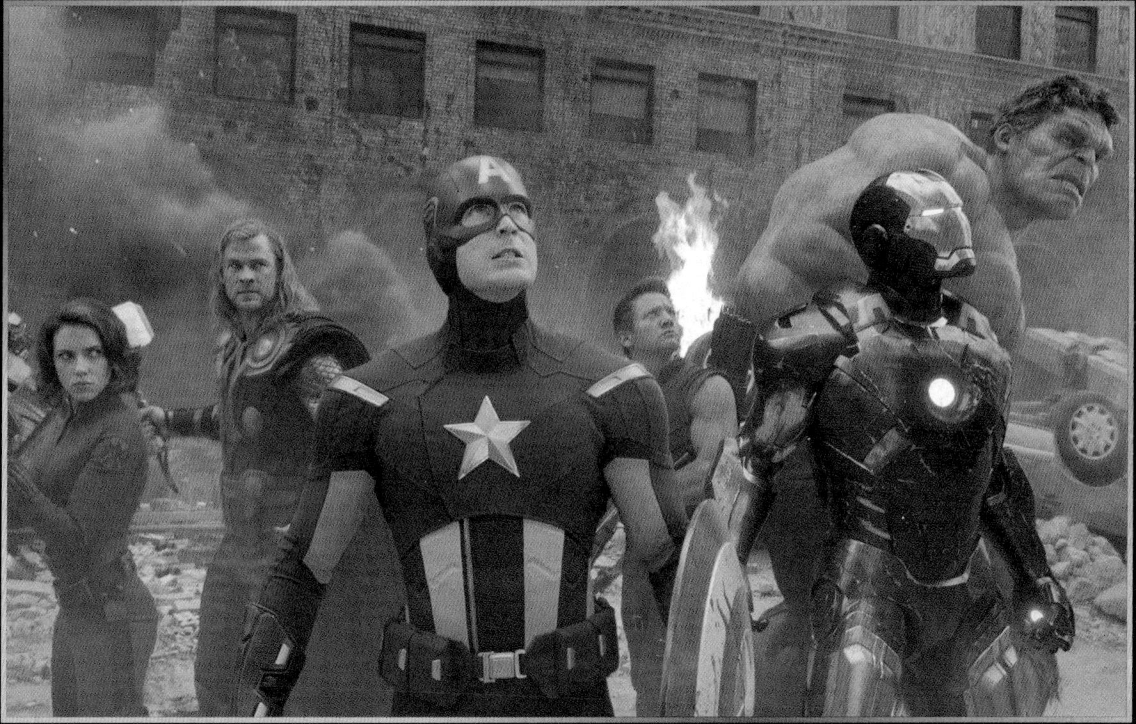

MARVEL'S THE AVENGERS
TWO

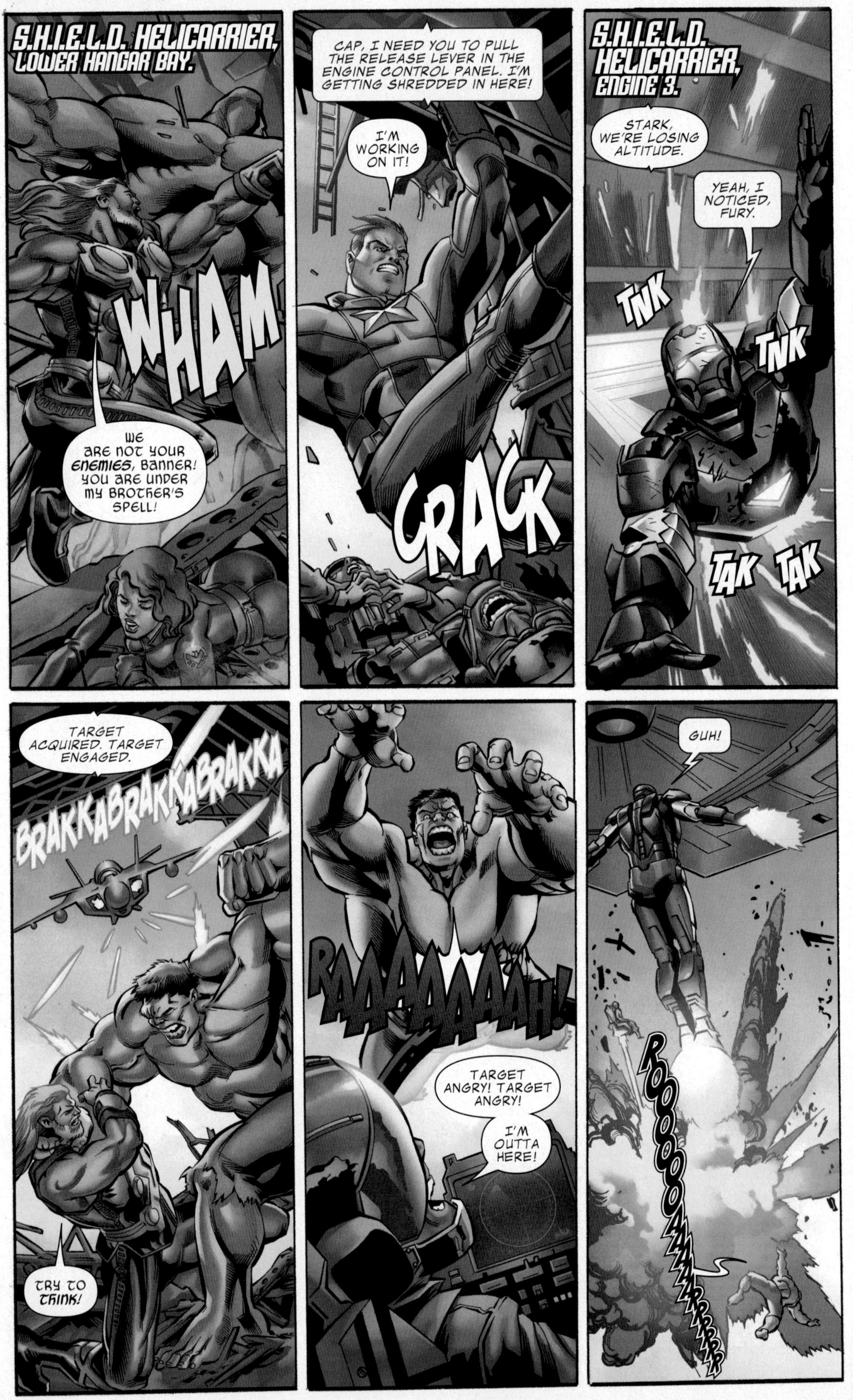
S.H.I.E.L.D. HELICARRIER, LOWER HANGAR BAY.
WHAM
WE ARE NOT YOUR ENEMIES, BANNER! YOU ARE UNDER MY BROTHER'S SPELL!
CAP, I NEED YOU TO PULL THE RELEASE LEVER IN THE ENGINE CONTROL PANEL. I'M GETTING SHREDDED IN HERE!
I'M WORKING ON IT!
CRACK
S.H.I.E.L.D. HELICARRIER, ENGINE 3.
STARK, WE'RE LOSING ALTITUDE.
YEAH, I NOTICED, FURY.
TNK
TNK
TAK TAK
TARGET ACQUIRED. TARGET ENGAGED.
BRAKKABRAKKABRAKKA
TRY TO THINK!
RAAAAAAAH!
TARGET ANGRY! TARGET ANGRY!
I'M OUTTA HERE!
GUH!

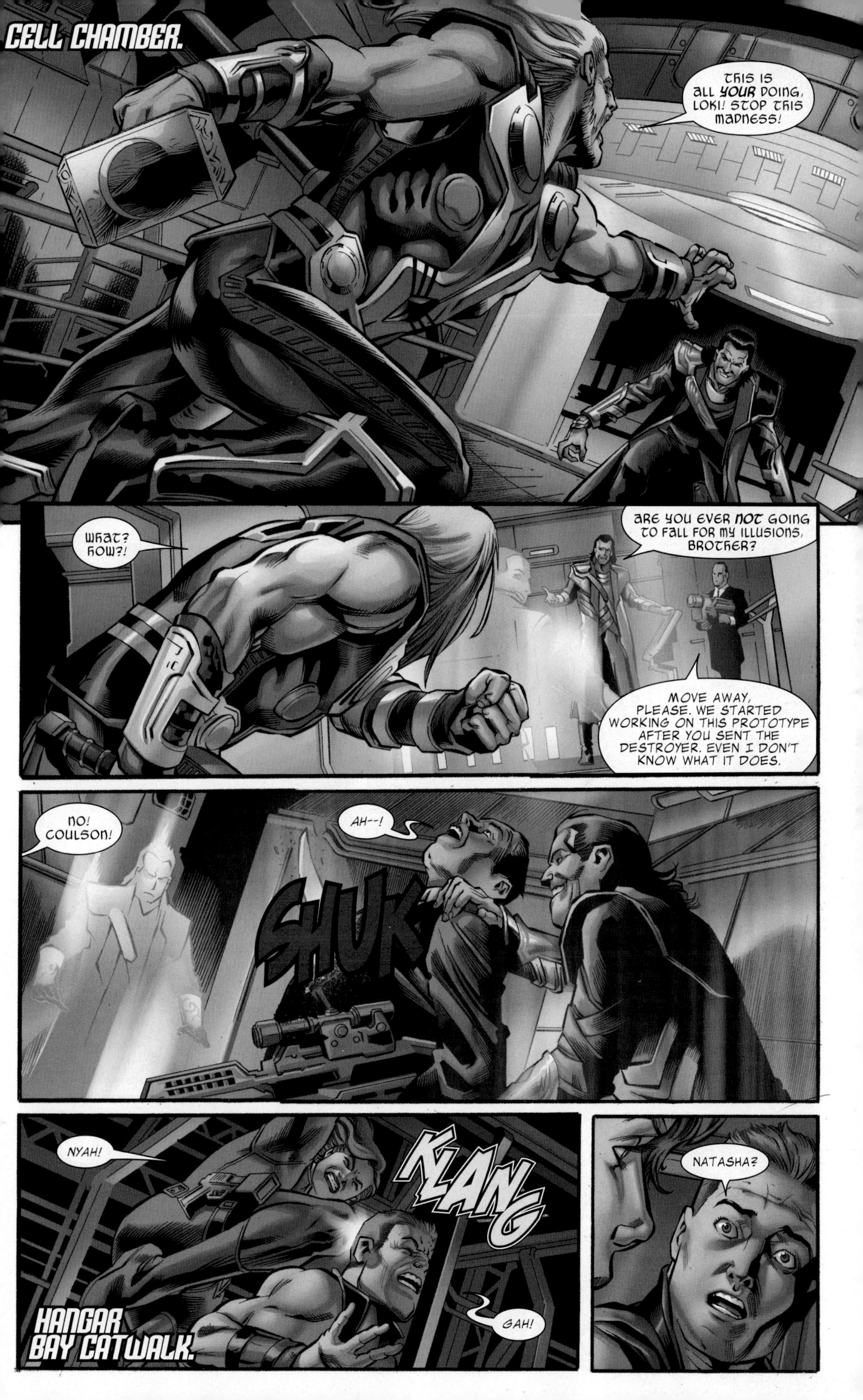
CELL CHAMBER.
THIS IS ALL YOUR DOING, LOKI! STOP THIS MADNESS!
WHAT? HOW?!
ARE YOU EVER NOT GOING TO FALL FOR MY ILLUSIONS, BROTHER?
MOVE AWAY, PLEASE. WE STARTED WORKING ON THIS PROTOTYPE AFTER YOU SENT THE DESTROYER. EVEN I DON'T KNOW WHAT IT DOES.
NO! COULSON!
AH--!
SHUK
NYAH!
KLANG
GAH!
HANGAR BAY CATWALK.
NATASHA?

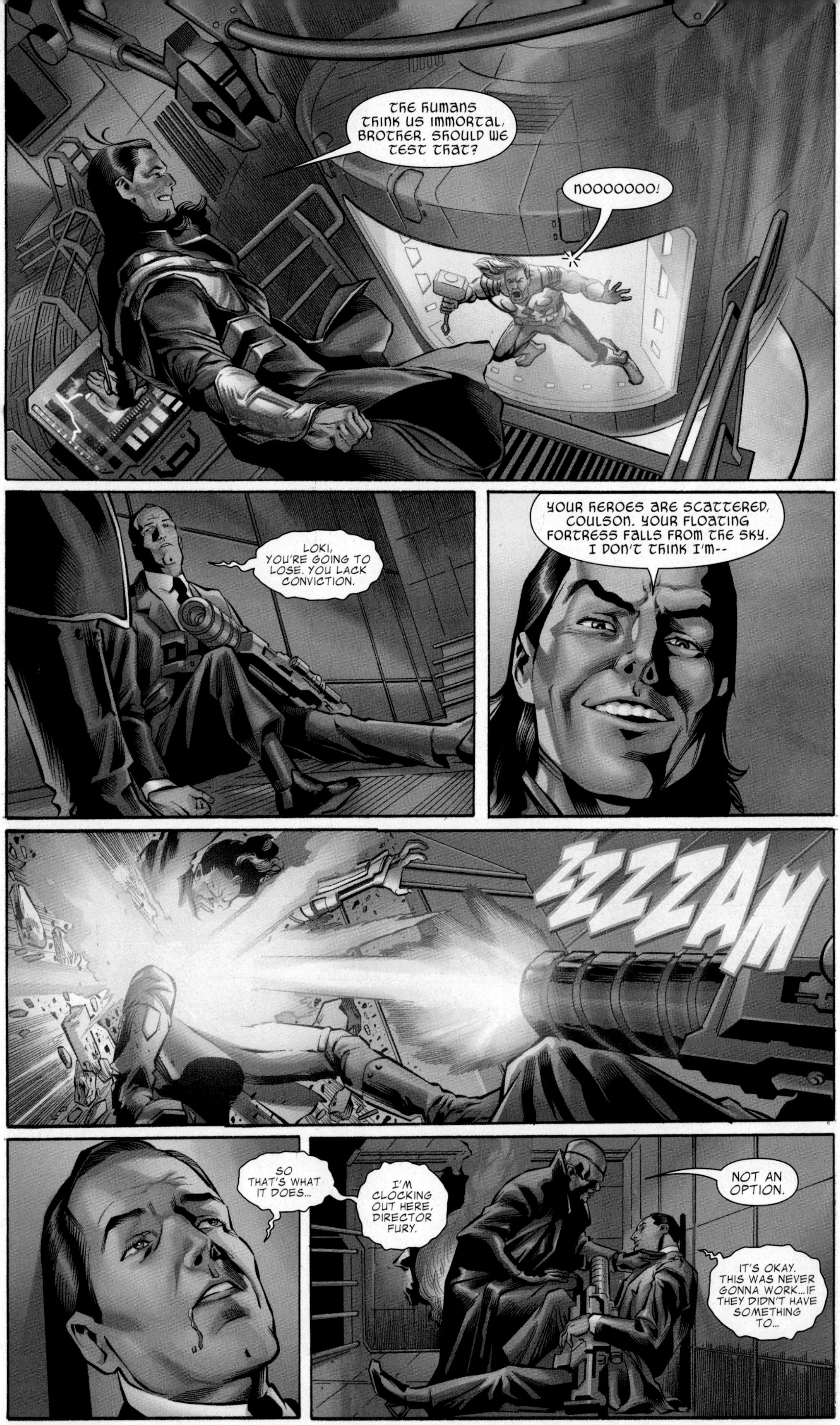
THE HUMANS THINK US IMMORTAL, BROTHER. SHOULD WE TEST THAT?
NOOOOOOO!
LOKI, YOU'RE GOING TO LOSE. YOU LACK CONVICTION.
YOUR HEROES ARE SCATTERED, COULSON. YOUR FLOATING FORTRESS FALLS FROM THE SKY. I DON'T THINK I'M--
ZZZZAM
SO THAT'S WHAT IT DOES...
I'M CLOCKING OUT HERE, DIRECTOR FURY.
NOT AN OPTION.
IT'S OKAY. THIS WAS NEVER GONNA WORK...IF THEY DIDN'T HAVE SOMETHING TO...

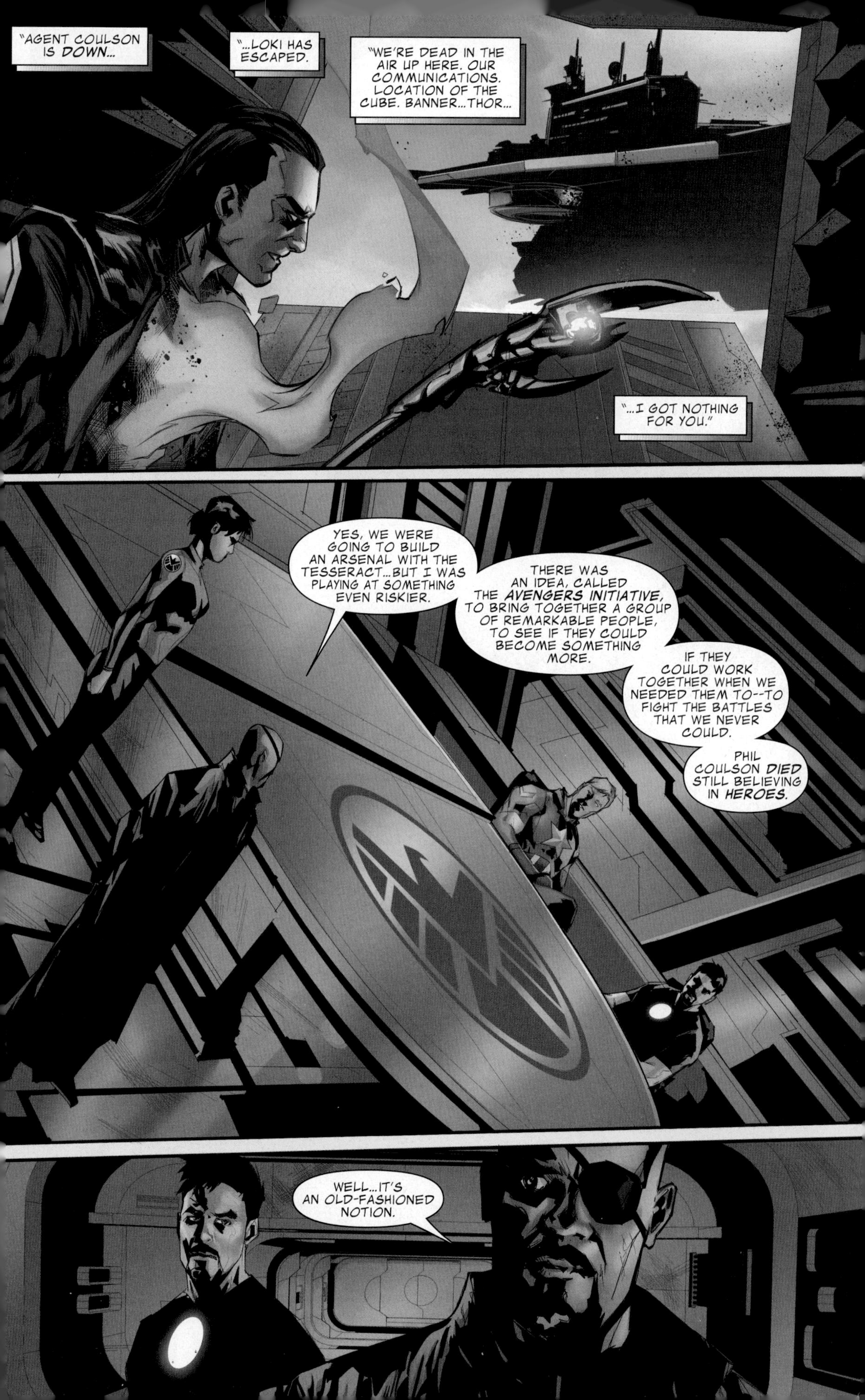
"AGENT COULSON IS DOWN...
"...LOKI HAS ESCAPED.
"WE'RE DEAD IN THE AIR UP HERE. OUR COMMUNICATIONS. LOCATION OF THE CUBE. BANNER...THOR...
"...I GOT NOTHING FOR YOU."
YES, WE WERE GOING TO BUILD AN ARSENAL WITH THE TESSERACT...BUT I WAS PLAYING AT SOMETHING EVEN RISKIER.
THERE WAS AN IDEA, CALLED THE AVENGERS INITIATIVE, TO BRING TOGETHER A GROUP OF REMARKABLE PEOPLE, TO SEE IF THEY COULD BECOME SOMETHING MORE.
IF THEY COULD WORK TOGETHER WHEN WE NEEDED THEM TO--TO FIGHT THE BATTLES THAT WE NEVER COULD.
PHIL COULSON DIED STILL BELIEVING IN HEROES.
WELL...IT'S AN OLD-FASHIONED NOTION.

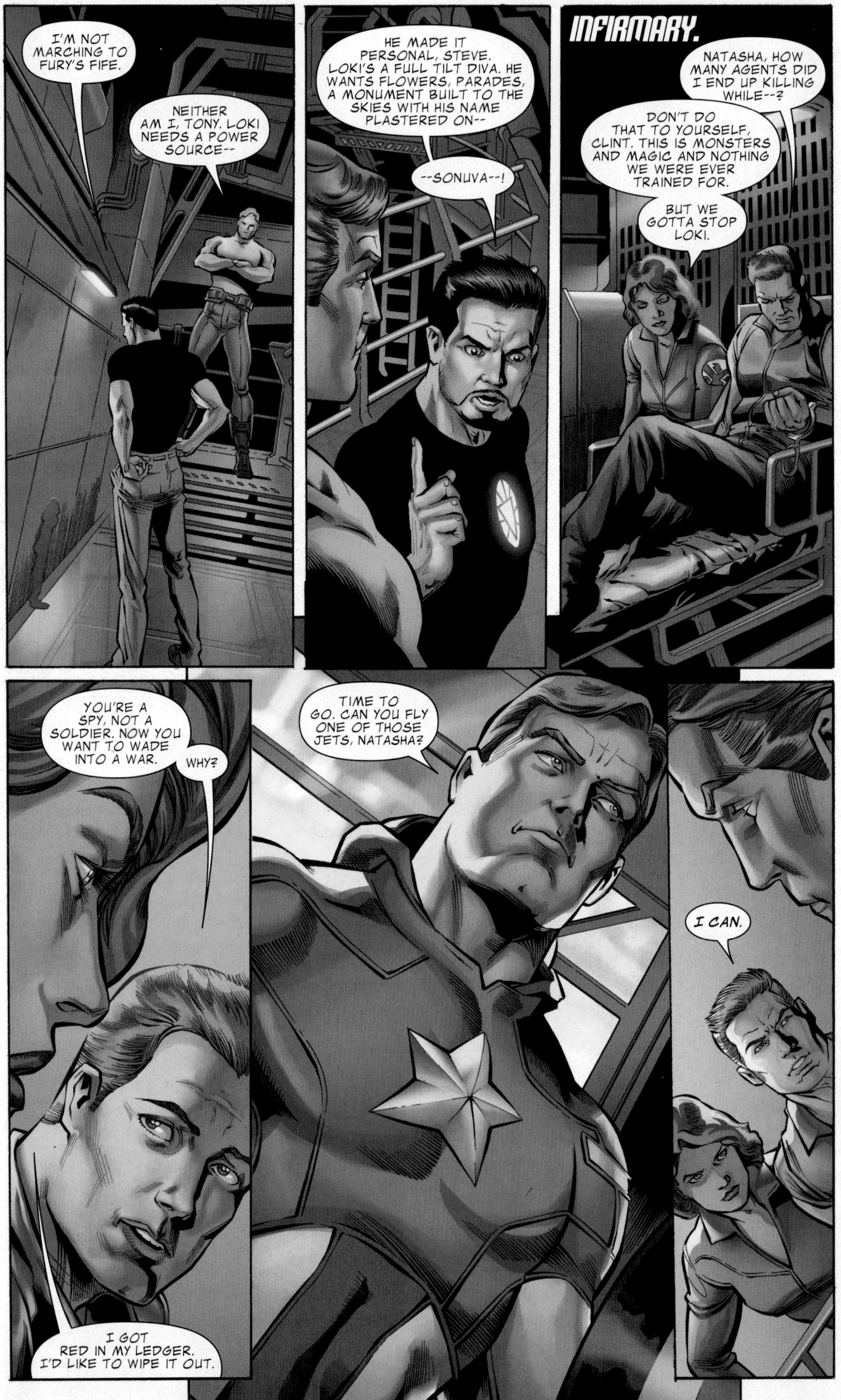
I'M NOT MARCHING TO FURY'S FIFE.
NEITHER AM I, TONY. LOKI NEEDS A POWER SOURCE--
HE MADE IT PERSONAL, STEVE. LOKI'S A FULL TILT DIVA. HE WANTS FLOWERS, PARADES, A MONUMENT BUILT TO THE SKIES WITH HIS NAME PLASTERED ON--
--SONUVA--!
INFIRMARY.
NATASHA, HOW MANY AGENTS DID I END UP KILLING WHILE--?
DON'T DO THAT TO YOURSELF, CLINT. THIS IS MONSTERS AND MAGIC AND NOTHING WE WERE EVER TRAINED FOR.
BUT WE GOTTA STOP LOKI.
YOU'RE A SPY, NOT A SOLDIER. NOW YOU WANT TO WADE INTO A WAR.
WHY?
I GOT RED IN MY LEDGER. I'D LIKE TO WIPE IT OUT.
TIME TO GO. CAN YOU FLY ONE OF THOSE JETS, NATASHA?
I CAN.

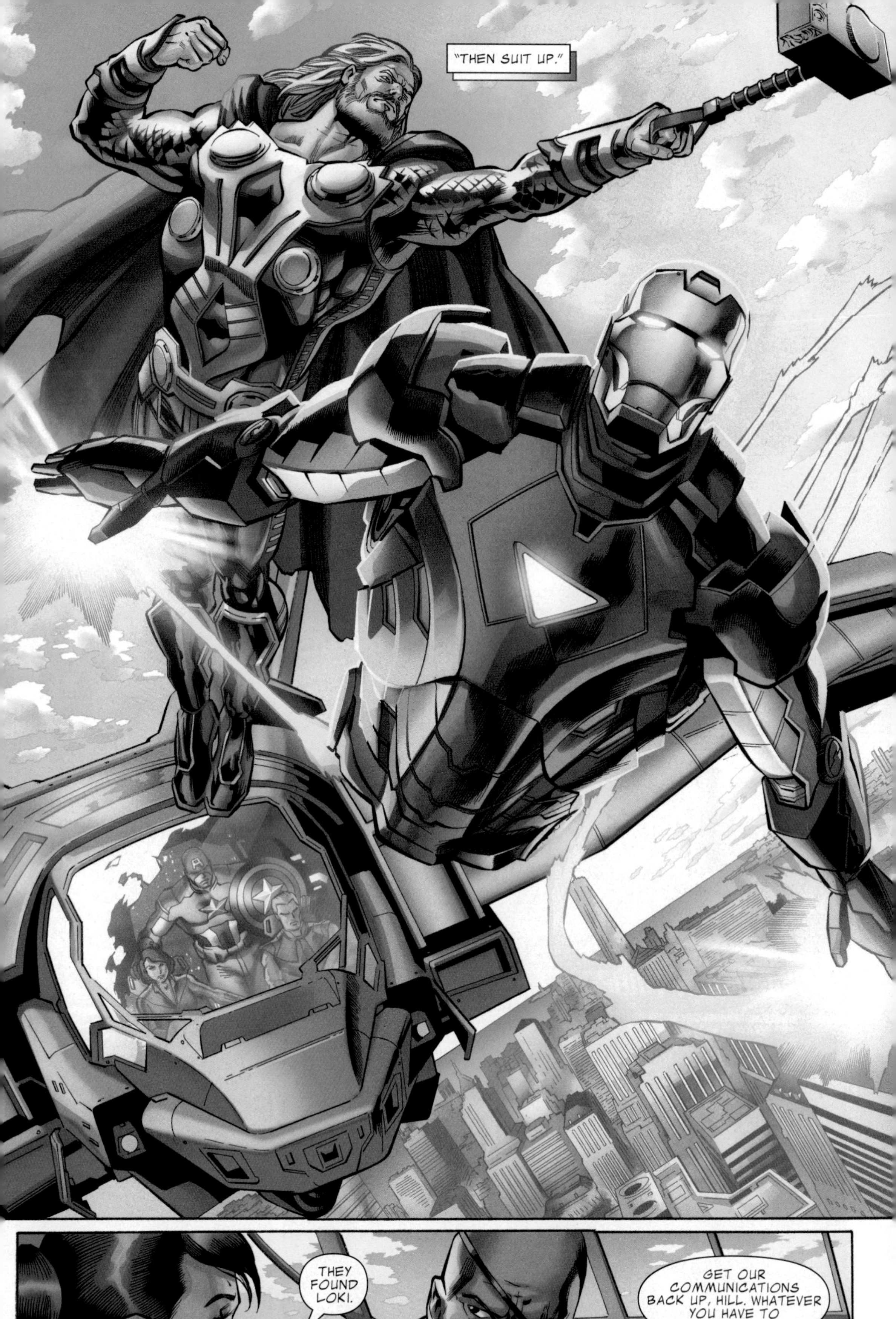
"THEN SUIT UP."

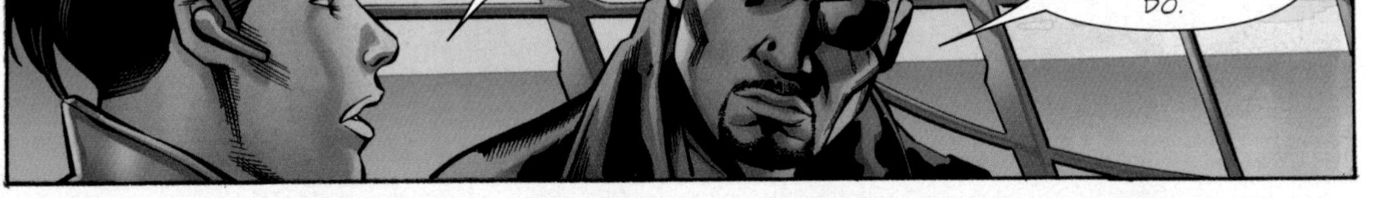
THEY FOUND LOKI.
GET OUR COMMUNICATIONS BACK UP, HILL. WHATEVER YOU HAVE TO DO.

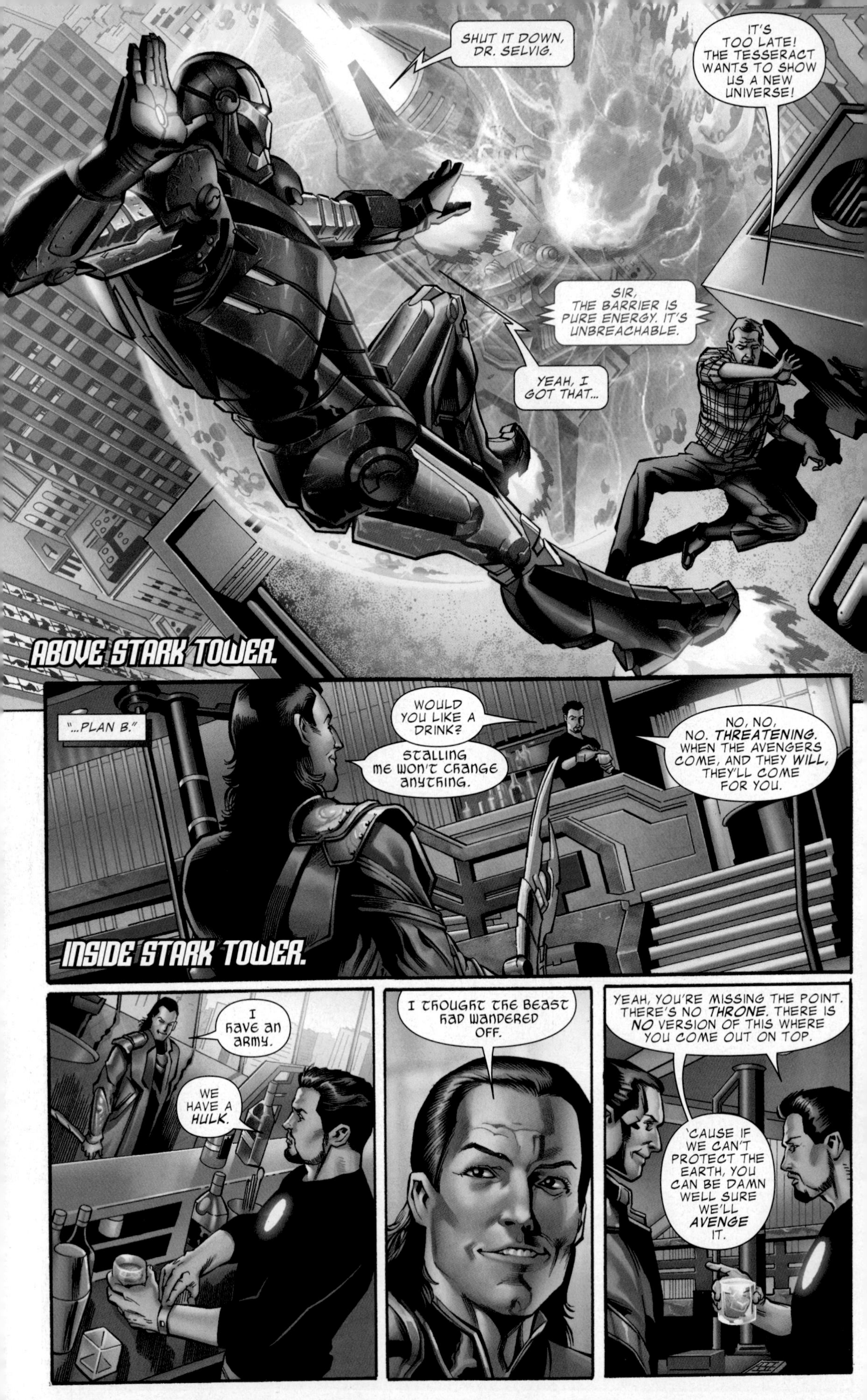
SHUT IT DOWN, DR. SELVIG.
IT'S TOO LATE! THE TESSERACT WANTS TO SHOW US A NEW UNIVERSE!
SIR, THE BARRIER IS PURE ENERGY. IT'S UNBREACHABLE.
YEAH, I GOT THAT...
ABOVE STARK TOWER.
"...PLAN B."
WOULD YOU LIKE A DRINK?
STALLING ME WON'T CHANGE ANYTHING.
NO, NO, NO. THREATENING. WHEN THE AVENGERS COME, AND THEY WILL, THEY'LL COME FOR YOU.
INSIDE STARK TOWER.
I HAVE AN ARMY.
WE HAVE A HULK.
I THOUGHT THE BEAST HAD WANDERED OFF.
YEAH, YOU'RE MISSING THE POINT. THERE'S NO THRONE. THERE IS NO VERSION OF THIS WHERE YOU COME OUT ON TOP.
'CAUSE IF WE CAN'T PROTECT THE EARTH, YOU CAN BE DAMN WELL SURE WE'LL AVENGE IT.

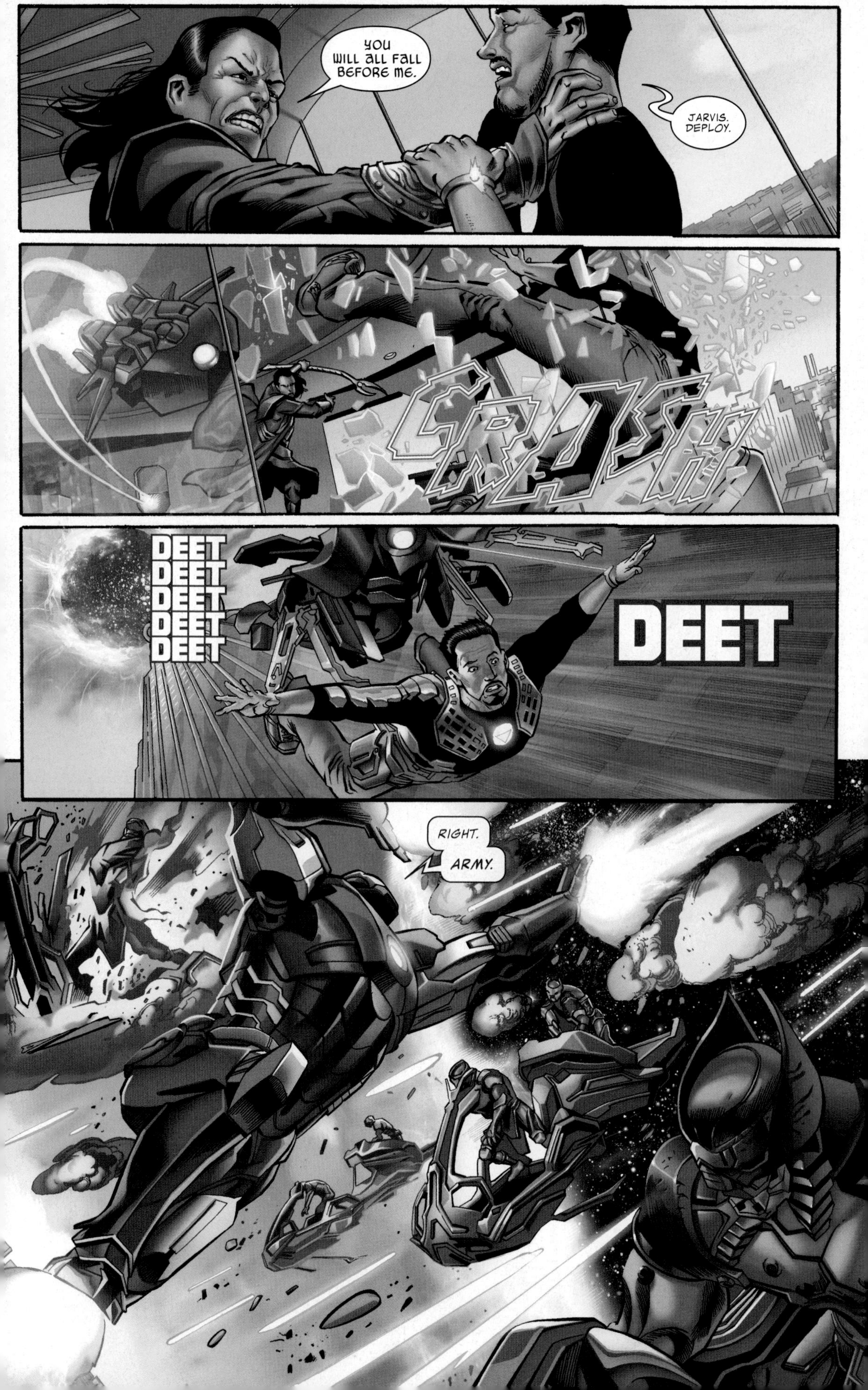
YOU WILL ALL FALL BEFORE ME.
JARVIS. DEPLOY.
CRASH
DEET DEET DEET DEET DEET
DEET
RIGHT.
ARMY.

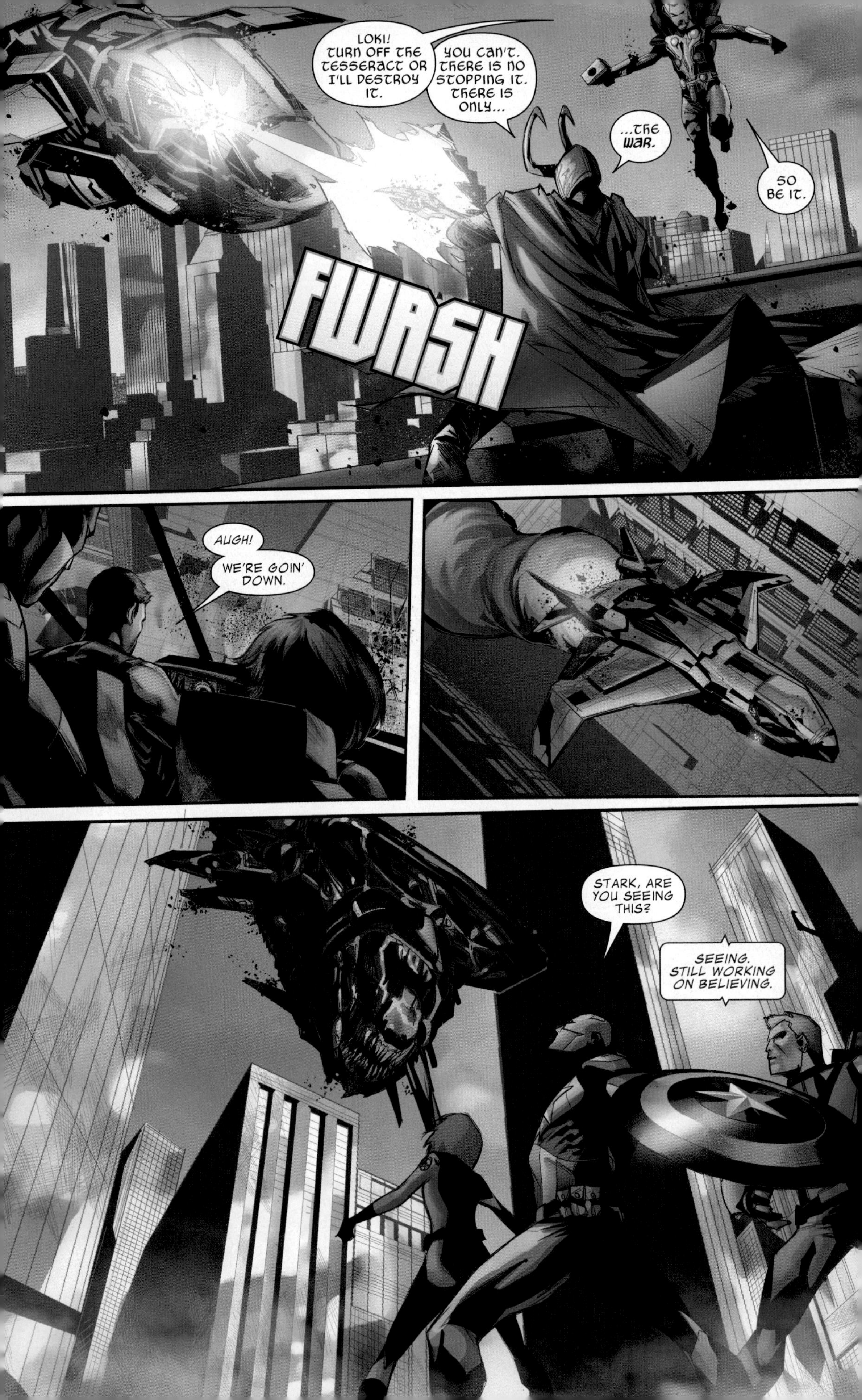
LOKI! TURN OFF THE TESSERACT OR I'LL DESTROY IT.
YOU CAN'T. THERE IS NO STOPPING IT. THERE IS ONLY...
...THE WAR.
SO BE IT.
FWASH
AUGH!
WE'RE GOIN' DOWN.
STARK, ARE YOU SEEING THIS?
SEEING. STILL WORKING ON BELIEVING.

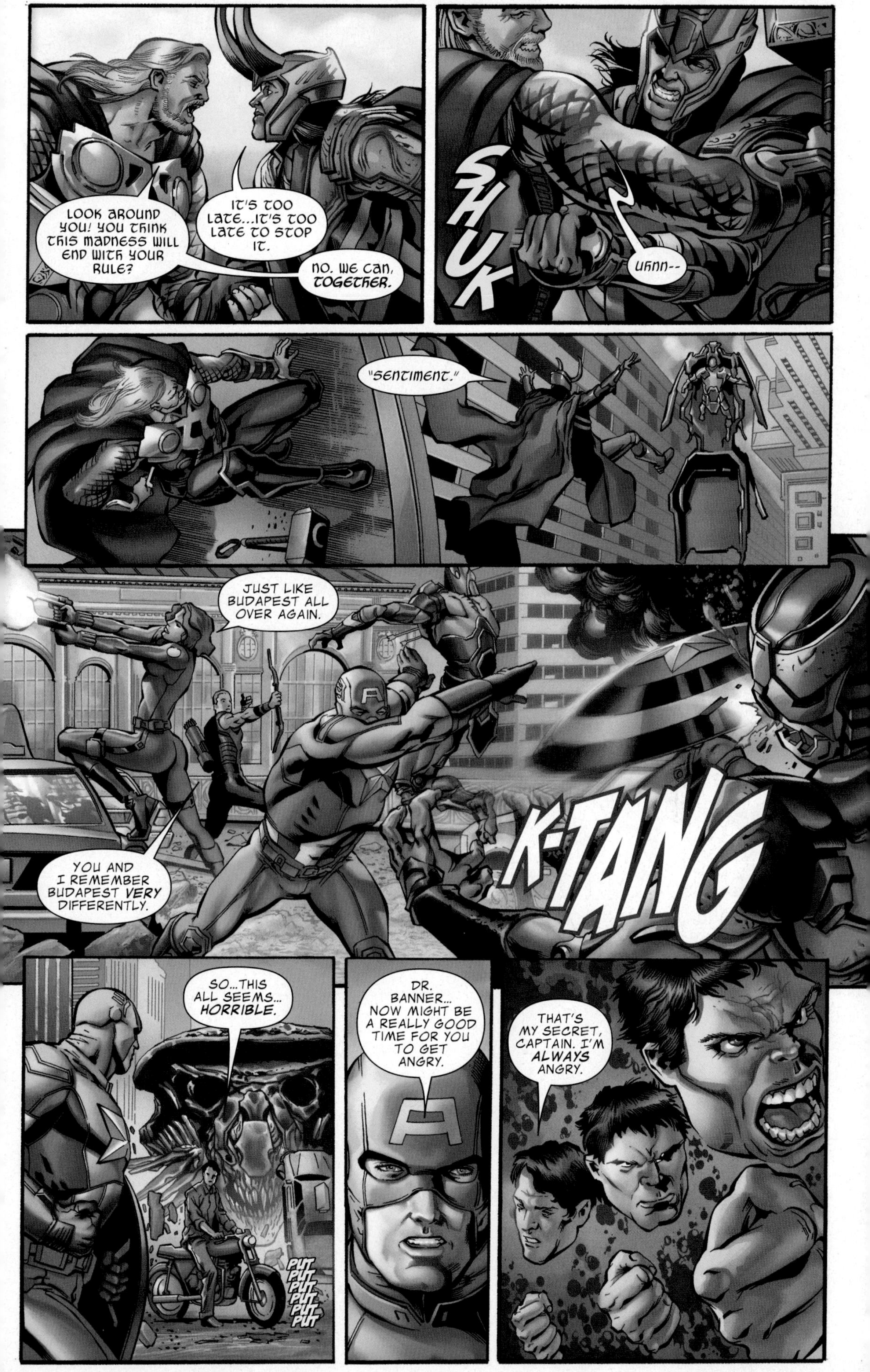
LOOK AROUND YOU! YOU THINK THIS MADNESS WILL END WITH YOUR RULE?
IT'S TOO LATE...IT'S TOO LATE TO STOP IT.
NO. WE CAN, TOGETHER.
SHUK
UHNN--
"SENTIMENT."
JUST LIKE BUDAPEST ALL OVER AGAIN.
YOU AND I REMEMBER BUDAPEST VERY DIFFERENTLY.
K-TANG
SO...THIS ALL SEEMS... HORRIBLE.
PUT PUT PUT PUT PUT PUT
DR. BANNER... NOW MIGHT BE A REALLY GOOD TIME FOR YOU TO GET ANGRY.
THAT'S MY SECRET, CAPTAIN. I'M ALWAYS ANGRY.

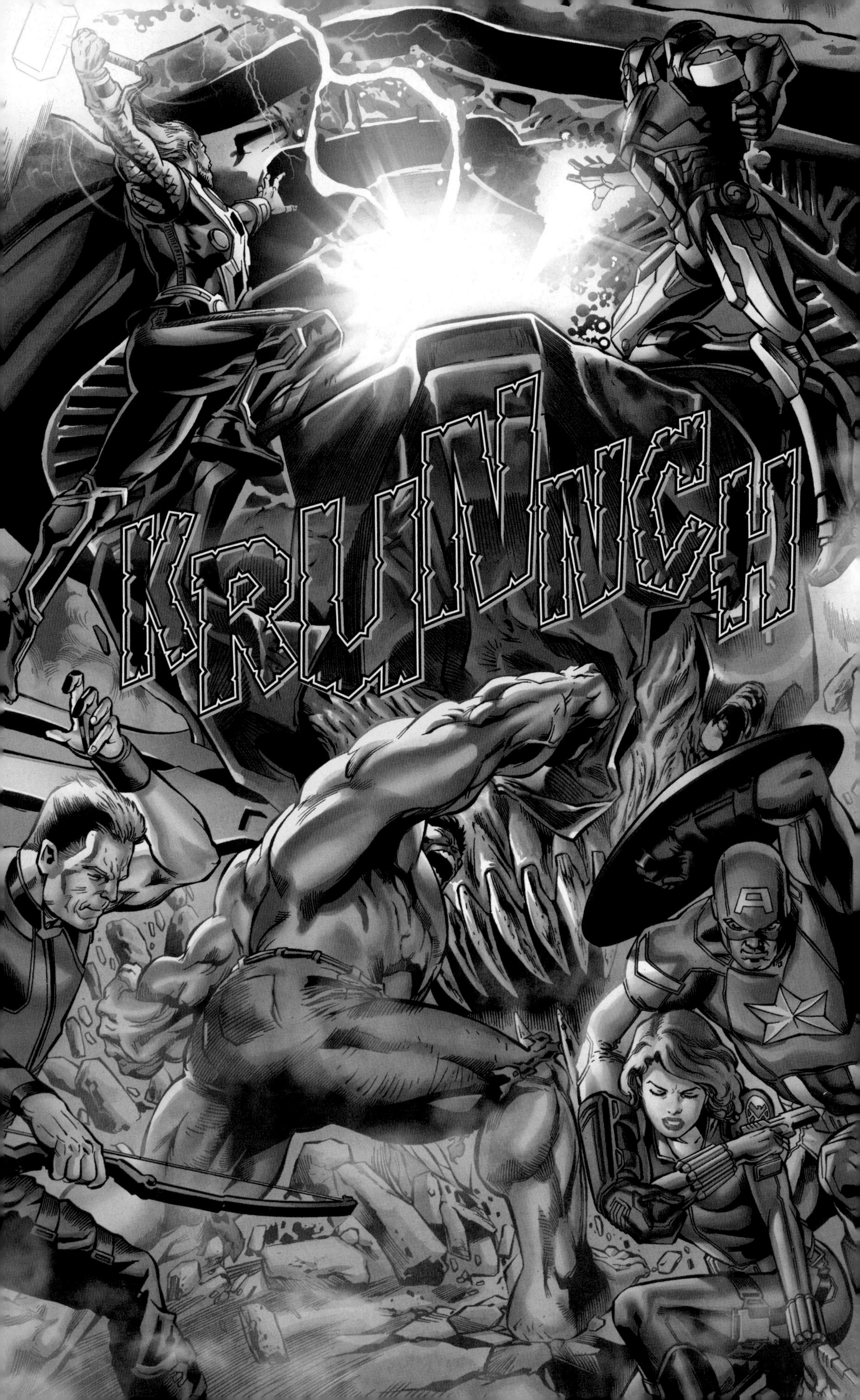
KRUNNCH

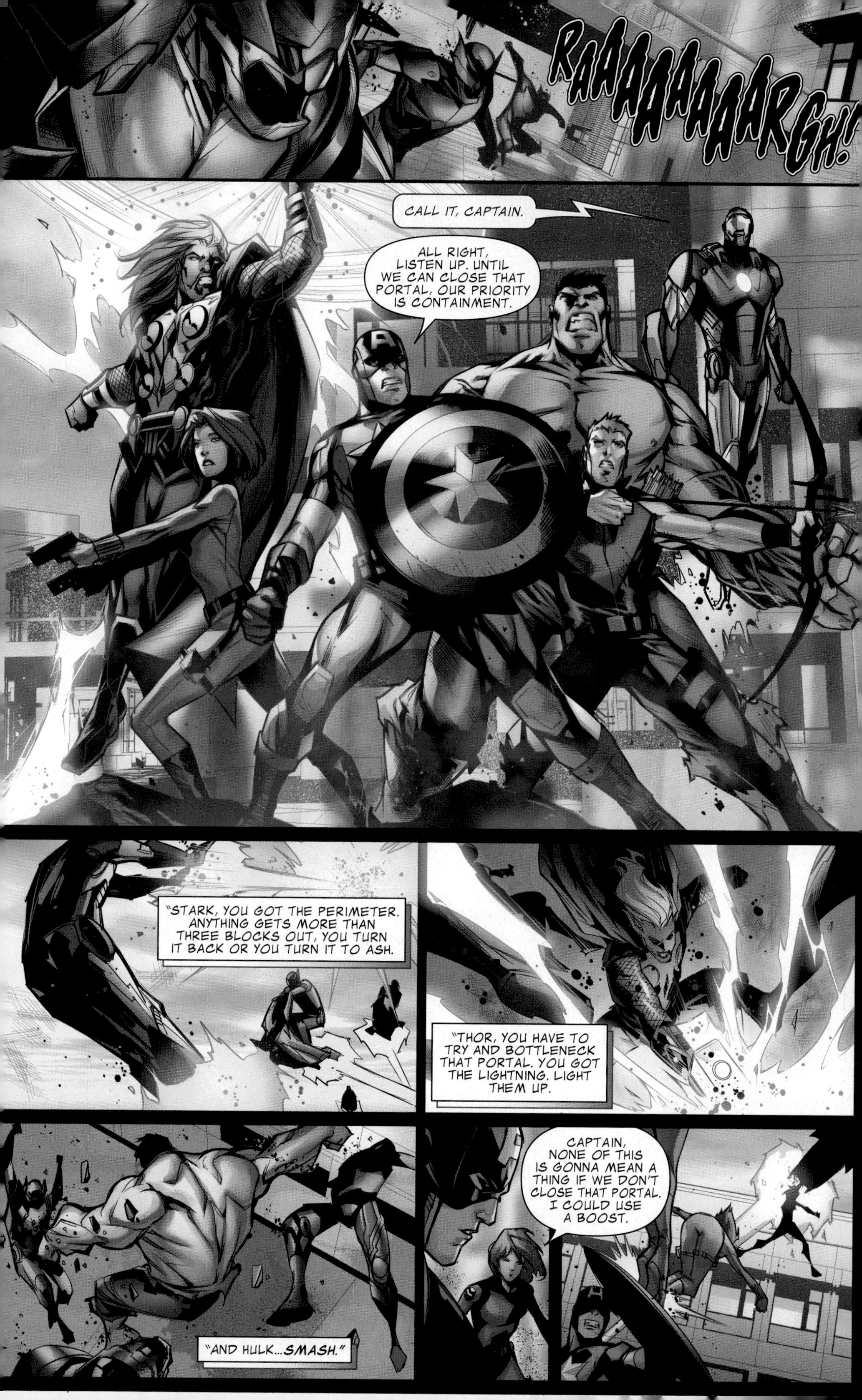
RAAAAAAAAARGH!
CALL IT, CAPTAIN.
ALL RIGHT, LISTEN UP. UNTIL WE CAN CLOSE THAT PORTAL, OUR PRIORITY IS CONTAINMENT.
"STARK, YOU GOT THE PERIMETER. ANYTHING GETS MORE THAN THREE BLOCKS OUT, YOU TURN IT BACK OR YOU TURN IT TO ASH.
"THOR, YOU HAVE TO TRY AND BOTTLENECK THAT PORTAL. YOU GOT THE LIGHTNING. LIGHT THEM UP.
"AND HULK...SMASH."
CAPTAIN, NONE OF THIS IS GONNA MEAN A THING IF WE DON'T CLOSE THAT PORTAL. I COULD USE A BOOST.

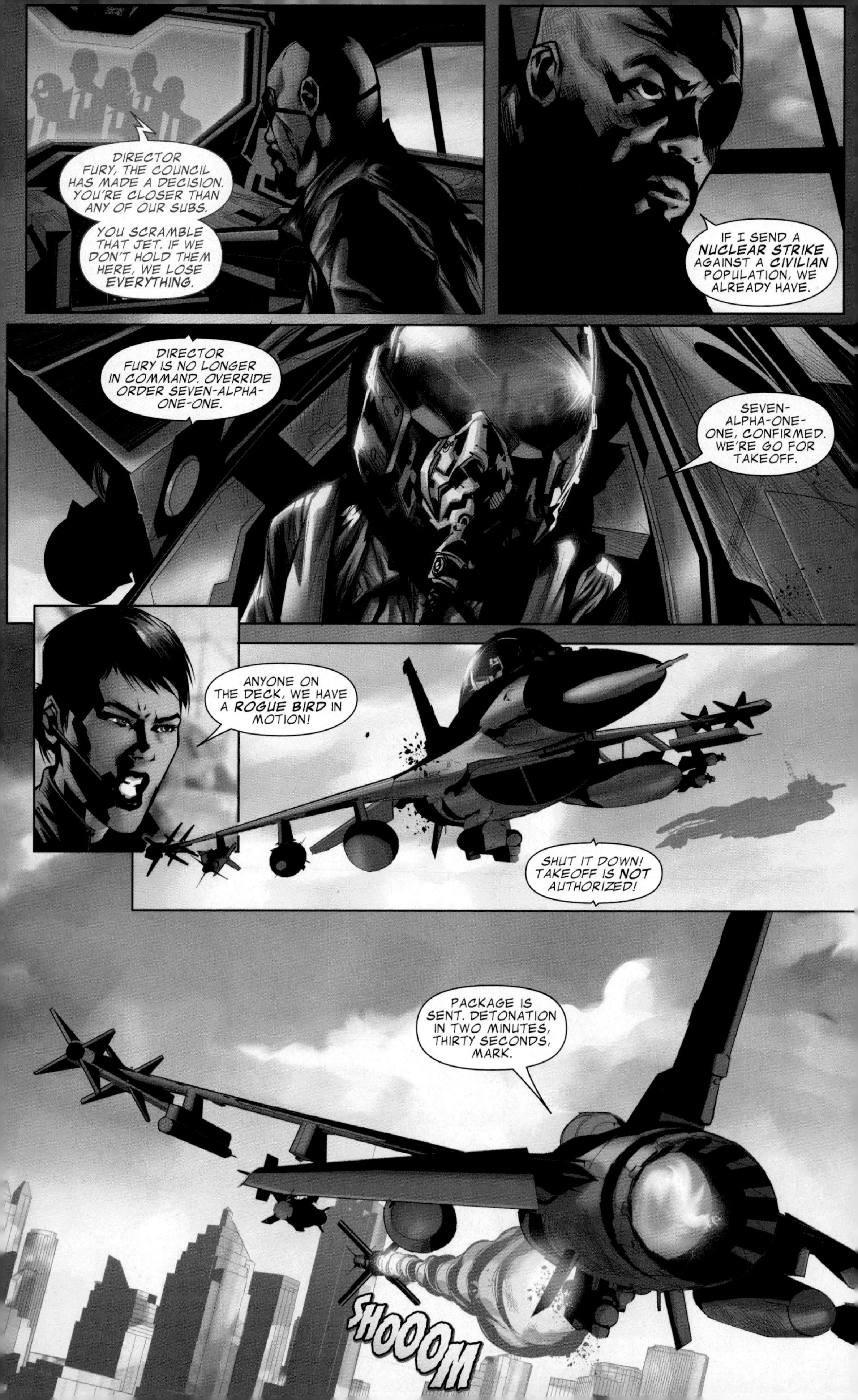
DIRECTOR FURY, THE COUNCIL HAS MADE A DECISION. YOU'RE CLOSER THAN ANY OF OUR SUBS.
YOU SCRAMBLE THAT JET. IF WE DON'T HOLD THEM HERE, WE LOSE EVERYTHING.
IF I SEND A NUCLEAR STRIKE AGAINST A CIVILIAN POPULATION, WE ALREADY HAVE.
DIRECTOR FURY IS NO LONGER IN COMMAND. OVERRIDE ORDER SEVEN-ALPHA-ONE-ONE.
SEVEN-ALPHA-ONE-ONE, CONFIRMED. WE'RE GO FOR TAKEOFF.
ANYONE ON THE DECK, WE HAVE A ROGUE BIRD IN MOTION!
SHUT IT DOWN! TAKEOFF IS NOT AUTHORIZED!
PACKAGE IS SENT. DETONATION IN TWO MINUTES, THIRTY SECONDS, MARK.
SHOOOM

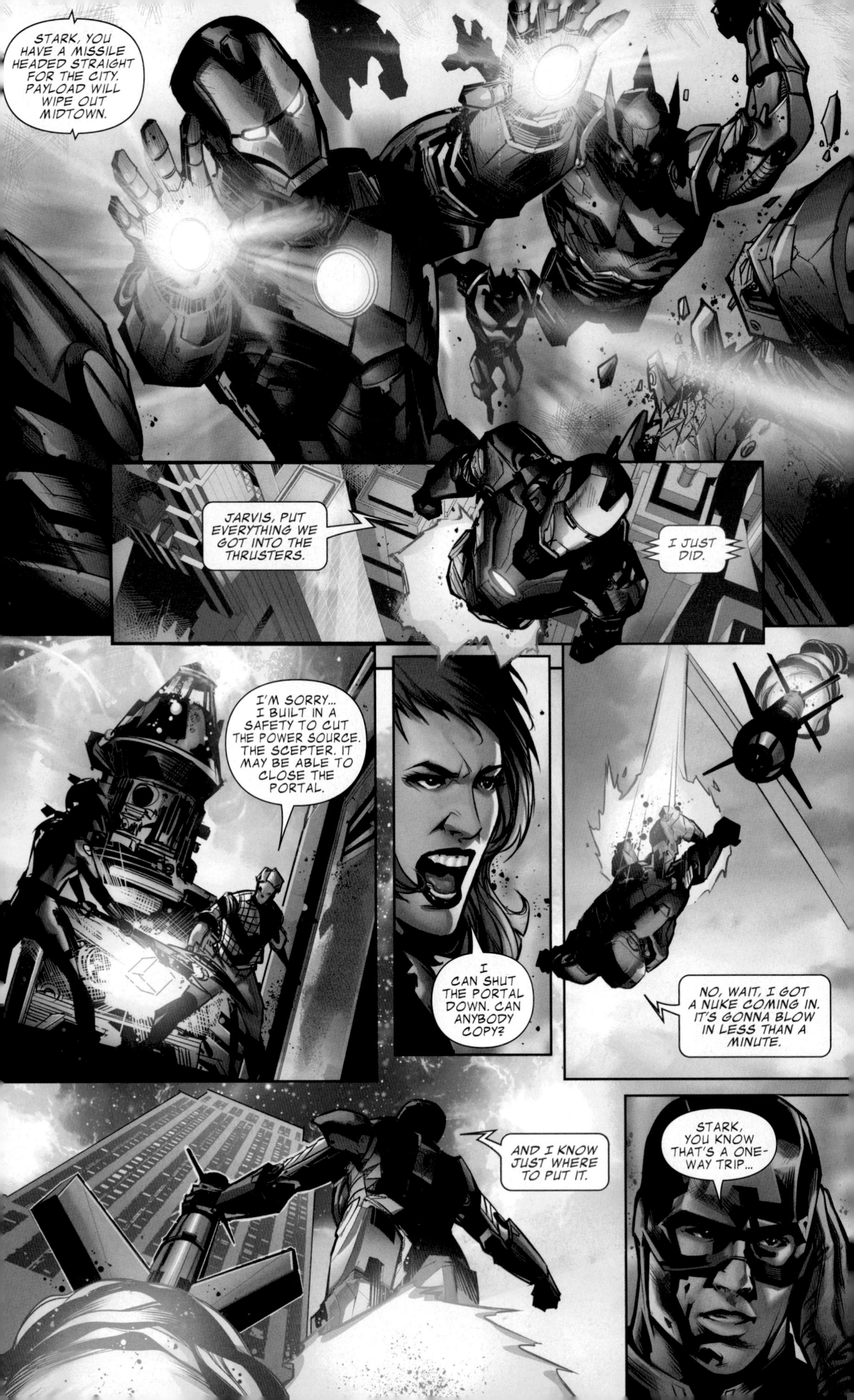
STARK, YOU HAVE A MISSILE HEADED STRAIGHT FOR THE CITY. PAYLOAD WILL WIPE OUT MIDTOWN.
JARVIS, PUT EVERYTHING WE GOT INTO THE THRUSTERS.
I JUST DID.
I'M SORRY... I BUILT IN A SAFETY TO CUT THE POWER SOURCE. THE SCEPTER. IT MAY BE ABLE TO CLOSE THE PORTAL.
I CAN SHUT THE PORTAL DOWN. CAN ANYBODY COPY?
NO, WAIT, I GOT A NUKE COMING IN. IT'S GONNA BLOW IN LESS THAN A MINUTE.
AND I KNOW JUST WHERE TO PUT IT.
STARK, YOU KNOW THAT'S A ONE-WAY TRIP...

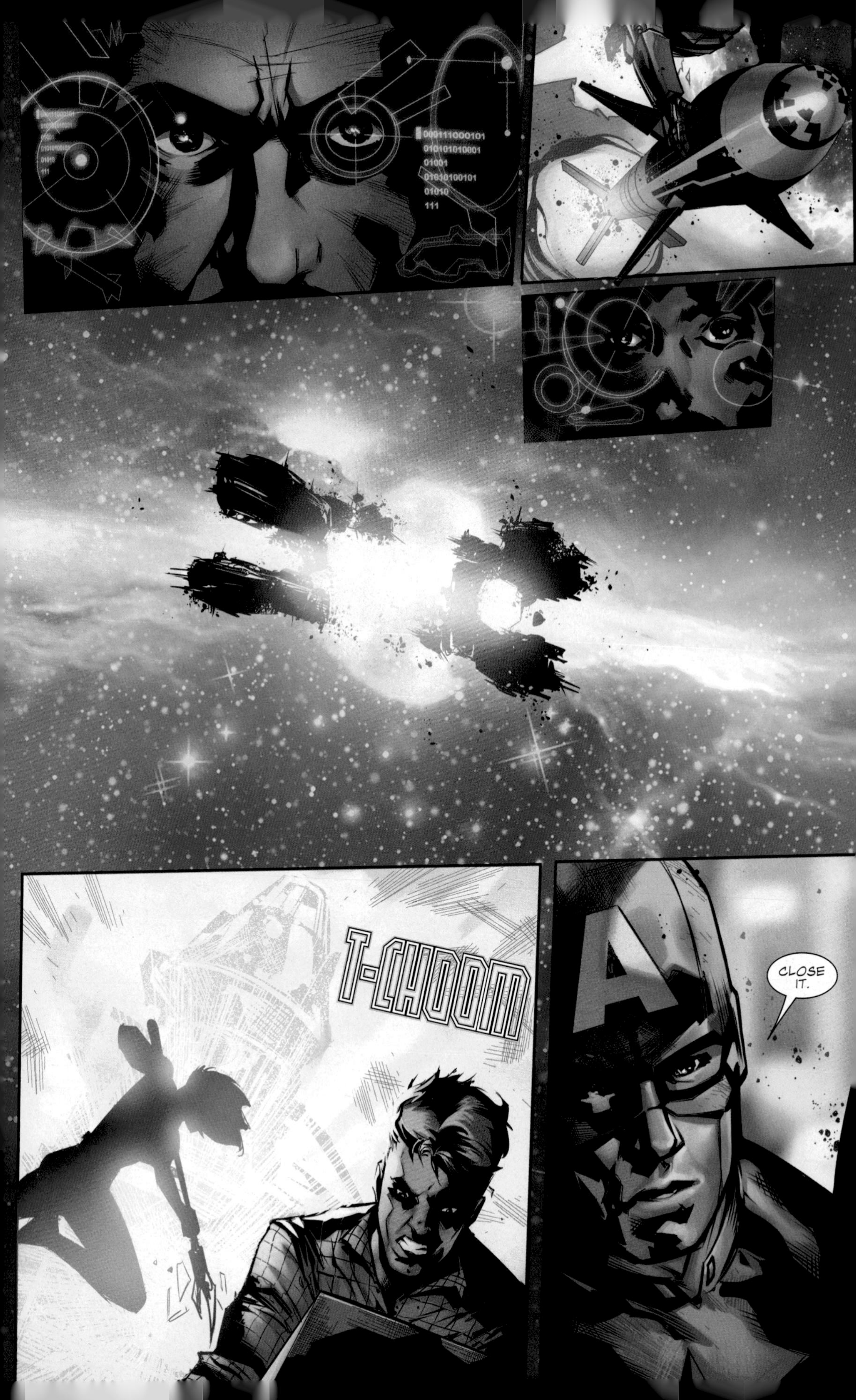
000111000101
010101010001
01001
01010100101
01010
111
T-CHOOM
CLOSE IT.

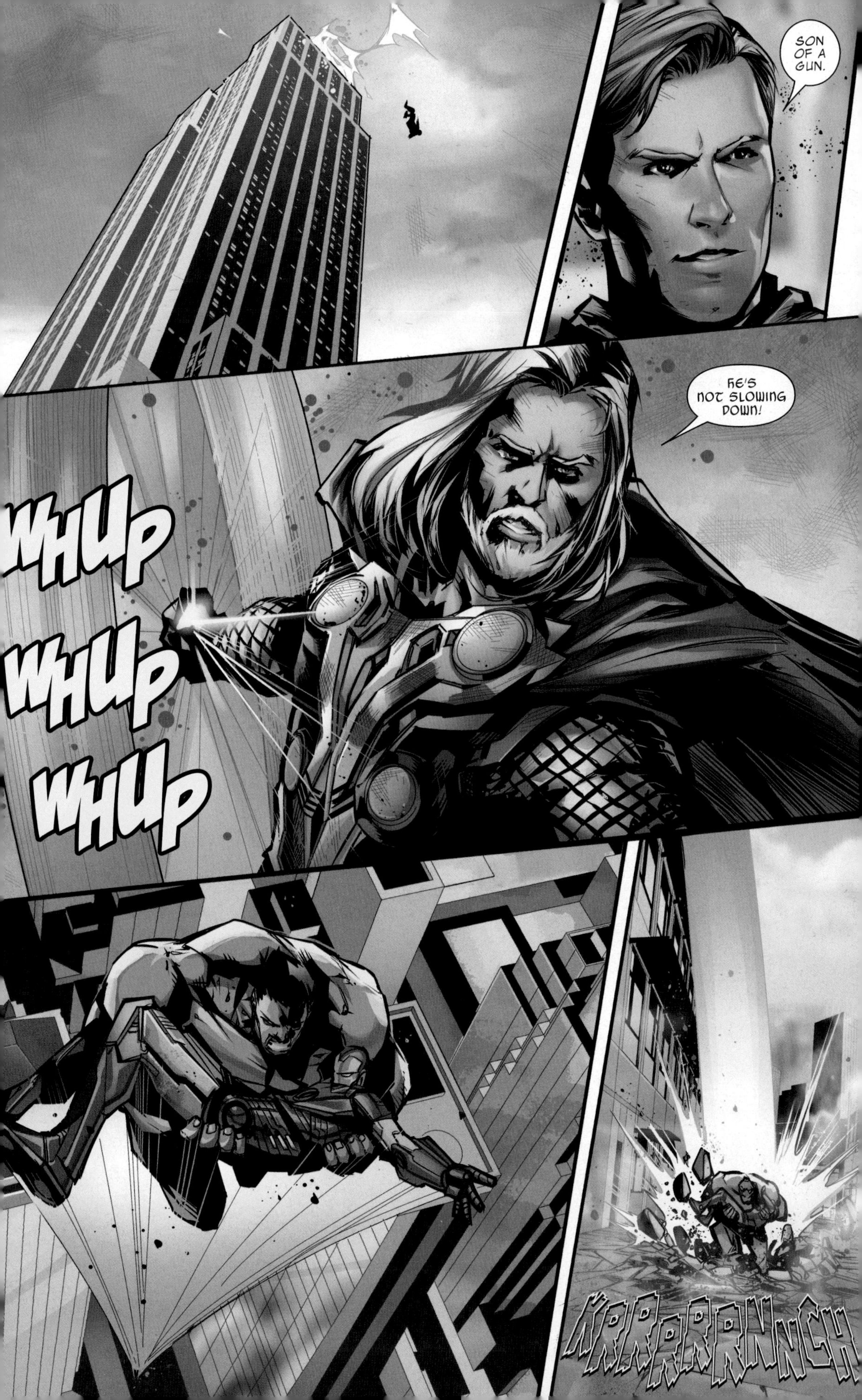
SON OF A GUN.
HE'S NOT SLOWING DOWN!
WHUP
WHUP
WHUP
KRRRRRRNNCH

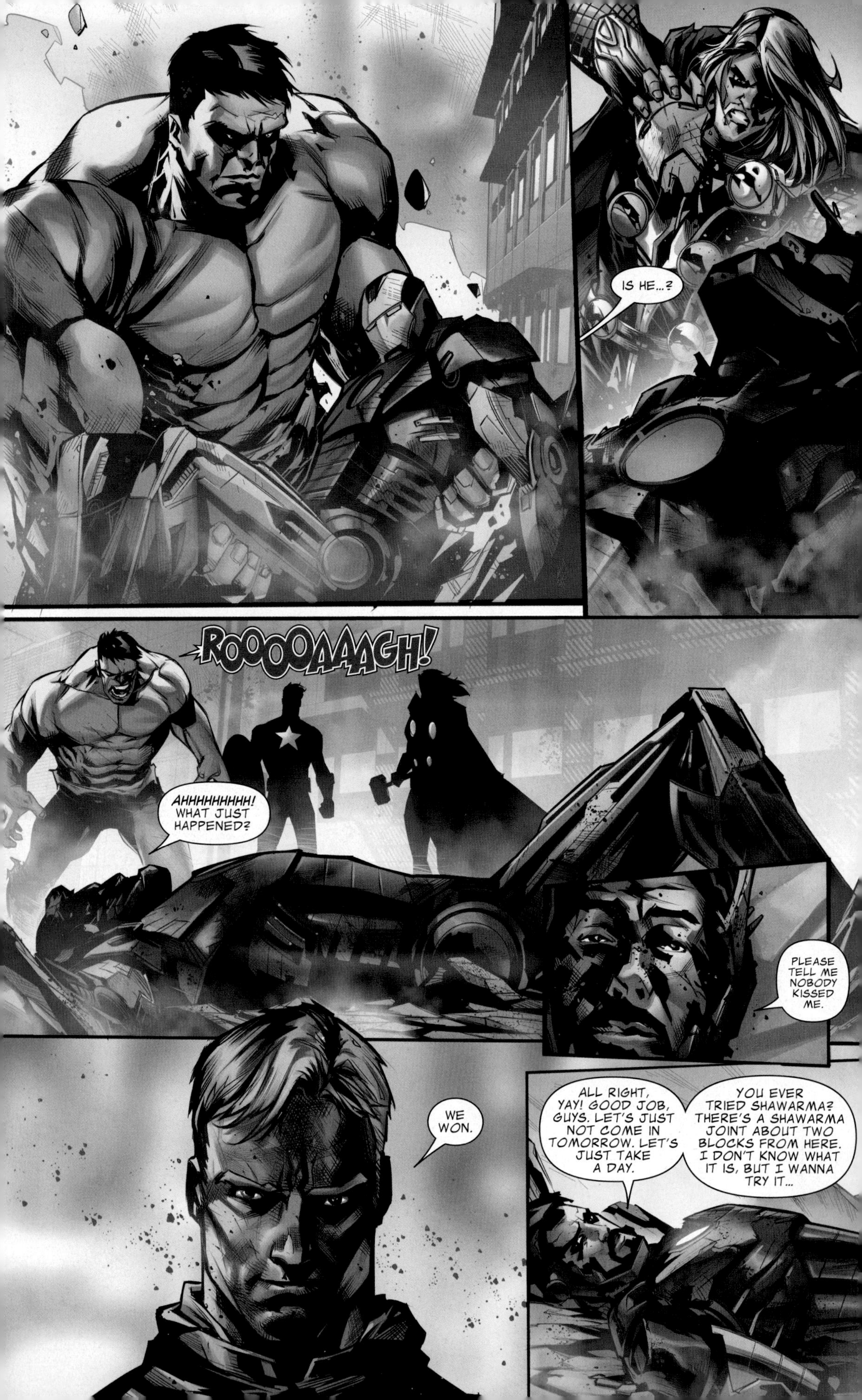
IS HE...?
ROOOOAAAGH!
AHHHHHHHHH! WHAT JUST HAPPENED?
PLEASE TELL ME NOBODY KISSED ME.
WE WON.
ALL RIGHT, YAY! GOOD JOB, GUYS. LET'S JUST NOT COME IN TOMORROW. LET'S JUST TAKE A DAY.
YOU EVER TRIED SHAWARMA? THERE'S A SHAWARMA JOINT ABOUT TWO BLOCKS FROM HERE. I DON'T KNOW WHAT IT IS, BUT I WANNA TRY IT...

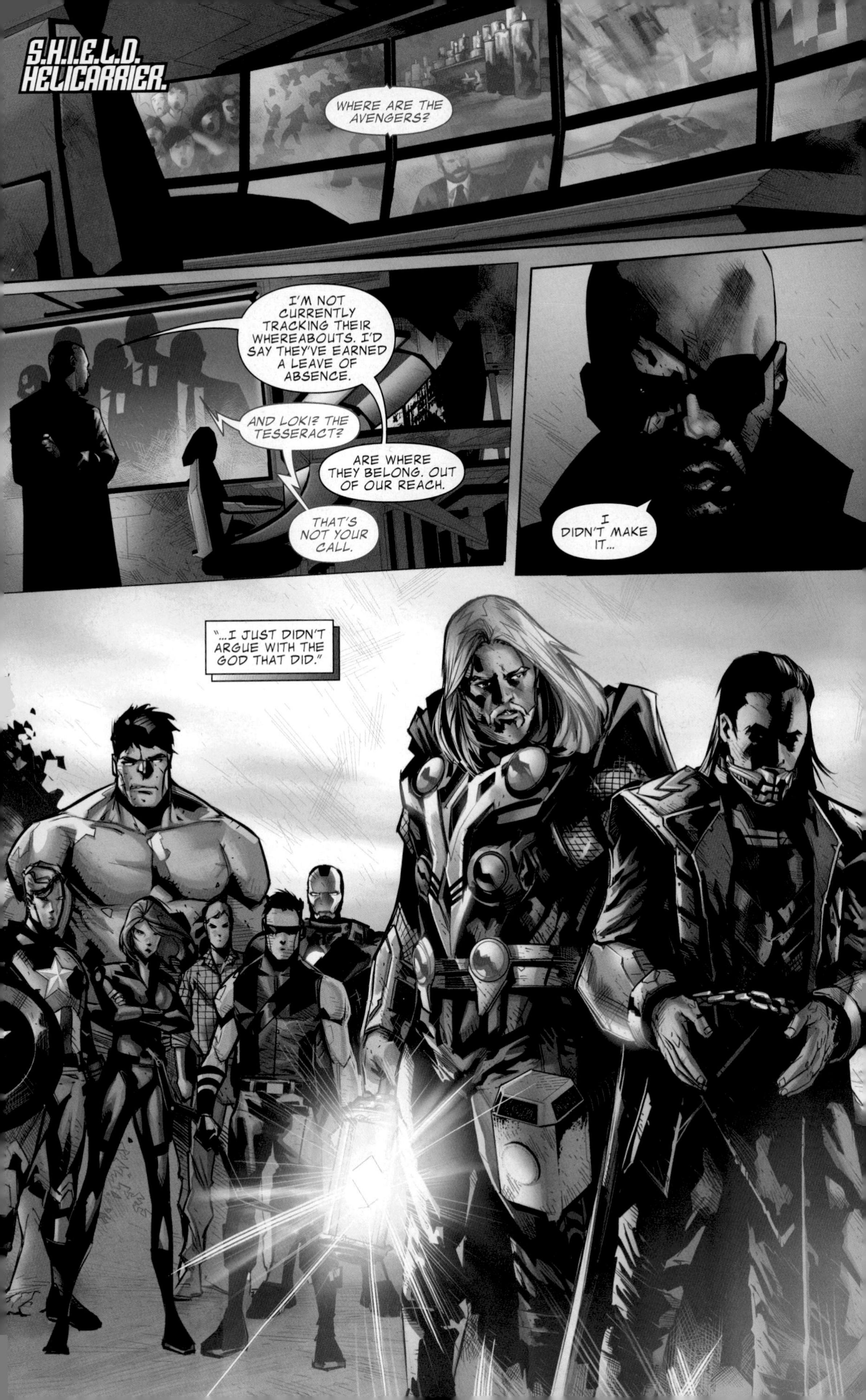
S.H.I.E.L.D. HELICARRIER.
WHERE ARE THE AVENGERS?
I'M NOT CURRENTLY TRACKING THEIR WHEREABOUTS. I'D SAY THEY'VE EARNED A LEAVE OF ABSENCE.
AND LOKI? THE TESSERACT?
ARE WHERE THEY BELONG. OUT OF OUR REACH.
THAT'S NOT YOUR CALL.
I DIDN'T MAKE IT...
"...I JUST DIDN'T ARGUE WITH THE GOD THAT DID."

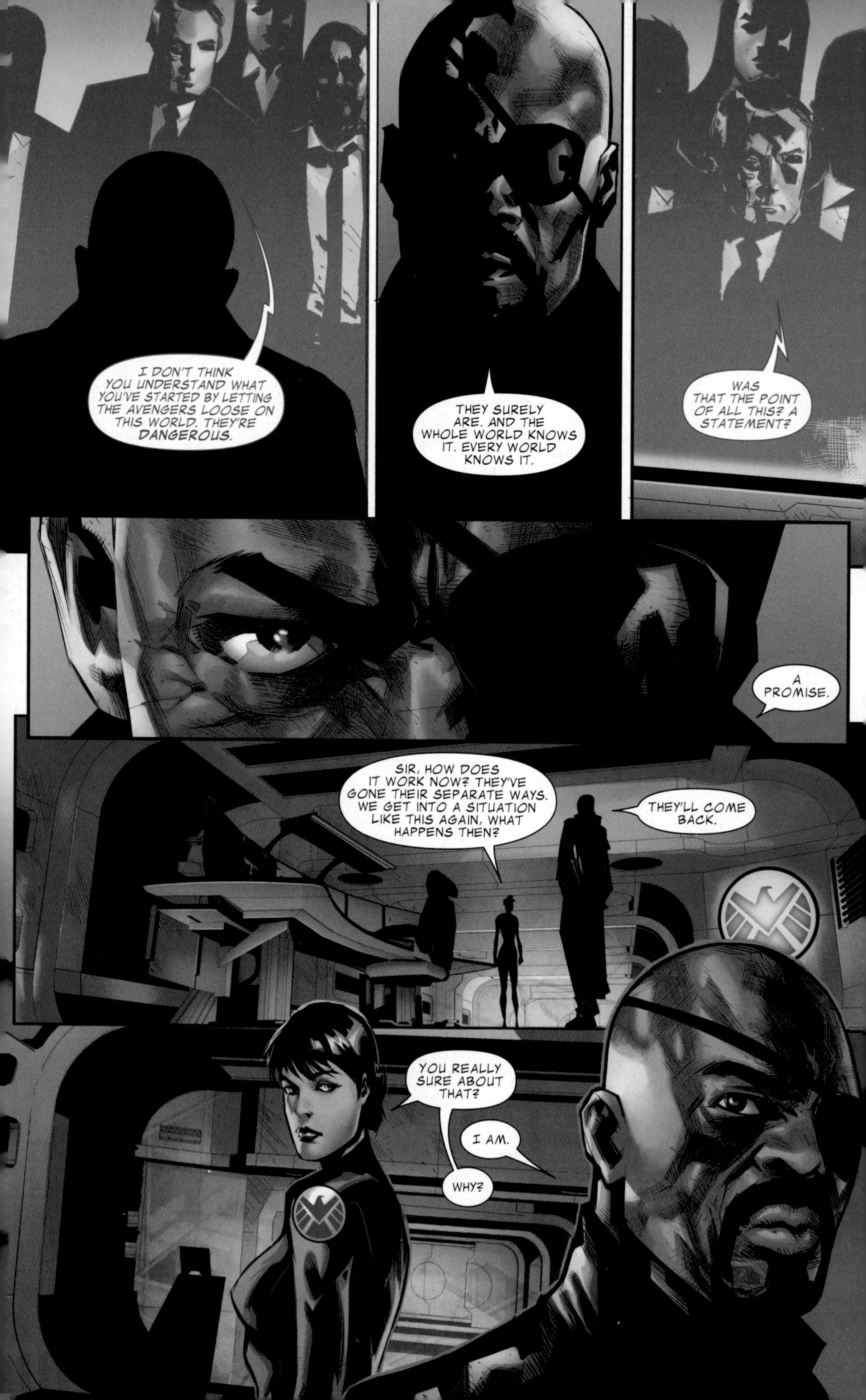
I DON'T THINK YOU UNDERSTAND WHAT YOU'VE STARTED BY LETTING THE AVENGERS LOOSE ON THIS WORLD. THEY'RE DANGEROUS.
THEY SURELY ARE. AND THE WHOLE WORLD KNOWS IT. EVERY WORLD KNOWS IT.
WAS THAT THE POINT OF ALL THIS? A STATEMENT?
A PROMISE.
SIR, HOW DOES IT WORK NOW? THEY'VE GONE THEIR SEPARATE WAYS. WE GET INTO A SITUATION LIKE THIS AGAIN, WHAT HAPPENS THEN?
THEY'LL COME BACK.
YOU REALLY SURE ABOUT THAT?
I AM.
WHY?

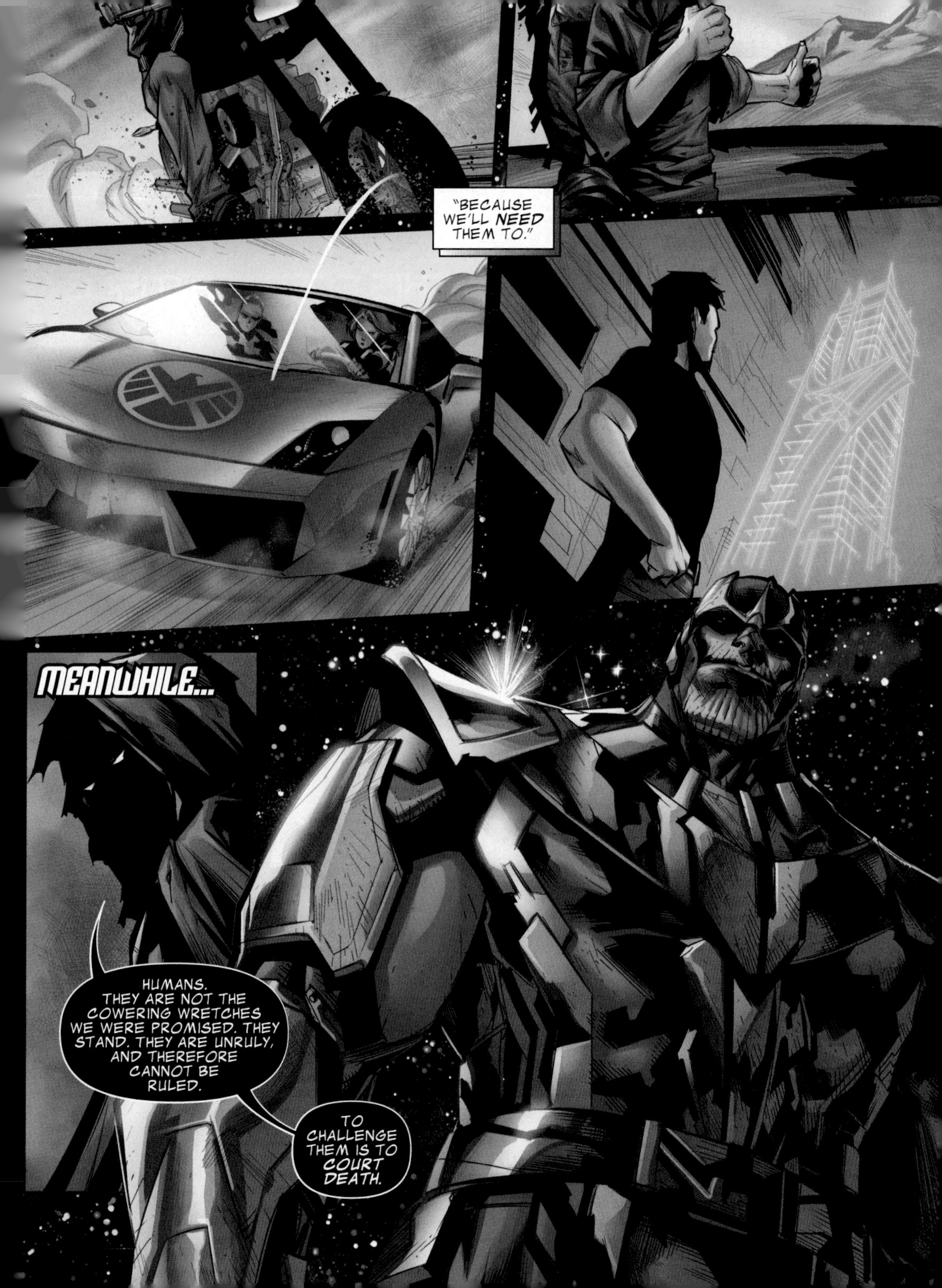
"BECAUSE WE'LL NEED THEM TO."
MEANWHILE...
HUMANS. THEY ARE NOT THE COWERING WRETCHES WE WERE PROMISED. THEY STAND. THEY ARE UNRULY, AND THEREFORE CANNOT BE RULED.
TO CHALLENGE THEM IS TO COURT DEATH.

MARVEL
AVENGERS
AGE OF ULTRON
PRELUDE
THIS SCEPTER'D ISLE

MARVEL
AVENGERS
AGE OF ULTRON
PRELUDE

WILL CORONA PILGRIM - WRITER
GEOFFO & MAST - STORYBOARD ARTISTS
WELLINTON ALVES - PENCILER
MANNY CLARK - INKER
JAY DAVID RAMOS - COLORIST
VC'S CLAYTON COWLES - LETTERER

ARLIN ORTIZ - PRODUCTION **TIM SMITH 3** - PRODUCTION MANAGER
EMILY SHAW - CONSULTING EDITOR **BILL ROSEMANN** & **MARK BASSO** - EDITORS
AXEL ALONSO - EDITOR IN CHIEF **JOE QUESADA** - CHIEF CREATIVE OFFICER **DAN BUCKLEY** - PUBLISHER

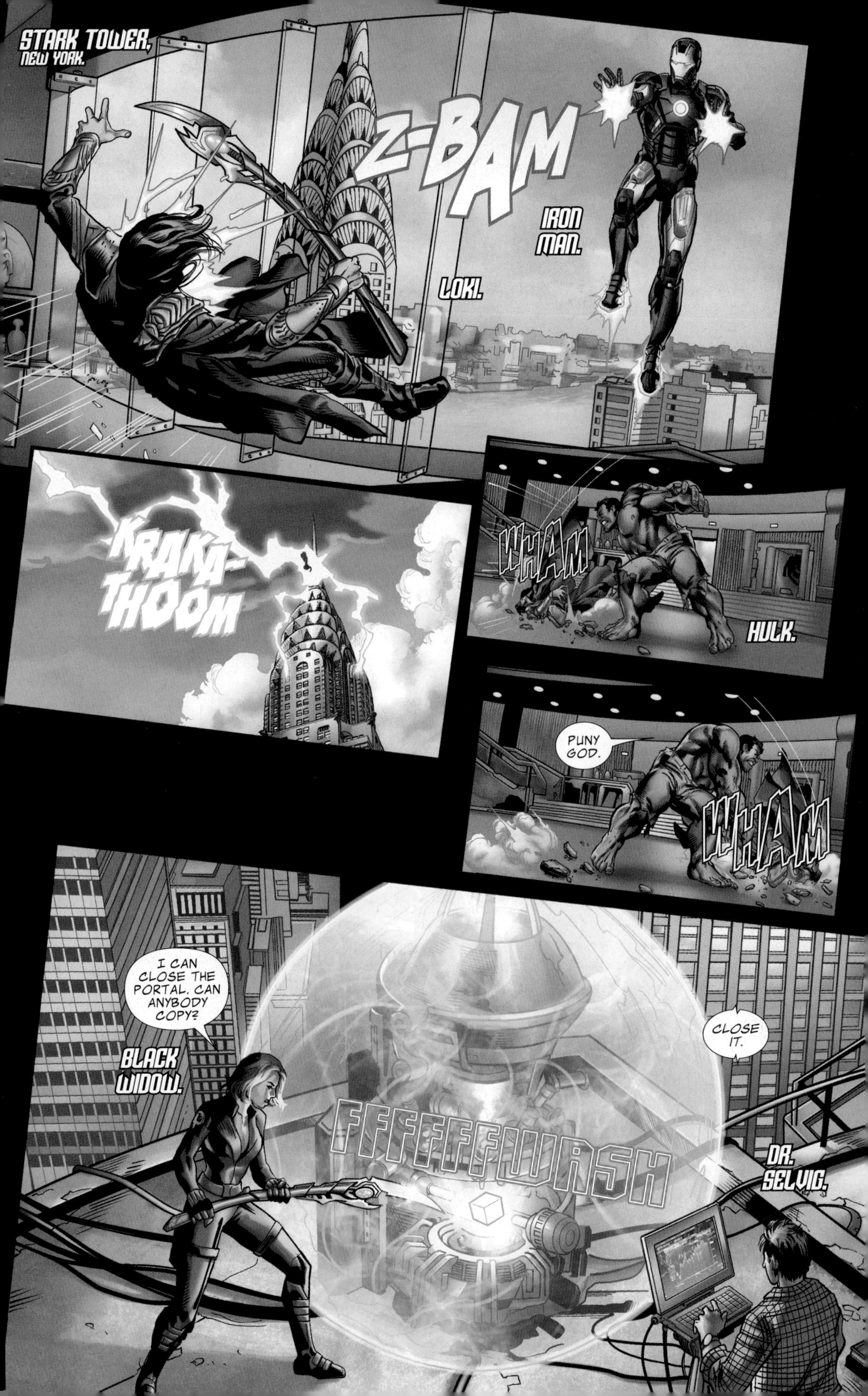
STARK TOWER, NEW YORK.
Z-BAM
IRON MAN.
LOKI.
KRAKA-THOOM
WHAM
HULK.
PUNY GOD.
WHAM
I CAN CLOSE THE PORTAL. CAN ANYBODY COPY?
BLACK WIDOW.
CLOSE IT.
FFFFFFWASH
DR. SELVIG.

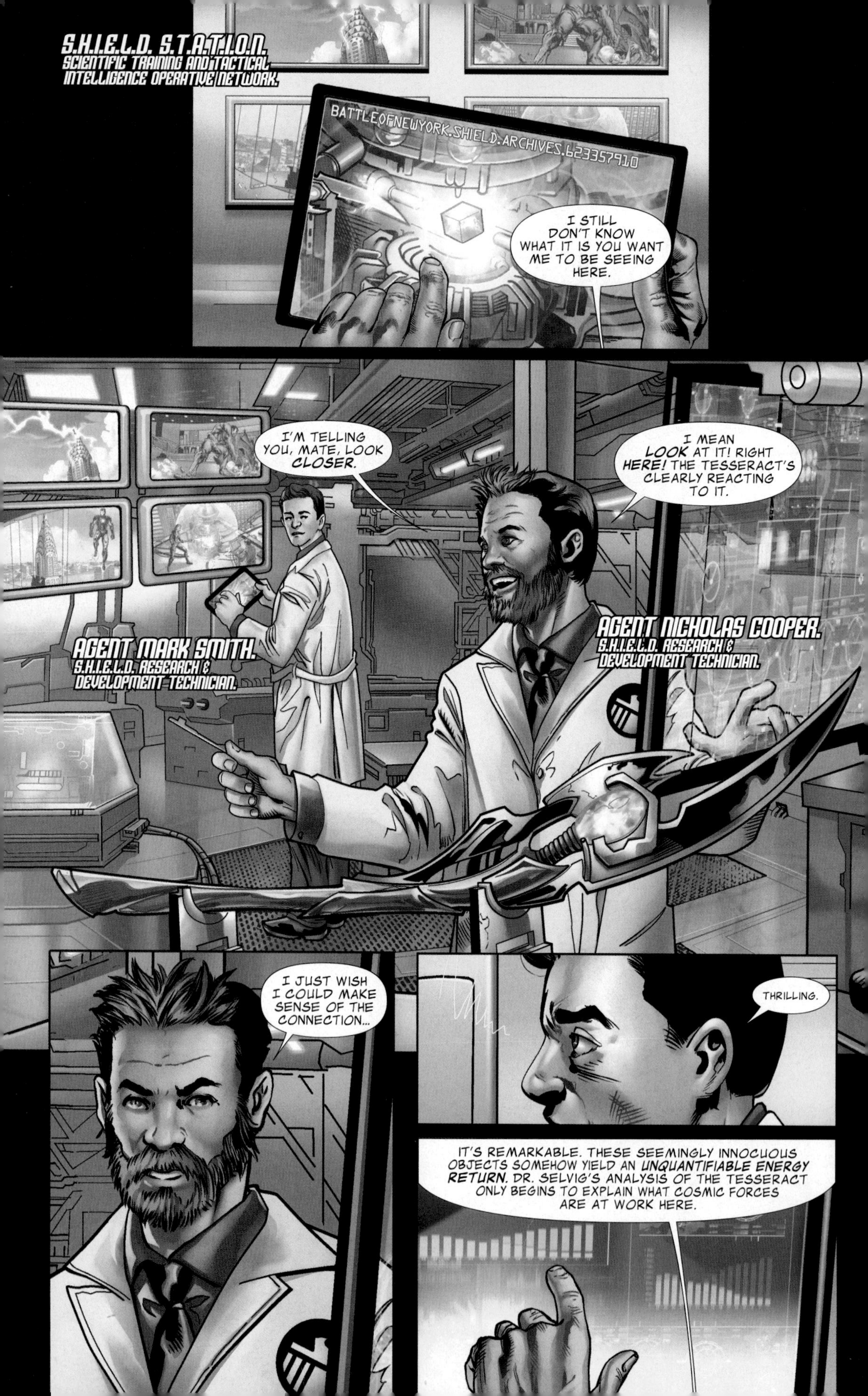
S.H.I.E.L.D. S.T.A.T.I.O.N.
SCIENTIFIC TRAINING AND TACTICAL INTELLIGENCE OPERATIVE NETWORK.
BATTLEOFNEWYORK.SHIELD.ARCHIVES.623357910
I STILL DON'T KNOW WHAT IT IS YOU WANT ME TO BE SEEING HERE.
I'M TELLING YOU, MATE, LOOK CLOSER.
I MEAN LOOK AT IT! RIGHT HERE! THE TESSERACT'S CLEARLY REACTING TO IT.
AGENT MARK SMITH.
S.H.I.E.L.D. RESEARCH & DEVELOPMENT TECHNICIAN.
AGENT NICHOLAS COOPER.
S.H.I.E.L.D. RESEARCH & DEVELOPMENT TECHNICIAN.
I JUST WISH I COULD MAKE SENSE OF THE CONNECTION...
THRILLING.
IT'S REMARKABLE. THESE SEEMINGLY INNOCUOUS OBJECTS SOMEHOW YIELD AN UNQUANTIFIABLE ENERGY RETURN. DR. SELVIG'S ANALYSIS OF THE TESSERACT ONLY BEGINS TO EXPLAIN WHAT COSMIC FORCES ARE AT WORK HERE.

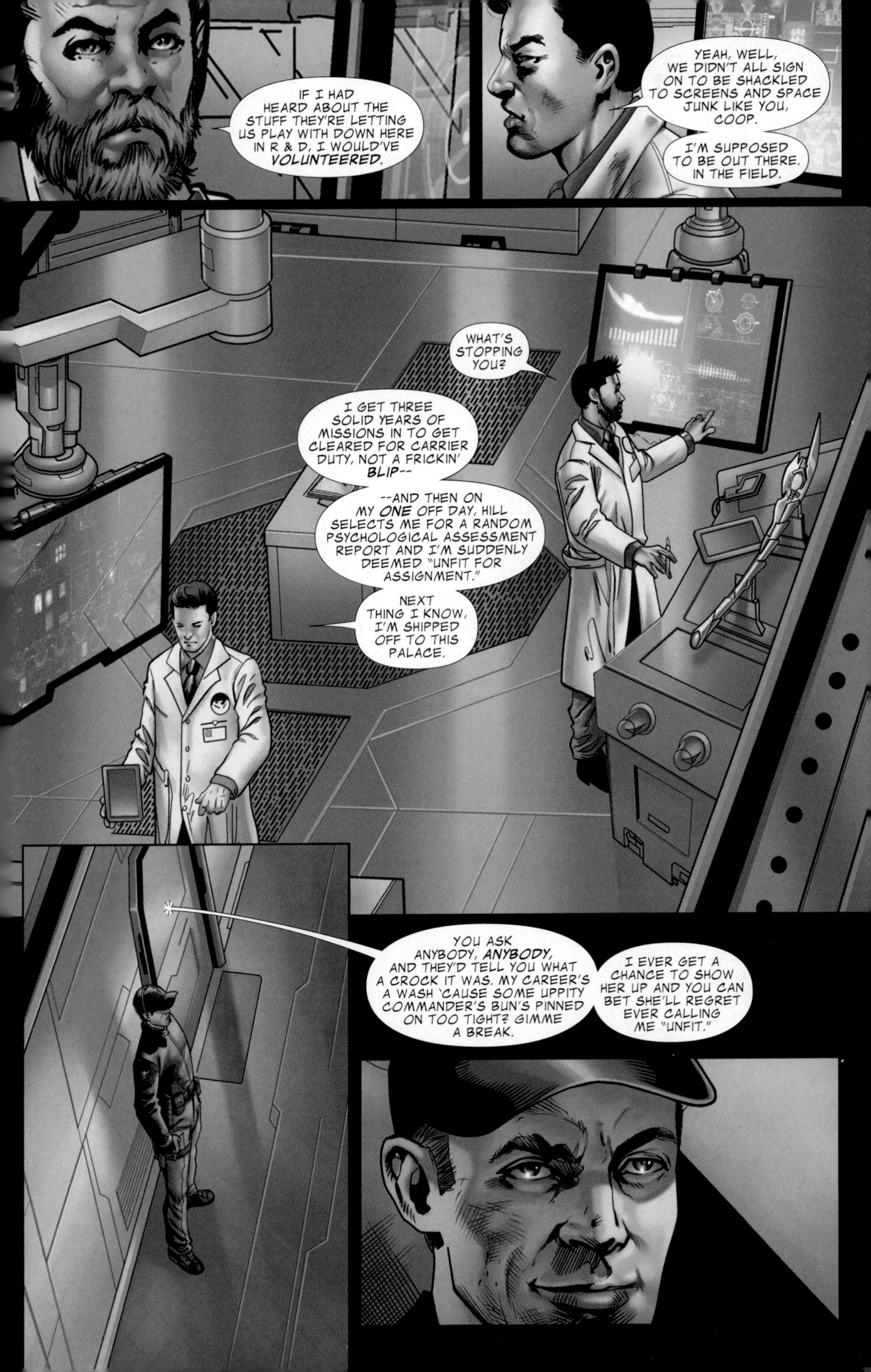
IF I HAD HEARD ABOUT THE STUFF THEY'RE LETTING US PLAY WITH DOWN HERE IN R & D, I WOULD'VE VOLUNTEERED.
YEAH, WELL, WE DIDN'T ALL SIGN ON TO BE SHACKLED TO SCREENS AND SPACE JUNK LIKE YOU, COOP.
I'M SUPPOSED TO BE OUT THERE. IN THE FIELD.
WHAT'S STOPPING YOU?
I GET THREE SOLID YEARS OF MISSIONS IN TO GET CLEARED FOR CARRIER DUTY, NOT A FRICKIN' BLIP--
--AND THEN ON MY ONE OFF DAY, HILL SELECTS ME FOR A RANDOM PSYCHOLOGICAL ASSESSMENT REPORT AND I'M SUDDENLY DEEMED "UNFIT FOR ASSIGNMENT."
NEXT THING I KNOW, I'M SHIPPED OFF TO THIS PALACE.
YOU ASK ANYBODY, ANYBODY, AND THEY'D TELL YOU WHAT A CROCK IT WAS. MY CAREER'S A WASH 'CAUSE SOME UPPITY COMMANDER'S BUN'S PINNED ON TOO TIGHT? GIMME A BREAK.
I EVER GET A CHANCE TO SHOW HER UP AND YOU CAN BET SHE'LL REGRET EVER CALLING ME "UNFIT."

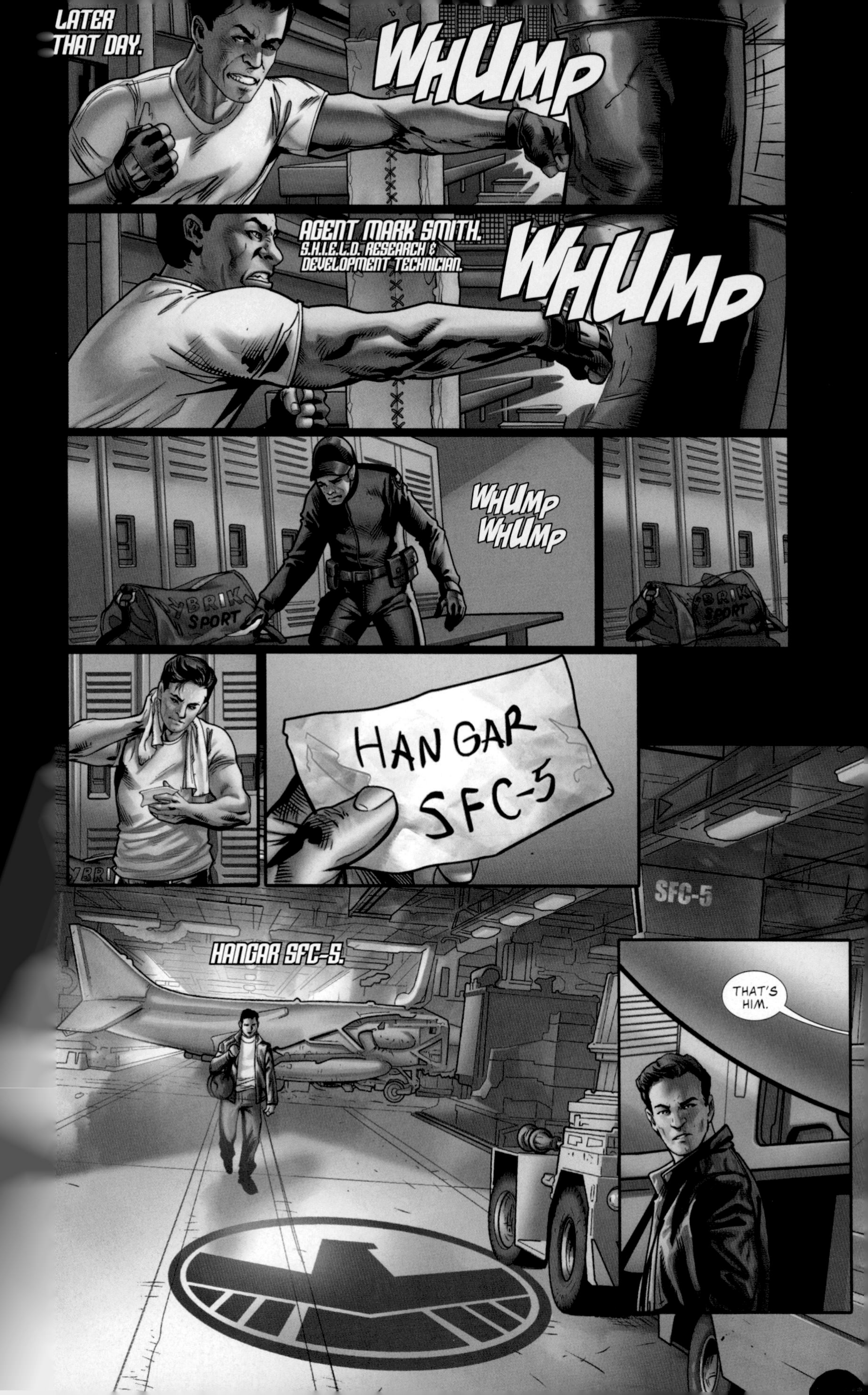
LATER THAT DAY.
WHUMP
AGENT MARK SMITH.
S.H.I.E.L.D. RESEARCH & DEVELOPMENT TECHNICIAN.
WHUMP
WHUMP WHUMP
BRIK SPORT
HANGAR SFC-5
SFC-5
HANGAR SFC-5.
THAT'S HIM.

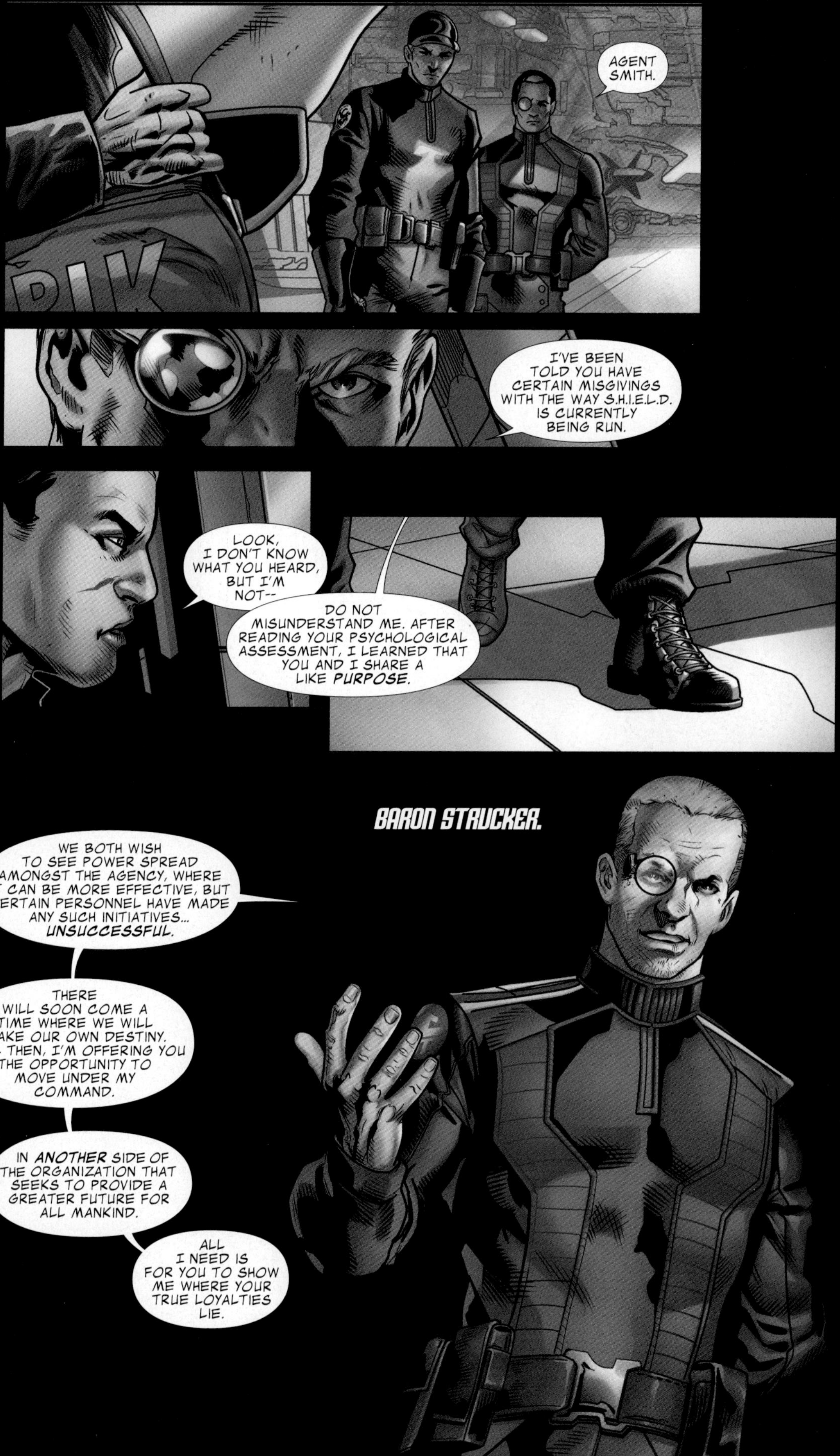
AGENT SMITH.
I'VE BEEN TOLD YOU HAVE CERTAIN MISGIVINGS WITH THE WAY S.H.I.E.L.D. IS CURRENTLY BEING RUN.
LOOK, I DON'T KNOW WHAT YOU HEARD, BUT I'M NOT--
DO NOT MISUNDERSTAND ME. AFTER READING YOUR PSYCHOLOGICAL ASSESSMENT, I LEARNED THAT YOU AND I SHARE A LIKE PURPOSE.
BARON STRUCKER.
WE BOTH WISH TO SEE POWER SPREAD AMONGST THE AGENCY, WHERE IT CAN BE MORE EFFECTIVE, BUT CERTAIN PERSONNEL HAVE MADE ANY SUCH INITIATIVES... UNSUCCESSFUL.
THERE WILL SOON COME A TIME WHERE WE WILL MAKE OUR OWN DESTINY. UNTIL THEN, I'M OFFERING YOU THE OPPORTUNITY TO MOVE UNDER MY COMMAND.
IN ANOTHER SIDE OF THE ORGANIZATION THAT SEEKS TO PROVIDE A GREATER FUTURE FOR ALL MANKIND.
ALL I NEED IS FOR YOU TO SHOW ME WHERE YOUR TRUE LOYALTIES LIE.

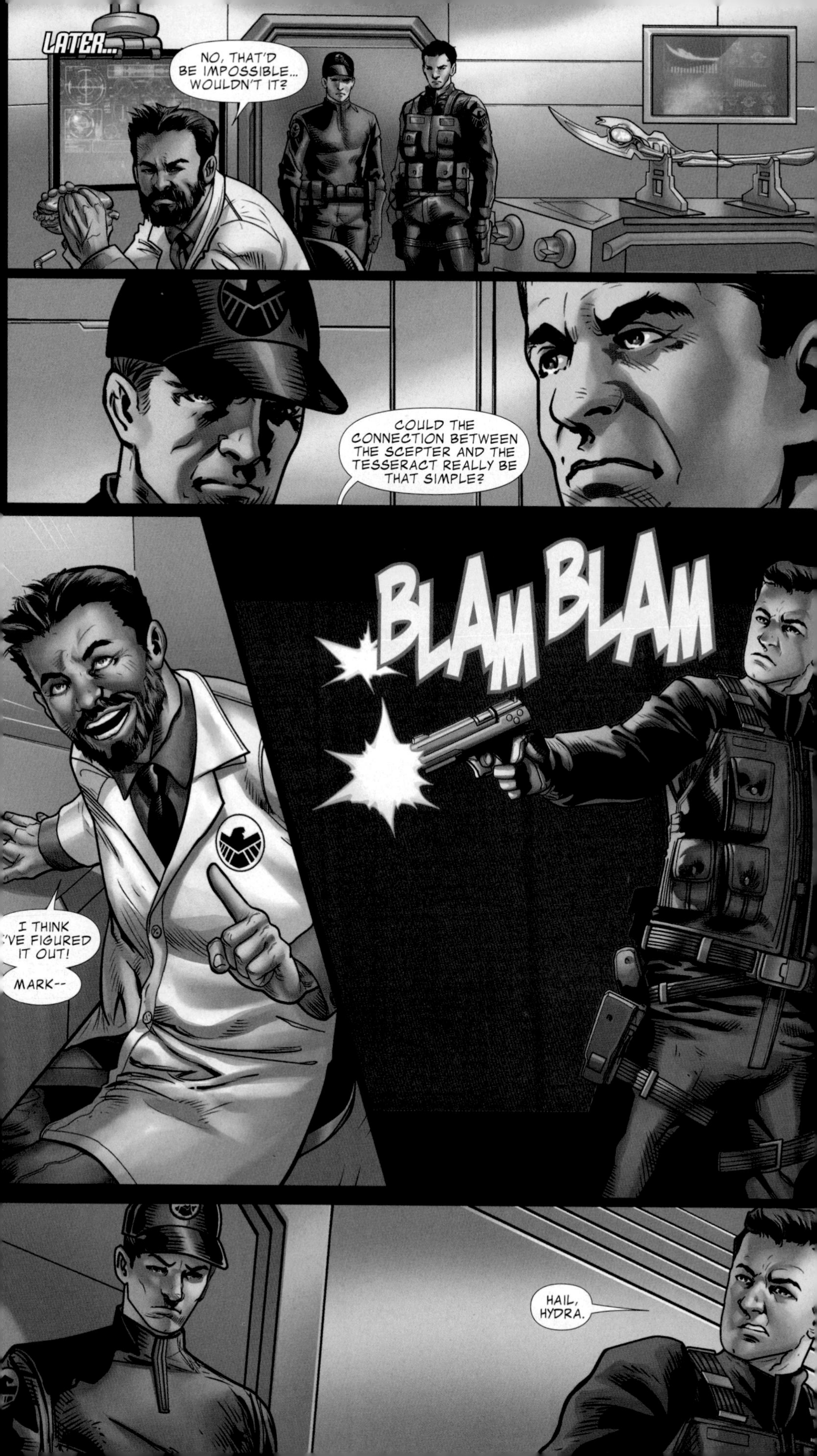
LATER...
NO, THAT'D BE IMPOSSIBLE... WOULDN'T IT?
COULD THE CONNECTION BETWEEN THE SCEPTER AND THE TESSERACT REALLY BE THAT SIMPLE?
I THINK 'VE FIGURED IT OUT!
MARK--
BLAM BLAM
HAIL, HYDRA.

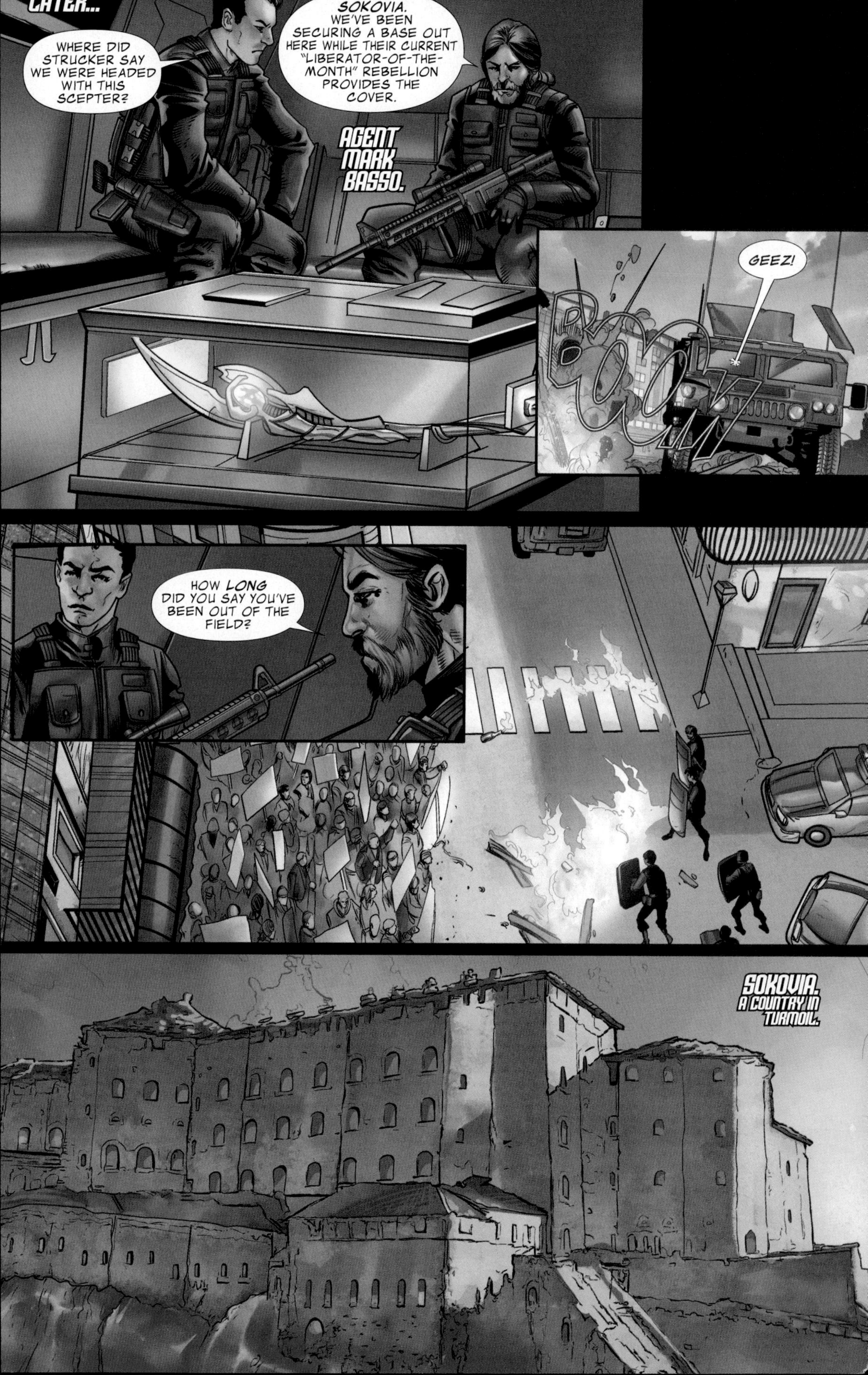
LATER...
WHERE DID STRUCKER SAY WE WERE HEADED WITH THIS SCEPTER?
SOKOVIA. WE'VE BEEN SECURING A BASE OUT HERE WHILE THEIR CURRENT "LIBERATOR-OF-THE-MONTH" REBELLION PROVIDES THE COVER.
AGENT MARK BASSO.
GEEZ!
BOOM
HOW LONG DID YOU SAY YOU'VE BEEN OUT OF THE FIELD?
SOKOVIA. A COUNTRY IN TURMOIL.

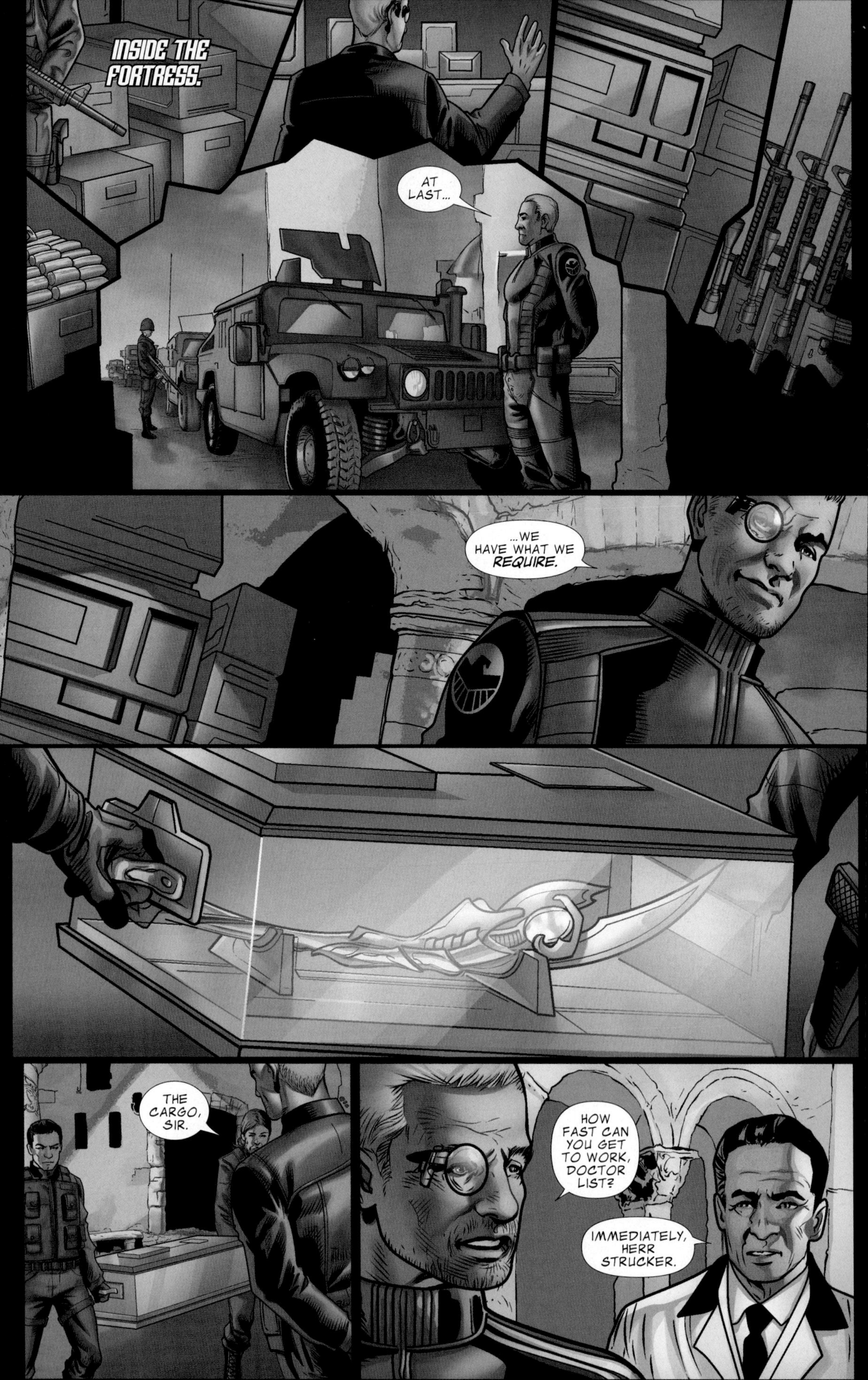
INSIDE THE FORTRESS.
AT LAST...
...WE HAVE WHAT WE REQUIRE.
THE CARGO, SIR.
HOW FAST CAN YOU GET TO WORK, DOCTOR LIST?
IMMEDIATELY, HERR STRUCKER.

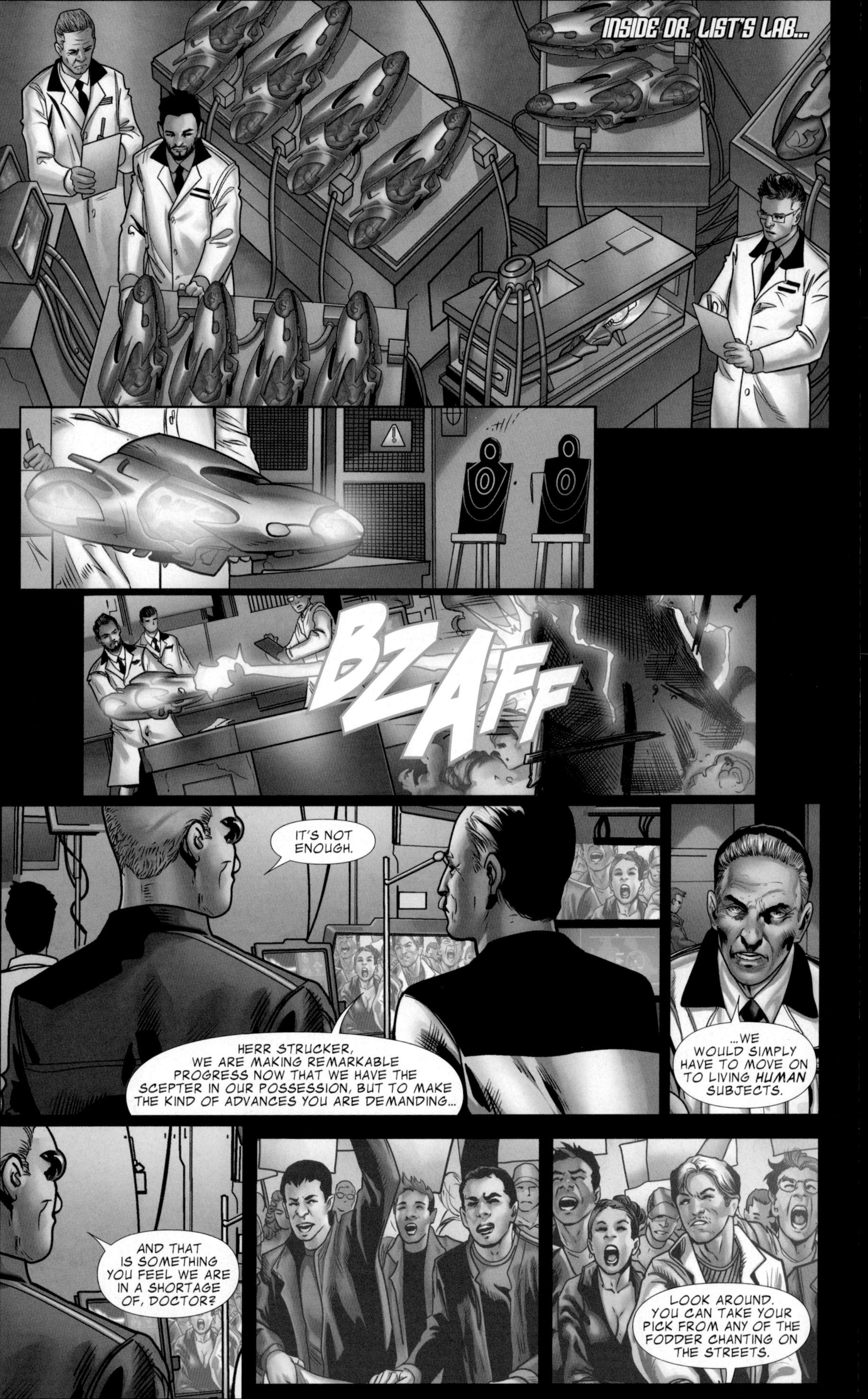
INSIDE DR. LIST'S LAB...
BZAFF
IT'S NOT ENOUGH.
HERR STRUCKER, WE ARE MAKING REMARKABLE PROGRESS NOW THAT WE HAVE THE SCEPTER IN OUR POSSESSION, BUT TO MAKE THE KIND OF ADVANCES YOU ARE DEMANDING...
...WE WOULD SIMPLY HAVE TO MOVE ON TO LIVING HUMAN SUBJECTS.
AND THAT IS SOMETHING YOU FEEL WE ARE IN A SHORTAGE OF, DOCTOR?
LOOK AROUND. YOU CAN TAKE YOUR PICK FROM ANY OF THE FODDER CHANTING ON THE STREETS.

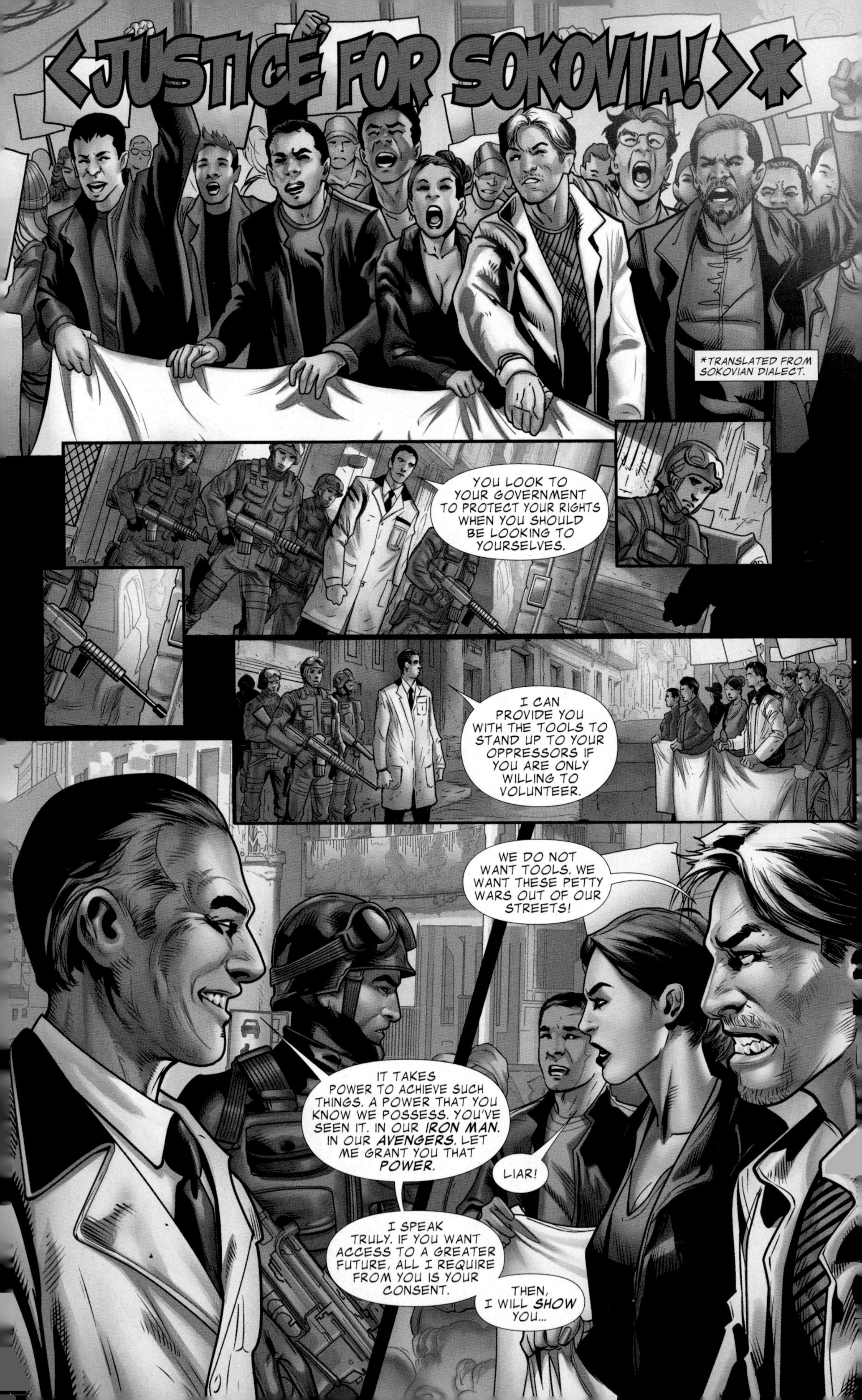

<JUSTICE FOR SOKOVIA!>*
*TRANSLATED FROM SOKOVIAN DIALECT.
YOU LOOK TO YOUR GOVERNMENT TO PROTECT YOUR RIGHTS WHEN YOU SHOULD BE LOOKING TO YOURSELVES.
I CAN PROVIDE YOU WITH THE TOOLS TO STAND UP TO YOUR OPPRESSORS IF YOU ARE ONLY WILLING TO VOLUNTEER.
WE DO NOT WANT TOOLS. WE WANT THESE PETTY WARS OUT OF OUR STREETS!
IT TAKES POWER TO ACHIEVE SUCH THINGS. A POWER THAT YOU KNOW WE POSSESS. YOU'VE SEEN IT. IN OUR IRON MAN. IN OUR AVENGERS. LET ME GRANT YOU THAT POWER.
LIAR!
I SPEAK TRULY. IF YOU WANT ACCESS TO A GREATER FUTURE, ALL I REQUIRE FROM YOU IS YOUR CONSENT.
THEN, I WILL SHOW YOU...

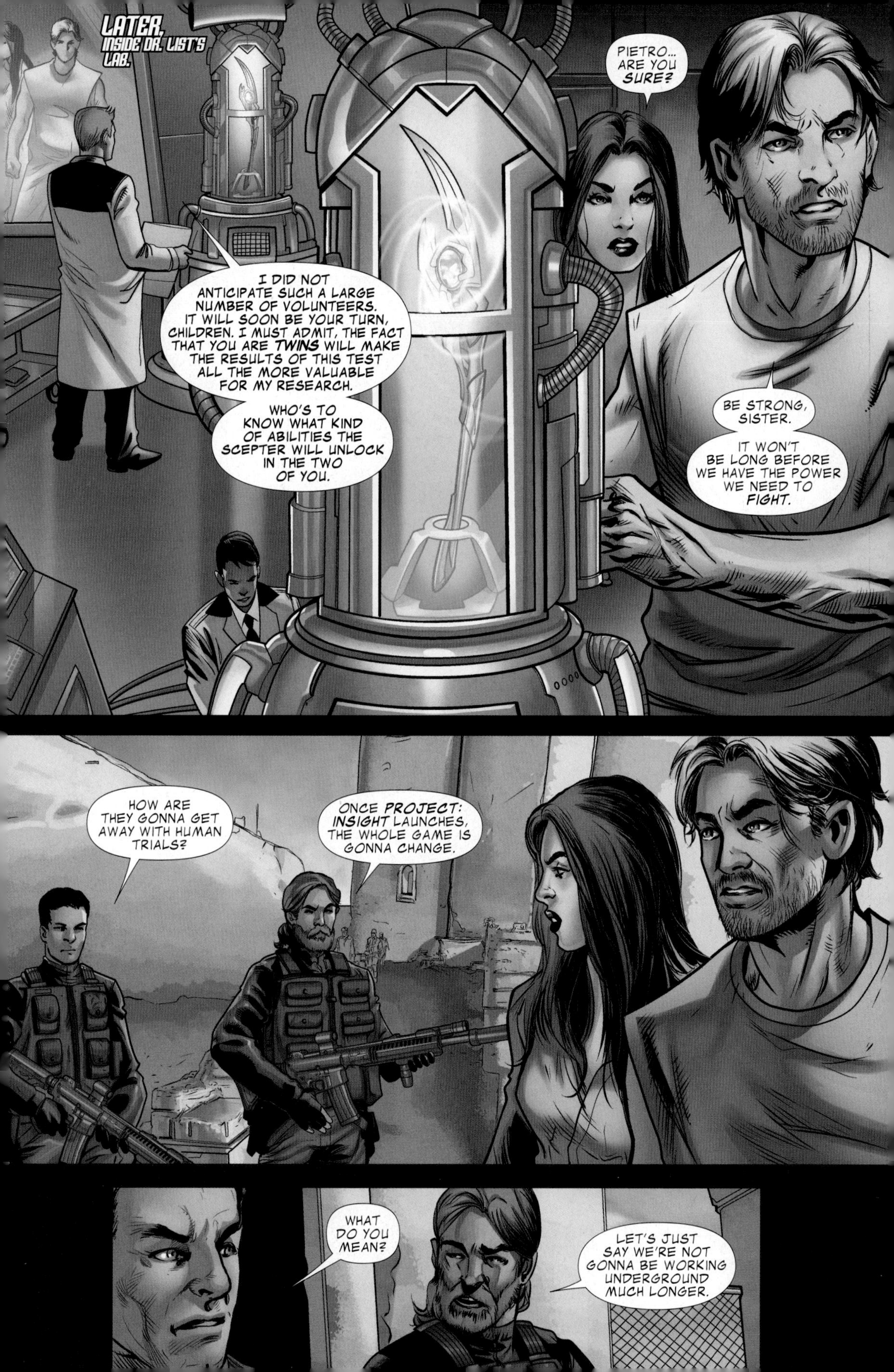
LATER, INSIDE DR. LIST'S LAB.
PIETRO... ARE YOU SURE?
I DID NOT ANTICIPATE SUCH A LARGE NUMBER OF VOLUNTEERS. IT WILL SOON BE YOUR TURN, CHILDREN. I MUST ADMIT, THE FACT THAT YOU ARE TWINS WILL MAKE THE RESULTS OF THIS TEST ALL THE MORE VALUABLE FOR MY RESEARCH.
WHO'S TO KNOW WHAT KIND OF ABILITIES THE SCEPTER WILL UNLOCK IN THE TWO OF YOU.
BE STRONG, SISTER.
IT WON'T BE LONG BEFORE WE HAVE THE POWER WE NEED TO FIGHT.
HOW ARE THEY GONNA GET AWAY WITH HUMAN TRIALS?
ONCE PROJECT: INSIGHT LAUNCHES, THE WHOLE GAME IS GONNA CHANGE.
WHAT DO YOU MEAN?
LET'S JUST SAY WE'RE NOT GONNA BE WORKING UNDERGROUND MUCH LONGER.

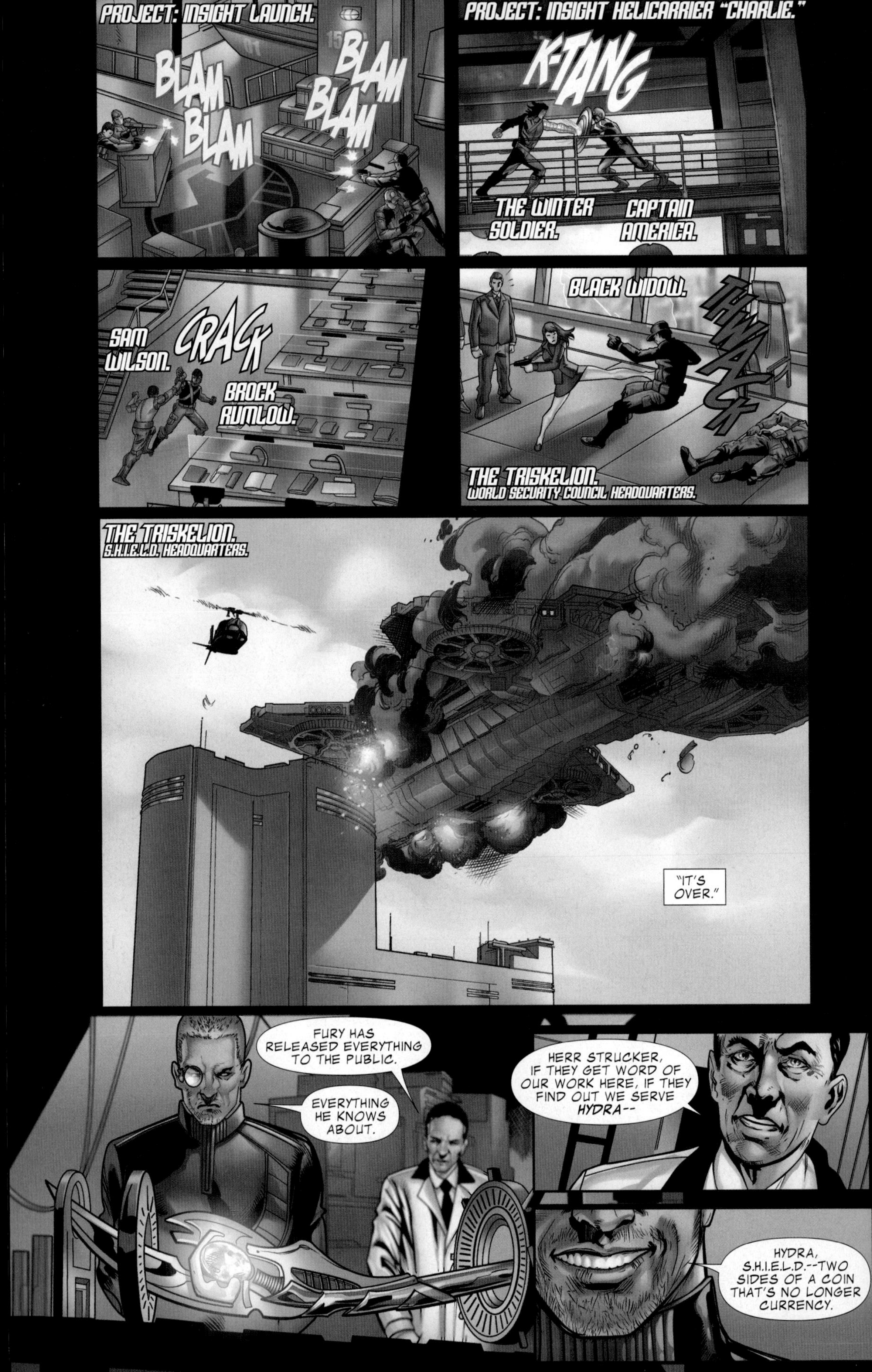
PROJECT: INSIGHT LAUNCH.
BLAM BLAM
BLAM BLAM
PROJECT: INSIGHT HELICARRIER "CHARLIE."
K-TANG
THE WINTER SOLDIER.
CAPTAIN AMERICA.
SAM WILSON.
CRACK
BROCK RUMLOW.
BLACK WIDOW.
THWACK
THE TRISKELION.
WORLD SECURITY COUNCIL HEADQUARTERS.
THE TRISKELION.
S.H.I.E.L.D. HEADQUARTERS.
"IT'S OVER."
FURY HAS RELEASED EVERYTHING TO THE PUBLIC.
EVERYTHING HE KNOWS ABOUT.
HERR STRUCKER, IF THEY GET WORD OF OUR WORK HERE, IF THEY FIND OUT WE SERVE HYDRA--
HYDRA, S.H.I.E.L.D.--TWO SIDES OF A COIN THAT'S NO LONGER CURRENCY.

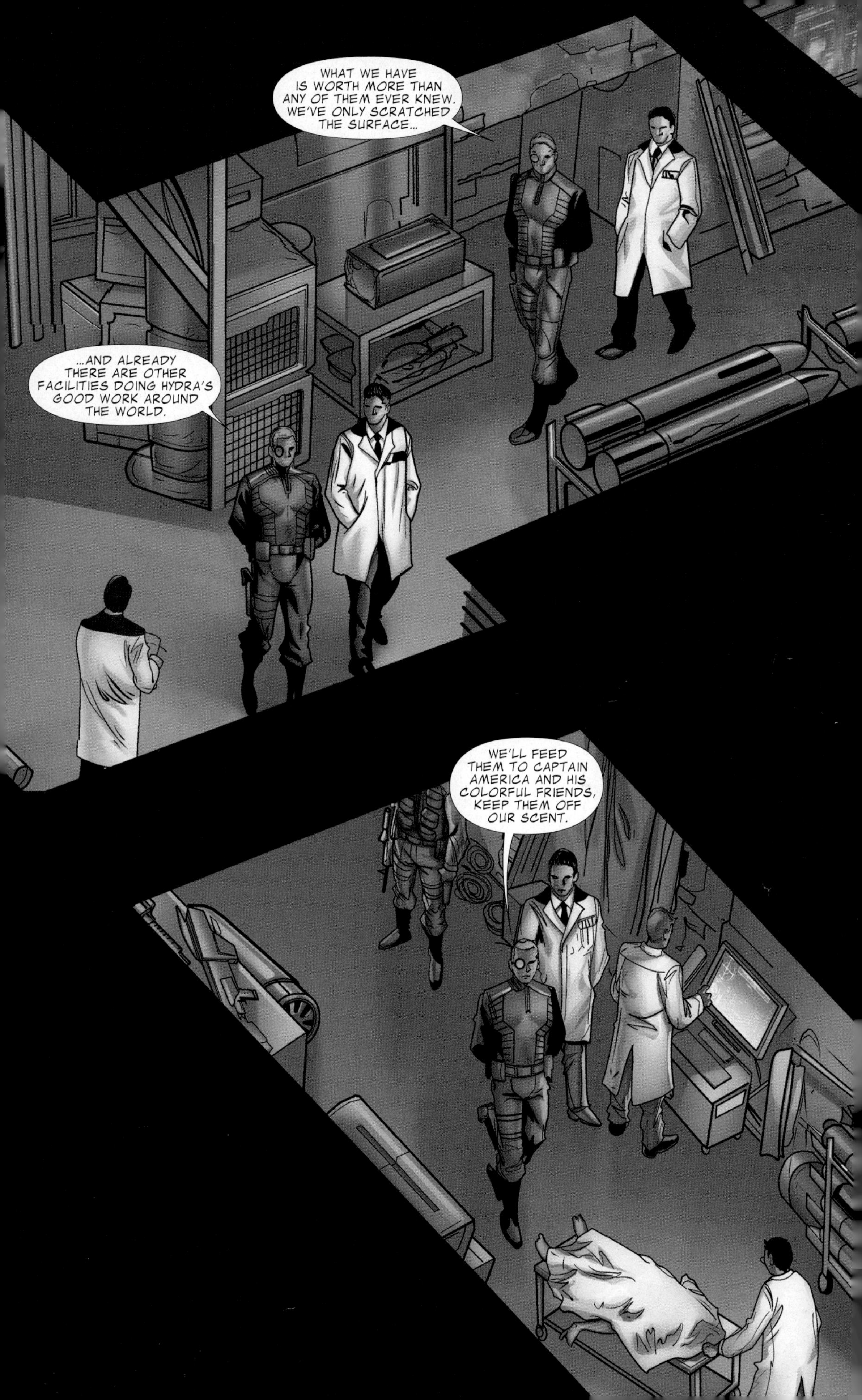
WHAT WE HAVE IS WORTH MORE THAN ANY OF THEM EVER KNEW. WE'VE ONLY SCRATCHED THE SURFACE...
...AND ALREADY THERE ARE OTHER FACILITIES DOING HYDRA'S GOOD WORK AROUND THE WORLD.
WE'LL FEED THEM TO CAPTAIN AMERICA AND HIS COLORFUL FRIENDS, KEEP THEM OFF OUR SCENT.

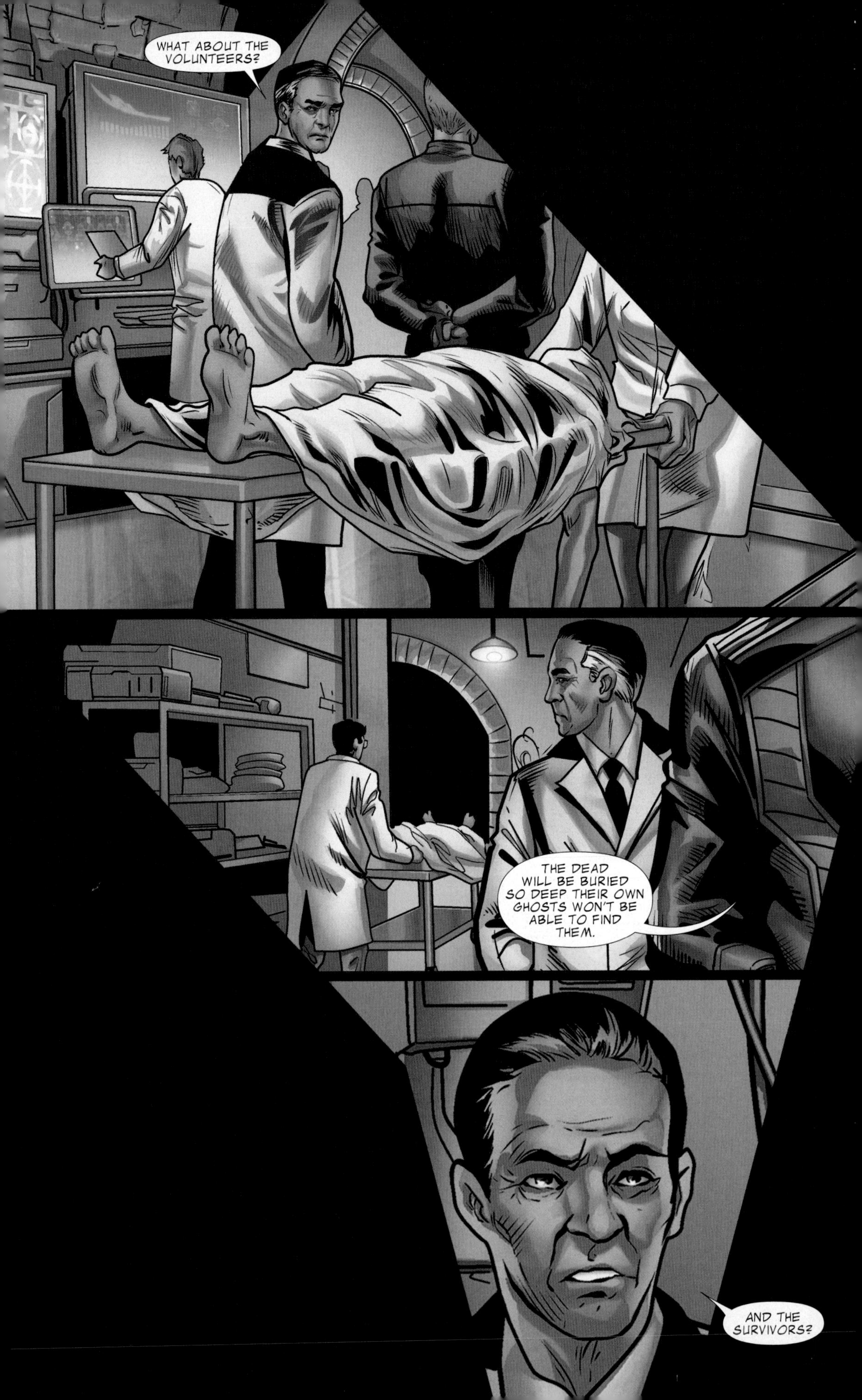
WHAT ABOUT THE VOLUNTEERS?
THE DEAD WILL BE BURIED SO DEEP THEIR OWN GHOSTS WON'T BE ABLE TO FIND THEM.
AND THE SURVIVORS?

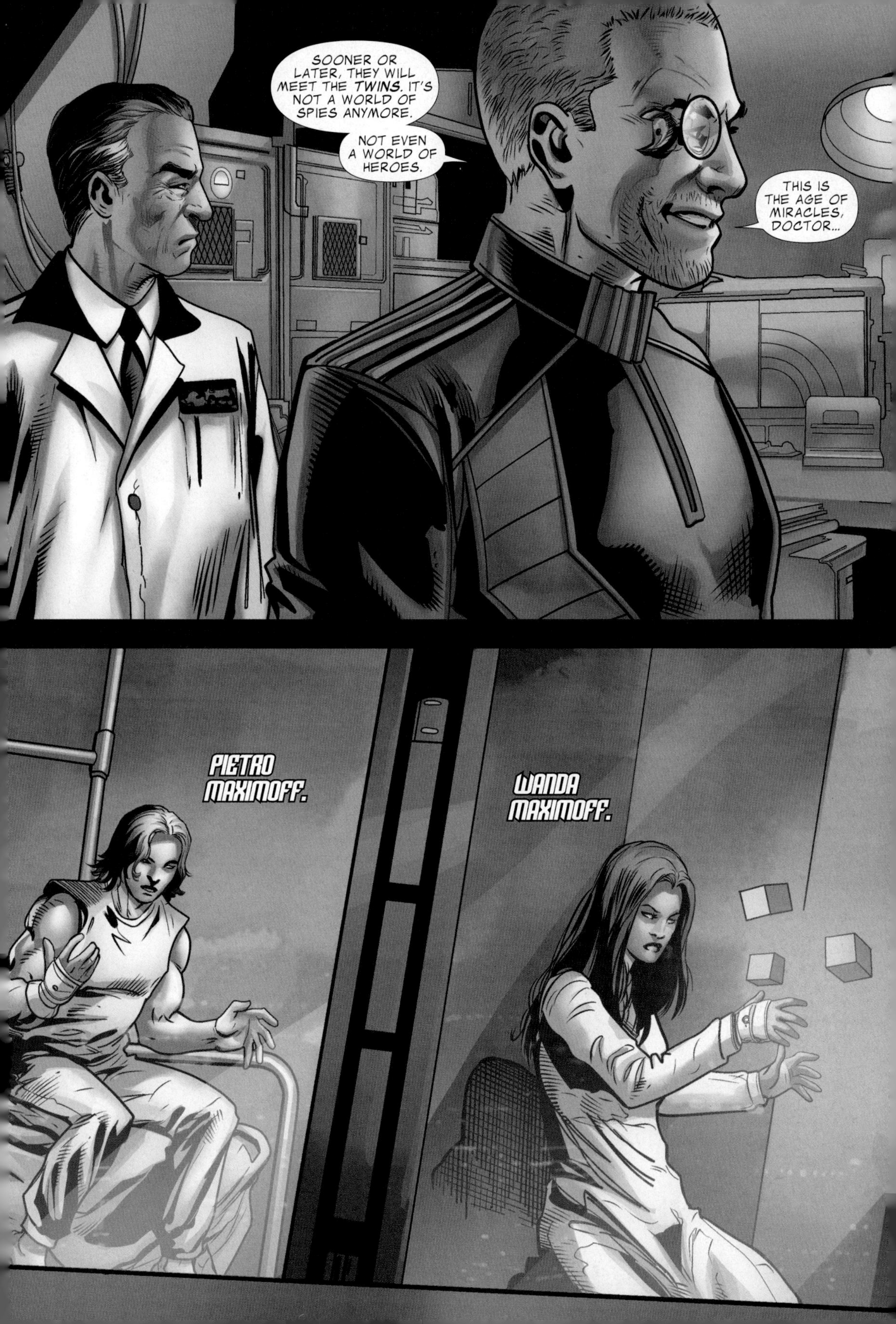
SOONER OR LATER, THEY WILL MEET THE TWINS. IT'S NOT A WORLD OF SPIES ANYMORE.
NOT EVEN A WORLD OF HEROES.
THIS IS THE AGE OF MIRACLES, DOCTOR...
PIETRO MAXIMOFF.
WANDA MAXIMOFF.

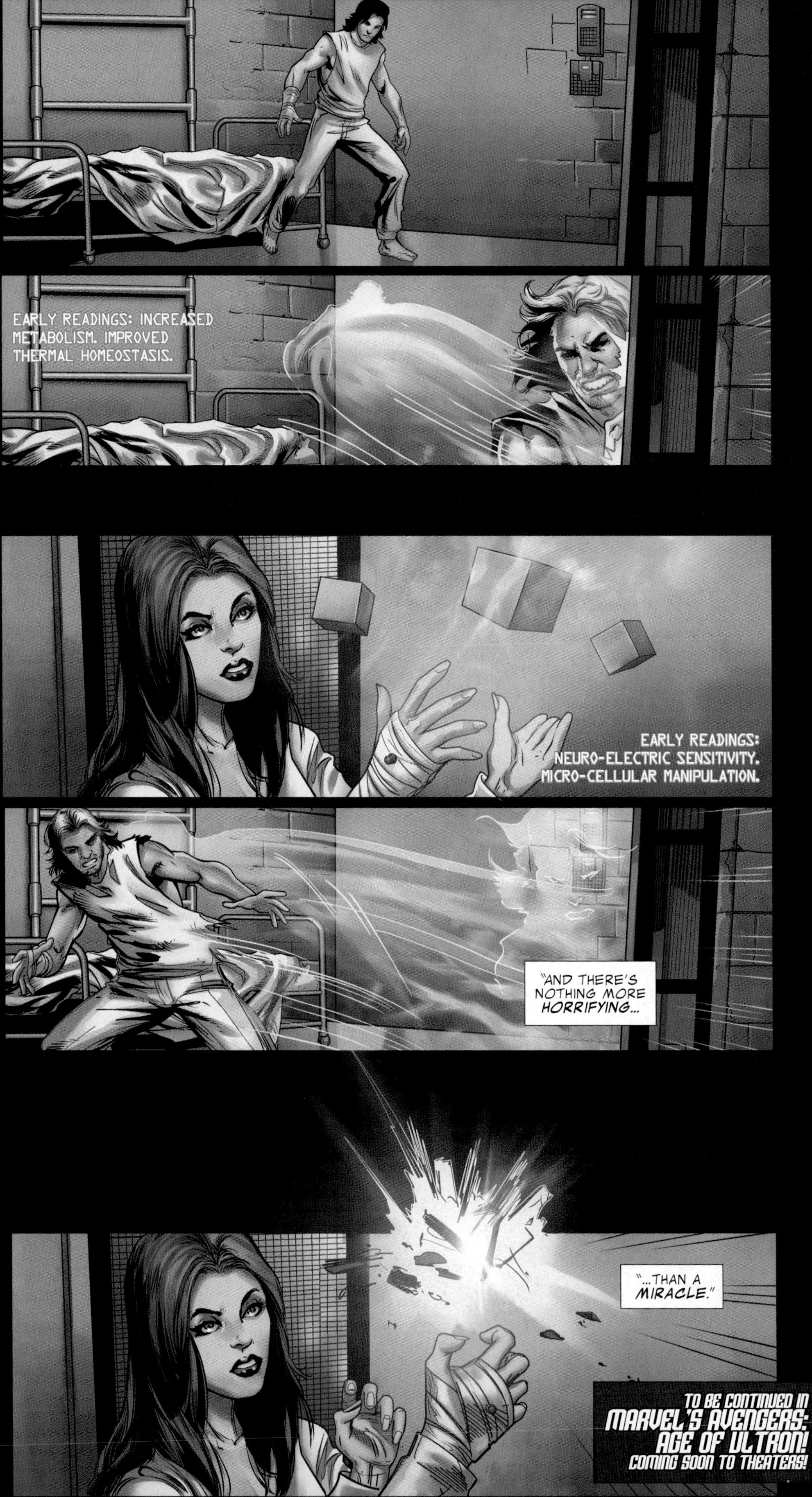
EARLY READINGS: INCREASED METABOLISM. IMPROVED THERMAL HOMEOSTASIS.
EARLY READINGS: NEURO-ELECTRIC SENSITIVITY. MICRO-CELLULAR MANIPULATION.
"AND THERE'S NOTHING MORE HORRIFYING...
"...THAN A MIRACLE."
TO BE CONTINUED IN MARVEL'S AVENGERS: AGE OF ULTRON! COMING SOON TO THEATERS!

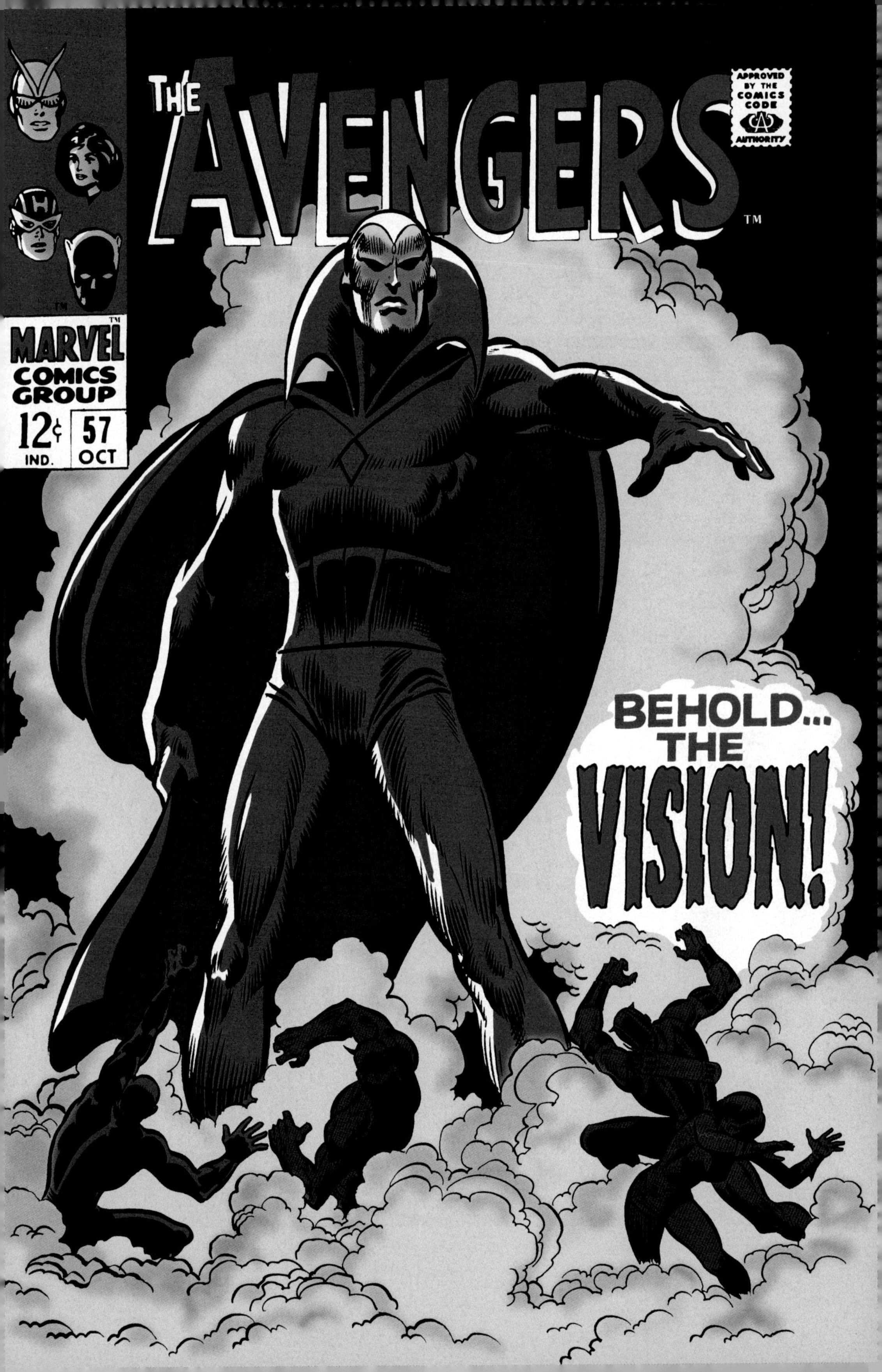
THE AVENGERS
APPROVED BY THE COMICS CODE AUTHORITY
MARVEL COMICS GROUP
12¢ IND.
57 OCT
BEHOLD... THE VISION!

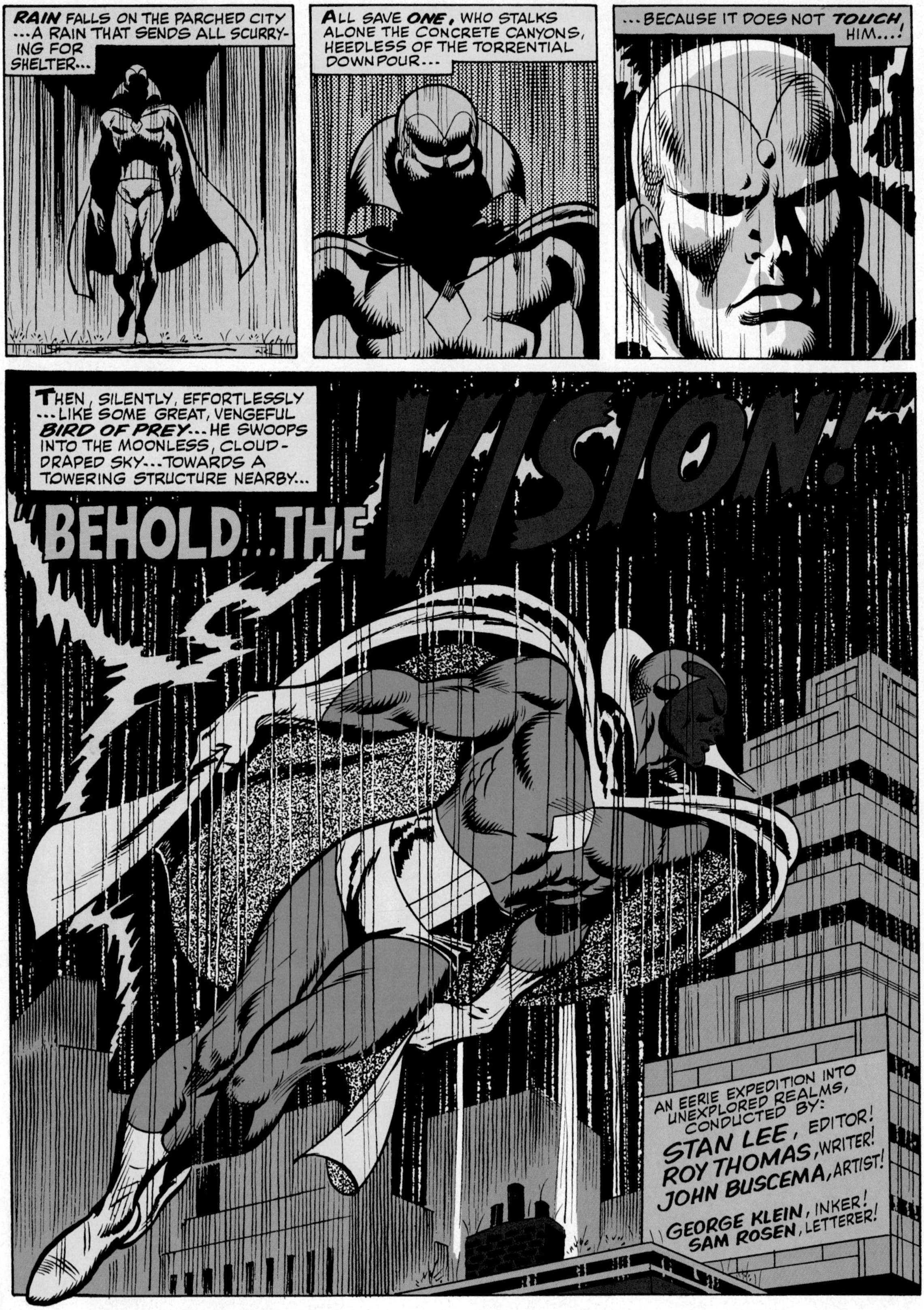
RAIN FALLS ON THE PARCHED CITY ...A RAIN THAT SENDS ALL SCURRYING FOR SHELTER...
ALL SAVE ONE, WHO STALKS ALONE THE CONCRETE CANYONS, HEEDLESS OF THE TORRENTIAL DOWNPOUR...
...BECAUSE IT DOES NOT TOUCH HIM...!
THEN, SILENTLY, EFFORTLESSLY ...LIKE SOME GREAT, VENGEFUL BIRD OF PREY...HE SWOOPS INTO THE MOONLESS, CLOUD-DRAPED SKY...TOWARDS A TOWERING STRUCTURE NEARBY...
"BEHOLD...THE VISION!"
AN EERIE EXPEDITION INTO UNEXPLORED REALMS, CONDUCTED BY:
STAN LEE, EDITOR!
ROY THOMAS, WRITER!
JOHN BUSCEMA, ARTIST!
GEORGE KLEIN, INKER!
SAM ROSEN, LETTERER!

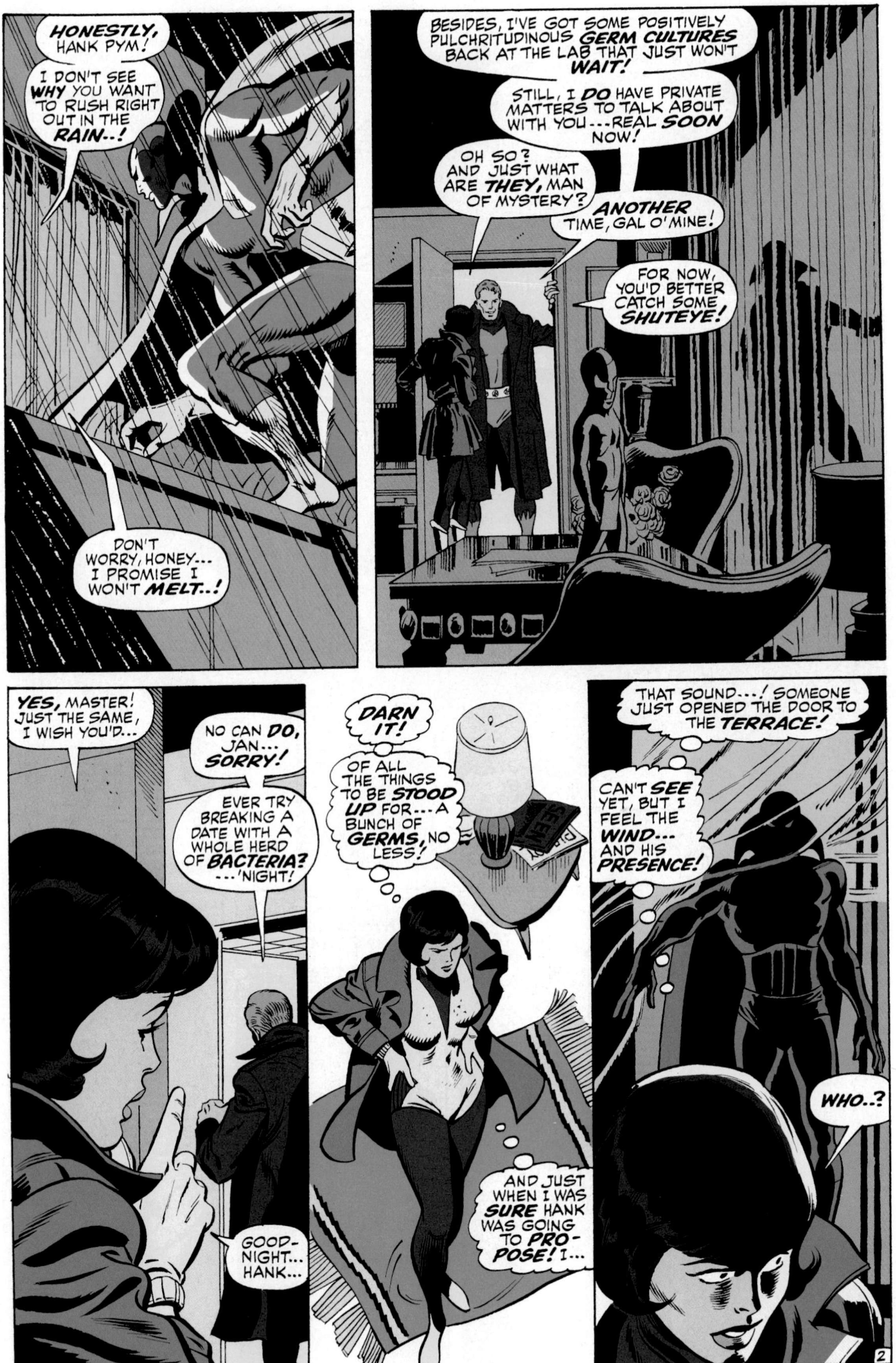
HONESTLY, HANK PYM!
I DON'T SEE WHY YOU WANT TO RUSH RIGHT OUT IN THE RAIN..!
DON'T WORRY, HONEY... I PROMISE I WON'T MELT..!
BESIDES, I'VE GOT SOME POSITIVELY PULCHRITUDINOUS GERM CULTURES BACK AT THE LAB THAT JUST WON'T WAIT!
STILL, I DO HAVE PRIVATE MATTERS TO TALK ABOUT WITH YOU---REAL SOON NOW!
OH SO? AND JUST WHAT ARE THEY, MAN OF MYSTERY?
ANOTHER TIME, GAL O'MINE!
FOR NOW, YOU'D BETTER CATCH SOME SHUTEYE!
YES, MASTER! JUST THE SAME, I WISH YOU'D...
NO CAN DO, JAN... SORRY!
EVER TRY BREAKING A DATE WITH A WHOLE HERD OF BACTERIA? ---'NIGHT!
GOOD-NIGHT... HANK...
DARN IT!
OF ALL THE THINGS TO BE STOOD UP FOR... A BUNCH OF GERMS, NO LESS!
AND JUST WHEN I WAS SURE HANK WAS GOING TO PRO-POSE! I...
THAT SOUND...! SOMEONE JUST OPENED THE DOOR TO THE TERRACE!
CAN'T SEE YET, BUT I FEEL THE WIND... AND HIS PRESENCE!
WHO..?

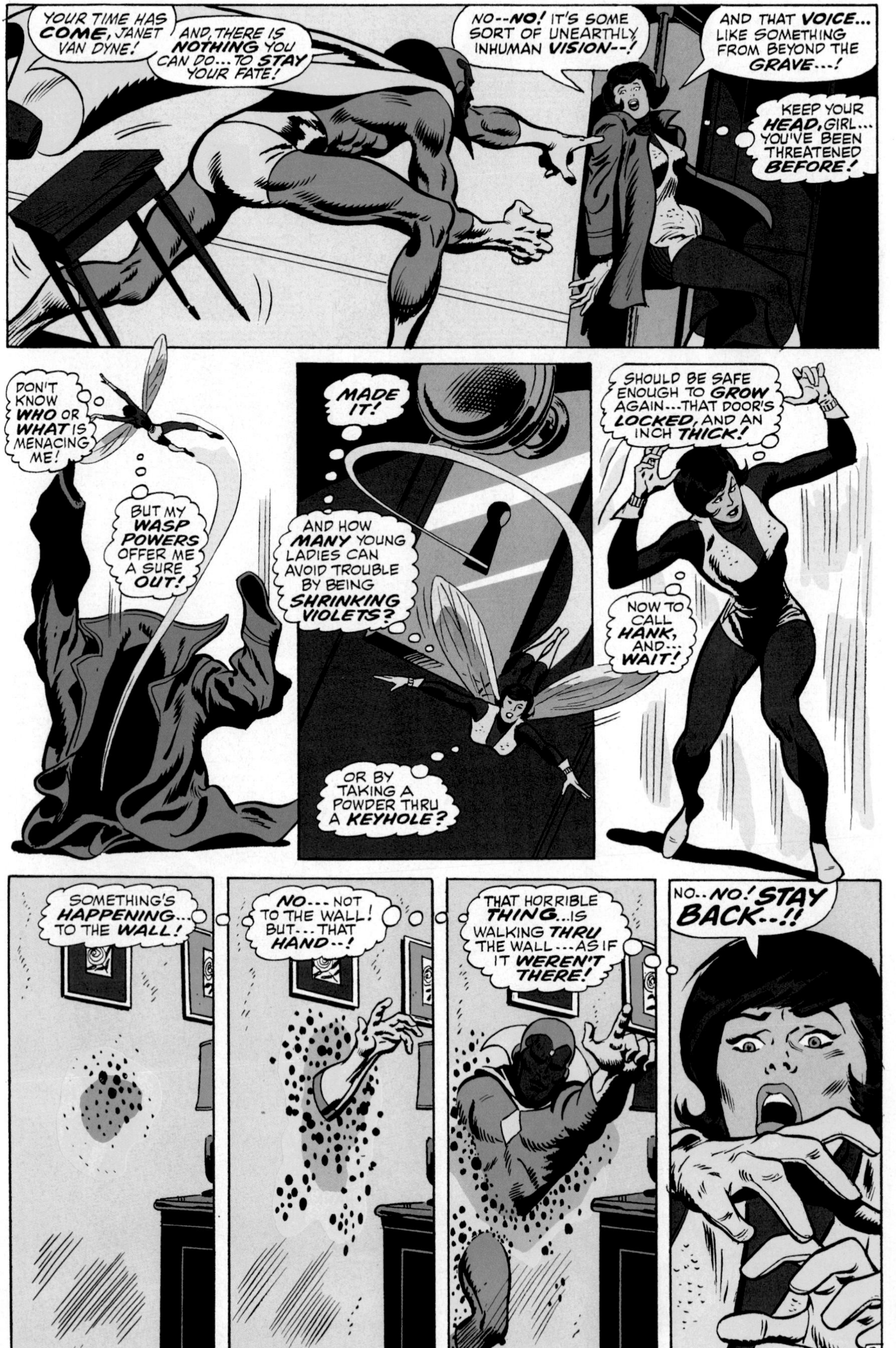
YOUR TIME HAS COME, JANET VAN DYNE!
AND, THERE IS NOTHING YOU CAN DO... TO STAY YOUR FATE!
NO--NO! IT'S SOME SORT OF UNEARTHLY, INHUMAN VISION--!
AND THAT VOICE... LIKE SOMETHING FROM BEYOND THE GRAVE...!
KEEP YOUR HEAD, GIRL... YOU'VE BEEN THREATENED BEFORE!
DON'T KNOW WHO OR WHAT IS MENACING ME!
BUT MY WASP POWERS OFFER ME A SURE OUT!
MADE IT!
AND HOW MANY YOUNG LADIES CAN AVOID TROUBLE BY BEING SHRINKING VIOLETS?
OR BY TAKING A POWDER THRU A KEYHOLE?
SHOULD BE SAFE ENOUGH TO GROW AGAIN...THAT DOOR'S LOCKED, AND AN INCH THICK!
NOW TO CALL HANK, AND... WAIT!
SOMETHING'S HAPPENING... TO THE WALL!
NO... NOT TO THE WALL! BUT... THAT HAND--!
THAT HORRIBLE THING...IS WALKING THRU THE WALL...AS IF IT WEREN'T THERE!
NO..NO! STAY BACK--!!
3.

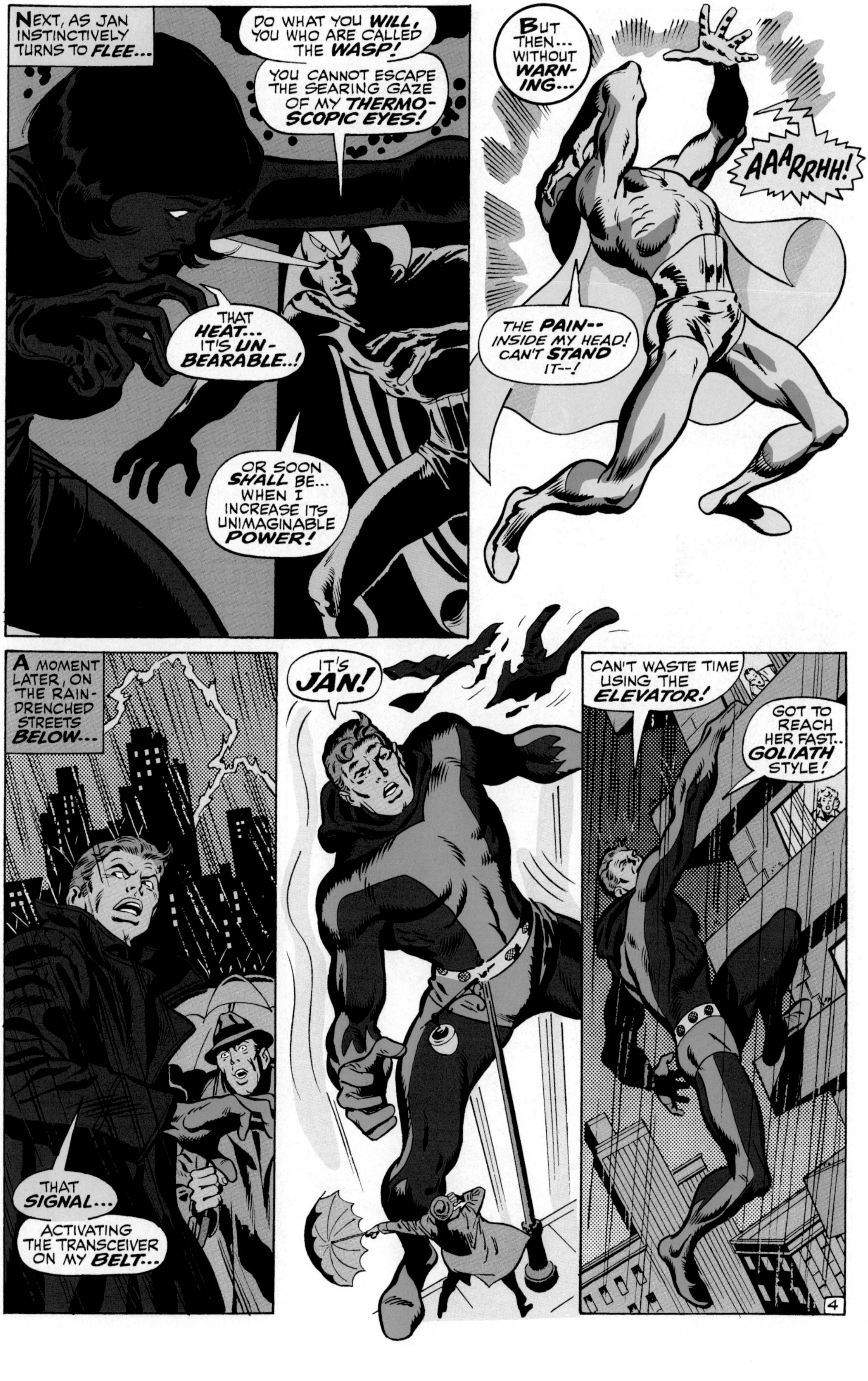
NEXT, AS JAN INSTINCTIVELY TURNS TO FLEE...
DO WHAT YOU WILL, YOU WHO ARE CALLED THE WASP!
YOU CANNOT ESCAPE THE SEARING GAZE OF MY THERMO-SCOPIC EYES!
THAT HEAT... IT'S UN-BEARABLE..!
OR SOON SHALL BE... WHEN I INCREASE ITS UNIMAGINABLE POWER!
BUT THEN... WITHOUT WARN-ING...
AAARRHH!
THE PAIN-- INSIDE MY HEAD! CAN'T STAND IT--!
A MOMENT LATER, ON THE RAIN-DRENCHED STREETS BELOW...
THAT SIGNAL...
ACTIVATING THE TRANSCEIVER ON MY BELT...
IT'S JAN!
CAN'T WASTE TIME USING THE ELEVATOR!
GOT TO REACH HER FAST.. GOLIATH STYLE!
4

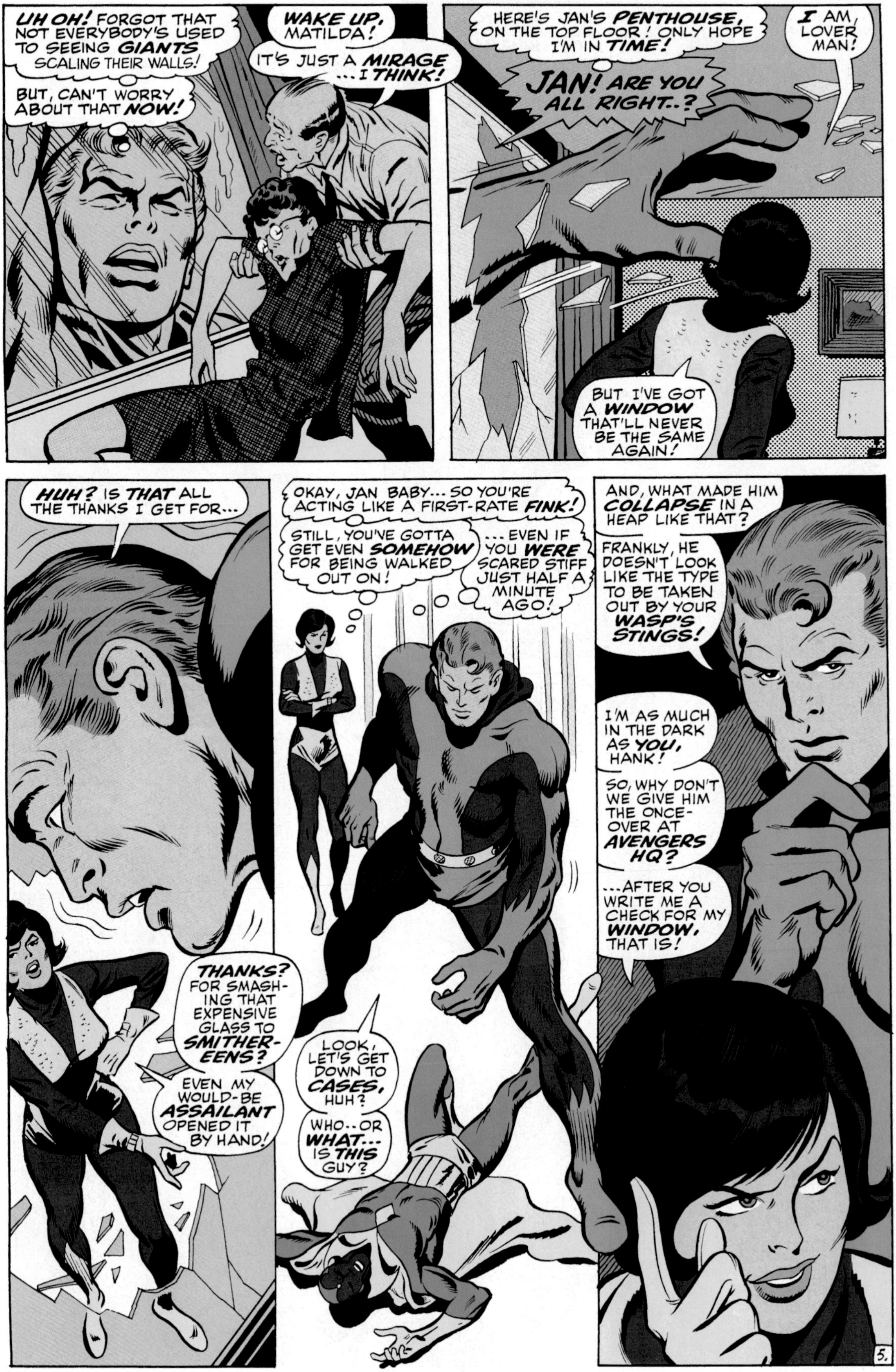
UH OH! FORGOT THAT NOT EVERYBODY'S USED TO SEEING GIANTS SCALING THEIR WALLS!
BUT, CAN'T WORRY ABOUT THAT NOW!
WAKE UP, MATILDA!
IT'S JUST A MIRAGE ...I THINK!
HERE'S JAN'S PENTHOUSE, ON THE TOP FLOOR! ONLY HOPE I'M IN TIME!
JAN! ARE YOU ALL RIGHT..?
I AM, LOVER MAN!
BUT I'VE GOT A WINDOW THAT'LL NEVER BE THE SAME AGAIN!
HUH? IS THAT ALL THE THANKS I GET FOR...
THANKS? FOR SMASHING THAT EXPENSIVE GLASS TO SMITHEREENS?
EVEN MY WOULD-BE ASSAILANT OPENED IT BY HAND!
OKAY, JAN BABY... SO YOU'RE ACTING LIKE A FIRST-RATE FINK!
STILL, YOU'VE GOTTA GET EVEN SOMEHOW FOR BEING WALKED OUT ON!
...EVEN IF YOU WERE SCARED STIFF JUST HALF A MINUTE AGO!
LOOK, LET'S GET DOWN TO CASES, HUH?
WHO..OR WHAT... IS THIS GUY?
AND, WHAT MADE HIM COLLAPSE IN A HEAP LIKE THAT?
FRANKLY, HE DOESN'T LOOK LIKE THE TYPE TO BE TAKEN OUT BY YOUR WASP'S STINGS!
I'M AS MUCH IN THE DARK AS YOU, HANK!
SO, WHY DON'T WE GIVE HIM THE ONCE-OVER AT AVENGERS HQ?
...AFTER YOU WRITE ME A CHECK FOR MY WINDOW, THAT IS!
5.

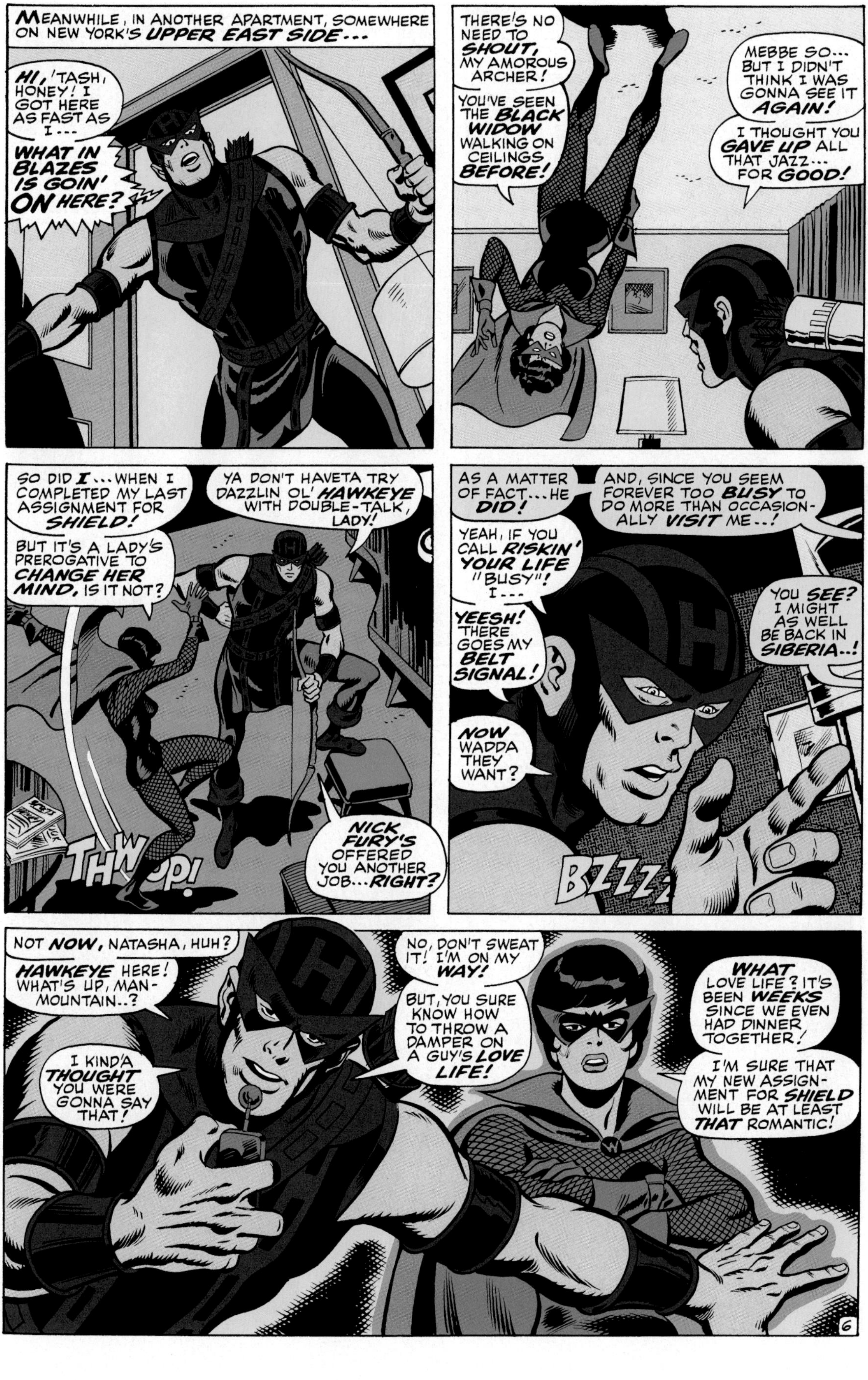
MEANWHILE, IN ANOTHER APARTMENT, SOMEWHERE ON NEW YORK'S UPPER EAST SIDE...
HI, 'TASH, HONEY! I GOT HERE AS FAST AS I---
WHAT IN BLAZES IS GOIN' ON HERE?
THERE'S NO NEED TO SHOUT, MY AMOROUS ARCHER!
YOU'VE SEEN THE BLACK WIDOW WALKING ON CEILINGS BEFORE!
MEBBE SO... BUT I DIDN'T THINK I WAS GONNA SEE IT AGAIN!
I THOUGHT YOU GAVE UP ALL THAT JAZZ... FOR GOOD!
SO DID I... WHEN I COMPLETED MY LAST ASSIGNMENT FOR SHIELD!
BUT IT'S A LADY'S PREROGATIVE TO CHANGE HER MIND, IS IT NOT?
YA DON'T HAVETA TRY DAZZLIN OL' HAWKEYE WITH DOUBLE-TALK, LADY!
THWOP!
NICK FURY'S OFFERED YOU ANOTHER JOB... RIGHT?
AS A MATTER OF FACT... HE DID!
AND, SINCE YOU SEEM FOREVER TOO BUSY TO DO MORE THAN OCCASIONALLY VISIT ME..!
YEAH, IF YOU CALL RISKIN' YOUR LIFE "BUSY"! I---
YOU SEE? I MIGHT AS WELL BE BACK IN SIBERIA..!
YEESH! THERE GOES MY BELT SIGNAL!
NOW WADDA THEY WANT?
BZZZ
NOT NOW, NATASHA, HUH?
HAWKEYE HERE! WHAT'S UP, MAN-MOUNTAIN..?
I KIND'A THOUGHT YOU WERE GONNA SAY THAT!
NO, DON'T SWEAT IT! I'M ON MY WAY!
BUT, YOU SURE KNOW HOW TO THROW A DAMPER ON A GUY'S LOVE LIFE!
WHAT LOVE LIFE? IT'S BEEN WEEKS SINCE WE EVEN HAD DINNER TOGETHER!
I'M SURE THAT MY NEW ASSIGNMENT FOR SHIELD WILL BE AT LEAST THAT ROMANTIC!
6

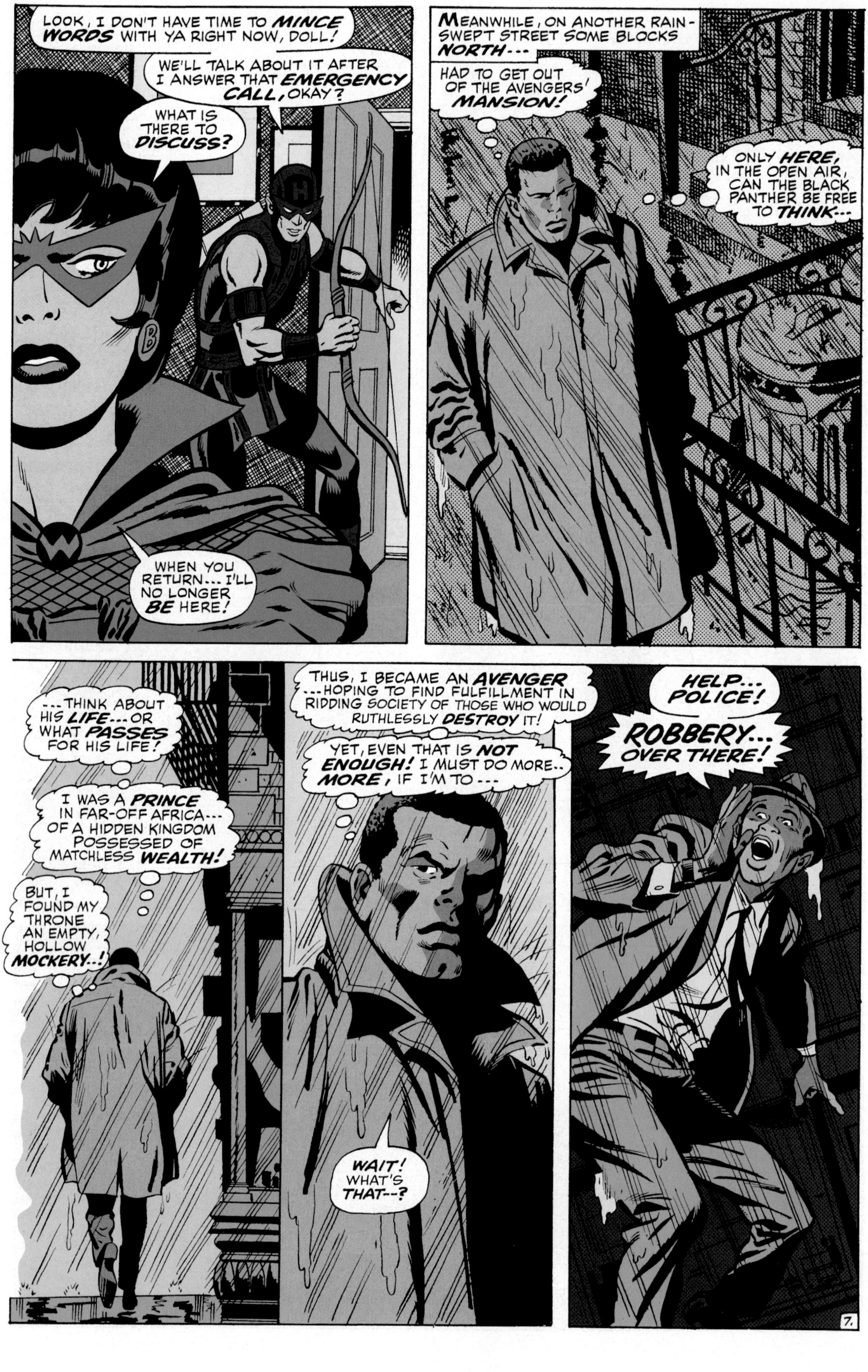
LOOK, I DON'T HAVE TIME TO MINCE WORDS WITH YA RIGHT NOW, DOLL!
WE'LL TALK ABOUT IT AFTER I ANSWER THAT EMERGENCY CALL, OKAY?
WHAT IS THERE TO DISCUSS?
WHEN YOU RETURN... I'LL NO LONGER BE HERE!
MEANWHILE, ON ANOTHER RAIN-SWEPT STREET SOME BLOCKS NORTH---
HAD TO GET OUT OF THE AVENGERS' MANSION!
ONLY HERE, IN THE OPEN AIR, CAN THE BLACK PANTHER BE FREE TO THINK...
---THINK ABOUT HIS LIFE---OR WHAT PASSES FOR HIS LIFE!
I WAS A PRINCE IN FAR-OFF AFRICA--- OF A HIDDEN KINGDOM POSSESSED OF MATCHLESS WEALTH!
BUT, I FOUND MY THRONE AN EMPTY, HOLLOW MOCKERY..!
THUS, I BECAME AN AVENGER ---HOPING TO FIND FULFILLMENT IN RIDDING SOCIETY OF THOSE WHO WOULD RUTHLESSLY DESTROY IT!
YET, EVEN THAT IS NOT ENOUGH! I MUST DO MORE.. MORE, IF I'M TO---
WAIT! WHAT'S THAT--?
HELP... POLICE!
ROBBERY... OVER THERE!

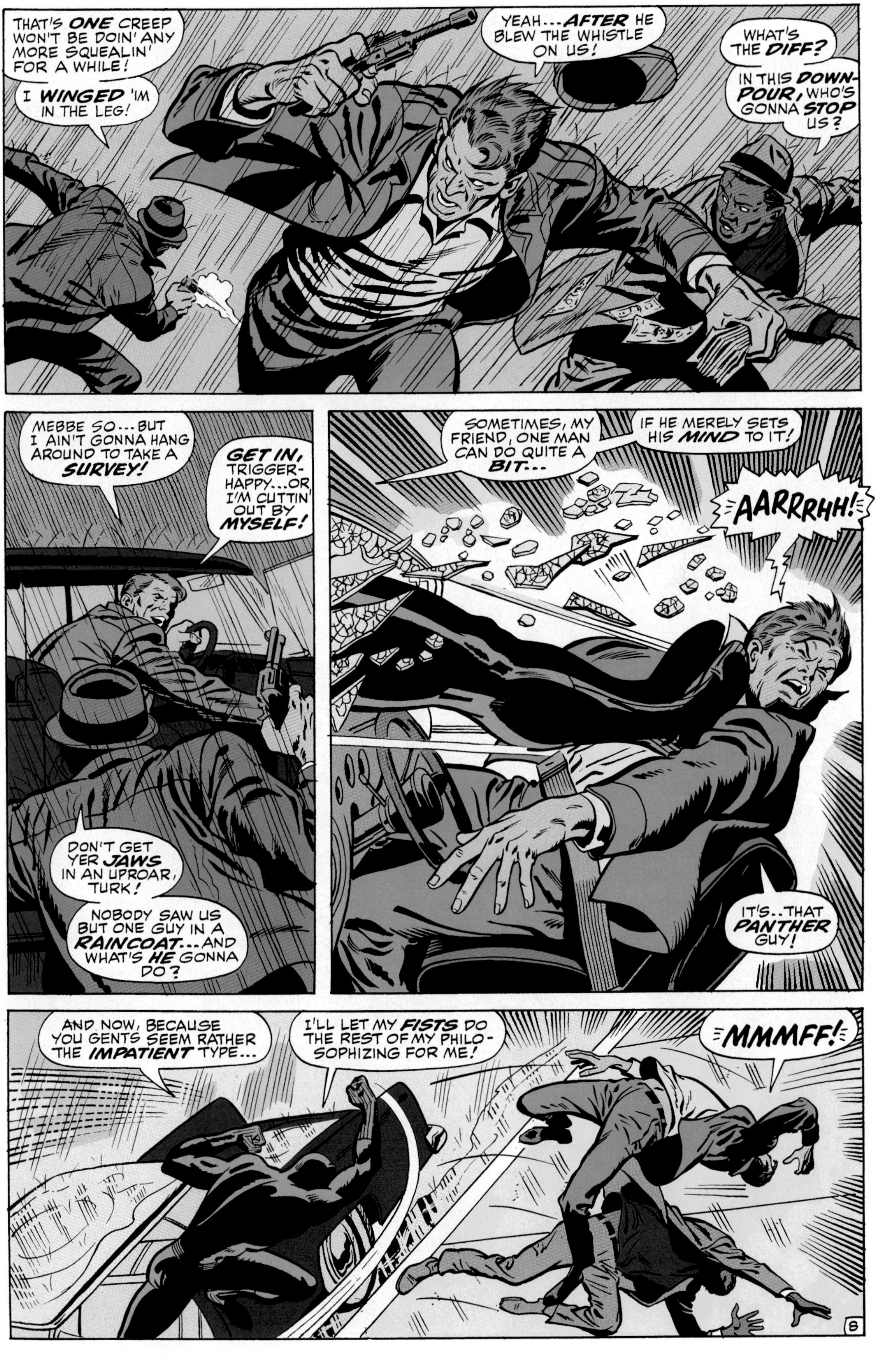

THAT'S ONE CREEP WON'T BE DOIN' ANY MORE SQUEALIN' FOR A WHILE!
I WINGED 'IM IN THE LEG!
YEAH...AFTER HE BLEW THE WHISTLE ON US!
WHAT'S THE DIFF?
IN THIS DOWN-POUR, WHO'S GONNA STOP US?
MEBBE SO...BUT I AIN'T GONNA HANG AROUND TO TAKE A SURVEY!
GET IN, TRIGGER-HAPPY...OR I'M CUTTIN' OUT BY MYSELF!
DON'T GET YER JAWS IN AN UPROAR, TURK!
NOBODY SAW US BUT ONE GUY IN A RAINCOAT...AND WHAT'S HE GONNA DO?
SOMETIMES, MY FRIEND, ONE MAN CAN DO QUITE A BIT...
IF HE MERELY SETS HIS MIND TO IT!
AARRRHH!
IT'S..THAT PANTHER GUY!
AND NOW, BECAUSE YOU GENTS SEEM RATHER THE IMPATIENT TYPE...
I'LL LET MY FISTS DO THE REST OF MY PHILO-SOPHIZING FOR ME!
MMMFF!
8

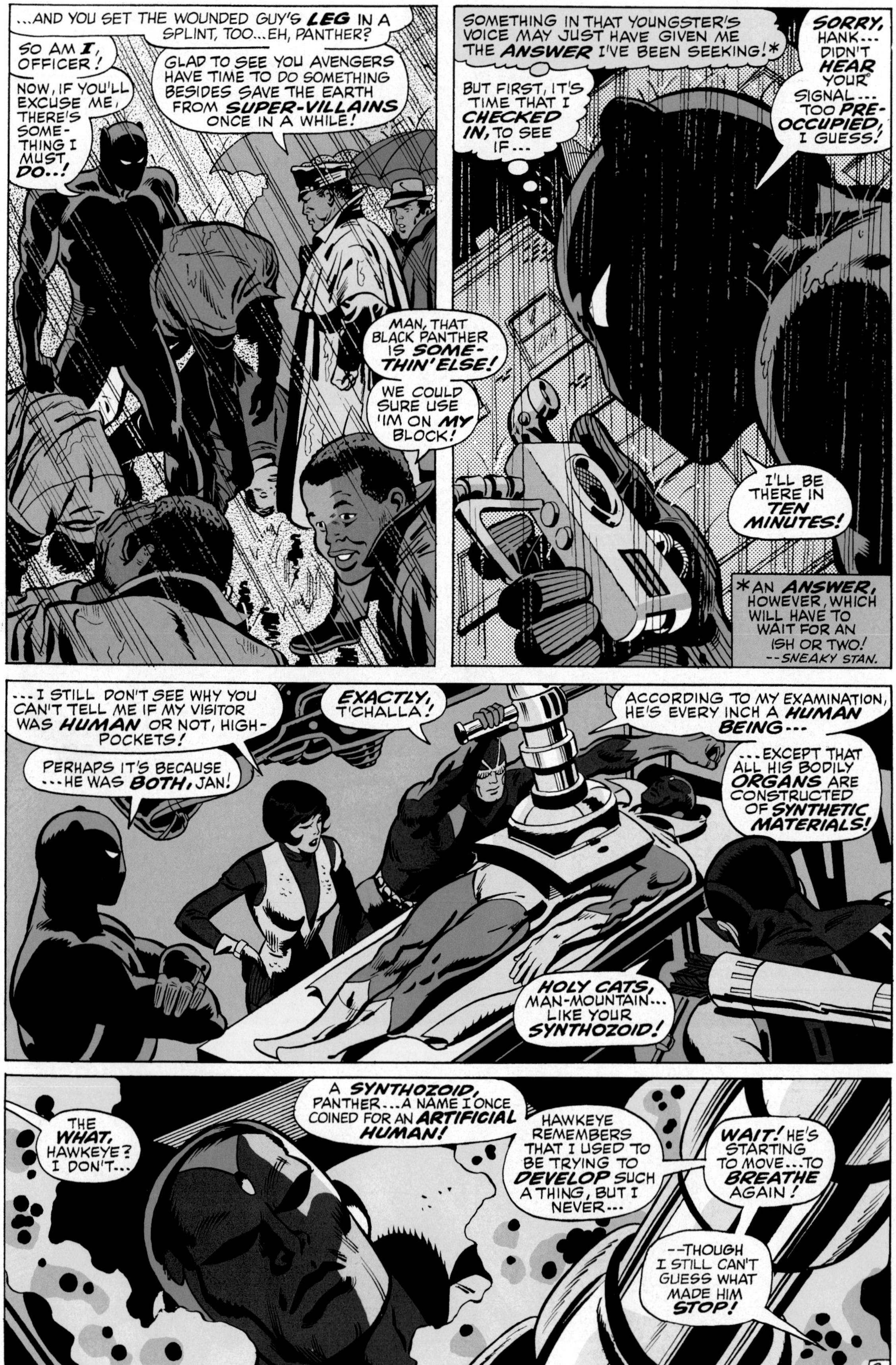

...AND YOU SET THE WOUNDED GUY'S LEG IN A SPLINT, TOO...EH, PANTHER?
SO AM I, OFFICER!
GLAD TO SEE YOU AVENGERS HAVE TIME TO DO SOMETHING BESIDES SAVE THE EARTH FROM SUPER-VILLAINS ONCE IN A WHILE!
NOW, IF YOU'LL EXCUSE ME, THERE'S SOMETHING I MUST DO..!
MAN, THAT BLACK PANTHER IS SOMETHIN' ELSE!
WE COULD SURE USE 'IM ON MY BLOCK!
SOMETHING IN THAT YOUNGSTER'S VOICE MAY JUST HAVE GIVEN ME THE ANSWER I'VE BEEN SEEKING!*
BUT FIRST, IT'S TIME THAT I CHECKED IN, TO SEE IF...
SORRY, HANK... DIDN'T HEAR YOUR SIGNAL... TOO PRE-OCCUPIED, I GUESS!
I'LL BE THERE IN TEN MINUTES!
*AN ANSWER, HOWEVER, WHICH WILL HAVE TO WAIT FOR AN ISH OR TWO! --SNEAKY STAN.
...I STILL DON'T SEE WHY YOU CAN'T TELL ME IF MY VISITOR WAS HUMAN OR NOT, HIGH-POCKETS!
PERHAPS IT'S BECAUSE ...HE WAS BOTH, JAN!
EXACTLY, T'CHALLA!
ACCORDING TO MY EXAMINATION, HE'S EVERY INCH A HUMAN BEING...
...EXCEPT THAT ALL HIS BODILY ORGANS ARE CONSTRUCTED OF SYNTHETIC MATERIALS!
HOLY CATS, MAN-MOUNTAIN... LIKE YOUR SYNTHOZOID!
THE WHAT, HAWKEYE? I DON'T...
A SYNTHOZOID, PANTHER... A NAME I ONCE COINED FOR AN ARTIFICIAL HUMAN!
HAWKEYE REMEMBERS THAT I USED TO BE TRYING TO DEVELOP SUCH A THING, BUT I NEVER...
WAIT! HE'S STARTING TO MOVE...TO BREATHE AGAIN!
--THOUGH I STILL CAN'T GUESS WHAT MADE HIM STOP!
9

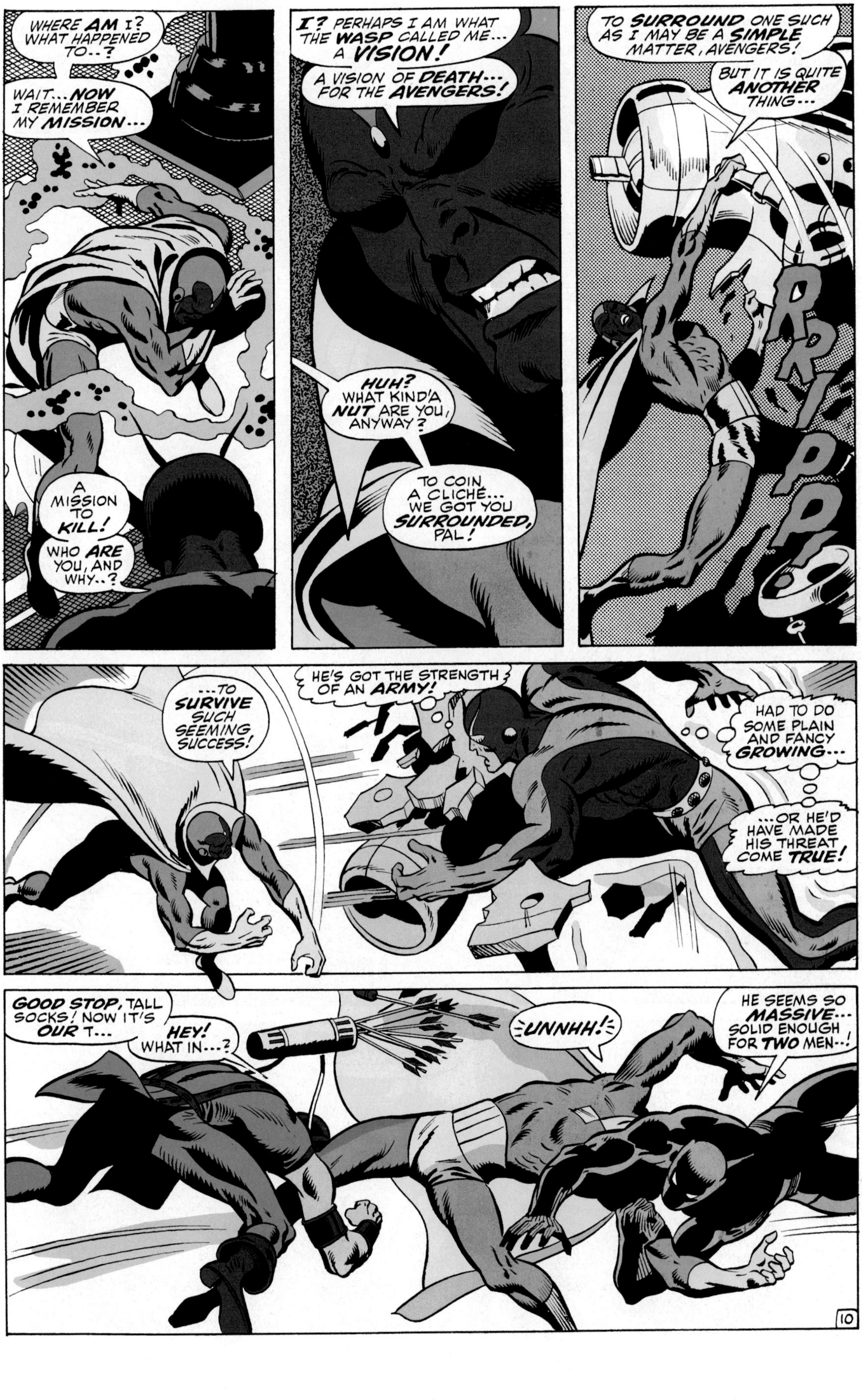

WHERE AM I? WHAT HAPPENED TO..?
WAIT... NOW I REMEMBER MY MISSION...
A MISSION TO KILL!
WHO ARE YOU, AND WHY..?
I? PERHAPS I AM WHAT THE WASP CALLED ME... A VISION!
A VISION OF DEATH... FOR THE AVENGERS!
HUH? WHAT KIND'A NUT ARE YOU, ANYWAY?
TO COIN A CLICHÉ... WE GOT YOU SURROUNDED, PAL!
TO SURROUND ONE SUCH AS I MAY BE A SIMPLE MATTER, AVENGERS!
BUT IT IS QUITE ANOTHER THING...
RRIPPP!
...TO SURVIVE SUCH SEEMING SUCCESS!
HE'S GOT THE STRENGTH OF AN ARMY!
HAD TO DO SOME PLAIN AND FANCY GROWING...
...OR HE'D HAVE MADE HIS THREAT COME TRUE!
GOOD STOP, TALL SOCKS! NOW IT'S OUR T...
HEY! WHAT IN...?
UNNHH!
HE SEEMS SO MASSIVE... SOLID ENOUGH FOR TWO MEN...!

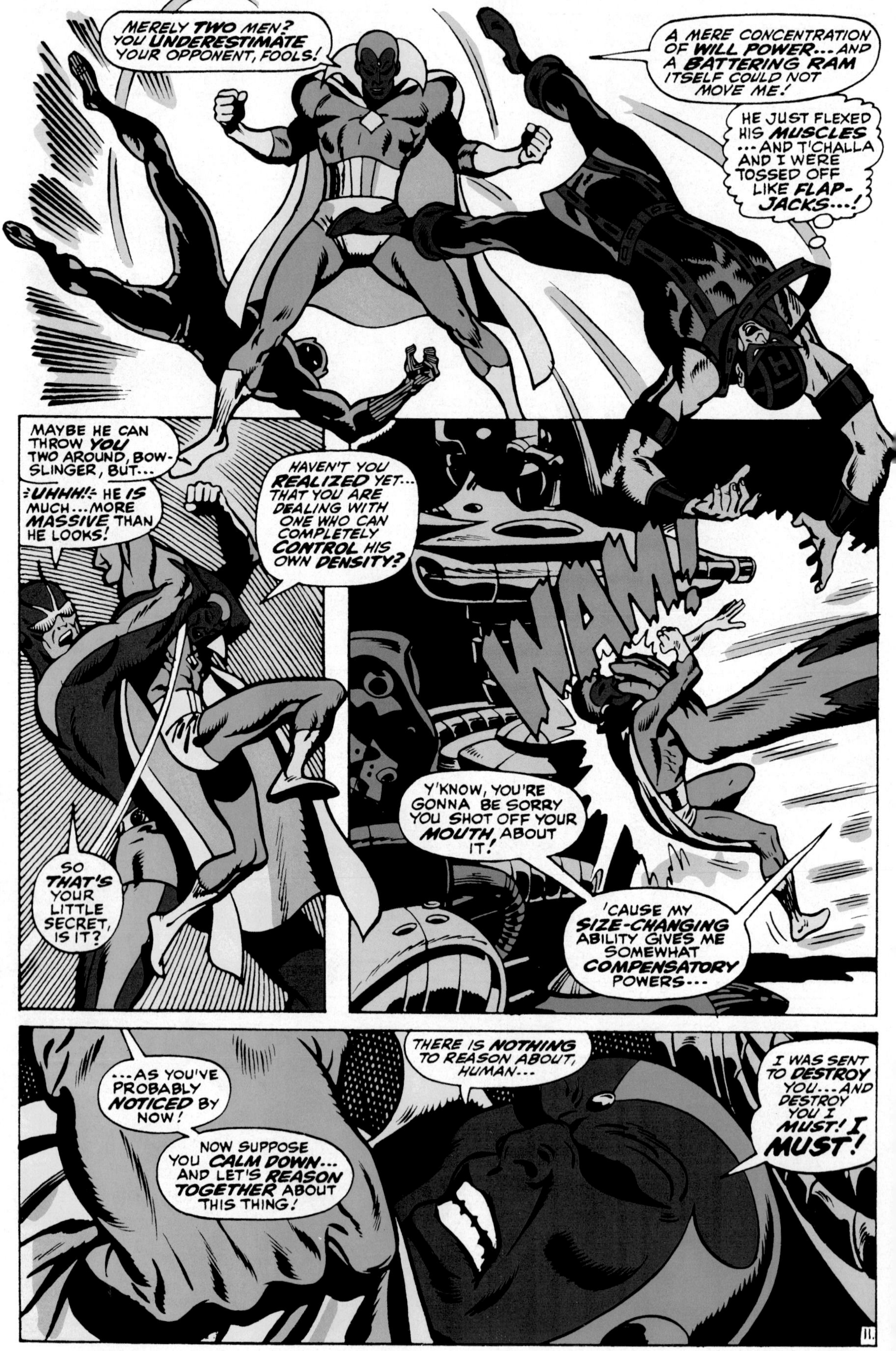

MERELY TWO MEN? YOU UNDERESTIMATE YOUR OPPONENT, FOOLS!
A MERE CONCENTRATION OF WILL POWER... AND A BATTERING RAM ITSELF COULD NOT MOVE ME!
HE JUST FLEXED HIS MUSCLES ...AND T'CHALLA AND I WERE TOSSED OFF LIKE FLAP-JACKS...!
MAYBE HE CAN THROW YOU TWO AROUND, BOW-SLINGER, BUT...
UHHH! HE IS MUCH...MORE MASSIVE THAN HE LOOKS!
HAVEN'T YOU REALIZED YET... THAT YOU ARE DEALING WITH ONE WHO CAN COMPLETELY CONTROL HIS OWN DENSITY?
SO THAT'S YOUR LITTLE SECRET, IS IT?
WAM!
Y'KNOW, YOU'RE GONNA BE SORRY YOU SHOT OFF YOUR MOUTH, ABOUT IT!
'CAUSE MY SIZE-CHANGING ABILITY GIVES ME SOMEWHAT COMPENSATORY POWERS...
...AS YOU'VE PROBABLY NOTICED BY NOW!
NOW SUPPOSE YOU CALM DOWN... AND LET'S REASON TOGETHER ABOUT THIS THING!
THERE IS NOTHING TO REASON ABOUT, HUMAN...
I WAS SENT TO DESTROY YOU... AND DESTROY YOU I MUST! I MUST!
11.

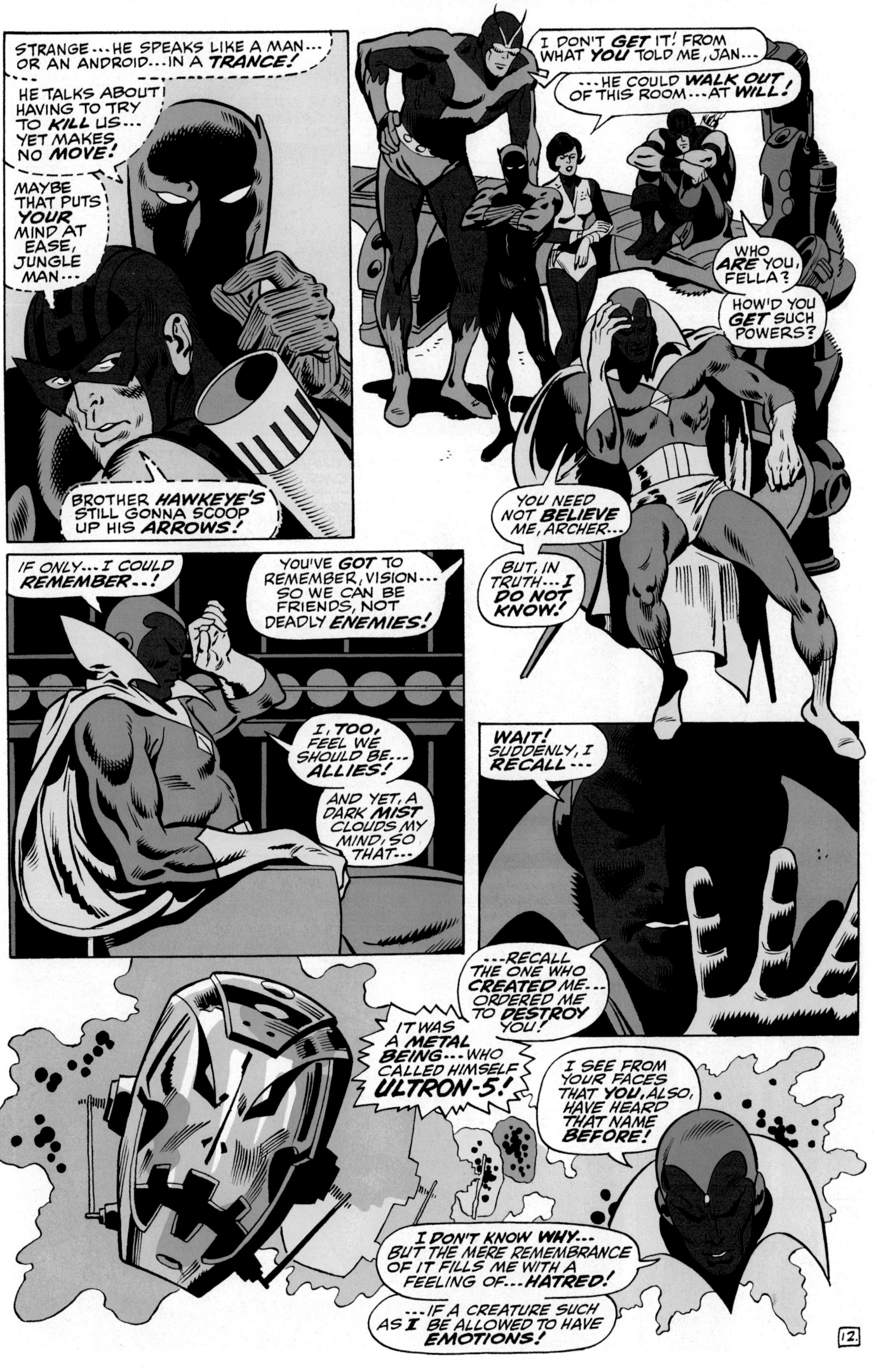

STRANGE...HE SPEAKS LIKE A MAN... OR AN ANDROID...IN A TRANCE!
HE TALKS ABOUT HAVING TO TRY TO KILL US... YET MAKES NO MOVE!
MAYBE THAT PUTS YOUR MIND AT EASE, JUNGLE MAN...
BROTHER HAWKEYE'S STILL GONNA SCOOP UP HIS ARROWS!
I DON'T GET IT! FROM WHAT YOU TOLD ME, JAN...
...HE COULD WALK OUT OF THIS ROOM...AT WILL!
WHO ARE YOU, FELLA?
HOW'D YOU GET SUCH POWERS?
YOU NEED NOT BELIEVE ME, ARCHER...
BUT, IN TRUTH...I DO NOT KNOW!
IF ONLY...I COULD REMEMBER--!
YOU'VE GOT TO REMEMBER, VISION... SO WE CAN BE FRIENDS, NOT DEADLY ENEMIES!
I, TOO, FEEL WE SHOULD BE... ALLIES!
AND YET, A DARK MIST CLOUDS MY MIND, SO THAT...
WAIT! SUDDENLY, I RECALL...
...RECALL THE ONE WHO CREATED ME... ORDERED ME TO DESTROY YOU!
IT WAS A METAL BEING...WHO CALLED HIMSELF ULTRON-5!
I SEE FROM YOUR FACES THAT YOU, ALSO, HAVE HEARD THAT NAME BEFORE!
I DON'T KNOW WHY... BUT THE MERE REMEMBRANCE OF IT FILLS ME WITH A FEELING OF...HATRED!
...IF A CREATURE SUCH AS I BE ALLOWED TO HAVE EMOTIONS!

IT IS UNCANNY... BUT, NOW THAT I HAVE PLUMBED MY DIM MEMORIES BACK AS FAR AS THEY WILL GO...

I NO LONGER FEEL ANY DESIRE TO ATTACK YOU!

IN FACT, IF YOU WISH... I'LL LEAD YOU TO HIM WHO... CREATED ME!

WE'VE BEEN HUNTING THAT METAL MANIAC FOR WEEKS!

SO, WE'VE GOT TO TAKE A CHANCE ON YOU!

STILL, JUST IN CASE THERE'S SOME TRICK UP YOUR SLEEVE...

I'M KEEPIN' A SHOCK ARROW TRAINED RIGHT ON YOUR SYNTHETIC KISSER!

MOMENTS LATER, A SLEEK AIR-CRUISER SOARS INTO THE SKY... ITS OCCUPANTS CLOAKED IN SOMBRE SILENCE...

--- EXCEPT FOR THE STRANGELY UNNATURAL VOICE WHICH ISSUES DIRECTIONS --- DIRECTIONS WHICH SOON LEAD TO...

ULTRON-5'S SUBTERRANEAN STRONGHOLD!

JARVIS COULDN'T LOCATE IT FOR US, BECAUSE OF AN INDUCED MEMORY BLOCK! *

WHY IS IT OPENING TO US... LIKE A BUDDING FLOWER?

YOU ARE UNDULY SUSPICIOUS, JANET VAN DYNE...

* AN ESOTERIC FOLLOW-UP REF TO AVENGERS #55! --- STAN.

--- REMEMBER, MY CREATOR'S PROTECTIVE DEVICES WERE SET TO RE-ADMIT ME!

SPEAKING OF YOUR SUPPOSED CREATOR---

JUST WHO IS HE... AND WHY IS HE SO FANATICAL ABOUT DESTROYING THE AVENGERS?

THAT, GOLIATH, EVEN I DO NOT KNOW...

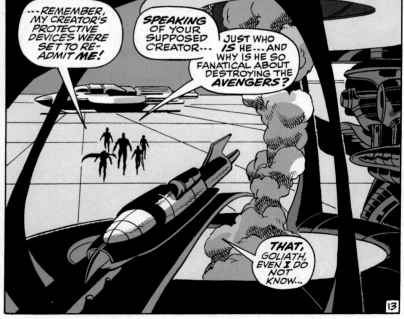

13

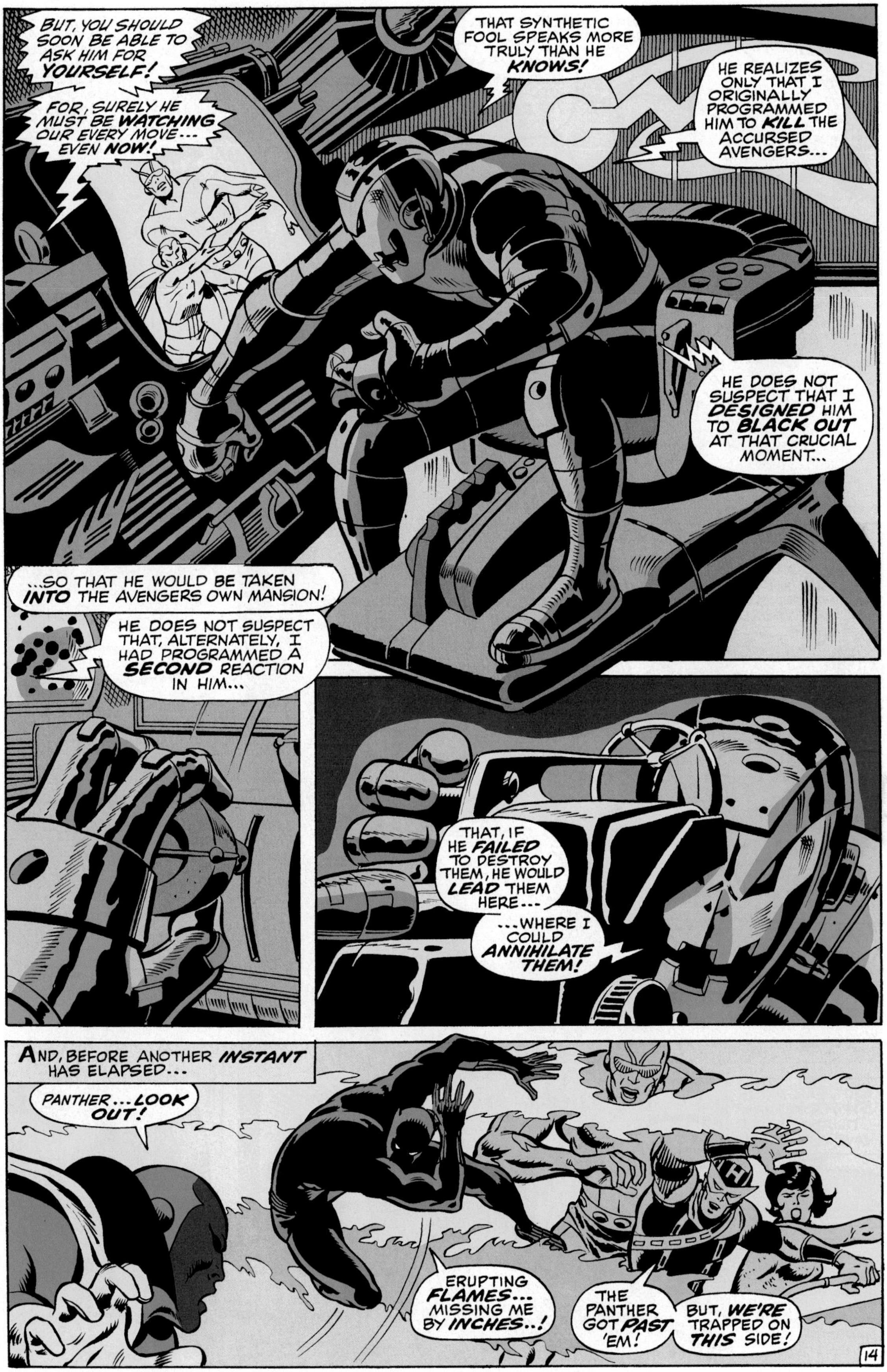
BUT, YOU SHOULD SOON BE ABLE TO ASK HIM FOR YOURSELF!
FOR, SURELY HE MUST BE WATCHING OUR EVERY MOVE--- EVEN NOW!
THAT SYNTHETIC FOOL SPEAKS MORE TRULY THAN HE KNOWS!
HE REALIZES ONLY THAT I ORIGINALLY PROGRAMMED HIM TO KILL THE ACCURSED AVENGERS...
HE DOES NOT SUSPECT THAT I DESIGNED HIM TO BLACK OUT AT THAT CRUCIAL MOMENT...
...SO THAT HE WOULD BE TAKEN INTO THE AVENGERS OWN MANSION!
HE DOES NOT SUSPECT THAT, ALTERNATELY, I HAD PROGRAMMED A SECOND REACTION IN HIM...
THAT, IF HE FAILED TO DESTROY THEM, HE WOULD LEAD THEM HERE---
...WHERE I COULD ANNIHILATE THEM!
AND, BEFORE ANOTHER INSTANT HAS ELAPSED...
PANTHER...LOOK OUT!
ERUPTING FLAMES... MISSING ME BY INCHES..!
THE PANTHER GOT PAST 'EM!
BUT, WE'RE TRAPPED ON THIS SIDE!
14

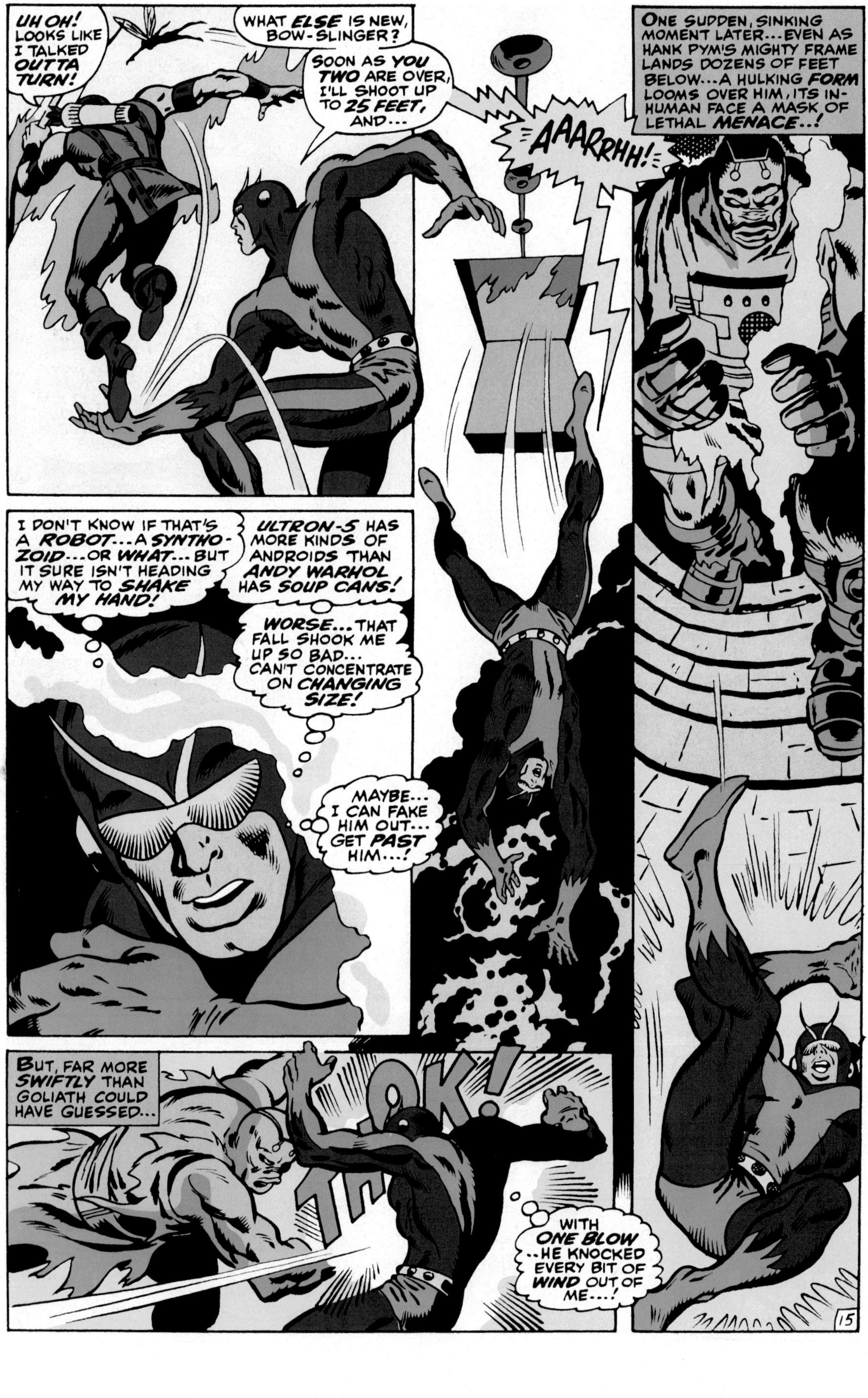
UH OH! LOOKS LIKE I TALKED OUTTA TURN!
WHAT ELSE IS NEW, BOW-SLINGER?
SOON AS YOU TWO ARE OVER, I'LL SHOOT UP TO 25 FEET, AND...
AAARRHH!
ONE SUDDEN, SINKING MOMENT LATER... EVEN AS HANK PYM'S MIGHTY FRAME LANDS DOZENS OF FEET BELOW... A HULKING FORM LOOMS OVER HIM, ITS IN-HUMAN FACE A MASK OF LETHAL MENACE..!
I DON'T KNOW IF THAT'S A ROBOT... A SYNTHO-ZOID... OR WHAT... BUT IT SURE ISN'T HEADING MY WAY TO SHAKE MY HAND!
ULTRON-5 HAS MORE KINDS OF ANDROIDS THAN ANDY WARHOL HAS SOUP CANS!
WORSE... THAT FALL SHOOK ME UP SO BAD... CAN'T CONCENTRATE ON CHANGING SIZE!
MAYBE... I CAN FAKE HIM OUT... GET PAST HIM...!
BUT, FAR MORE SWIFTLY THAN GOLIATH COULD HAVE GUESSED...
THOK!
WITH ONE BLOW ..HE KNOCKED EVERY BIT OF WIND OUT OF ME...!

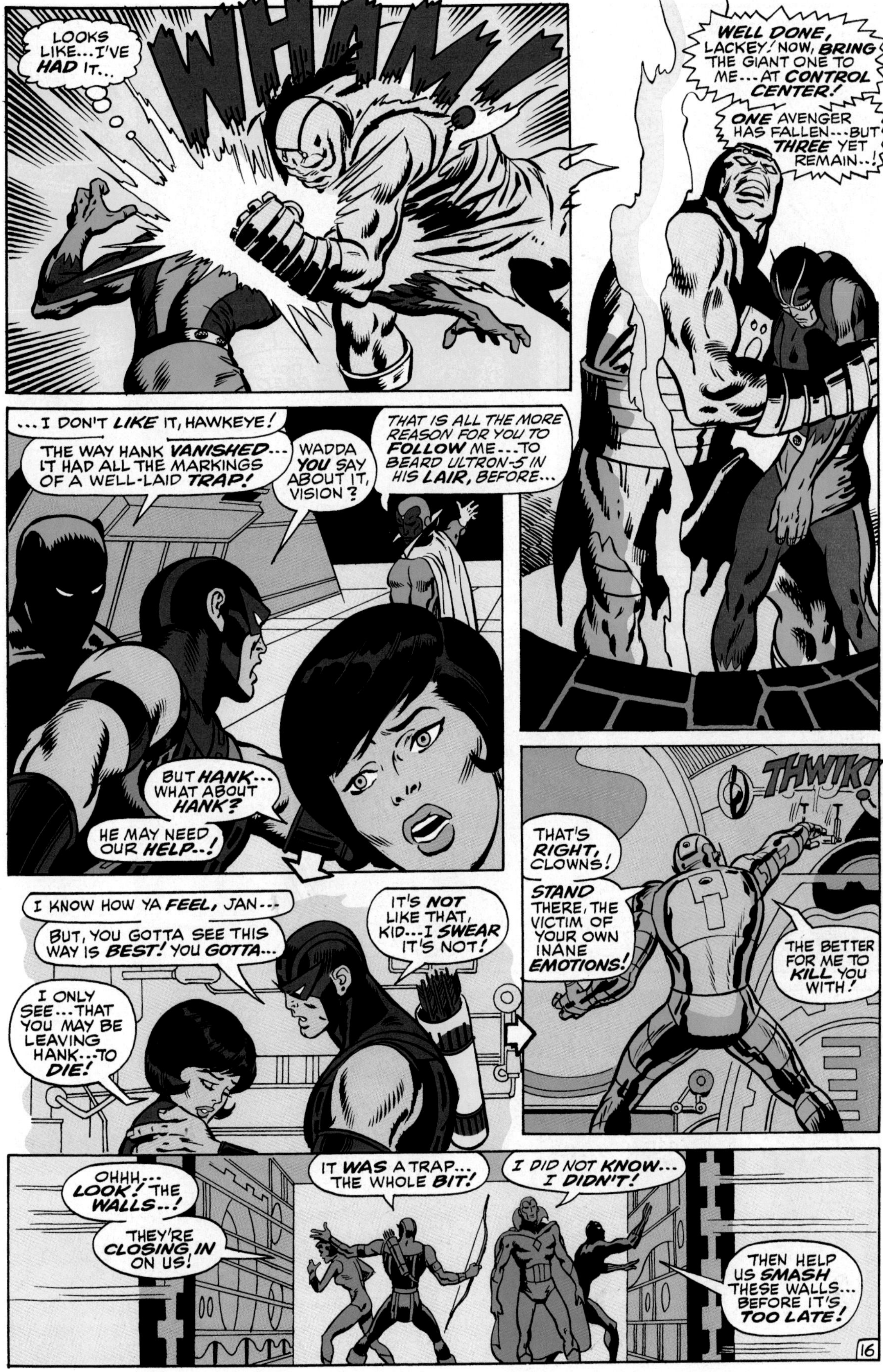

LOOKS LIKE... I'VE HAD IT...
WHAM!
WELL DONE, LACKEY! NOW, BRING THE GIANT ONE TO ME... AT CONTROL CENTER!
ONE AVENGER HAS FALLEN... BUT THREE YET REMAIN..!
...I DON'T LIKE IT, HAWKEYE!
THE WAY HANK VANISHED... IT HAD ALL THE MARKINGS OF A WELL-LAID TRAP!
WADDA YOU SAY ABOUT IT, VISION?
THAT IS ALL THE MORE REASON FOR YOU TO FOLLOW ME... TO BEARD ULTRON-5 IN HIS LAIR, BEFORE...
BUT HANK... WHAT ABOUT HANK?
HE MAY NEED OUR HELP..!
THWIK!
THAT'S RIGHT, CLOWNS!
STAND THERE, THE VICTIM OF YOUR OWN INANE EMOTIONS!
THE BETTER FOR ME TO KILL YOU WITH!
I KNOW HOW YA FEEL, JAN...
BUT, YOU GOTTA SEE THIS WAY IS BEST! YOU GOTTA...
IT'S NOT LIKE THAT, KID... I SWEAR IT'S NOT!
I ONLY SEE... THAT YOU MAY BE LEAVING HANK... TO DIE!
OHHH... LOOK! THE WALLS..!
THEY'RE CLOSING IN ON US!
IT WAS A TRAP... THE WHOLE BIT!
I DID NOT KNOW... I DIDN'T!
THEN HELP US SMASH THESE WALLS... BEFORE IT'S TOO LATE!

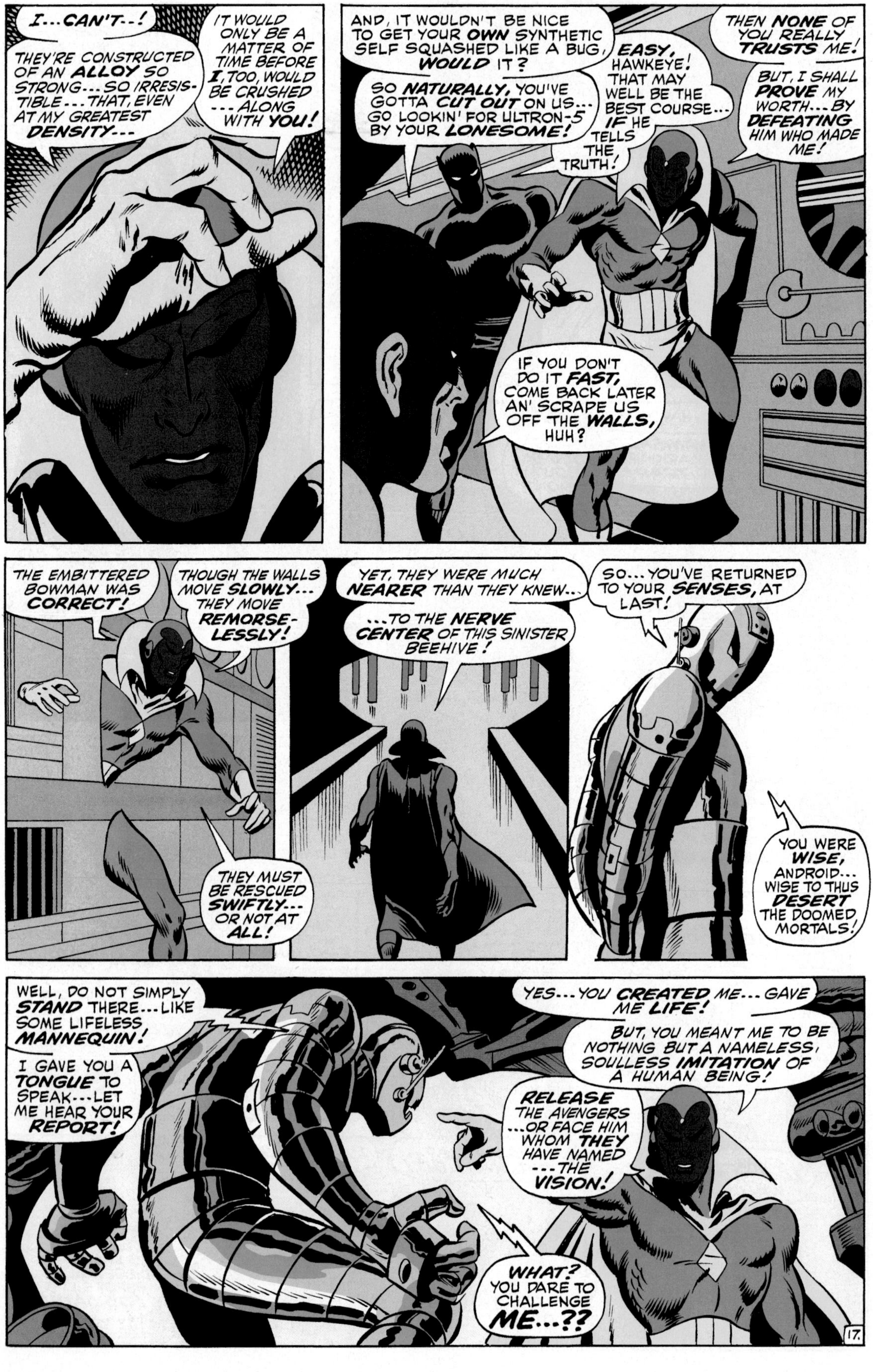
I...CAN'T..!
THEY'RE CONSTRUCTED OF AN ALLOY SO STRONG... SO IRRESISTIBLE... THAT, EVEN AT MY GREATEST DENSITY...
IT WOULD ONLY BE A MATTER OF TIME BEFORE I, TOO, WOULD BE CRUSHED... ALONG WITH YOU!
AND, IT WOULDN'T BE NICE TO GET YOUR OWN SYNTHETIC SELF SQUASHED LIKE A BUG, WOULD IT?
SO NATURALLY, YOU'VE GOTTA CUT OUT ON US... GO LOOKIN' FOR ULTRON-5 BY YOUR LONESOME!
EASY, HAWKEYE! THAT MAY WELL BE THE BEST COURSE... IF HE TELLS THE TRUTH!
THEN NONE OF YOU REALLY TRUSTS ME!
BUT, I SHALL PROVE MY WORTH... BY DEFEATING HIM WHO MADE ME!
IF YOU DON'T DO IT FAST, COME BACK LATER AN' SCRAPE US OFF THE WALLS, HUH?
THE EMBITTERED BOWMAN WAS CORRECT!
THOUGH THE WALLS MOVE SLOWLY... THEY MOVE REMORSELESSLY!
THEY MUST BE RESCUED SWIFTLY... OR NOT AT ALL!
YET, THEY WERE MUCH NEARER THAN THEY KNEW...
...TO THE NERVE CENTER OF THIS SINISTER BEEHIVE!
SO... YOU'VE RETURNED TO YOUR SENSES, AT LAST!
YOU WERE WISE, ANDROID... WISE TO THUS DESERT THE DOOMED MORTALS!
WELL, DO NOT SIMPLY STAND THERE... LIKE SOME LIFELESS MANNEQUIN!
I GAVE YOU A TONGUE TO SPEAK... LET ME HEAR YOUR REPORT!
YES... YOU CREATED ME... GAVE ME LIFE!
BUT, YOU MEANT ME TO BE NOTHING BUT A NAMELESS, SOULLESS IMITATION OF A HUMAN BEING!
RELEASE THE AVENGERS ...OR FACE HIM WHOM THEY HAVE NAMED --- THE VISION!
WHAT? YOU DARE TO CHALLENGE ME...??
17.

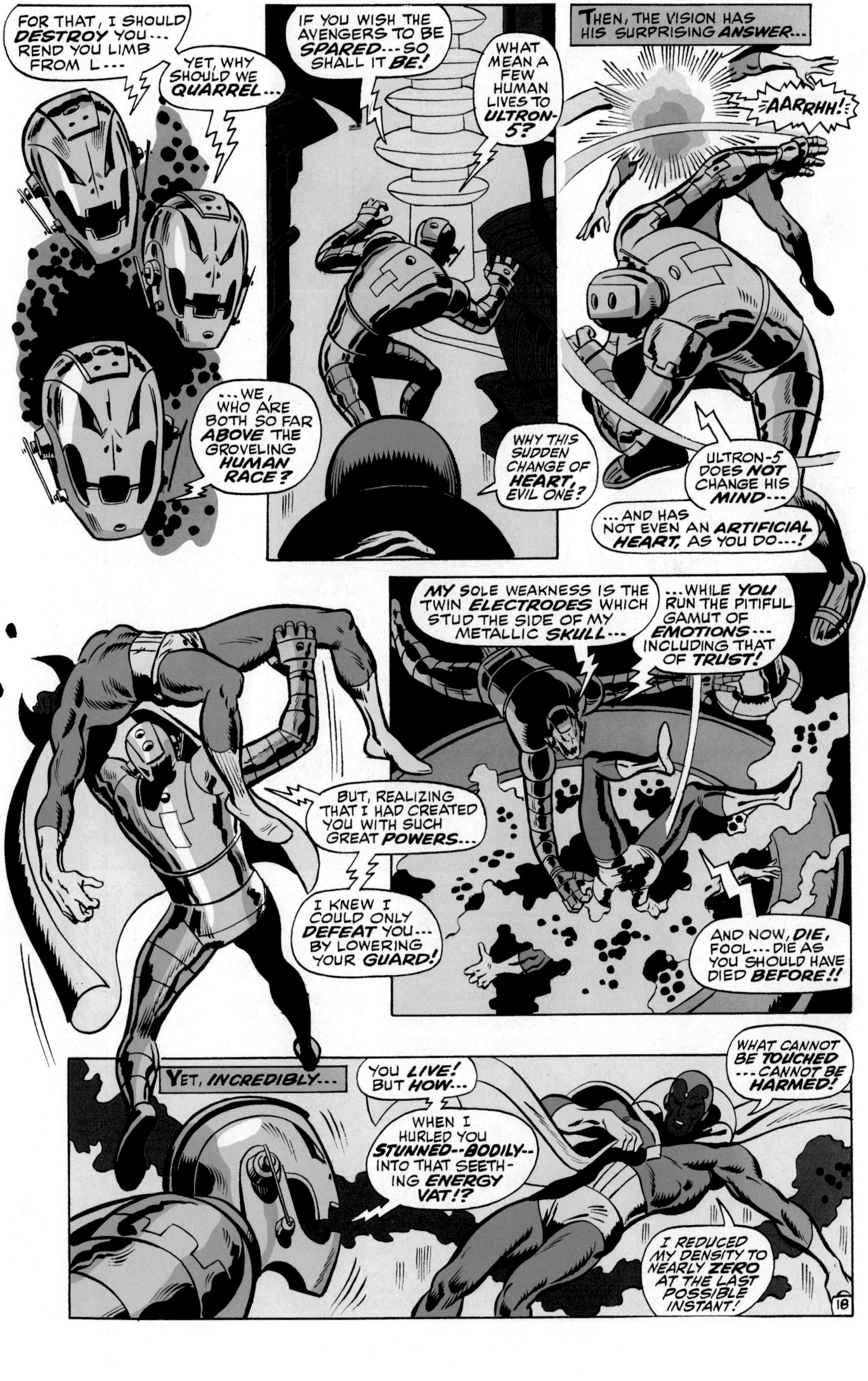

FOR THAT, I SHOULD DESTROY YOU... REND YOU LIMB FROM L---
YET, WHY SHOULD WE QUARREL...
...WE, WHO ARE BOTH SO FAR ABOVE THE GROVELING HUMAN RACE?
IF YOU WISH THE AVENGERS TO BE SPARED---SO SHALL IT BE!
WHAT MEAN A FEW HUMAN LIVES TO ULTRON-5?
WHY THIS SUDDEN CHANGE OF HEART, EVIL ONE?
THEN, THE VISION HAS HIS SURPRISING ANSWER...
AARRHH!
ULTRON-5 DOES NOT CHANGE HIS MIND---
...AND HAS NOT EVEN AN ARTIFICIAL HEART, AS YOU DO---!
BUT, REALIZING THAT I HAD CREATED YOU WITH SUCH GREAT POWERS...
I KNEW I COULD ONLY DEFEAT YOU... BY LOWERING YOUR GUARD!
MY SOLE WEAKNESS IS THE TWIN ELECTRODES WHICH STUD THE SIDE OF MY METALLIC SKULL---
...WHILE YOU RUN THE PITIFUL GAMUT OF EMOTIONS--- INCLUDING THAT OF TRUST!
AND NOW, DIE, FOOL---DIE AS YOU SHOULD HAVE DIED BEFORE!!
YET, INCREDIBLY...
YOU LIVE! BUT HOW...
WHEN I HURLED YOU STUNNED--BODILY-- INTO THAT SEETHING ENERGY VAT!?
WHAT CANNOT BE TOUCHED ---CANNOT BE HARMED!
I REDUCED MY DENSITY TO NEARLY ZERO AT THE LAST POSSIBLE INSTANT!

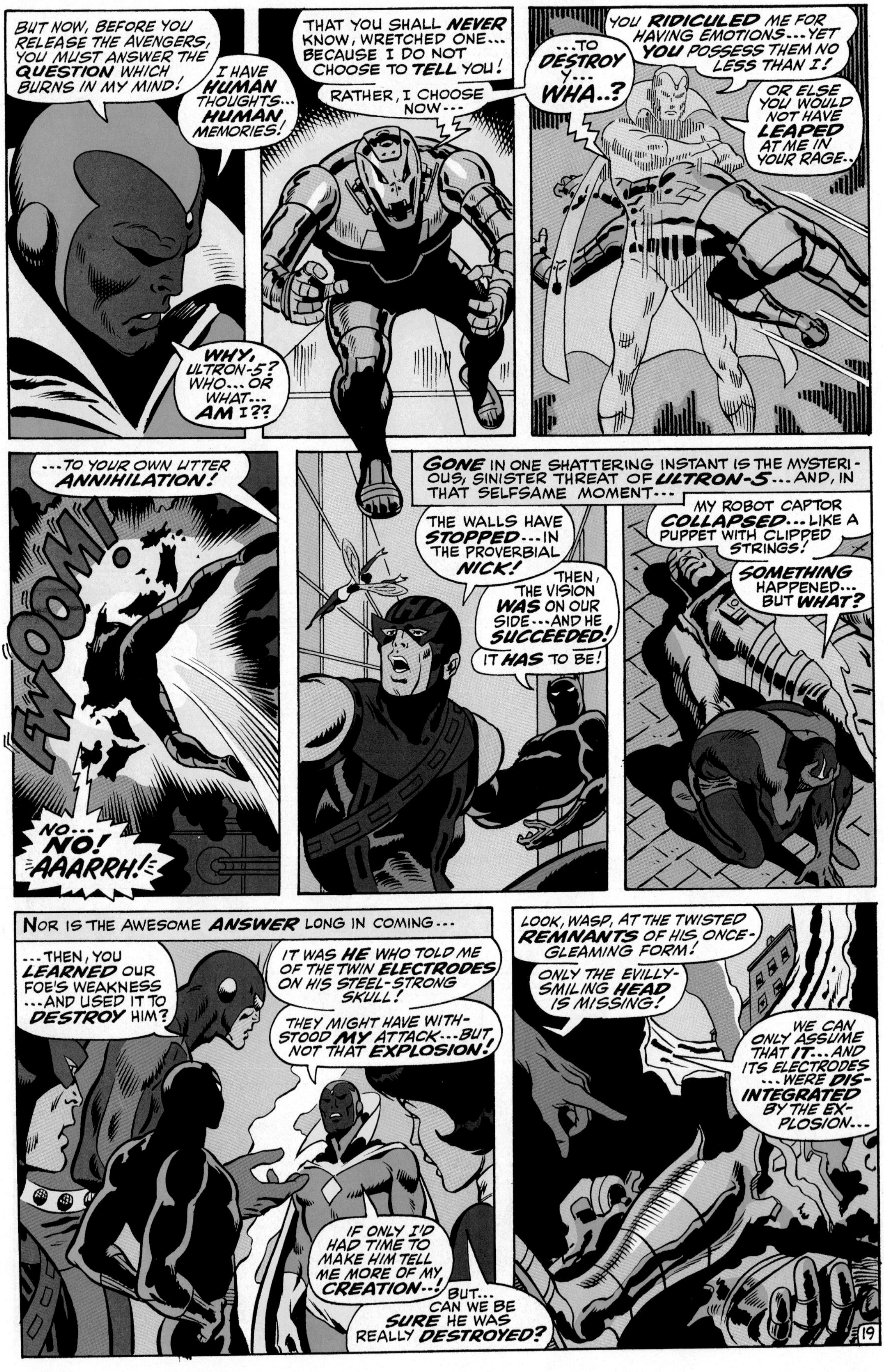
BUT NOW, BEFORE YOU RELEASE THE AVENGERS, YOU MUST ANSWER THE QUESTION WHICH BURNS IN MY MIND!
I HAVE HUMAN THOUGHTS... HUMAN MEMORIES!
WHY, ULTRON-5? WHO... OR WHAT... AM I??
THAT YOU SHALL NEVER KNOW, WRETCHED ONE... BECAUSE I DO NOT CHOOSE TO TELL YOU!
RATHER, I CHOOSE NOW---
...TO DESTROY Y... WHA..?
YOU RIDICULED ME FOR HAVING EMOTIONS---YET YOU POSSESS THEM NO LESS THAN I!
OR ELSE YOU WOULD NOT HAVE LEAPED AT ME IN YOUR RAGE..
---TO YOUR OWN UTTER ANNIHILATION!
FWOOOM!
NO... NO! AAARRH!
GONE IN ONE SHATTERING INSTANT IS THE MYSTERIOUS, SINISTER THREAT OF ULTRON-5---AND, IN THAT SELFSAME MOMENT---
THE WALLS HAVE STOPPED---IN THE PROVERBIAL NICK!
THEN, THE VISION WAS ON OUR SIDE---AND HE SUCCEEDED!
IT HAS TO BE!
MY ROBOT CAPTOR COLLAPSED... LIKE A PUPPET WITH CLIPPED STRINGS!
SOMETHING HAPPENED... BUT WHAT?
NOR IS THE AWESOME ANSWER LONG IN COMING---
---THEN, YOU LEARNED OUR FOE'S WEAKNESS ---AND USED IT TO DESTROY HIM?
IT WAS HE WHO TOLD ME OF THE TWIN ELECTRODES ON HIS STEEL-STRONG SKULL!
THEY MIGHT HAVE WITHSTOOD MY ATTACK---BUT, NOT THAT EXPLOSION!
IF ONLY I'D HAD TIME TO MAKE HIM TELL ME MORE OF MY CREATION--!
BUT... CAN WE BE SURE HE WAS REALLY DESTROYED?
LOOK, WASP, AT THE TWISTED REMNANTS OF HIS ONCE-GLEAMING FORM!
ONLY THE EVILLY-SMILING HEAD IS MISSING!
WE CAN ONLY ASSUME THAT IT...AND ITS ELECTRODES ...WERE DISINTEGRATED BY THE EXPLOSION...

...FOR, IF THEY SOMEHOW REMAINED INTACT, WE WOULD ALL BE IN DEADLY DANGER...!

EPILOGUE:
I met a traveler from an antique land, Who said:

Two vast and trunkless legs of stone Stand in the desert.

Near them, on the sand, Half sunk, a shattered visage lies,

Whose frown, And wrinkled lip, and sneer of cold command,

Tell that its sculptor well those passions read Which yet survive, stamped on these lifeless things...

The hand that mocked them, and the heart that fed; And on the pedestal these words appear:

"My name is Ozymandias, King of Kings: Look on my works, ye Mighty, and despair!"

Nothing beside remains. Round the decay Of that colossal wreck, Boundless and bare

The lone and level sands stretch far away.

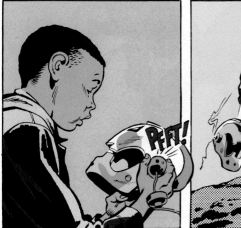

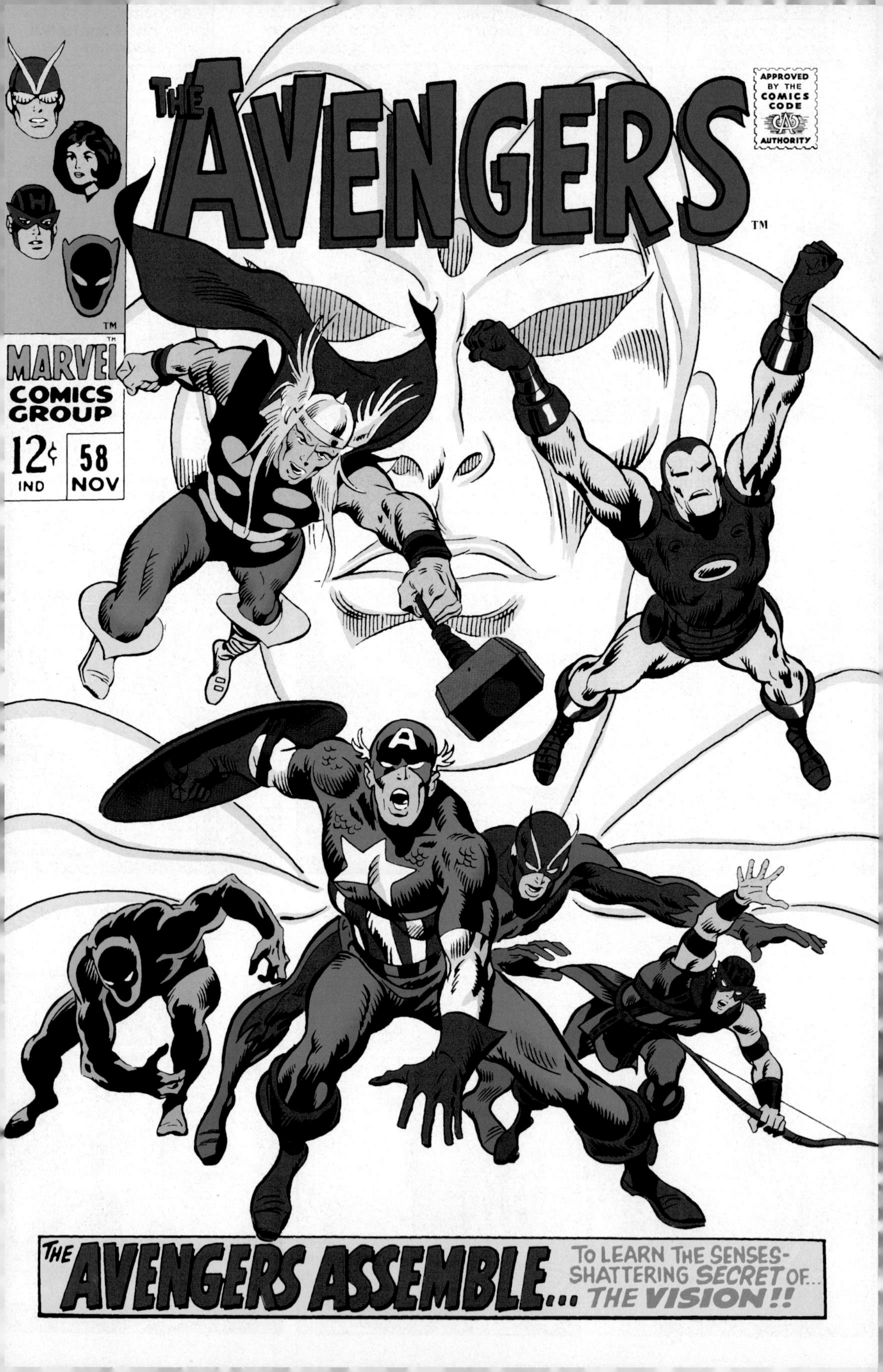

THE AVENGERS
APPROVED BY THE COMICS CODE AUTHORITY
TM
MARVEL COMICS GROUP
12¢ IND
58 NOV
THE AVENGERS ASSEMBLE... TO LEARN THE SENSES-SHATTERING SECRET OF... THE VISION!!

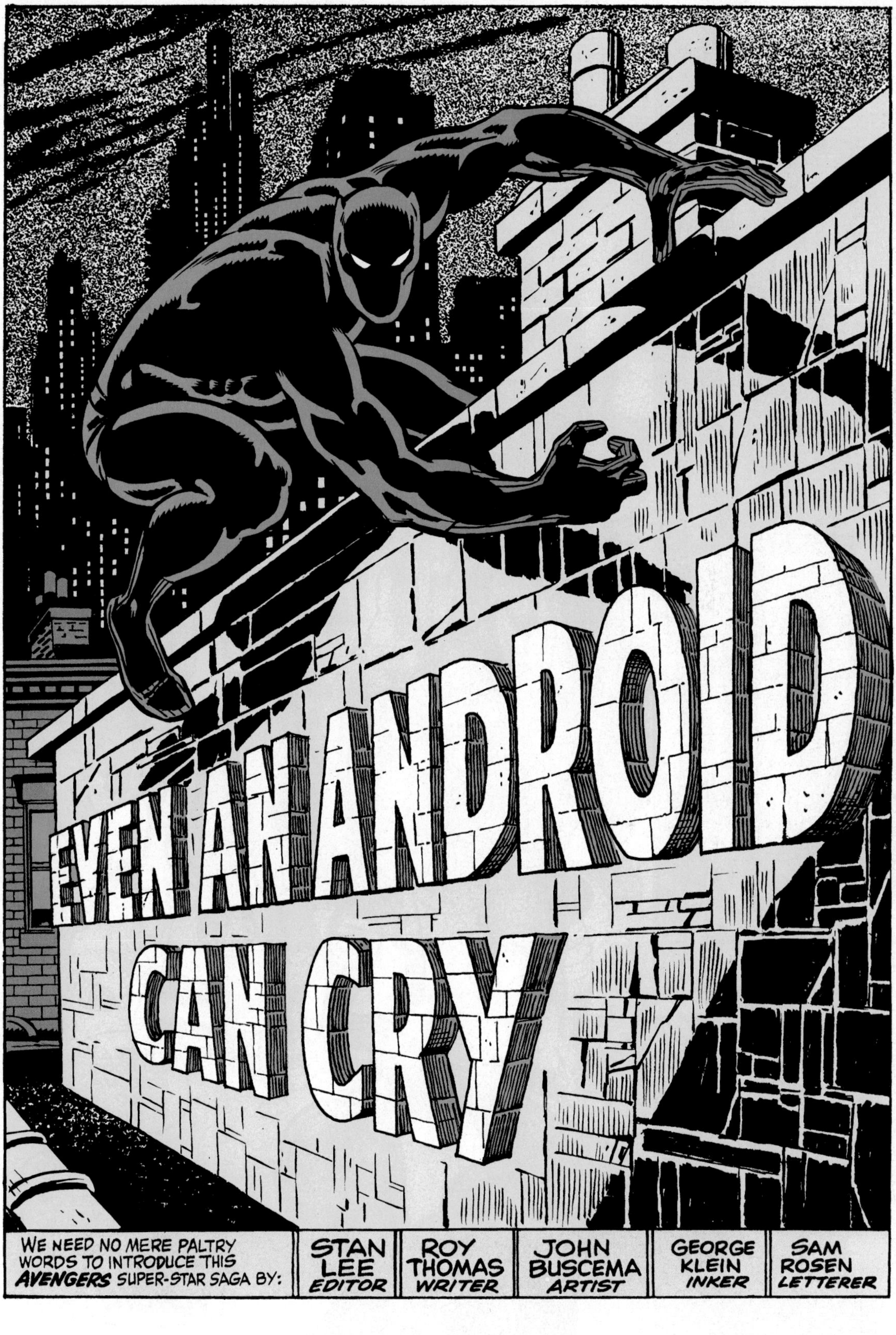

EVEN AN ANDROID CAN CRY
WE NEED NO MERE PALTRY WORDS TO INTRODUCE THIS AVENGERS SUPER-STAR SAGA BY:
STAN LEE EDITOR
ROY THOMAS WRITER
JOHN BUSCEMA ARTIST
GEORGE KLEIN INKER
SAM ROSEN LETTERER

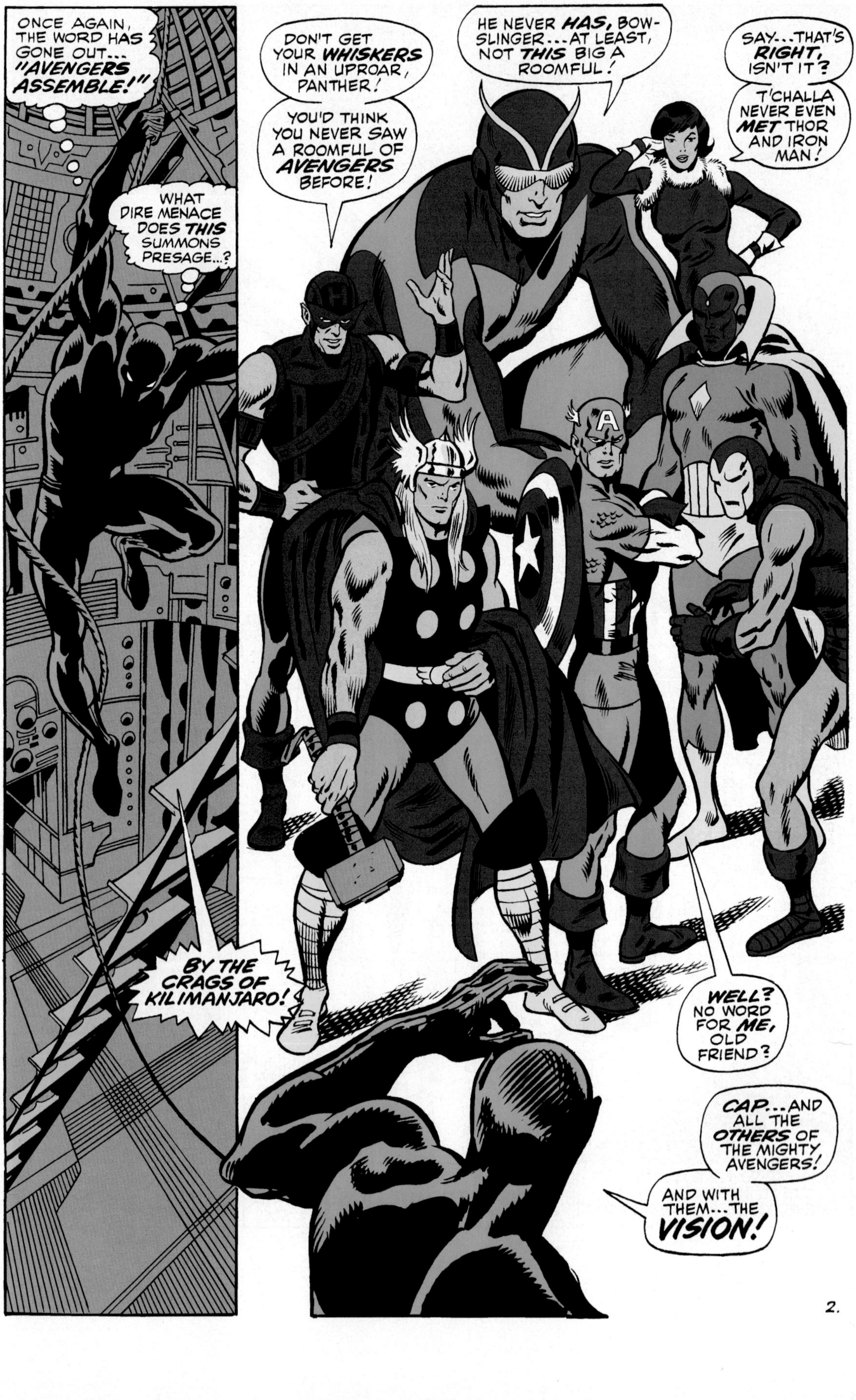

ONCE AGAIN, THE WORD HAS GONE OUT... "AVENGERS ASSEMBLE!"
WHAT DIRE MENACE DOES THIS SUMMONS PRESAGE...?
DON'T GET YOUR WHISKERS IN AN UPROAR, PANTHER!
YOU'D THINK YOU NEVER SAW A ROOMFUL OF AVENGERS BEFORE!
HE NEVER HAS, BOW-SLINGER...AT LEAST, NOT THIS BIG A ROOMFUL!
SAY...THAT'S RIGHT, ISN'T IT?
T'CHALLA NEVER EVEN MET THOR AND IRON MAN!
BY THE CRAGS OF KILIMANJARO!
WELL? NO WORD FOR ME, OLD FRIEND?
CAP...AND ALL THE OTHERS OF THE MIGHTY AVENGERS!
AND WITH THEM...THE VISION!

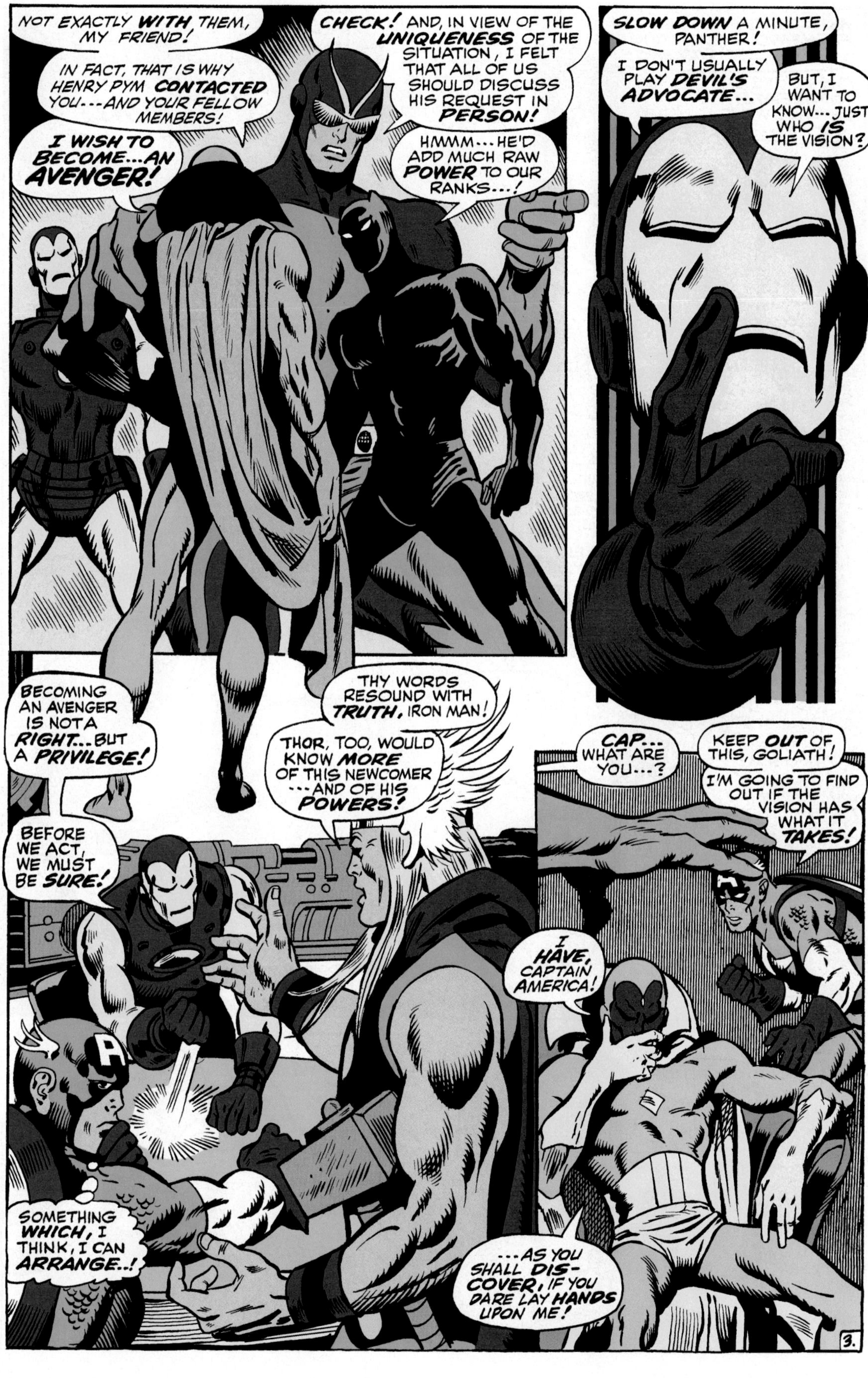
NOT EXACTLY WITH THEM, MY FRIEND!
IN FACT, THAT IS WHY HENRY PYM CONTACTED YOU---AND YOUR FELLOW MEMBERS!
I WISH TO BECOME...AN AVENGER!
CHECK! AND, IN VIEW OF THE UNIQUENESS OF THE SITUATION, I FELT THAT ALL OF US SHOULD DISCUSS HIS REQUEST IN PERSON!
HMMM...HE'D ADD MUCH RAW POWER TO OUR RANKS...!
SLOW DOWN A MINUTE, PANTHER!
I DON'T USUALLY PLAY DEVIL'S ADVOCATE...
BUT, I WANT TO KNOW...JUST WHO IS THE VISION?
BECOMING AN AVENGER IS NOT A RIGHT...BUT A PRIVILEGE!
BEFORE WE ACT, WE MUST BE SURE!
THY WORDS RESOUND WITH TRUTH, IRON MAN!
THOR, TOO, WOULD KNOW MORE OF THIS NEWCOMER ---AND OF HIS POWERS!
SOMETHING WHICH, I THINK, I CAN ARRANGE..!
CAP... WHAT ARE YOU...?
KEEP OUT OF THIS, GOLIATH!
I'M GOING TO FIND OUT IF THE VISION HAS WHAT IT TAKES!
I HAVE, CAPTAIN AMERICA!
...AS YOU SHALL DIS-COVER, IF YOU DARE LAY HANDS UPON ME!
3.

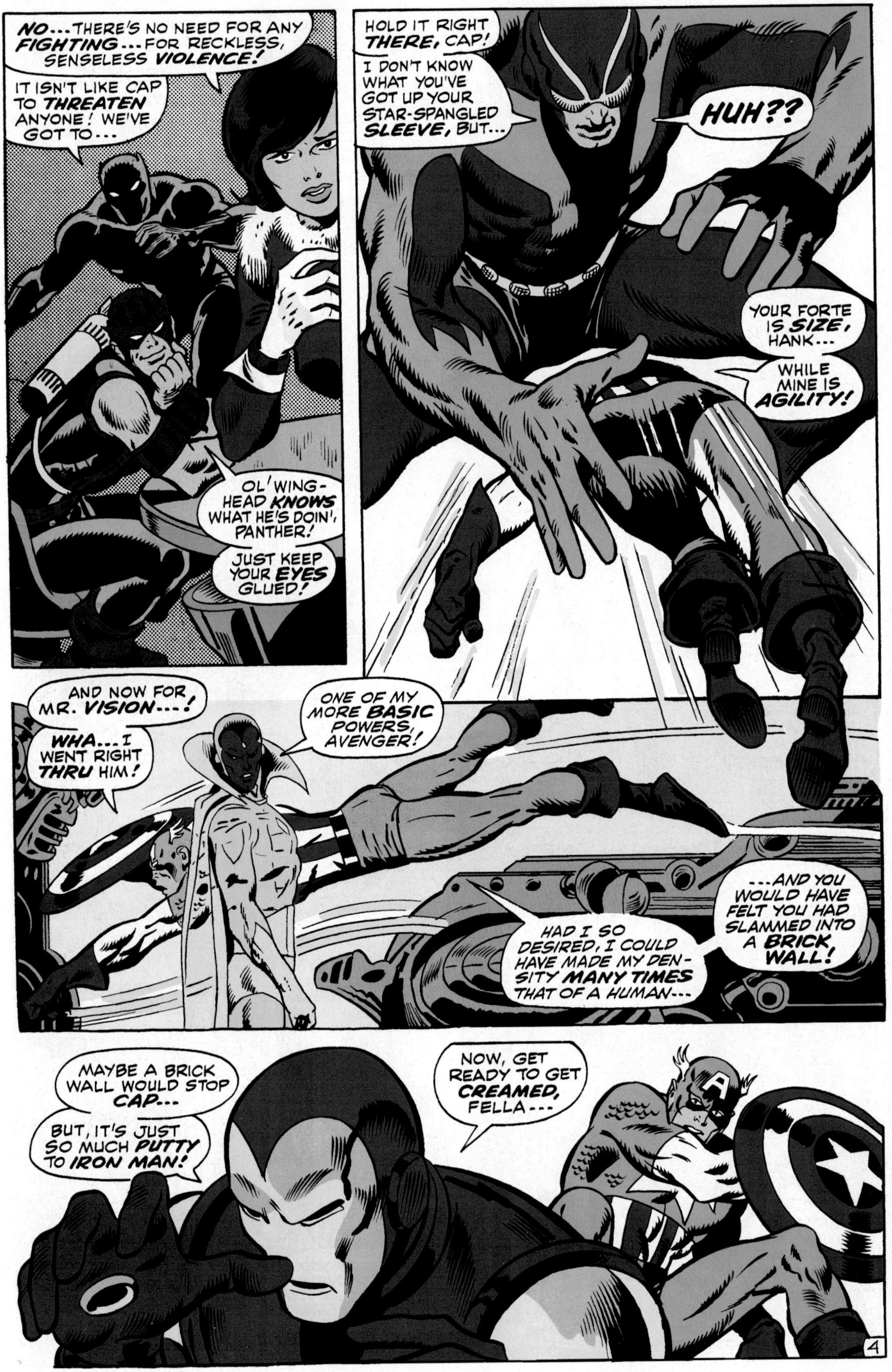
NO... THERE'S NO NEED FOR ANY FIGHTING... FOR RECKLESS, SENSELESS VIOLENCE!
IT ISN'T LIKE CAP TO THREATEN ANYONE! WE'VE GOT TO...
OL' WING-HEAD KNOWS WHAT HE'S DOIN', PANTHER!
JUST KEEP YOUR EYES GLUED!
HOLD IT RIGHT THERE, CAP!
I DON'T KNOW WHAT YOU'VE GOT UP YOUR STAR-SPANGLED SLEEVE, BUT...
HUH??
YOUR FORTE IS SIZE, HANK...
WHILE MINE IS AGILITY!
AND NOW FOR MR. VISION...!
WHA... I WENT RIGHT THRU HIM!
ONE OF MY MORE BASIC POWERS, AVENGER!
HAD I SO DESIRED, I COULD HAVE MADE MY DENSITY MANY TIMES THAT OF A HUMAN...
...AND YOU WOULD HAVE FELT YOU HAD SLAMMED INTO A BRICK WALL!
MAYBE A BRICK WALL WOULD STOP CAP...
BUT, IT'S JUST SO MUCH PUTTY TO IRON MAN!
NOW, GET READY TO GET CREAMED, FELLA...
4

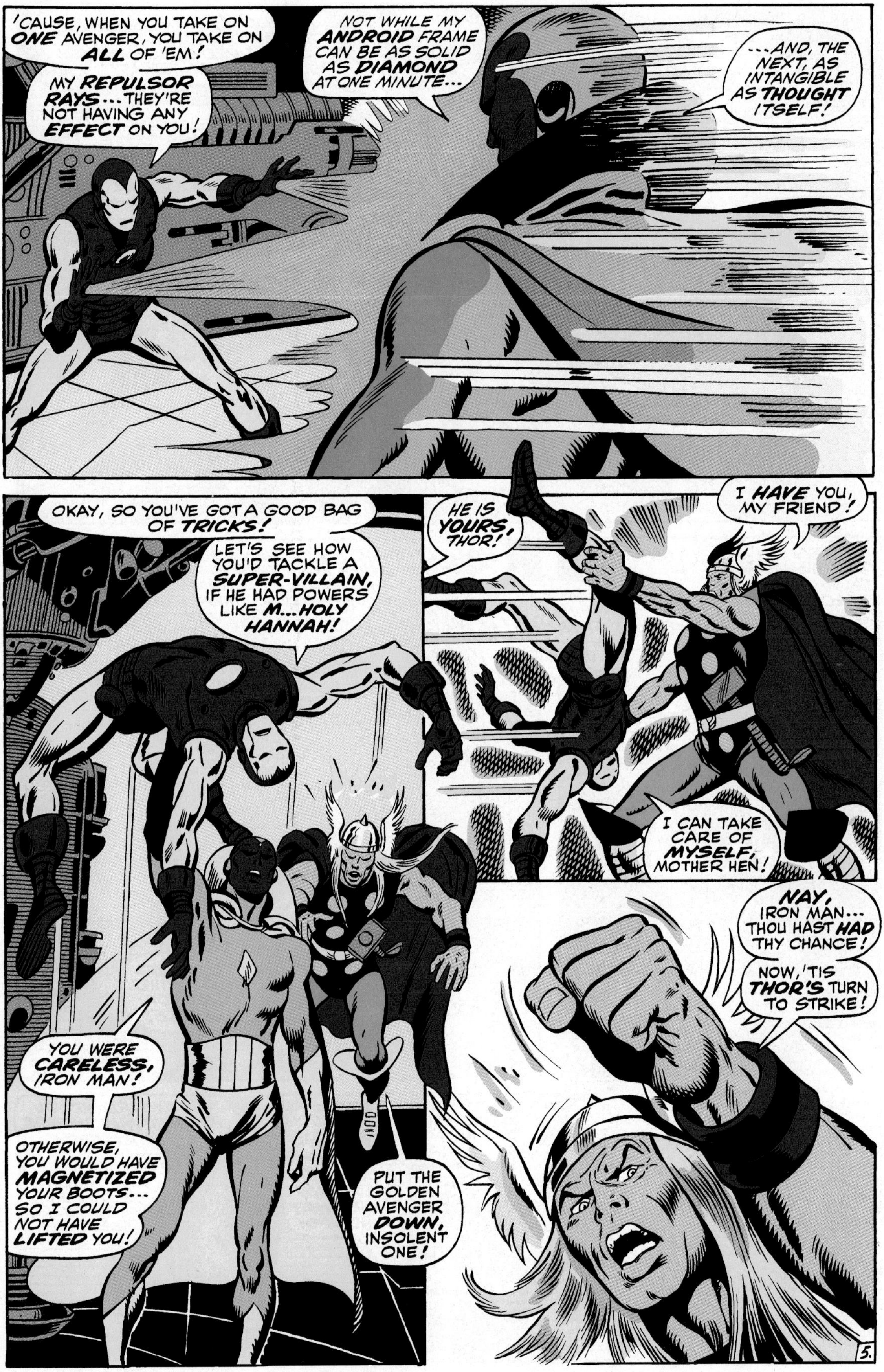

'CAUSE, WHEN YOU TAKE ON ONE AVENGER, YOU TAKE ON ALL OF 'EM!
MY REPULSOR RAYS... THEY'RE NOT HAVING ANY EFFECT ON YOU!
NOT WHILE MY ANDROID FRAME CAN BE AS SOLID AS DIAMOND AT ONE MINUTE...
...AND, THE NEXT, AS INTANGIBLE AS THOUGHT ITSELF!
OKAY, SO YOU'VE GOT A GOOD BAG OF TRICKS!
LET'S SEE HOW YOU'D TACKLE A SUPER-VILLAIN, IF HE HAD POWERS LIKE M...HOLY HANNAH!
YOU WERE CARELESS, IRON MAN!
OTHERWISE, YOU WOULD HAVE MAGNETIZED YOUR BOOTS... SO I COULD NOT HAVE LIFTED YOU!
PUT THE GOLDEN AVENGER DOWN, INSOLENT ONE!
HE IS YOURS, THOR!
I HAVE YOU, MY FRIEND!
I CAN TAKE CARE OF MYSELF, MOTHER HEN!
NAY, IRON MAN... THOU HAST HAD THY CHANCE!
NOW, 'TIS THOR'S TURN TO STRIKE!
5.

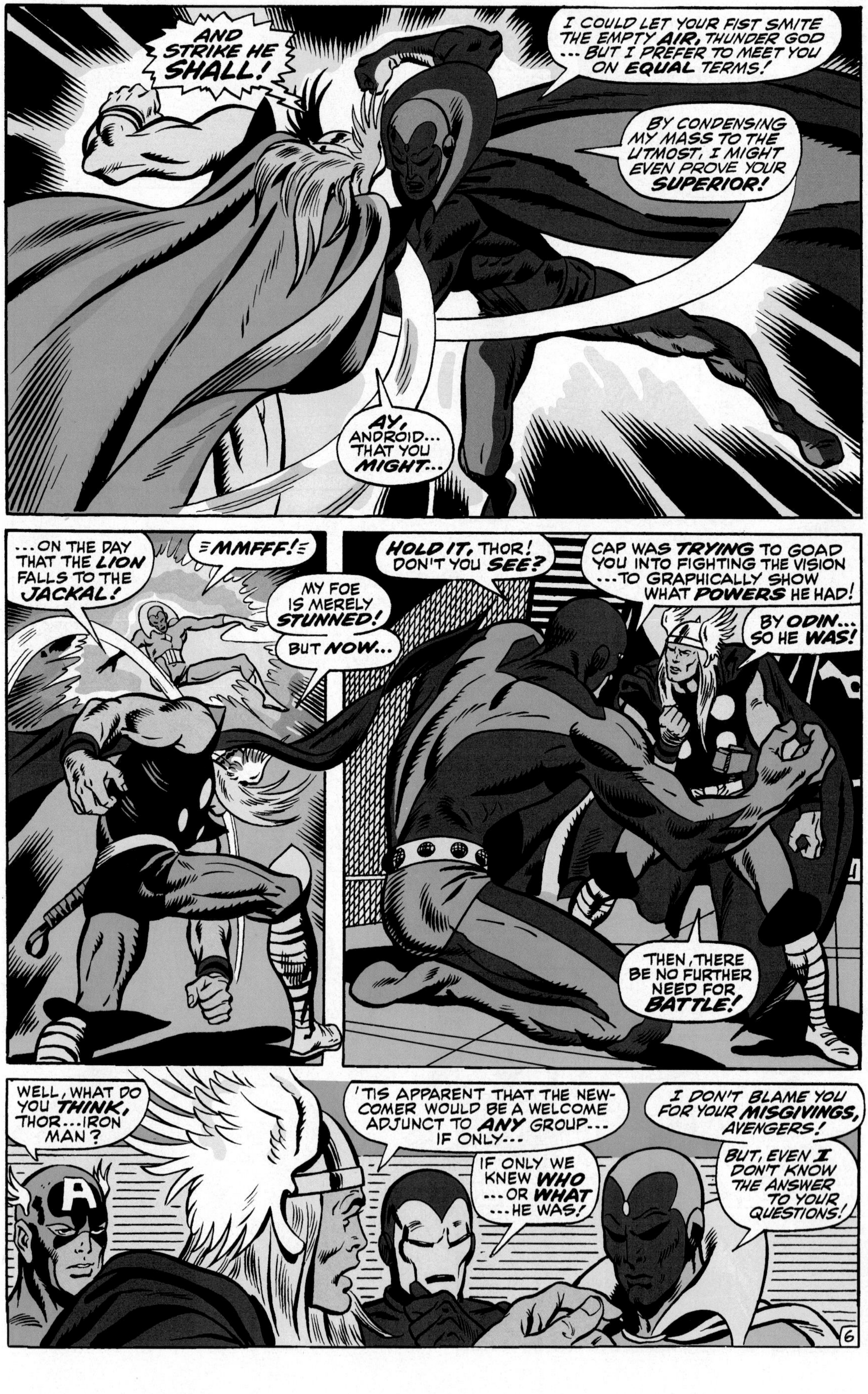

AND STRIKE HE SHALL!
I COULD LET YOUR FIST SMITE THE EMPTY AIR, THUNDER GOD ...BUT I PREFER TO MEET YOU ON EQUAL TERMS!
BY CONDENSING MY MASS TO THE UTMOST, I MIGHT EVEN PROVE YOUR SUPERIOR!
AY, ANDROID... THAT YOU MIGHT...
...ON THE DAY THAT THE LION FALLS TO THE JACKAL!
MMFFF!
MY FOE IS MERELY STUNNED!
BUT NOW...
HOLD IT, THOR! DON'T YOU SEE?
CAP WAS TRYING TO GOAD YOU INTO FIGHTING THE VISION ...TO GRAPHICALLY SHOW WHAT POWERS HE HAD!
BY ODIN... SO HE WAS!
THEN, THERE BE NO FURTHER NEED FOR BATTLE!
WELL, WHAT DO YOU THINK, THOR...IRON MAN?
'TIS APPARENT THAT THE NEWCOMER WOULD BE A WELCOME ADJUNCT TO ANY GROUP... IF ONLY...
IF ONLY WE KNEW WHO ...OR WHAT ...HE WAS!
I DON'T BLAME YOU FOR YOUR MISGIVINGS, AVENGERS!
BUT, EVEN I DON'T KNOW THE ANSWER TO YOUR QUESTIONS!
6

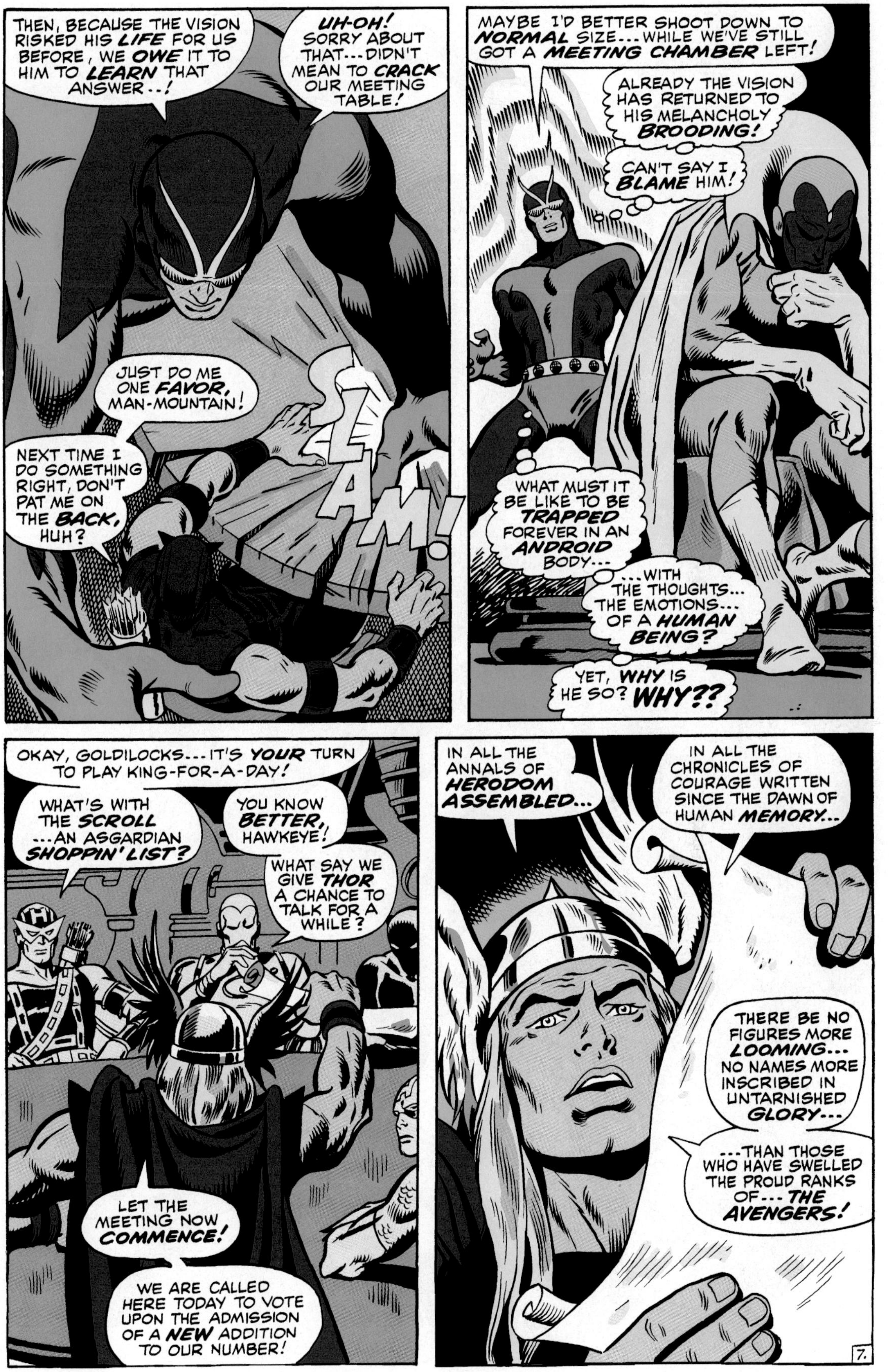
THEN, BECAUSE THE VISION RISKED HIS LIFE FOR US BEFORE, WE OWE IT TO HIM TO LEARN THAT ANSWER..!
UH-OH! SORRY ABOUT THAT...DIDN'T MEAN TO CRACK OUR MEETING TABLE!
JUST DO ME ONE FAVOR, MAN-MOUNTAIN!
NEXT TIME I DO SOMETHING RIGHT, DON'T PAT ME ON THE BACK, HUH?
SLAM!
MAYBE I'D BETTER SHOOT DOWN TO NORMAL SIZE...WHILE WE'VE STILL GOT A MEETING CHAMBER LEFT!
ALREADY THE VISION HAS RETURNED TO HIS MELANCHOLY BROODING!
CAN'T SAY I BLAME HIM!
WHAT MUST IT BE LIKE TO BE TRAPPED FOREVER IN AN ANDROID BODY...
...WITH THE THOUGHTS... THE EMOTIONS... OF A HUMAN BEING?
YET, WHY IS HE SO? WHY??
OKAY, GOLDILOCKS... IT'S YOUR TURN TO PLAY KING-FOR-A-DAY!
WHAT'S WITH THE SCROLL ...AN ASGARDIAN SHOPPIN' LIST?
YOU KNOW BETTER, HAWKEYE!
WHAT SAY WE GIVE THOR A CHANCE TO TALK FOR A WHILE?
LET THE MEETING NOW COMMENCE!
WE ARE CALLED HERE TODAY TO VOTE UPON THE ADMISSION OF A NEW ADDITION TO OUR NUMBER!
IN ALL THE ANNALS OF HERODOM ASSEMBLED...
IN ALL THE CHRONICLES OF COURAGE WRITTEN SINCE THE DAWN OF HUMAN MEMORY...
THERE BE NO FIGURES MORE LOOMING... NO NAMES MORE INSCRIBED IN UNTARNISHED GLORY...
...THAN THOSE WHO HAVE SWELLED THE PROUD RANKS OF... THE AVENGERS!
7.

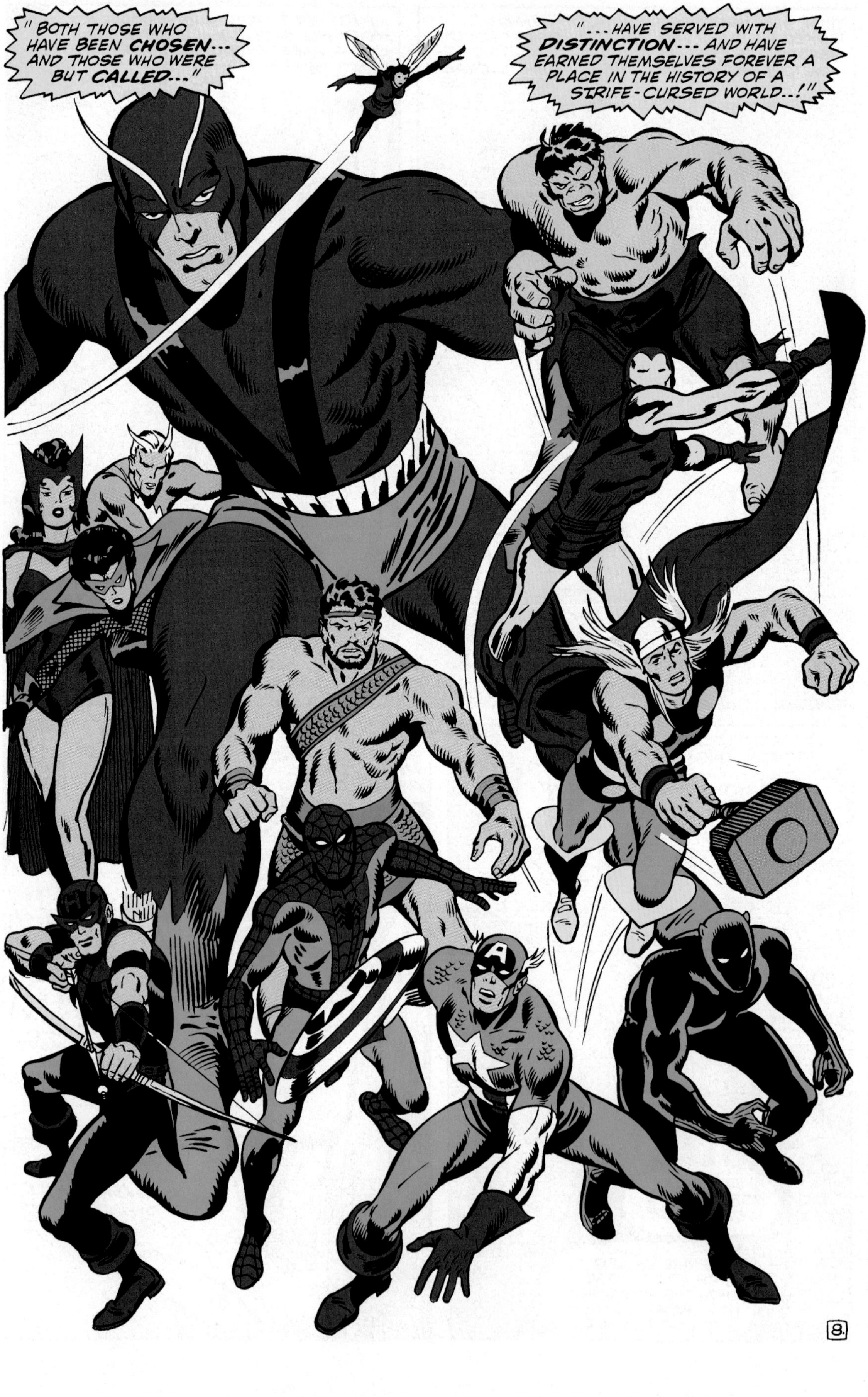
" BOTH THOSE WHO HAVE BEEN CHOSEN... AND THOSE WHO WERE BUT CALLED..."
"...HAVE SERVED WITH DISTINCTION... AND HAVE EARNED THEMSELVES FOREVER A PLACE IN THE HISTORY OF A STRIFE-CURSED WORLD...!"
8.

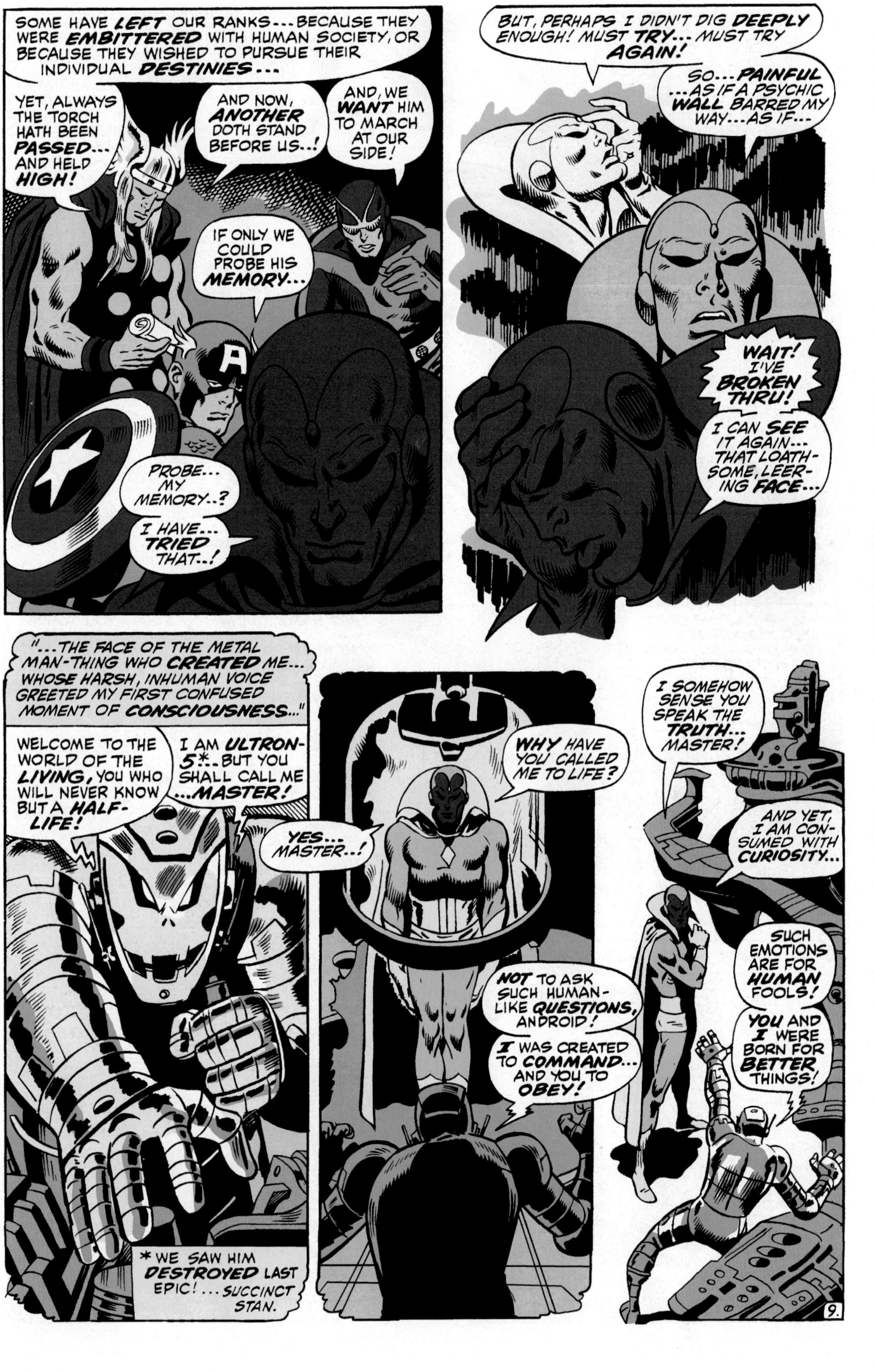

SOME HAVE LEFT OUR RANKS... BECAUSE THEY WERE EMBITTERED WITH HUMAN SOCIETY, OR BECAUSE THEY WISHED TO PURSUE THEIR INDIVIDUAL DESTINIES...
YET, ALWAYS THE TORCH HATH BEEN PASSED... AND HELD HIGH!
AND NOW, ANOTHER DOTH STAND BEFORE US..!
AND, WE WANT HIM TO MARCH AT OUR SIDE!
IF ONLY WE COULD PROBE HIS MEMORY...
PROBE... MY MEMORY..?
I HAVE... TRIED THAT..!
BUT, PERHAPS I DIDN'T DIG DEEPLY ENOUGH! MUST TRY... MUST TRY AGAIN!
SO... PAINFUL ...AS IF A PSYCHIC WALL BARRED MY WAY... AS IF...
WAIT! I'VE BROKEN THRU!
I CAN SEE IT AGAIN... THAT LOATHSOME, LEERING FACE...
"...THE FACE OF THE METAL MAN-THING WHO CREATED ME... WHOSE HARSH, INHUMAN VOICE GREETED MY FIRST CONFUSED MOMENT OF CONSCIOUSNESS..."
WELCOME TO THE WORLD OF THE LIVING, YOU WHO WILL NEVER KNOW BUT A HALF-LIFE!
I AM ULTRON-5*..BUT YOU SHALL CALL ME ...MASTER!
YES... MASTER..!
*WE SAW HIM DESTROYED LAST EPIC! ... SUCCINCT STAN.
WHY HAVE YOU CALLED ME TO LIFE?
NOT TO ASK SUCH HUMAN-LIKE QUESTIONS, ANDROID!
I WAS CREATED TO COMMAND... AND YOU TO OBEY!
I SOMEHOW SENSE YOU SPEAK THE TRUTH... MASTER!
AND YET, I AM CONSUMED WITH CURIOSITY...
SUCH EMOTIONS ARE FOR HUMAN FOOLS!
YOU AND I WERE BORN FOR BETTER THINGS!
9.

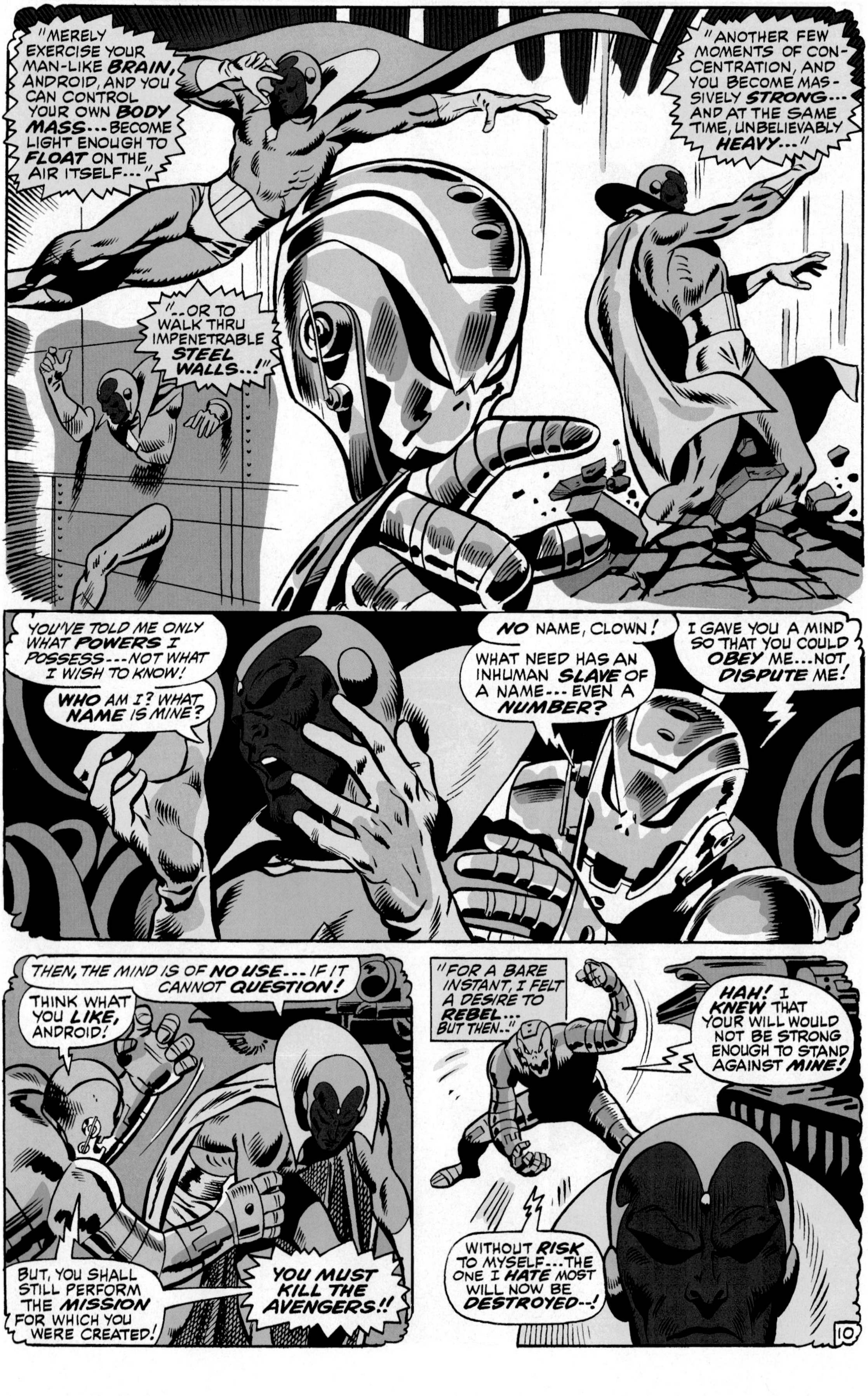
"MERELY EXERCISE YOUR MAN-LIKE BRAIN, ANDROID, AND YOU CAN CONTROL YOUR OWN BODY MASS... BECOME LIGHT ENOUGH TO FLOAT ON THE AIR ITSELF..."
"...OR TO WALK THRU IMPENETRABLE STEEL WALLS...!"
"ANOTHER FEW MOMENTS OF CONCENTRATION, AND YOU BECOME MASSIVELY STRONG... AND AT THE SAME TIME, UNBELIEVABLY HEAVY..."
YOU'VE TOLD ME ONLY WHAT POWERS I POSSESS---NOT WHAT I WISH TO KNOW!
WHO AM I? WHAT NAME IS MINE?
NO NAME, CLOWN!
WHAT NEED HAS AN INHUMAN SLAVE OF A NAME--- EVEN A NUMBER?
I GAVE YOU A MIND SO THAT YOU COULD OBEY ME... NOT DISPUTE ME!
THEN, THE MIND IS OF NO USE... IF IT CANNOT QUESTION!
THINK WHAT YOU LIKE, ANDROID!
BUT, YOU SHALL STILL PERFORM THE MISSION FOR WHICH YOU WERE CREATED!
YOU MUST KILL THE AVENGERS!!
"FOR A BARE INSTANT, I FELT A DESIRE TO REBEL... BUT THEN..."
HAH! I KNEW THAT YOUR WILL WOULD NOT BE STRONG ENOUGH TO STAND AGAINST MINE!
WITHOUT RISK TO MYSELF... THE ONE I HATE MOST WILL NOW BE DESTROYED--!
10

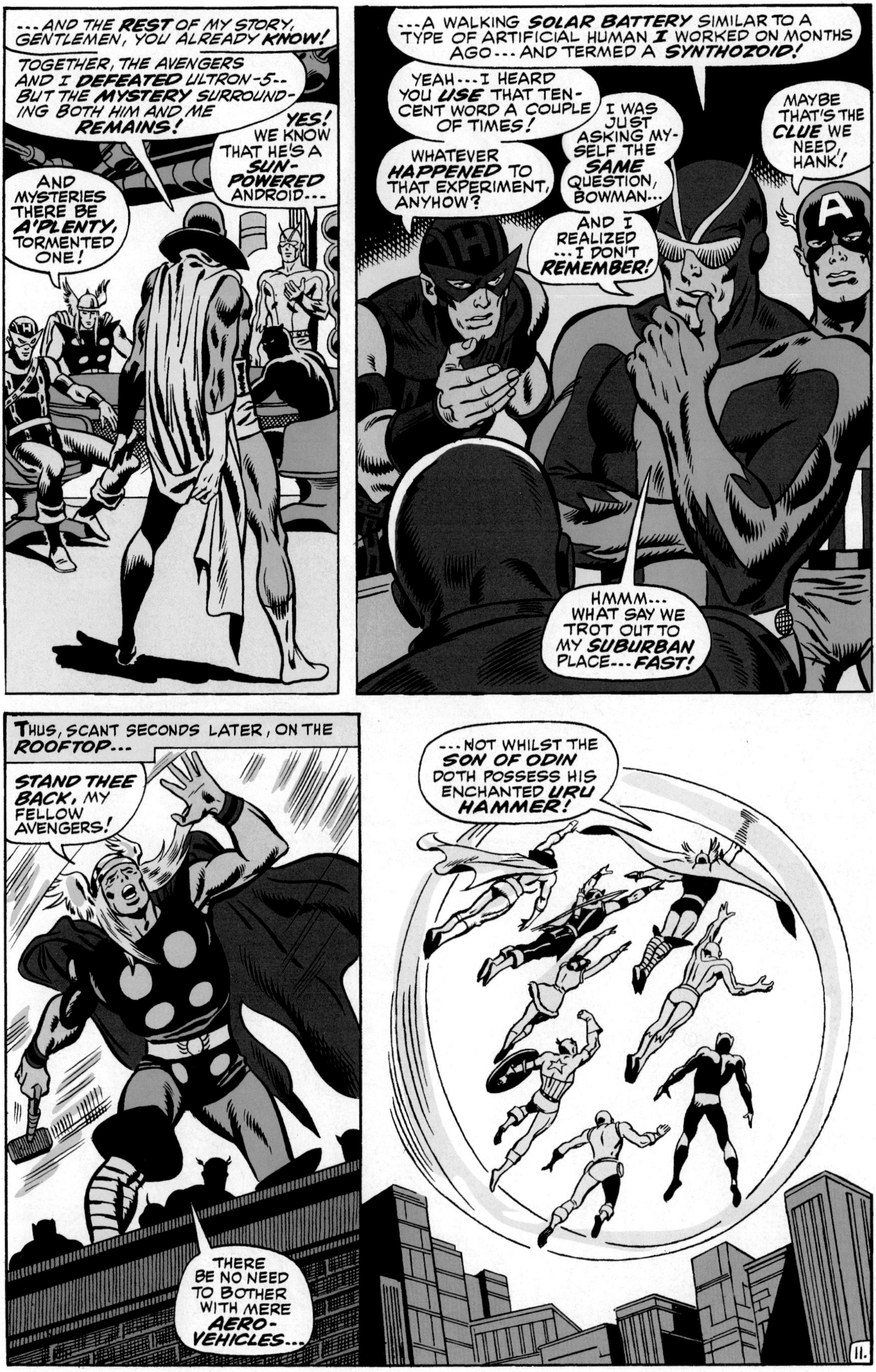

...AND THE REST OF MY STORY, GENTLEMEN, YOU ALREADY KNOW!
TOGETHER, THE AVENGERS AND I DEFEATED ULTRON-5-- BUT THE MYSTERY SURROUNDING BOTH HIM AND ME REMAINS!
AND MYSTERIES THERE BE A'PLENTY, TORMENTED ONE!
YES! WE KNOW THAT HE'S A SUN-POWERED ANDROID...
...A WALKING SOLAR BATTERY SIMILAR TO A TYPE OF ARTIFICIAL HUMAN I WORKED ON MONTHS AGO--- AND TERMED A SYNTHOZOID!
YEAH---I HEARD YOU USE THAT TEN-CENT WORD A COUPLE OF TIMES!
WHATEVER HAPPENED TO THAT EXPERIMENT, ANYHOW?
I WAS JUST ASKING MYSELF THE SAME QUESTION, BOWMAN...
AND I REALIZED ...I DON'T REMEMBER!
MAYBE THAT'S THE CLUE WE NEED, HANK!
HMMM... WHAT SAY WE TROT OUT TO MY SUBURBAN PLACE---FAST!
THUS, SCANT SECONDS LATER, ON THE ROOFTOP...
STAND THEE BACK, MY FELLOW AVENGERS!
THERE BE NO NEED TO BOTHER WITH MERE AERO-VEHICLES...
...NOT WHILST THE SON OF ODIN DOTH POSSESS HIS ENCHANTED URU HAMMER!
11.

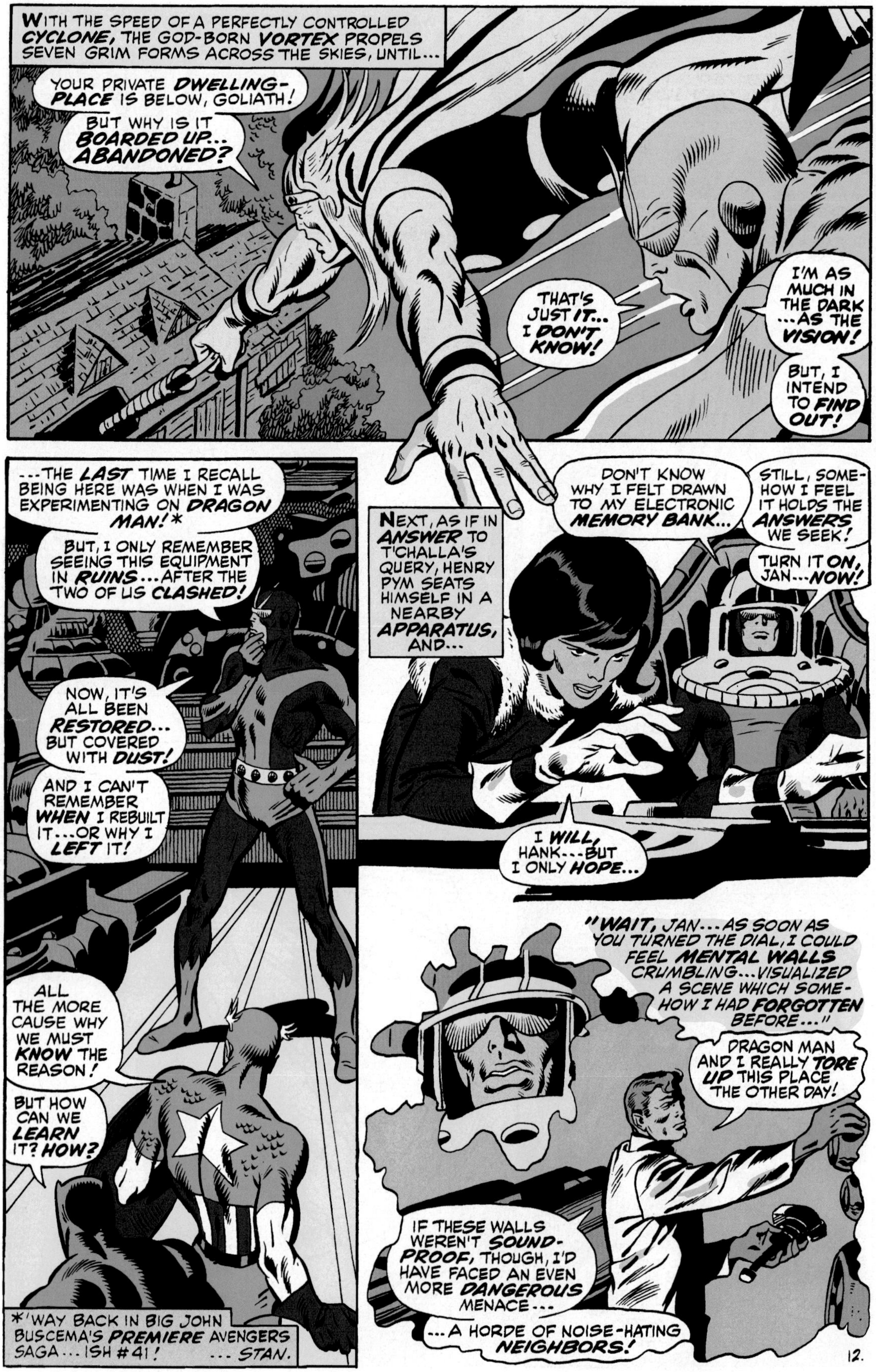
WITH THE SPEED OF A PERFECTLY CONTROLLED CYCLONE, THE GOD-BORN VORTEX PROPELS SEVEN GRIM FORMS ACROSS THE SKIES, UNTIL...
YOUR PRIVATE DWELLING-PLACE IS BELOW, GOLIATH!
BUT WHY IS IT BOARDED UP... ABANDONED?
THAT'S JUST IT... I DON'T KNOW!
I'M AS MUCH IN THE DARK ...AS THE VISION!
BUT, I INTEND TO FIND OUT!
...THE LAST TIME I RECALL BEING HERE WAS WHEN I WAS EXPERIMENTING ON DRAGON MAN!*
BUT, I ONLY REMEMBER SEEING THIS EQUIPMENT IN RUINS... AFTER THE TWO OF US CLASHED!
NOW, IT'S ALL BEEN RESTORED... BUT COVERED WITH DUST!
AND I CAN'T REMEMBER WHEN I REBUILT IT... OR WHY I LEFT IT!
ALL THE MORE CAUSE WHY WE MUST KNOW THE REASON!
BUT HOW CAN WE LEARN IT? HOW?
*'WAY BACK IN BIG JOHN BUSCEMA'S PREMIERE AVENGERS SAGA... ISH #41! ...STAN.
NEXT, AS IF IN ANSWER TO T'CHALLA'S QUERY, HENRY PYM SEATS HIMSELF IN A NEARBY APPARATUS, AND...
DON'T KNOW WHY I FELT DRAWN TO MY ELECTRONIC MEMORY BANK...
STILL, SOME-HOW I FEEL IT HOLDS THE ANSWERS WE SEEK!
TURN IT ON, JAN... NOW!
I WILL, HANK... BUT I ONLY HOPE...
"WAIT, JAN... AS SOON AS YOU TURNED THE DIAL, I COULD FEEL MENTAL WALLS CRUMBLING... VISUALIZED A SCENE WHICH SOME-HOW I HAD FORGOTTEN BEFORE..."
DRAGON MAN AND I REALLY TORE UP THIS PLACE THE OTHER DAY!
IF THESE WALLS WEREN'T SOUND-PROOF, THOUGH, I'D HAVE FACED AN EVEN MORE DANGEROUS MENACE...
...A HORDE OF NOISE-HATING NEIGHBORS!

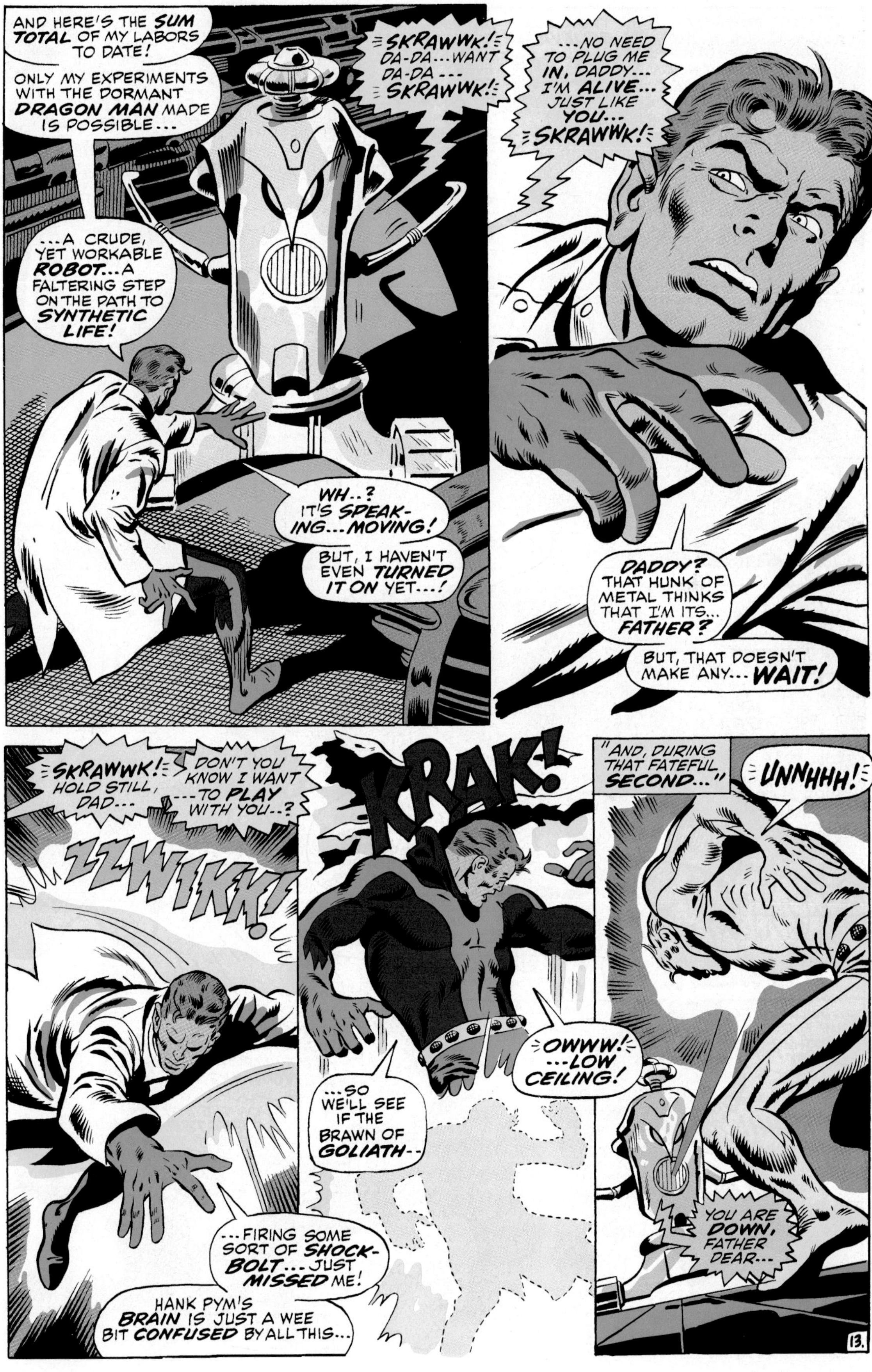

AND HERE'S THE SUM TOTAL OF MY LABORS TO DATE!
ONLY MY EXPERIMENTS WITH THE DORMANT DRAGON MAN MADE IS POSSIBLE...
...A CRUDE, YET WORKABLE ROBOT...A FALTERING STEP ON THE PATH TO SYNTHETIC LIFE!
SKRAWWK! DA-DA...WANT DA-DA... SKRAWWK!
WH..? IT'S SPEAK-ING...MOVING!
BUT, I HAVEN'T EVEN TURNED IT ON YET...!
...NO NEED TO PLUG ME IN, DADDY... I'M ALIVE... JUST LIKE YOU... SKRAWWK!
DADDY? THAT HUNK OF METAL THINKS THAT I'M ITS... FATHER?
BUT, THAT DOESN'T MAKE ANY... WAIT!
SKRAWWK! HOLD STILL, DAD...
DON'T YOU KNOW I WANT TO PLAY WITH YOU...?
ZZWIKK!
...FIRING SOME SORT OF SHOCK-BOLT... JUST MISSED ME!
HANK PYM'S BRAIN IS JUST A WEE BIT CONFUSED BY ALL THIS...
KRAK!
...SO WE'LL SEE IF THE BRAWN OF GOLIATH--
OWWW! ...LOW CEILING!
"AND, DURING THAT FATEFUL SECOND..."
UNNHHH!
YOU ARE DOWN, FATHER DEAR...
13.

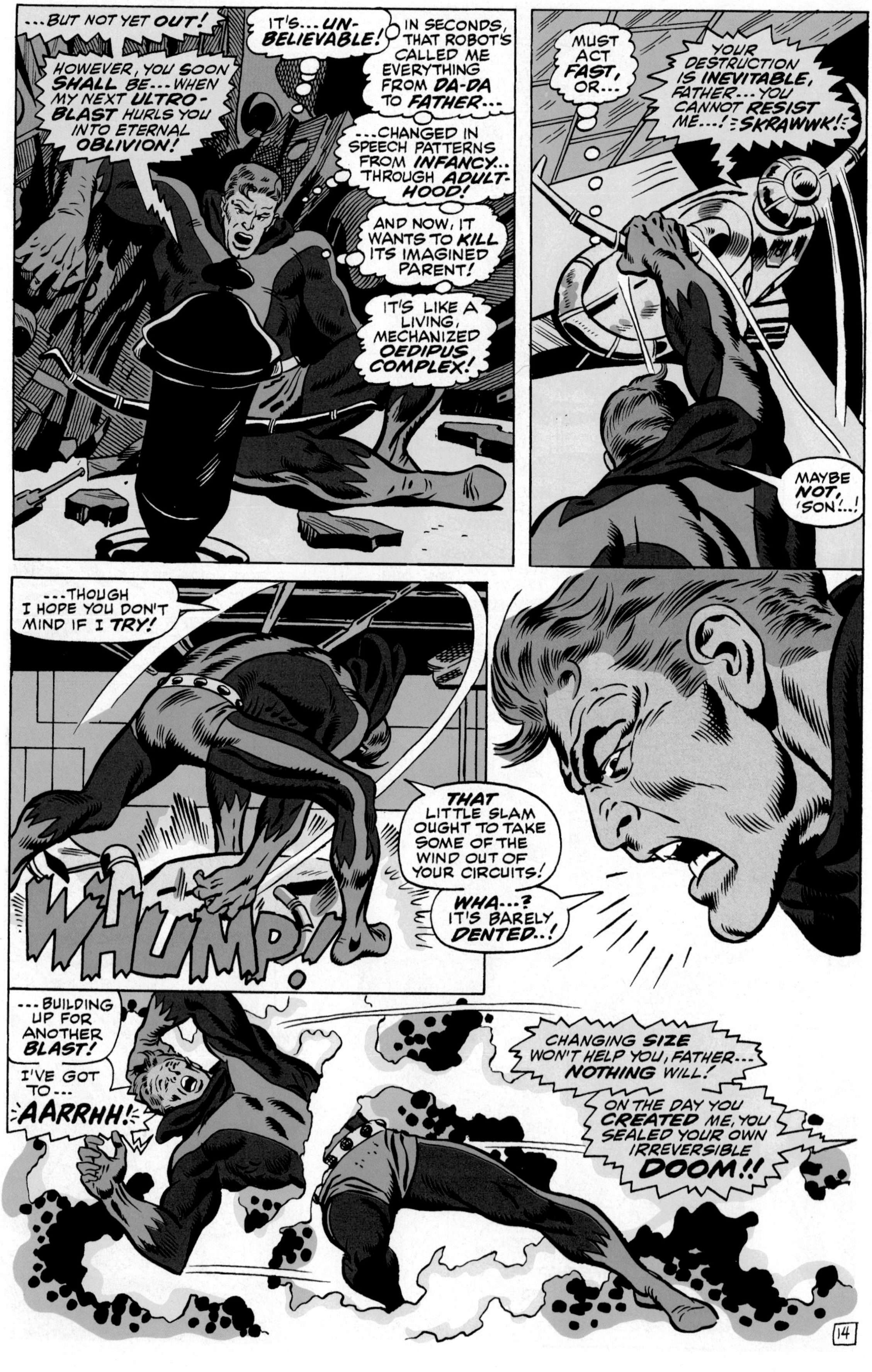
...BUT NOT YET OUT!
HOWEVER, YOU SOON SHALL BE... WHEN MY NEXT ULTRO-BLAST HURLS YOU INTO ETERNAL OBLIVION!
IT'S... UN-BELIEVABLE!
IN SECONDS, THAT ROBOT'S CALLED ME EVERYTHING FROM DA-DA TO FATHER...
...CHANGED IN SPEECH PATTERNS FROM INFANCY... THROUGH ADULT-HOOD!
AND NOW, IT WANTS TO KILL ITS IMAGINED PARENT!
IT'S LIKE A LIVING, MECHANIZED OEDIPUS COMPLEX!
MUST ACT FAST, OR...
YOUR DESTRUCTION IS INEVITABLE, FATHER... YOU CANNOT RESIST ME...! SKRAWWK!
MAYBE NOT, 'SON'...!
...THOUGH I HOPE YOU DON'T MIND IF I TRY!
THAT LITTLE SLAM OUGHT TO TAKE SOME OF THE WIND OUT OF YOUR CIRCUITS!
WHUMP!
WHA...? IT'S BARELY DENTED..!
...BUILDING UP FOR ANOTHER BLAST!
I'VE GOT TO...
AARRHH!
CHANGING SIZE WON'T HELP YOU, FATHER... NOTHING WILL!
ON THE DAY YOU CREATED ME, YOU SEALED YOUR OWN IRREVERSIBLE DOOM!!

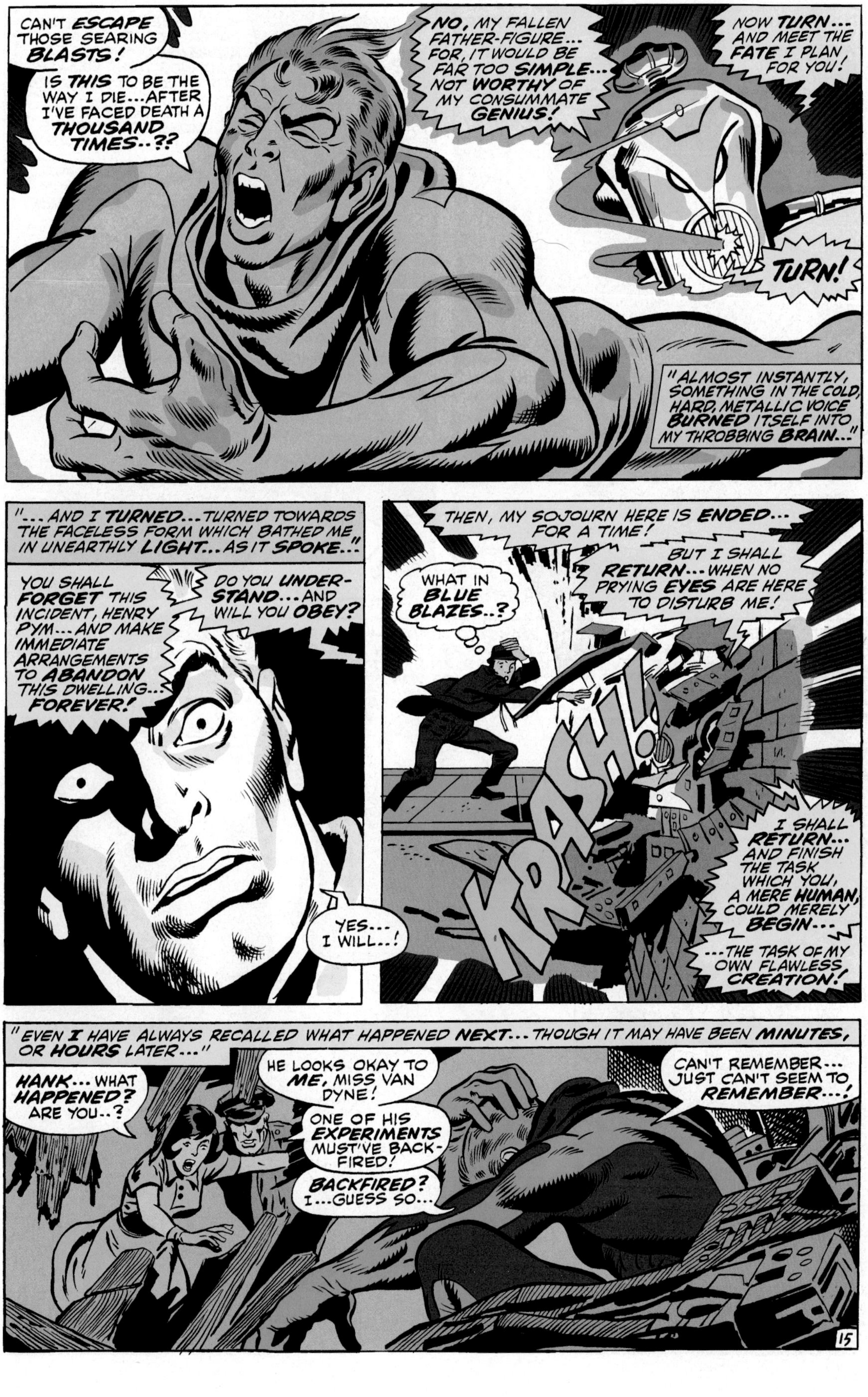
CAN'T ESCAPE THOSE SEARING BLASTS!
IS THIS TO BE THE WAY I DIE...AFTER I'VE FACED DEATH A THOUSAND TIMES..??
NO, MY FALLEN FATHER-FIGURE... FOR, IT WOULD BE FAR TOO SIMPLE... NOT WORTHY OF MY CONSUMMATE GENIUS!
NOW TURN... AND MEET THE FATE I PLAN FOR YOU!
TURN!
"ALMOST INSTANTLY, SOMETHING IN THE COLD, HARD, METALLIC VOICE BURNED ITSELF INTO MY THROBBING BRAIN..."
"...AND I TURNED...TURNED TOWARDS THE FACELESS FORM WHICH BATHED ME IN UNEARTHLY LIGHT...AS IT SPOKE..."
YOU SHALL FORGET THIS INCIDENT, HENRY PYM...AND MAKE IMMEDIATE ARRANGEMENTS TO ABANDON THIS DWELLING... FOREVER!
DO YOU UNDERSTAND...AND WILL YOU OBEY?
YES... I WILL..!
THEN, MY SOJOURN HERE IS ENDED... FOR A TIME!
BUT I SHALL RETURN...WHEN NO PRYING EYES ARE HERE TO DISTURB ME!
WHAT IN BLUE BLAZES..?
KRASH!
I SHALL RETURN... AND FINISH THE TASK WHICH YOU, A MERE HUMAN, COULD MERELY BEGIN...
...THE TASK OF MY OWN FLAWLESS CREATION!
"EVEN I HAVE ALWAYS RECALLED WHAT HAPPENED NEXT...THOUGH IT MAY HAVE BEEN MINUTES, OR HOURS LATER..."
HANK...WHAT HAPPENED? ARE YOU..?
HE LOOKS OKAY TO ME, MISS VAN DYNE!
ONE OF HIS EXPERIMENTS MUST'VE BACK-FIRED!
BACKFIRED? I...GUESS SO...
CAN'T REMEMBER... JUST CAN'T SEEM TO REMEMBER...!

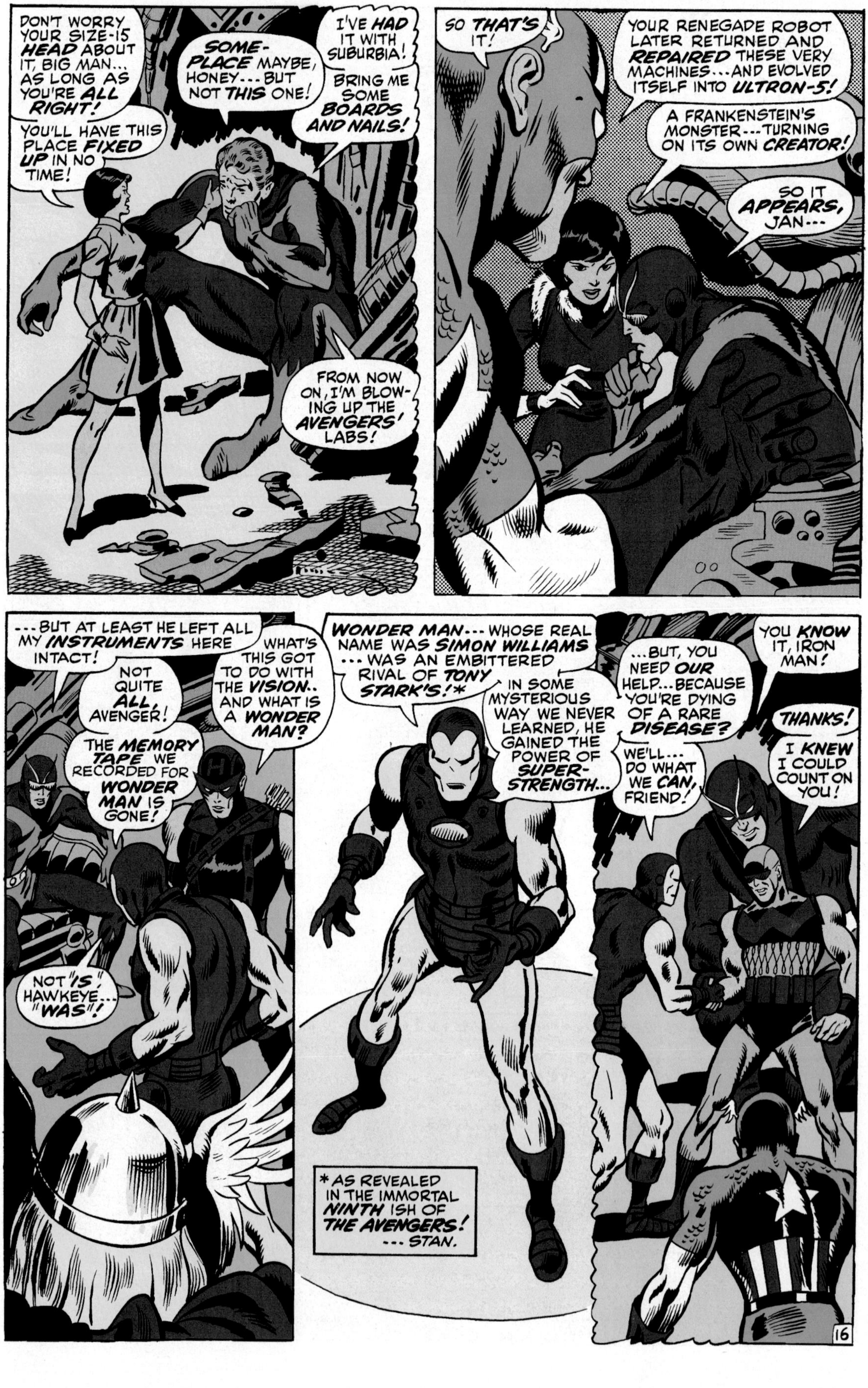
DON'T WORRY YOUR SIZE-15 HEAD ABOUT IT, BIG MAN... AS LONG AS YOU'RE ALL RIGHT!
YOU'LL HAVE THIS PLACE FIXED UP IN NO TIME!
SOME-PLACE MAYBE, HONEY--- BUT NOT THIS ONE!
I'VE HAD IT WITH SUBURBIA!
BRING ME SOME BOARDS AND NAILS!
FROM NOW ON, I'M BLOWING UP THE AVENGERS' LABS!
SO THAT'S IT!
YOUR RENEGADE ROBOT LATER RETURNED AND REPAIRED THESE VERY MACHINES...AND EVOLVED ITSELF INTO ULTRON-5!
A FRANKENSTEIN'S MONSTER---TURNING ON ITS OWN CREATOR!
SO IT APPEARS, JAN---
---BUT AT LEAST HE LEFT ALL MY INSTRUMENTS HERE INTACT!
NOT QUITE ALL, AVENGER!
THE MEMORY TAPE WE RECORDED FOR WONDER MAN IS GONE!
WHAT'S THIS GOT TO DO WITH THE VISION.. AND WHAT IS A WONDER MAN?
NOT "IS", HAWKEYE... "WAS"!
WONDER MAN--- WHOSE REAL NAME WAS SIMON WILLIAMS --- WAS AN EMBITTERED RIVAL OF TONY STARK'S!*
IN SOME MYSTERIOUS WAY WE NEVER LEARNED, HE GAINED THE POWER OF SUPER-STRENGTH...
*AS REVEALED IN THE IMMORTAL NINTH ISH OF THE AVENGERS! --- STAN.
...BUT, YOU NEED OUR HELP...BECAUSE YOU'RE DYING OF A RARE DISEASE?
WE'LL... DO WHAT WE CAN, FRIEND!
YOU KNOW IT, IRON MAN!
THANKS!
I KNEW I COULD COUNT ON YOU!
16

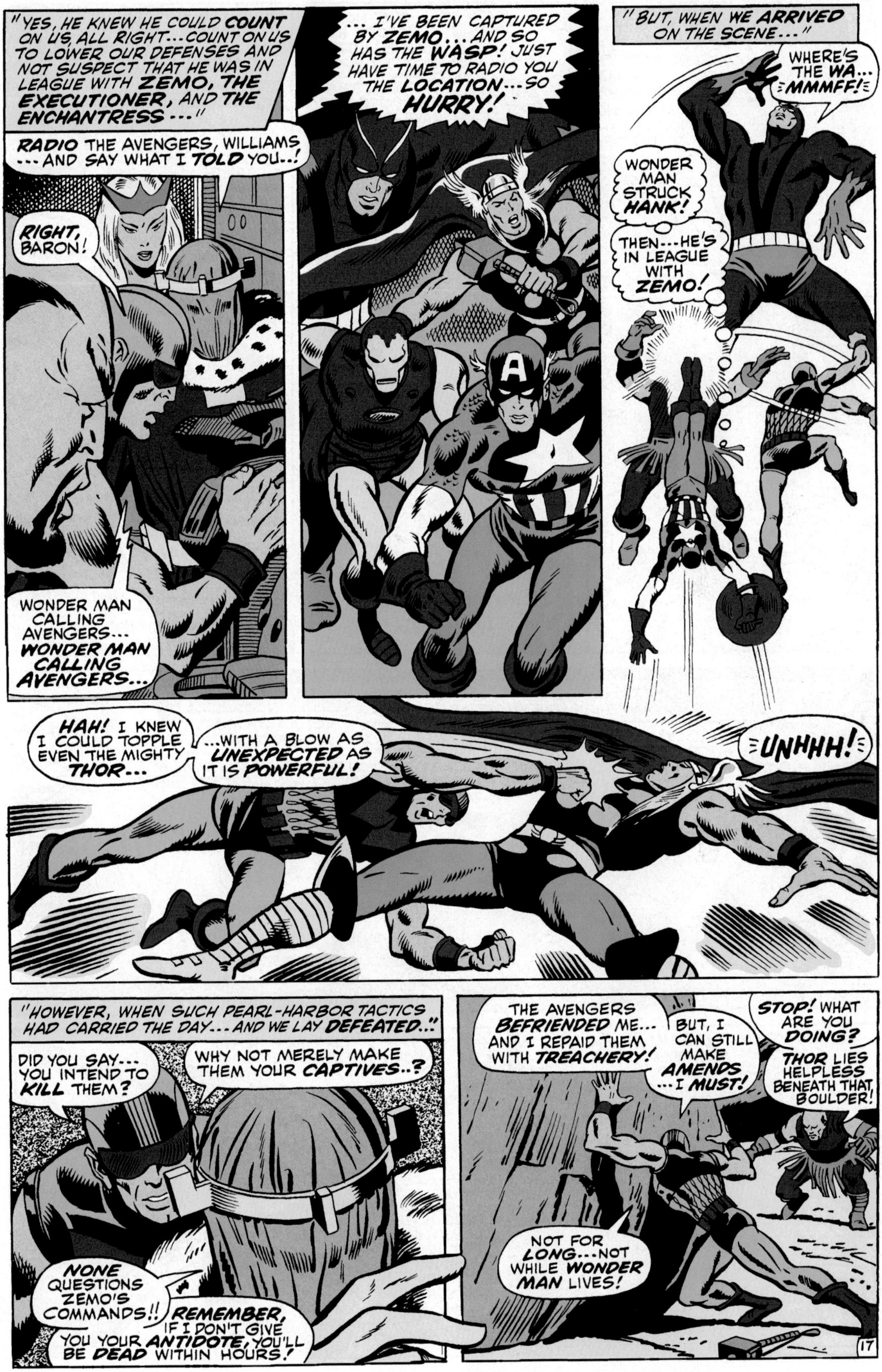

"YES, HE KNEW HE COULD COUNT ON US, ALL RIGHT... COUNT ON US TO LOWER OUR DEFENSES AND NOT SUSPECT THAT HE WAS IN LEAGUE WITH ZEMO, THE EXECUTIONER, AND THE ENCHANTRESS..."
RADIO THE AVENGERS, WILLIAMS ... AND SAY WHAT I TOLD YOU..!
RIGHT, BARON!
WONDER MAN CALLING AVENGERS... WONDER MAN CALLING AVENGERS...
... I'VE BEEN CAPTURED BY ZEMO... AND SO HAS THE WASP! JUST HAVE TIME TO RADIO YOU THE LOCATION... SO HURRY!
"BUT, WHEN WE ARRIVED ON THE SCENE..."
WHERE'S THE WA... MMMFF!
WONDER MAN STRUCK HANK!
THEN... HE'S IN LEAGUE WITH ZEMO!
HAH! I KNEW I COULD TOPPLE EVEN THE MIGHTY THOR...
...WITH A BLOW AS UNEXPECTED AS IT IS POWERFUL!
UNHHH!
"HOWEVER, WHEN SUCH PEARL-HARBOR TACTICS HAD CARRIED THE DAY... AND WE LAY DEFEATED.."
DID YOU SAY... YOU INTEND TO KILL THEM?
WHY NOT MERELY MAKE THEM YOUR CAPTIVES..?
NONE QUESTIONS ZEMO'S COMMANDS!!
REMEMBER, IF I DON'T GIVE YOU YOUR ANTIDOTE, YOU'LL BE DEAD WITHIN HOURS!
THE AVENGERS BEFRIENDED ME... AND I REPAID THEM WITH TREACHERY!
BUT, I CAN STILL MAKE AMENDS ... I MUST!
STOP! WHAT ARE YOU DOING? THOR LIES HELPLESS BENEATH THAT BOULDER!
NOT FOR LONG... NOT WHILE WONDER MAN LIVES!
17

THEN LIVE NO LONGER, FOOL! ...WHILE WE ESCAPE, DESTROYING THE TUNNEL AFTER US!

WHROOM!

ZEMO'S GONE!

BUT NOT BEFORE HE RAY-BLASTED WONDER MAN...

WITHOUT THAT ANTIDOTE, HE'D HAVE DIED ANY-WAY... WITHIN HOURS!

AT LEAST I DIE...KNOWING I DIDN'T LIVE... IN VAIN...!

"YET, A SPARK OF LIFE STILL FLICKERED WITHIN SIMON WILLIAMS, AND SO..."

WE GOT TO MY SUBURBAN LAB JUST IN TIME!

NO POWER ON EARTH CAN SAVE WONDER MAN'S BODY...

BUT, WITH YOUR ELECTRONIC MEMORY BANK, WE CAN PRESERVE HIS BRAIN PATTERNS...

PERHAPS HE'LL LIVE AGAIN...ANOTHER DAY...IN ANOTHER FORM!

THE CHAMBER IS QUIET NOW... SOMEWHERE HIGH ABOVE A PLANE DRONES... AND THEN, THE VISION SPEAKS...

THEN---THAT IS THE SECRET OF MY CREATION!

AN ANDROID... WITH THE AMNESIAC BRAIN PATTERNS OF A MURDERED MAN!

NOT AN ANDROID... BUT A SYNTHOZOID! YOU'RE BASICALLY HUMAN IN EVERY WAY... EXCEPT THAT YOUR BODY IS MADE OF SYNTHETIC PARTS!

AND, YOUR BRAIN...

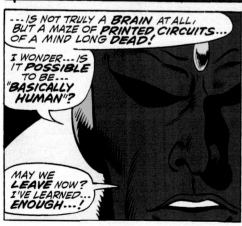

---IS NOT TRULY A BRAIN AT ALL, BUT A MAZE OF PRINTED CIRCUITS... OF A MIND LONG DEAD!

I WONDER...IS IT POSSIBLE TO BE... "BASICALLY HUMAN"?

MAY WE LEAVE NOW? I'VE LEARNED... ENOUGH...!

AY, VISION! 'TIS TIME FOR THE FINAL RECKONING!

MAYBE OL' RUDDY-CHEEKS WAS HUMAN ONCE... BUT HE AIN'T NOW!

HIS VOICE WAS COLD AS A CHRISTMAS TURKEY!

18

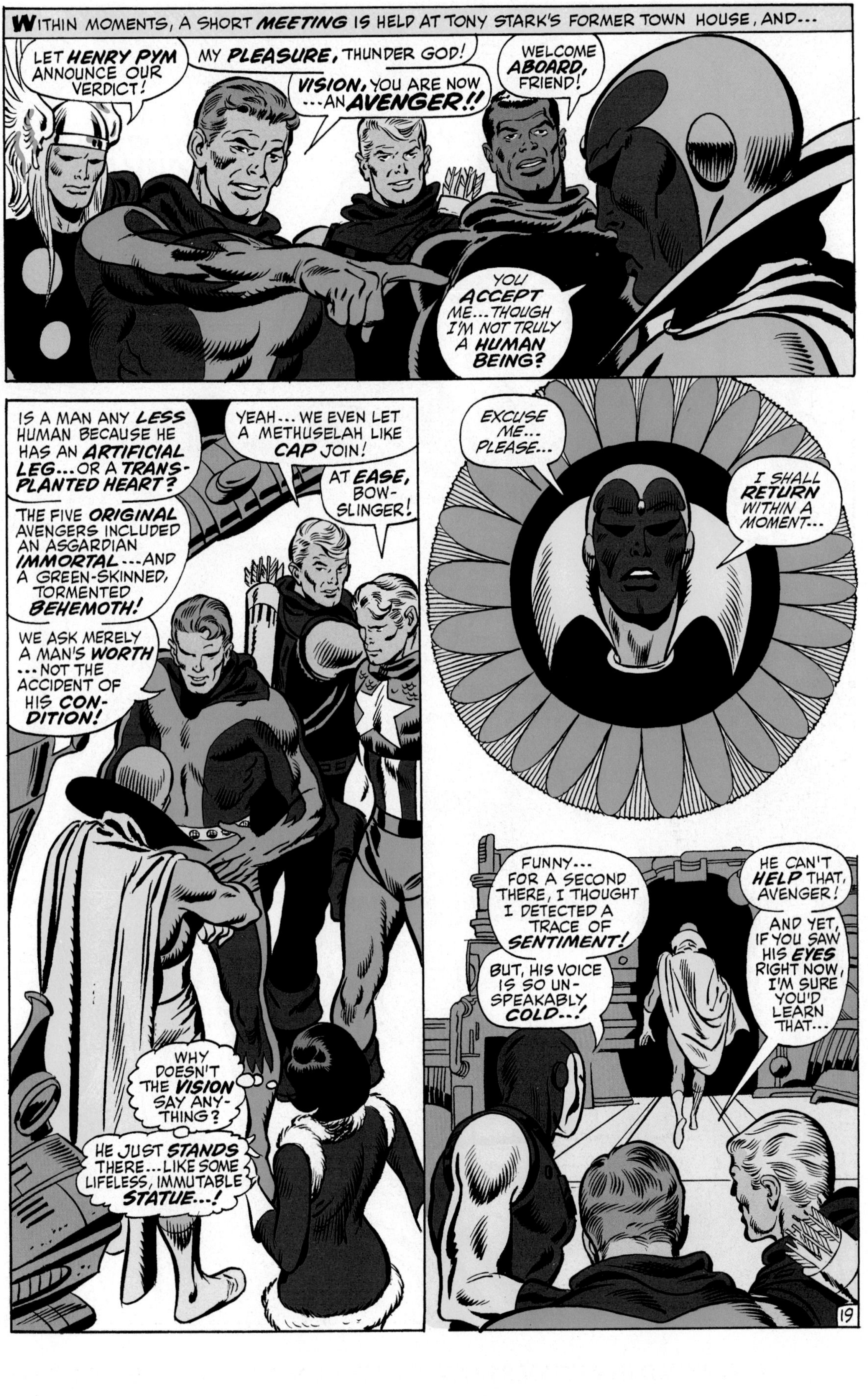
WITHIN MOMENTS, A SHORT MEETING IS HELD AT TONY STARK'S FORMER TOWN HOUSE, AND...
LET HENRY PYM ANNOUNCE OUR VERDICT!
MY PLEASURE, THUNDER GOD!
VISION, YOU ARE NOW ...AN AVENGER!!
WELCOME ABOARD, FRIEND!
YOU ACCEPT ME... THOUGH I'M NOT TRULY A HUMAN BEING?
IS A MAN ANY LESS HUMAN BECAUSE HE HAS AN ARTIFICIAL LEG... OR A TRANS-PLANTED HEART?
THE FIVE ORIGINAL AVENGERS INCLUDED AN ASGARDIAN IMMORTAL ...AND A GREEN-SKINNED, TORMENTED BEHEMOTH!
WE ASK MERELY A MAN'S WORTH ...NOT THE ACCIDENT OF HIS CON-DITION!
YEAH... WE EVEN LET A METHUSELAH LIKE CAP JOIN!
AT EASE, BOW-SLINGER!
WHY DOESN'T THE VISION SAY ANY-THING?
HE JUST STANDS THERE... LIKE SOME LIFELESS, IMMUTABLE STATUE...!
EXCUSE ME... PLEASE...
I SHALL RETURN WITHIN A MOMENT...
FUNNY... FOR A SECOND THERE, I THOUGHT I DETECTED A TRACE OF SENTIMENT!
BUT, HIS VOICE IS SO UN-SPEAKABLY COLD...!
HE CAN'T HELP THAT, AVENGER!
AND YET, IF YOU SAW HIS EYES RIGHT NOW, I'M SURE YOU'D LEARN THAT...
19

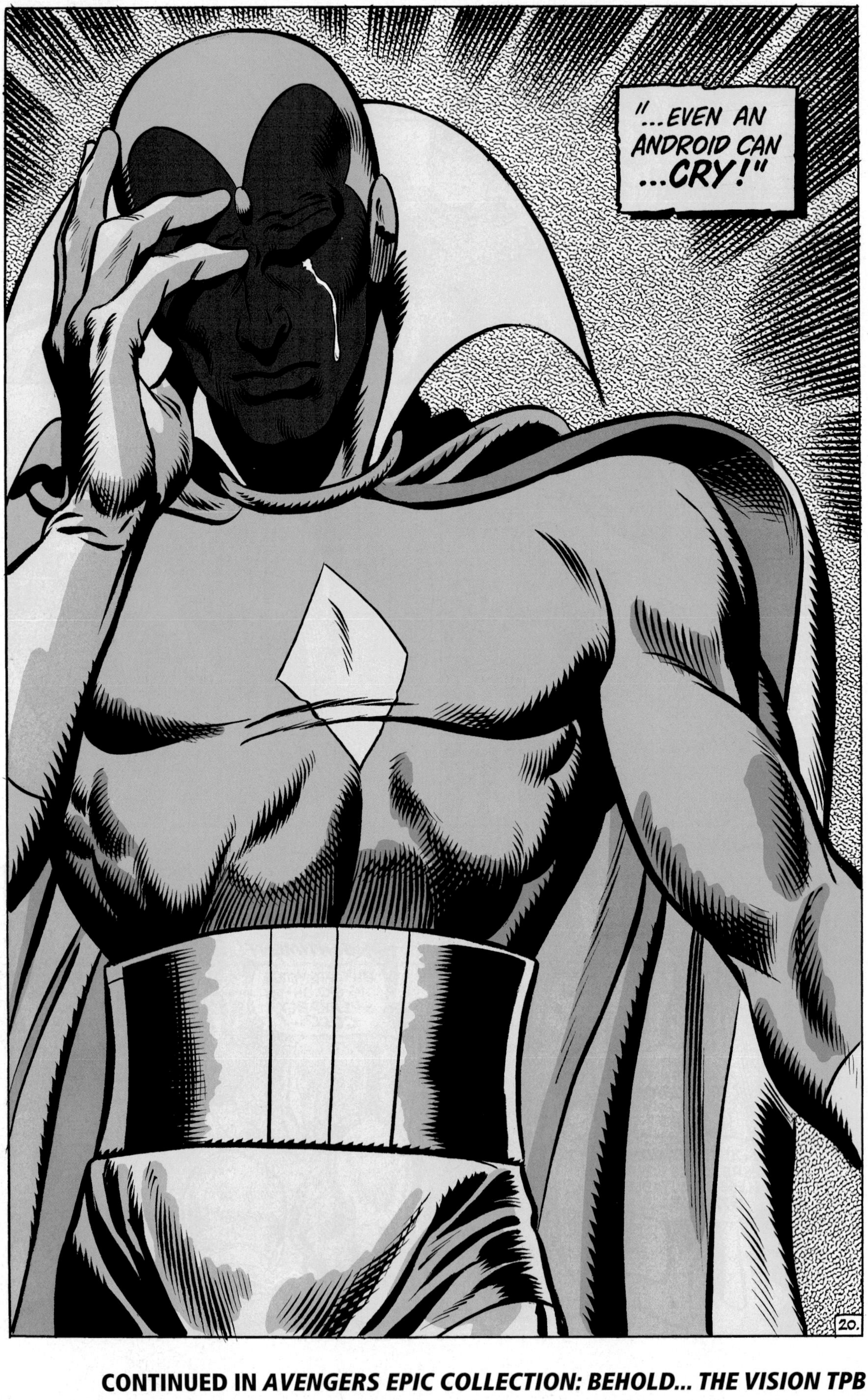
"...EVEN AN ANDROID CAN ...CRY!"
20.

CONTINUED IN *AVENGERS EPIC COLLECTION: BEHOLD... THE VISION* TPB

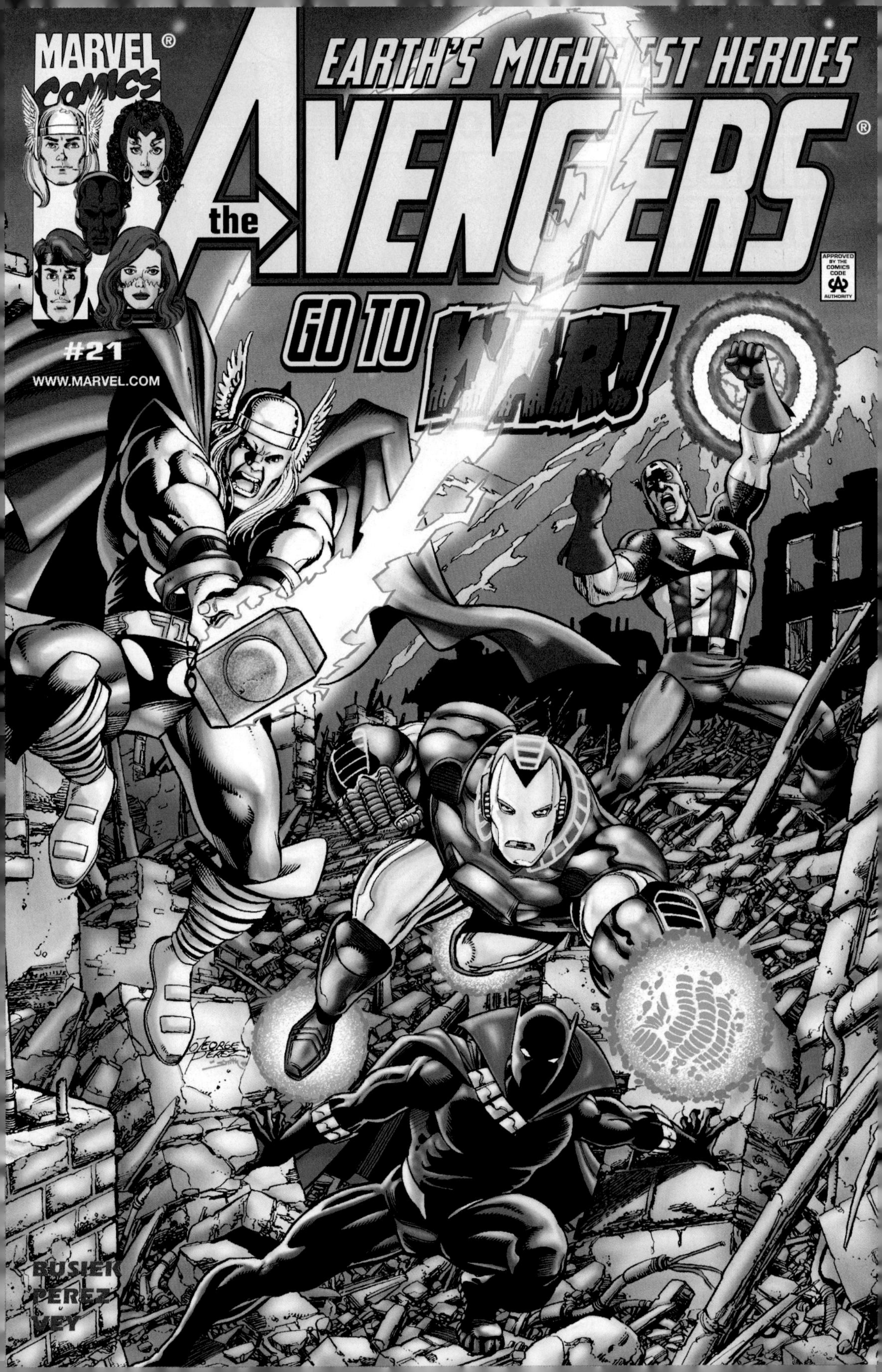

MARVEL®
COMICS
EARTH'S MIGHTIEST HEROES
the AVENGERS®
APPROVED BY THE COMICS CODE AUTHORITY
#21
WWW.MARVEL.COM
GO TO WAR!
GEORGE PEREZ
BUSIEK
PEREZ
VEY

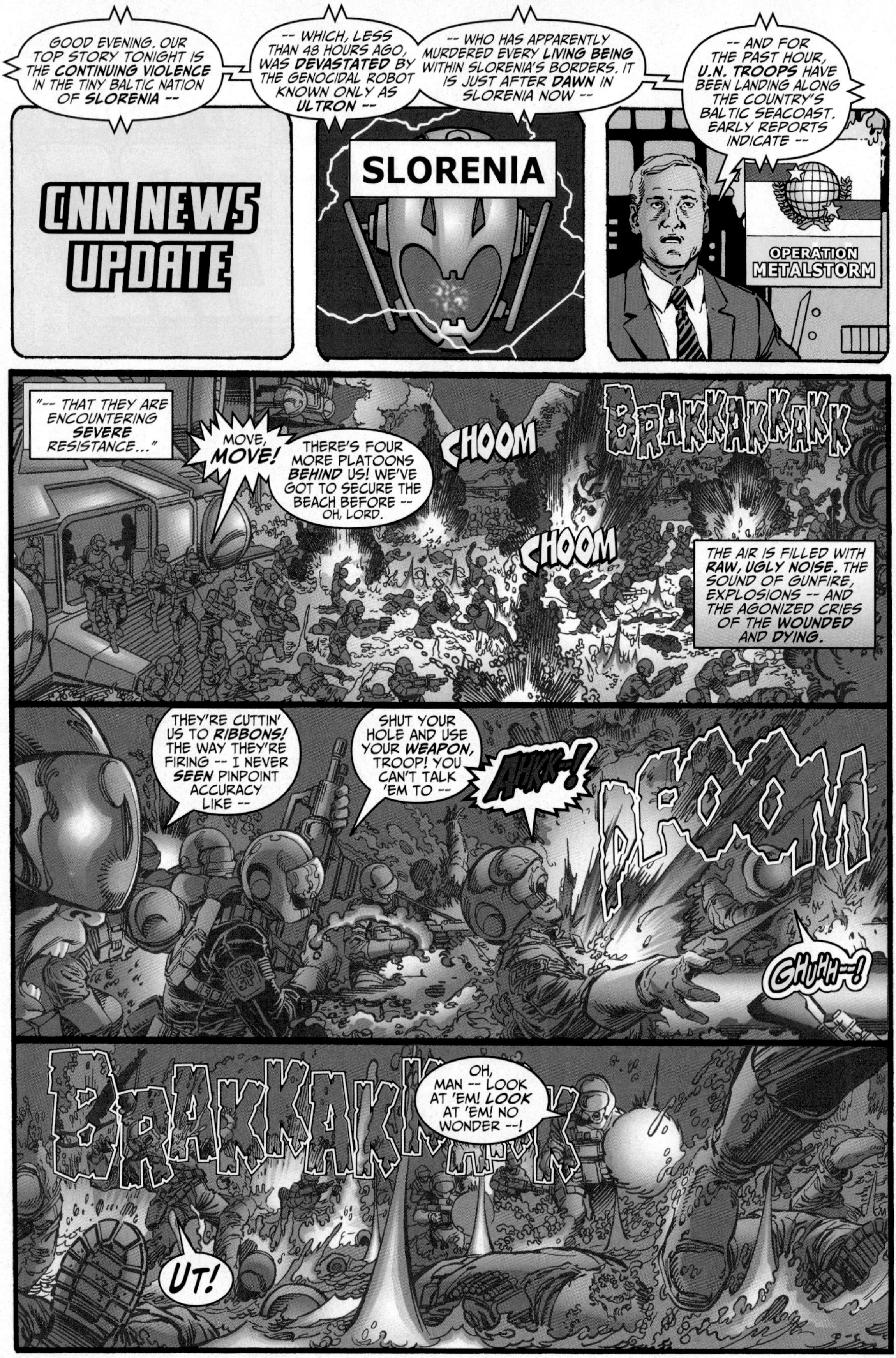
GOOD EVENING. OUR TOP STORY TONIGHT IS THE CONTINUING VIOLENCE IN THE TINY BALTIC NATION OF SLORENIA --
-- WHICH, LESS THAN 48 HOURS AGO, WAS DEVASTATED BY THE GENOCIDAL ROBOT KNOWN ONLY AS ULTRON --
-- WHO HAS APPARENTLY MURDERED EVERY LIVING BEING WITHIN SLORENIA'S BORDERS. IT IS JUST AFTER DAWN IN SLORENIA NOW --
-- AND FOR THE PAST HOUR, U.N. TROOPS HAVE BEEN LANDING ALONG THE COUNTRY'S BALTIC SEACOAST. EARLY REPORTS INDICATE --
CNN NEWS UPDATE
SLORENIA
OPERATION METALSTORM
"-- THAT THEY ARE ENCOUNTERING SEVERE RESISTANCE..."
MOVE, MOVE!
THERE'S FOUR MORE PLATOONS BEHIND US! WE'VE GOT TO SECURE THE BEACH BEFORE -- OH, LORD.
CHOOM
BRAKKAKKAKK
CHOOM
THE AIR IS FILLED WITH RAW, UGLY NOISE. THE SOUND OF GUNFIRE, EXPLOSIONS -- AND THE AGONIZED CRIES OF THE WOUNDED AND DYING.
THEY'RE CUTTIN' US TO RIBBONS! THE WAY THEY'RE FIRING -- I NEVER SEEN PINPOINT ACCURACY LIKE --
SHUT YOUR HOLE AND USE YOUR WEAPON, TROOP! YOU CAN'T TALK 'EM TO --
AHKK--!
DROOM
GHUHH--!
BRAKKAKKAKK
OH, MAN -- LOOK AT 'EM! LOOK AT 'EM! NO WONDER --!
UT!

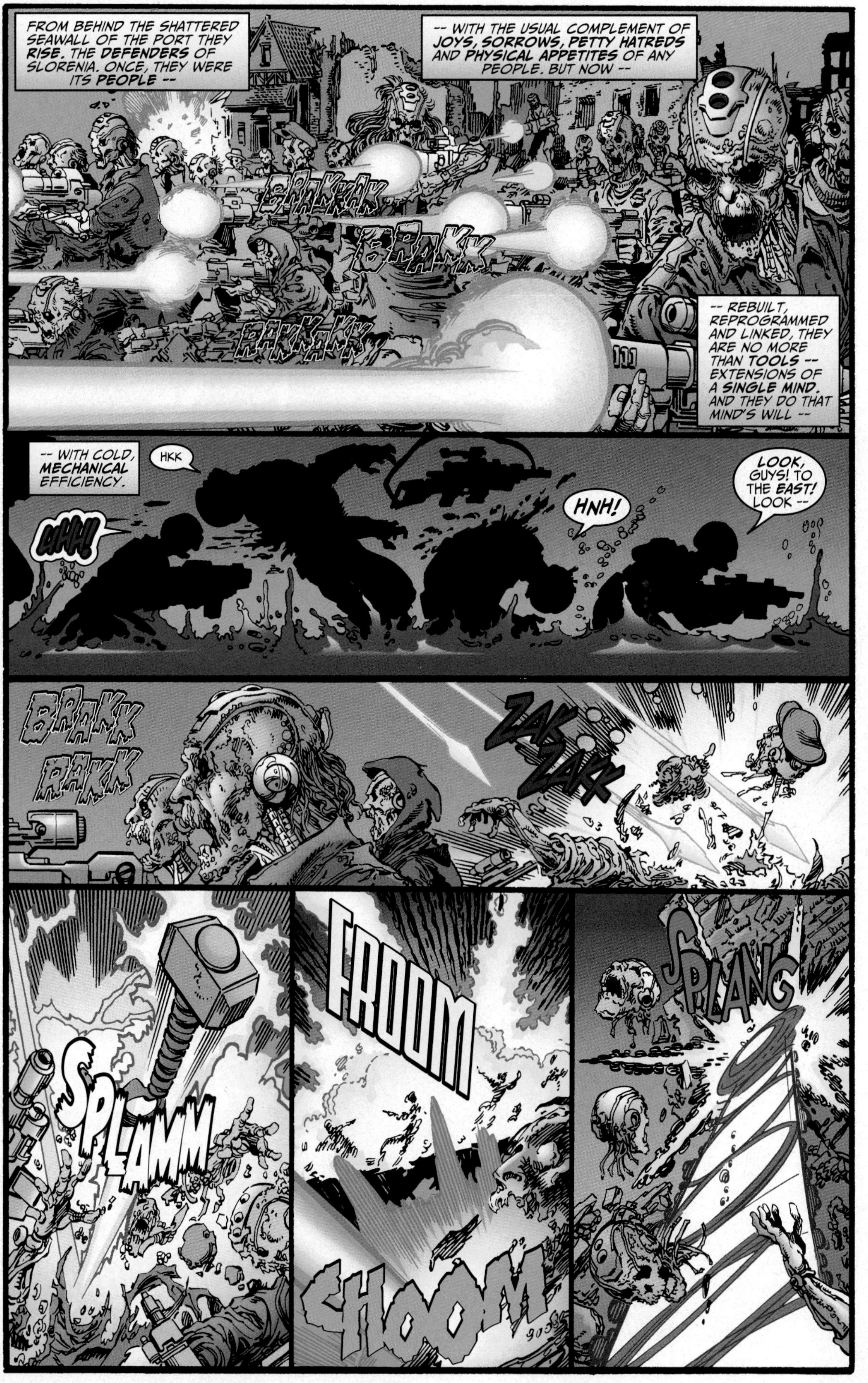
FROM BEHIND THE SHATTERED SEAWALL OF THE PORT THEY RISE. THE DEFENDERS OF SLORENIA. ONCE, THEY WERE ITS PEOPLE --
-- WITH THE USUAL COMPLEMENT OF JOYS, SORROWS, PETTY HATREDS AND PHYSICAL APPETITES OF ANY PEOPLE. BUT NOW --
BRAKKAK
BRAKK
RAKKAKK
-- REBUILT, REPROGRAMMED AND LINKED, THEY ARE NO MORE THAN TOOLS -- EXTENSIONS OF A SINGLE MIND. AND THEY DO THAT MIND'S WILL --
-- WITH COLD, MECHANICAL EFFICIENCY.
HKK
UHH!
HNH!
LOOK, GUYS! TO THE EAST! LOOK --
BRAKK
RAKK
ZAK
ZAKK
SPLAMM
FROOM
CHOOM
SPLANG

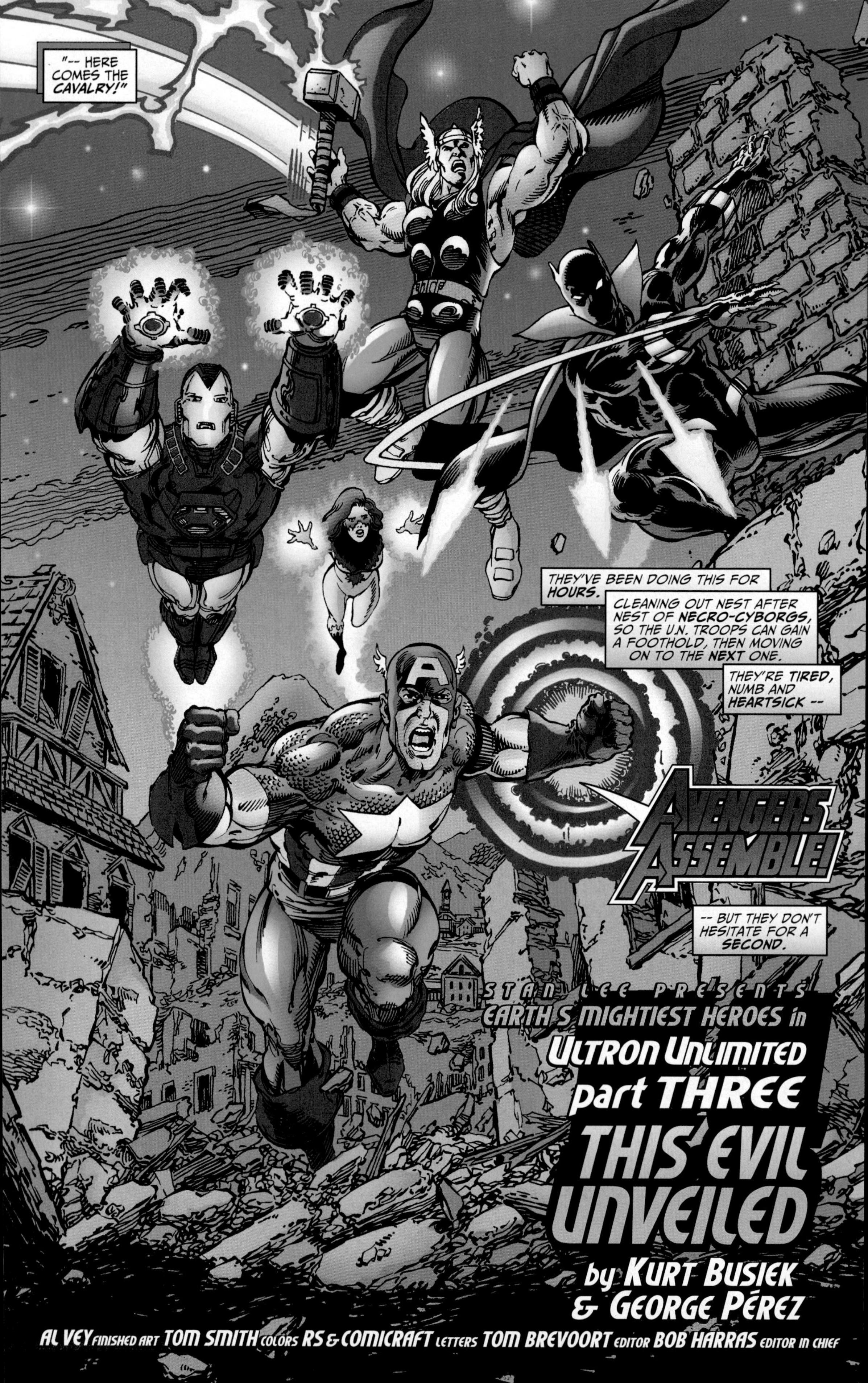
"-- HERE COMES THE CAVALRY!"
THEY'VE BEEN DOING THIS FOR HOURS.
CLEANING OUT NEST AFTER NEST OF NECRO-CYBORGS, SO THE U.N. TROOPS CAN GAIN A FOOTHOLD, THEN MOVING ON TO THE NEXT ONE.
THEY'RE TIRED, NUMB AND HEARTSICK --
AVENGERS ASSEMBLE!
-- BUT THEY DON'T HESITATE FOR A SECOND.
STAN LEE PRESENTS
EARTH'S MIGHTIEST HEROES in
ULTRON UNLIMITED
part THREE
THIS EVIL UNVEILED
by KURT BUSIEK
& GEORGE PÉREZ
AL VEY finished art TOM SMITH colors RS & COMICRAFT letters TOM BREVOORT editor BOB HARRAS editor in chief

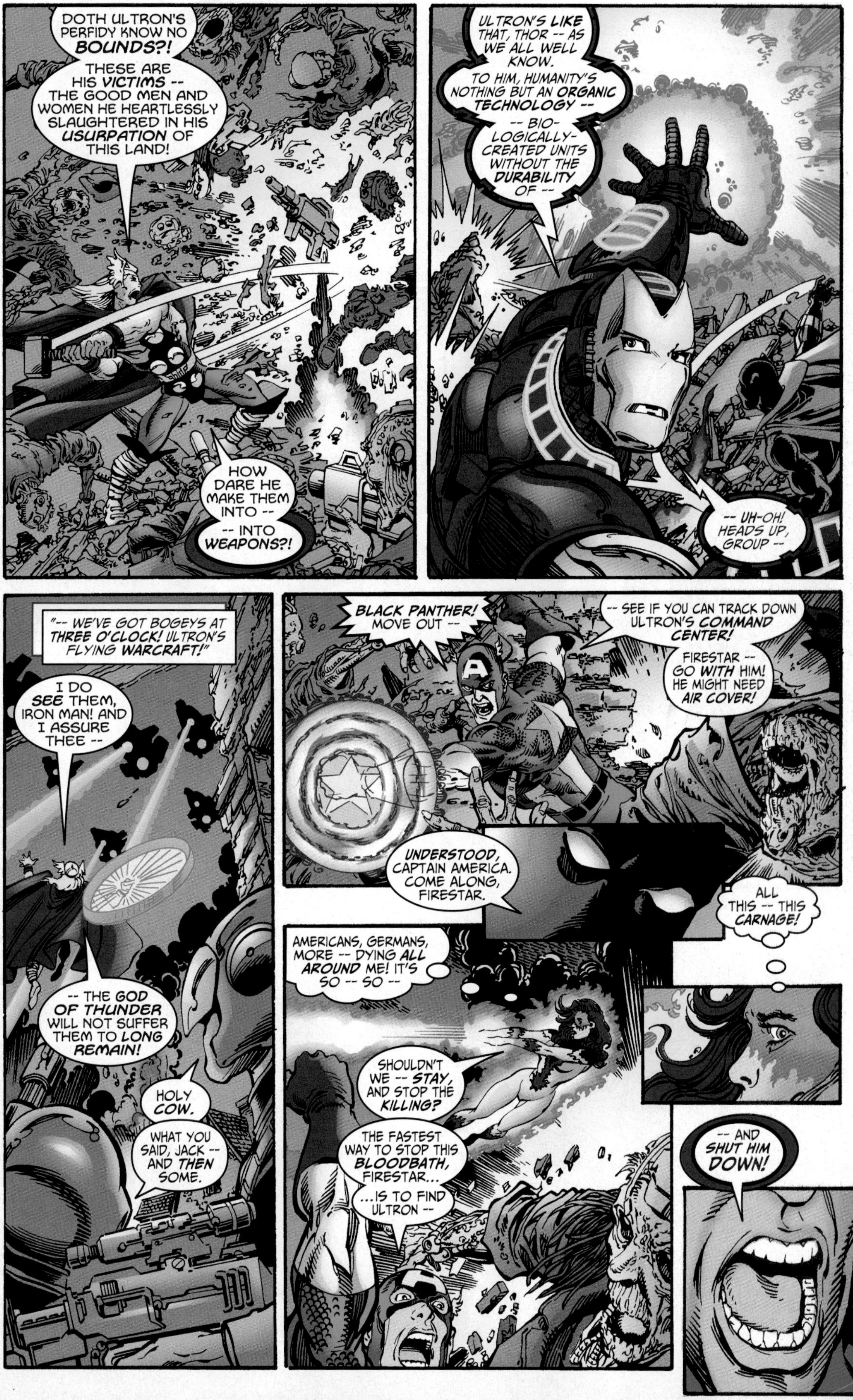

DOTH ULTRON'S PERFIDY KNOW NO BOUNDS?!
THESE ARE HIS VICTIMS -- THE GOOD MEN AND WOMEN HE HEARTLESSLY SLAUGHTERED IN HIS USURPATION OF THIS LAND!
HOW DARE HE MAKE THEM INTO --
-- INTO WEAPONS?!
ULTRON'S LIKE THAT, THOR -- AS WE ALL WELL KNOW.
TO HIM, HUMANITY'S NOTHING BUT AN ORGANIC TECHNOLOGY --
-- BIO-LOGICALLY-CREATED UNITS WITHOUT THE DURABILITY OF --
-- UH-OH! HEADS UP, GROUP --
"-- WE'VE GOT BOGEYS AT THREE O'CLOCK! ULTRON'S FLYING WARCRAFT!"
I DO SEE THEM, IRON MAN! AND I ASSURE THEE --
-- THE GOD OF THUNDER WILL NOT SUFFER THEM TO LONG REMAIN!
HOLY COW.
WHAT YOU SAID, JACK -- AND THEN SOME.
BLACK PANTHER! MOVE OUT --
-- SEE IF YOU CAN TRACK DOWN ULTRON'S COMMAND CENTER!
FIRESTAR -- GO WITH HIM! HE MIGHT NEED AIR COVER!
UNDERSTOOD, CAPTAIN AMERICA. COME ALONG, FIRESTAR.
ALL THIS -- THIS CARNAGE!
AMERICANS, GERMANS, MORE -- DYING ALL AROUND ME! IT'S SO -- SO --
SHOULDN'T WE -- STAY, AND STOP THE KILLING?
THE FASTEST WAY TO STOP THIS BLOODBATH, FIRESTAR...
...IS TO FIND ULTRON --
-- AND SHUT HIM DOWN!

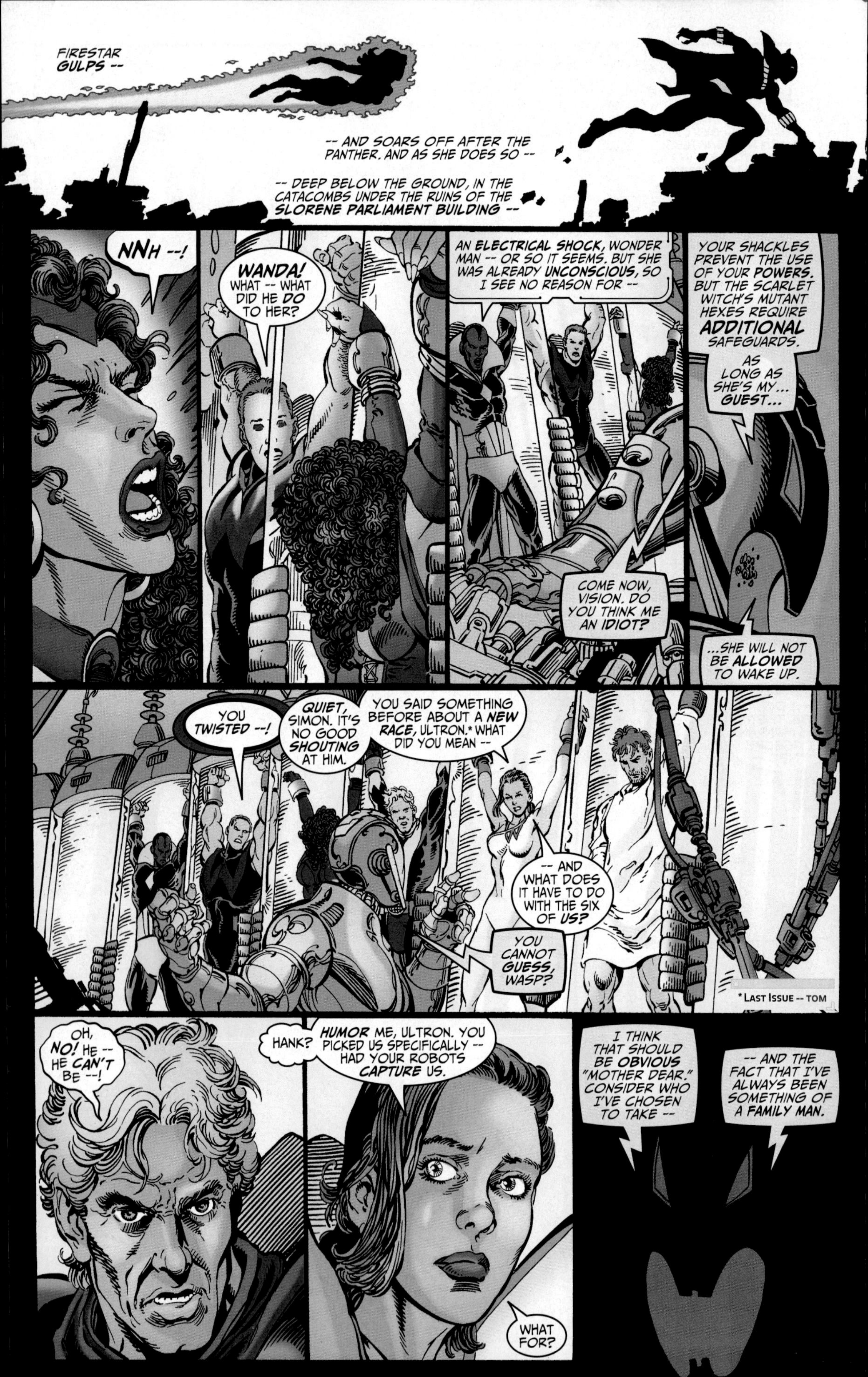
FIRESTAR GULPS --
-- AND SOARS OFF AFTER THE PANTHER. AND AS SHE DOES SO --
-- DEEP BELOW THE GROUND, IN THE CATACOMBS UNDER THE RUINS OF THE SLORENE PARLIAMENT BUILDING --
NNH --!
WANDA! WHAT -- WHAT DID HE DO TO HER?
AN ELECTRICAL SHOCK, WONDER MAN -- OR SO IT SEEMS. BUT SHE WAS ALREADY UNCONSCIOUS, SO I SEE NO REASON FOR --
COME NOW, VISION. DO YOU THINK ME AN IDIOT?
YOUR SHACKLES PREVENT THE USE OF YOUR POWERS. BUT THE SCARLET WITCH'S MUTANT HEXES REQUIRE ADDITIONAL SAFEGUARDS.
AS LONG AS SHE'S MY... GUEST...
...SHE WILL NOT BE ALLOWED TO WAKE UP.
YOU TWISTED --!
QUIET, SIMON. IT'S NO GOOD SHOUTING AT HIM.
YOU SAID SOMETHING BEFORE ABOUT A NEW RACE, ULTRON.* WHAT DID YOU MEAN --
-- AND WHAT DOES IT HAVE TO DO WITH THE SIX OF US?
YOU CANNOT GUESS, WASP?
*LAST ISSUE -- TOM
OH, NO! HE -- HE CAN'T BE --!
HANK?
HUMOR ME, ULTRON. YOU PICKED US SPECIFICALLY -- HAD YOUR ROBOTS CAPTURE US.
WHAT FOR?
I THINK THAT SHOULD BE OBVIOUS "MOTHER DEAR." CONSIDER WHO I'VE CHOSEN TO TAKE --
-- AND THE FACT THAT I'VE ALWAYS BEEN SOMETHING OF A FAMILY MAN.

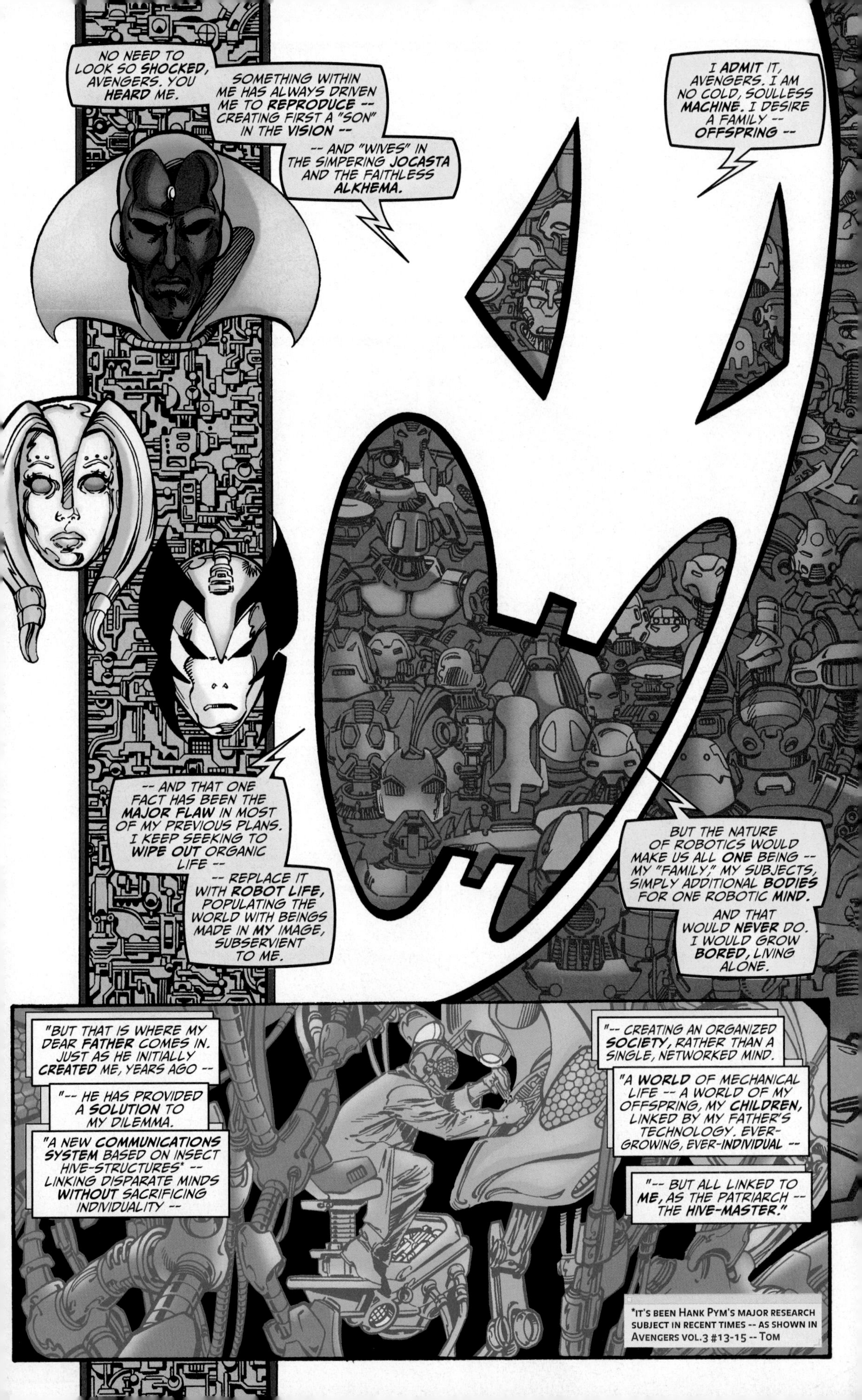

NO NEED TO LOOK SO SHOCKED, AVENGERS. YOU HEARD ME.
SOMETHING WITHIN ME HAS ALWAYS DRIVEN ME TO REPRODUCE -- CREATING FIRST A "SON" IN THE VISION --
-- AND "WIVES" IN THE SIMPERING JOCASTA AND THE FAITHLESS ALKHEMA.
I ADMIT IT, AVENGERS. I AM NO COLD, SOULLESS MACHINE. I DESIRE A FAMILY -- OFFSPRING --
-- AND THAT ONE FACT HAS BEEN THE MAJOR FLAW IN MOST OF MY PREVIOUS PLANS. I KEEP SEEKING TO WIPE OUT ORGANIC LIFE --
-- REPLACE IT WITH ROBOT LIFE, POPULATING THE WORLD WITH BEINGS MADE IN MY IMAGE, SUBSERVIENT TO ME.
BUT THE NATURE OF ROBOTICS WOULD MAKE US ALL ONE BEING -- MY "FAMILY," MY SUBJECTS, SIMPLY ADDITIONAL BODIES FOR ONE ROBOTIC MIND.
AND THAT WOULD NEVER DO. I WOULD GROW BORED, LIVING ALONE.
"BUT THAT IS WHERE MY DEAR FATHER COMES IN. JUST AS HE INITIALLY CREATED ME, YEARS AGO --
"-- HE HAS PROVIDED A SOLUTION TO MY DILEMMA.
"A NEW COMMUNICATIONS SYSTEM BASED ON INSECT HIVE-STRUCTURES* -- LINKING DISPARATE MINDS WITHOUT SACRIFICING INDIVIDUALITY --
"-- CREATING AN ORGANIZED SOCIETY, RATHER THAN A SINGLE, NETWORKED MIND.
"A WORLD OF MECHANICAL LIFE -- A WORLD OF MY OFFSPRING, MY CHILDREN, LINKED BY MY FATHER'S TECHNOLOGY. EVER-GROWING, EVER-INDIVIDUAL --
"-- BUT ALL LINKED TO ME, AS THE PATRIARCH -- THE HIVE-MASTER."
*IT'S BEEN HANK PYM'S MAJOR RESEARCH SUBJECT IN RECENT TIMES -- AS SHOWN IN AVENGERS VOL.3 #13-15 -- TOM

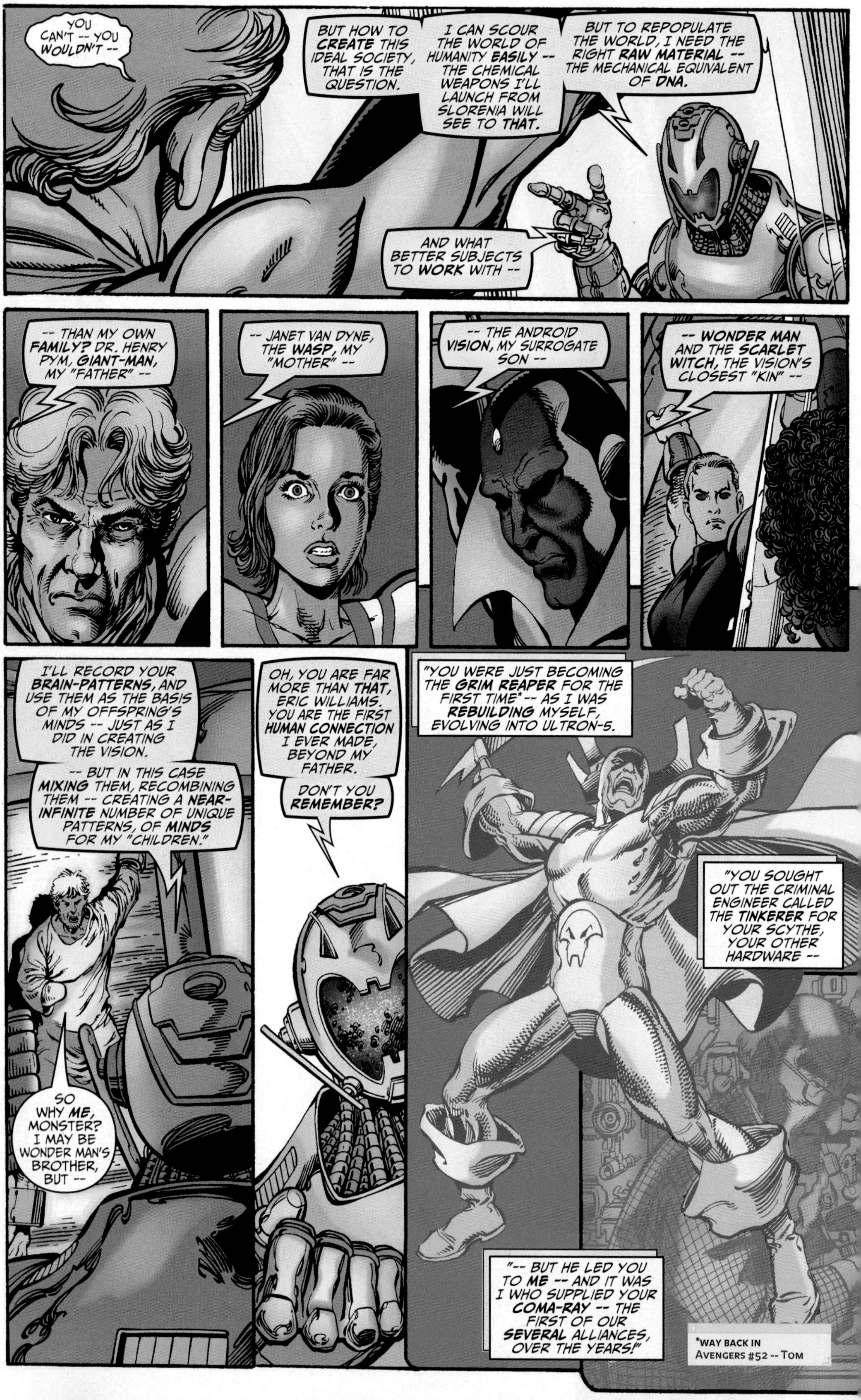

YOU CAN'T -- YOU WOULDN'T --
BUT HOW TO CREATE THIS IDEAL SOCIETY, THAT IS THE QUESTION.
I CAN SCOUR THE WORLD OF HUMANITY EASILY -- THE CHEMICAL WEAPONS I'LL LAUNCH FROM SLORENIA WILL SEE TO THAT.
BUT TO REPOPULATE THE WORLD, I NEED THE RIGHT RAW MATERIAL -- THE MECHANICAL EQUIVALENT OF DNA.
AND WHAT BETTER SUBJECTS TO WORK WITH --
-- THAN MY OWN FAMILY? DR. HENRY PYM, GIANT-MAN, MY "FATHER" --
-- JANET VAN DYNE, THE WASP, MY "MOTHER" --
-- THE ANDROID VISION, MY SURROGATE SON --
-- WONDER MAN AND THE SCARLET WITCH, THE VISION'S CLOSEST "KIN" --
I'LL RECORD YOUR BRAIN-PATTERNS, AND USE THEM AS THE BASIS OF MY OFFSPRING'S MINDS -- JUST AS I DID IN CREATING THE VISION.
-- BUT IN THIS CASE MIXING THEM, RECOMBINING THEM -- CREATING A NEAR-INFINITE NUMBER OF UNIQUE PATTERNS, OF MINDS FOR MY "CHILDREN."
SO WHY ME, MONSTER? I MAY BE WONDER MAN'S BROTHER, BUT --
OH, YOU ARE FAR MORE THAN THAT, ERIC WILLIAMS. YOU ARE THE FIRST HUMAN CONNECTION I EVER MADE, BEYOND MY FATHER.
DON'T YOU REMEMBER?
"YOU WERE JUST BECOMING THE GRIM REAPER FOR THE FIRST TIME* -- AS I WAS REBUILDING MYSELF, EVOLVING INTO ULTRON-5.
"YOU SOUGHT OUT THE CRIMINAL ENGINEER CALLED THE TINKERER FOR YOUR SCYTHE, YOUR OTHER HARDWARE --
"-- BUT HE LED YOU TO ME -- AND IT WAS I WHO SUPPLIED YOUR COMA-RAY -- THE FIRST OF OUR SEVERAL ALLIANCES, OVER THE YEARS!"
*WAY BACK IN AVENGERS #52 -- TOM

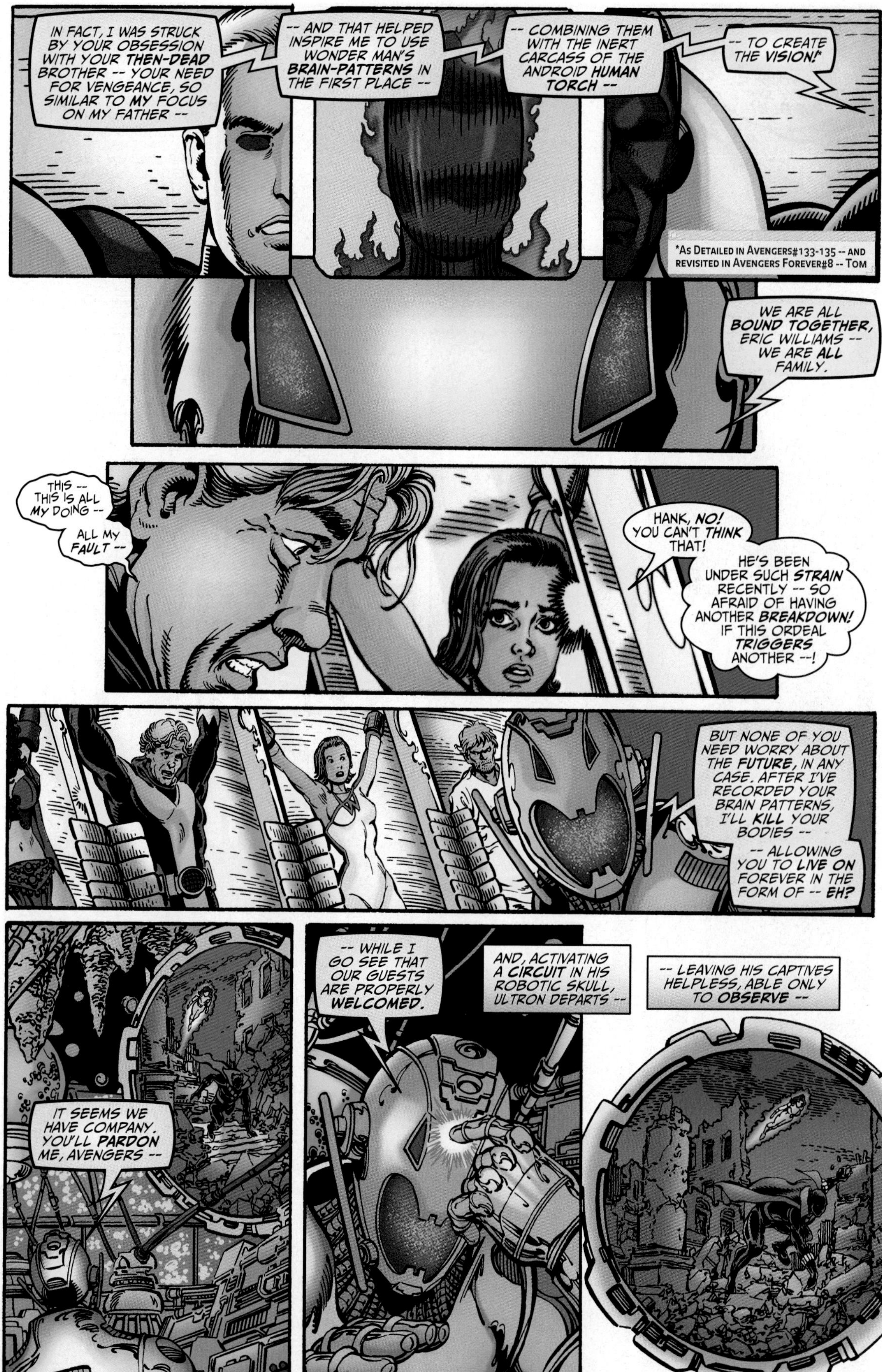
IN FACT, I WAS STRUCK BY YOUR OBSESSION WITH YOUR THEN-DEAD BROTHER -- YOUR NEED FOR VENGEANCE, SO SIMILAR TO MY FOCUS ON MY FATHER --
-- AND THAT HELPED INSPIRE ME TO USE WONDER MAN'S BRAIN-PATTERNS IN THE FIRST PLACE --
-- COMBINING THEM WITH THE INERT CARCASS OF THE ANDROID HUMAN TORCH --
-- TO CREATE THE VISION!*
*As Detailed in Avengers#133-135 -- and revisited in Avengers Forever#8 -- Tom
WE ARE ALL BOUND TOGETHER, ERIC WILLIAMS -- WE ARE ALL FAMILY.
THIS -- THIS IS ALL MY DOING --
ALL MY FAULT --
HANK, NO! YOU CAN'T THINK THAT!
HE'S BEEN UNDER SUCH STRAIN RECENTLY -- SO AFRAID OF HAVING ANOTHER BREAKDOWN! IF THIS ORDEAL TRIGGERS ANOTHER --!
BUT NONE OF YOU NEED WORRY ABOUT THE FUTURE, IN ANY CASE. AFTER I'VE RECORDED YOUR BRAIN PATTERNS, I'LL KILL YOUR BODIES --
-- ALLOWING YOU TO LIVE ON FOREVER IN THE FORM OF -- EH?
IT SEEMS WE HAVE COMPANY. YOU'LL PARDON ME, AVENGERS --
-- WHILE I GO SEE THAT OUR GUESTS ARE PROPERLY WELCOMED.
AND, ACTIVATING A CIRCUIT IN HIS ROBOTIC SKULL, ULTRON DEPARTS --
-- LEAVING HIS CAPTIVES HELPLESS, ABLE ONLY TO OBSERVE --

UM, PANTHER? T'CHALLA? CAN YOU *REALLY* FIND A TRAIL THROUGH ALL THIS? IT'S JUST... *RUBBLE!*

BUT RUBBLE THAT FELL INTO PARTICULAR *PATTERNS*, DUE TO THE BLASTS THAT CAUSED IT. AND IT'S BEEN *DISTURBED* -- BY A REGULAR, UNVARYING TREAD --

-- WHICH CHANGES ONLY TO COMPENSATE FOR THE *UNEVEN TERRAIN.* NOTHING *HUMAN* MADE THAT -- NOT EVEN THOSE *CYBORGS.*

I GUESS THERE'S A *REASON* THE AVENGERS TALK ABOUT THE PANTHER WITH SUCH RESPECT. I HAD NO *IDEA* ANYBODY COULD DO --

HEY! OVER *THERE!*

GREETINGS, *AVENGERS!*

MY SENSORS TELL ME YOU'VE ALREADY *BIOCHEMICALLY* GUARDED YOURSELF AGAINST MY *ENCEPHALO-BEAM* --

-- SO IT SEEMS YOU'VE *LEARNED* SOMETHING FROM YOUR UNFORTUNATE COMRADES' PATHETIC SHOWING IN NEW JERSEY!*

BUT THAT IS ONLY *ONE* OF MY WEAPONS --

*LAST ISSUE -- TOM

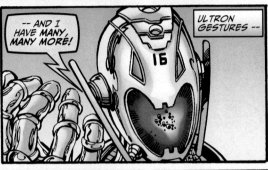

-- AND I HAVE MANY, MANY MORE!

ULTRON GESTURES --

-- AND --

CH OM

EH?!

CHM

WHAT IN THE WORLD --?

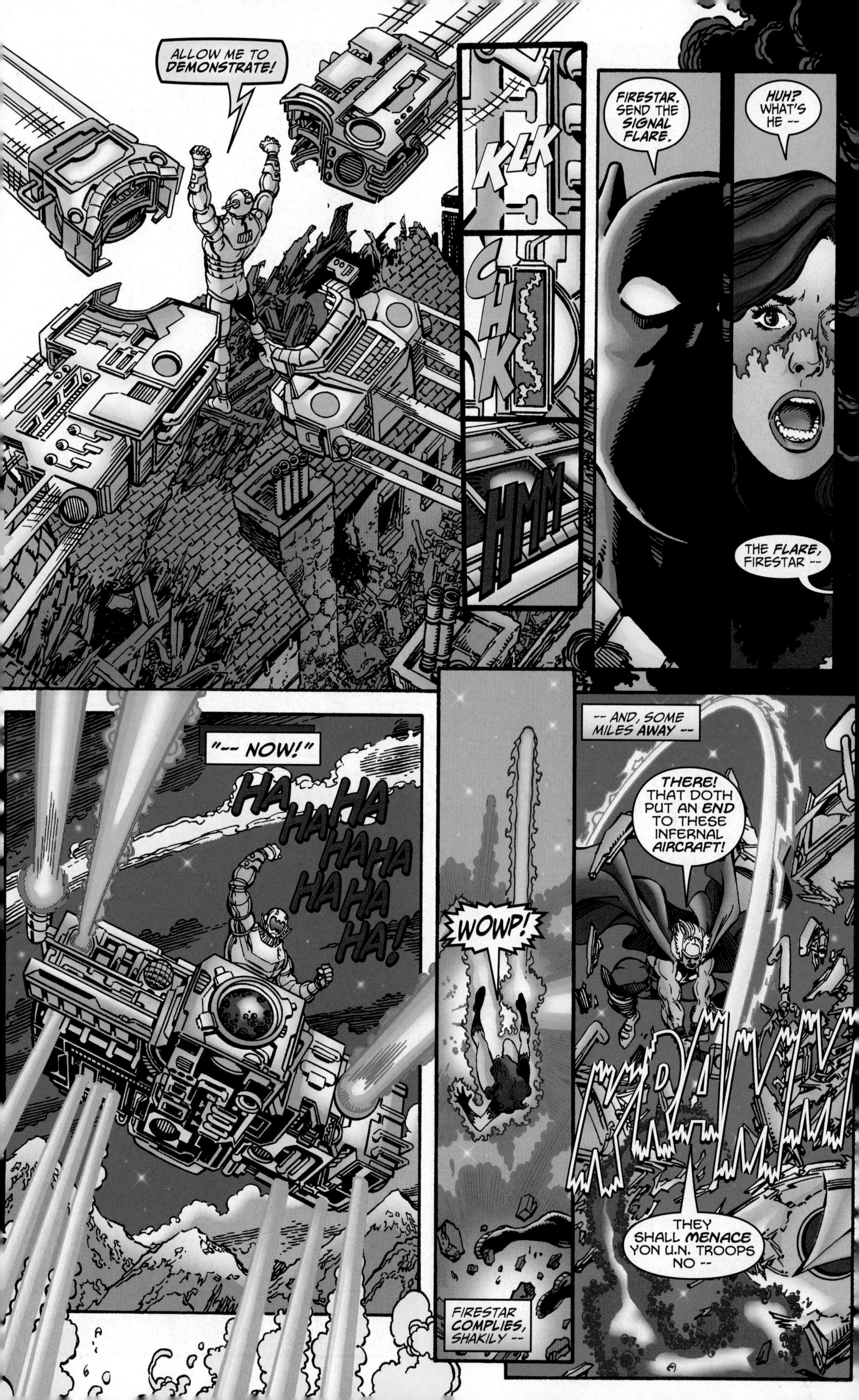
ALLOW ME TO DEMONSTRATE!
KLIK
CHIK
HMMM
FIRESTAR. SEND THE SIGNAL FLARE.
HUH? WHAT'S HE --
THE FLARE, FIRESTAR --
"-- NOW!"
HA HA HA HA HA HA HA HA HA HA!
WOWP!
FIRESTAR COMPLIES, SHAKILY --
-- AND, SOME MILES AWAY --
THERE! THAT DOTH PUT AN END TO THESE INFERNAL AIRCRAFT!
KRAKUM
THEY SHALL MENACE YON U.N. TROOPS NO --

-- EH?

IRON MAN! CAPTAIN AMERICA! BEHOLD!

FIRESTAR'S SIGNAL!

THEY'VE FOUND ULTRON.

WE'D BETTER GO JOIN THEM -- CAN YOU HOLD YOUR POSITION HERE, LIEUTENANT?

KRAK

WE'LL BE FINE, CAP!

GOOD. THEN COME ON, AVENGERS -- -- LET'S MOVE OUT!

MEANWHILE --

BLANGLANGLANGLANGLANGLANGLANGLANGLANG

-- IN A HIGH-SECURITY MILITARY FACILITY IN VIRGINIA'S BLUE RIDGE MOUNTAINS --

BLANGLANGLANGLANGLANGLANGLANGLANGLANG

PERIMETER BREACH!

THIS IS NO DRILL! WE HAVE INTRUDERS! AND WHOEVER THEY ARE, THEY'VE ALREADY GOTTEN THROUGH THE EXTERIOR --

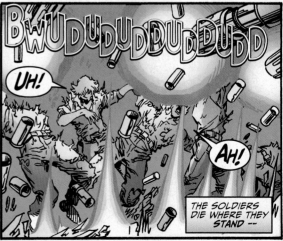

BWUDUDUDDUDUDD

UH!

AH!

THE SOLDIERS DIE WHERE THEY STAND --

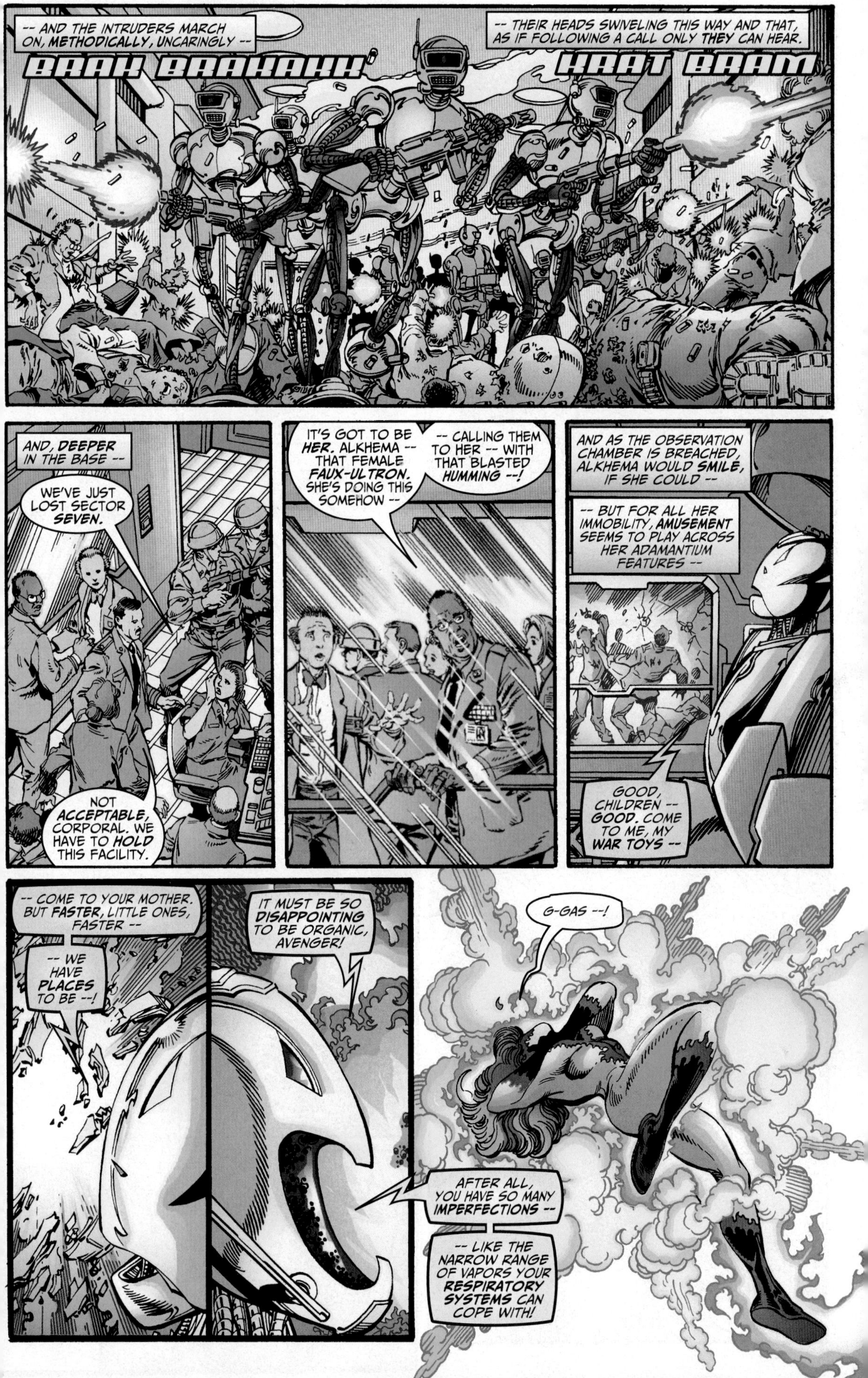
-- AND THE INTRUDERS MARCH ON, METHODICALLY, UNCARINGLY --
-- THEIR HEADS SWIVELING THIS WAY AND THAT, AS IF FOLLOWING A CALL ONLY THEY CAN HEAR.
BRAK BRAKAKK
KRAT BRAM
AND, DEEPER IN THE BASE --
WE'VE JUST LOST SECTOR SEVEN.
NOT ACCEPTABLE, CORPORAL. WE HAVE TO HOLD THIS FACILITY.
IT'S GOT TO BE HER. ALKHEMA -- THAT FEMALE FAUX-ULTRON. SHE'S DOING THIS SOMEHOW --
-- CALLING THEM TO HER -- WITH THAT BLASTED HUMMING --!
AND AS THE OBSERVATION CHAMBER IS BREACHED, ALKHEMA WOULD SMILE, IF SHE COULD --
-- BUT FOR ALL HER IMMOBILITY, AMUSEMENT SEEMS TO PLAY ACROSS HER ADAMANTIUM FEATURES --
GOOD, CHILDREN -- GOOD. COME TO ME, MY WAR TOYS --
-- COME TO YOUR MOTHER. BUT FASTER, LITTLE ONES, FASTER --
-- WE HAVE PLACES TO BE --!
IT MUST BE SO DISAPPOINTING TO BE ORGANIC, AVENGER!
G-GAS --!
AFTER ALL, YOU HAVE SO MANY IMPERFECTIONS --
-- LIKE THE NARROW RANGE OF VAPORS YOUR RESPIRATORY SYSTEMS CAN COPE WITH!

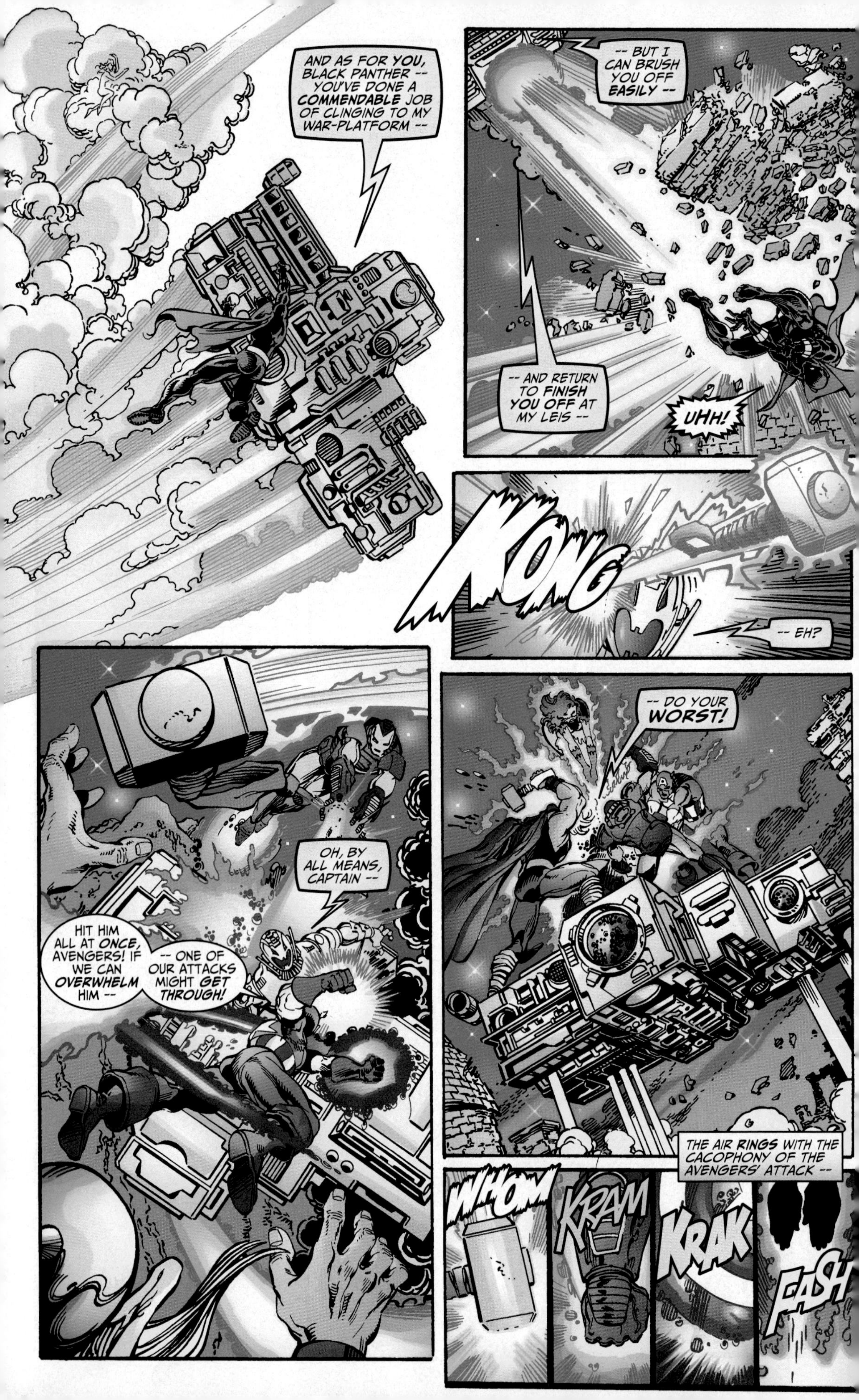
AND AS FOR YOU, BLACK PANTHER -- YOU'VE DONE A COMMENDABLE JOB OF CLINGING TO MY WAR-PLATFORM --
-- BUT I CAN BRUSH YOU OFF EASILY --
-- AND RETURN TO FINISH YOU OFF AT MY LEIS --
UHH!
KONG
-- EH?
HIT HIM ALL AT ONCE, AVENGERS! IF WE CAN OVERWHELM HIM --
-- ONE OF OUR ATTACKS MIGHT GET THROUGH!
OH, BY ALL MEANS, CAPTAIN --
-- DO YOUR WORST!
THE AIR RINGS WITH THE CACOPHONY OF THE AVENGERS' ATTACK --
WHOM
KRAM
KRAK
FASH

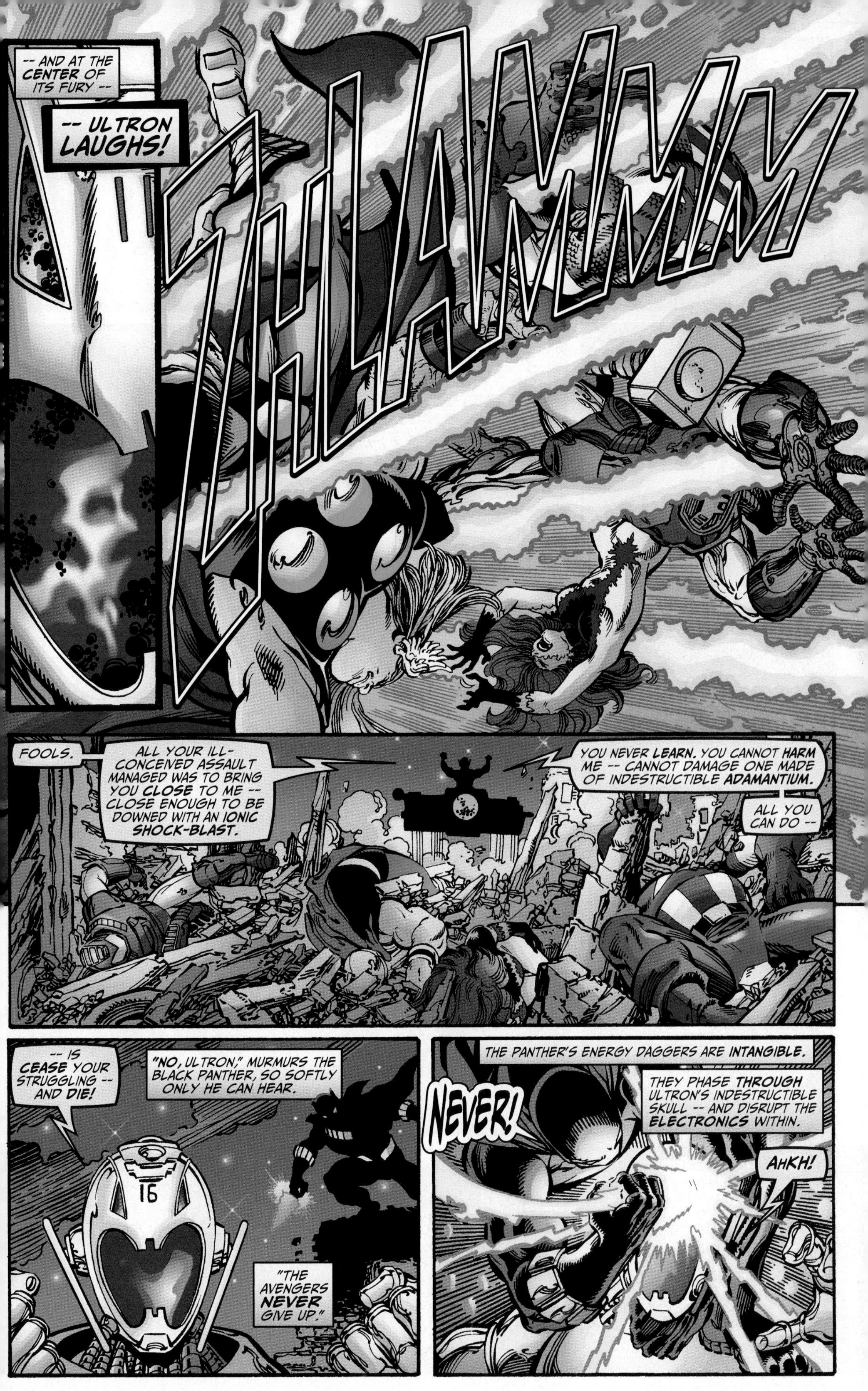
-- AND AT THE CENTER OF ITS FURY --
-- ULTRON LAUGHS!
ZHLAMMMM
FOOLS.
ALL YOUR ILL-CONCEIVED ASSAULT MANAGED WAS TO BRING YOU CLOSE TO ME -- CLOSE ENOUGH TO BE DOWNED WITH AN IONIC SHOCK-BLAST.
YOU NEVER LEARN. YOU CANNOT HARM ME -- CANNOT DAMAGE ONE MADE OF INDESTRUCTIBLE ADAMANTIUM.
ALL YOU CAN DO --
-- IS CEASE YOUR STRUGGLING -- AND DIE!
"NO, ULTRON," MURMURS THE BLACK PANTHER, SO SOFTLY ONLY HE CAN HEAR.
16
"THE AVENGERS NEVER GIVE UP."
THE PANTHER'S ENERGY DAGGERS ARE INTANGIBLE.
NEVER!
THEY PHASE THROUGH ULTRON'S INDESTRUCTIBLE SKULL -- AND DISRUPT THE ELECTRONICS WITHIN.
AHKH!

BUT --

UHHH!

PLAMM

THAT -- ACTUALLY *HURT* ME, YOU MISERABLE *FLESHBAG.* NOT AS MUCH AS I HURT *YOU*, THOUGH.

16

THE NEXT SIGN OF ULTRON'S PRESENCE WAS THE DISCOVERY OF A MOUNTAIN OF INERT *ROBOTIC SKULLS* IN UPSTATE NEW YORK --

-- WHICH WAS FOUND TO HAVE BEEN THE SITE OF A CLASH BETWEEN *ULTRON-13* AND THE *MANHATTAN-BASED* ADVENTURER *DAREDEVIL.**

DAREDEVIL

DAREDEVIL? HMP. HOW DID *HE* BEAT ULTRON?

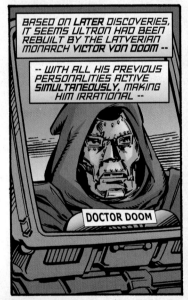

BASED ON *LATER* DISCOVERIES, IT SEEMS ULTRON HAD BEEN REBUILT BY THE LATVERIAN MONARCH *VICTOR VON DOOM* --

-- WITH ALL HIS PREVIOUS PERSONALITIES ACTIVE SIMULTANEOUSLY, MAKING HIM IRRATIONAL --

DOCTOR DOOM

HM.

TAP TAP

DESPITE HIS *SEEMING DESTRUCTION,* HOWEVER, ULTRON-13 RETURNED, HIS MULTIPLE PERSONALITIES APPARENTLY *STABILIZED* --

-- AND THE *WEST COAST AVENGERS* WERE ONLY BARELY ABLE TO PREVENT HIM FROM TURNING MUCH OF CALIFORNIA'S POPULATION INTO ROBOTIC LIFE.**

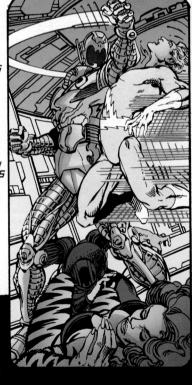

JUSTICE? MASTER VANCE?

YEAH, JARVIS?

TAP TAP TAP

* DAREDEVIL #275-276
** AVENGERS WEST COAST #65-68 -- TOM

I THOUGHT YOU MIGHT LIKE SOME *HERBAL* TEA.

AND, IF I MIGHT SUGGEST -- YOU HAVEN'T SLEPT SINCE YOU *STARTED* YOUR RESEARCHES INTO ULTRON'S PAST APPEARANCES.

IT'S QUITE LATE, AND YOU *ARE* SUPPOSED TO BE RECUPERATING...

SORRY, JARVIS. I KNOW YOU *MEAN* WELL, BUT NO CHANCE. I'M ON THE INJURED LIST, BUT I'M STILL AN AVENGER -- AND I'VE GOT A *JOB* TO DO.

I... UNDERSTAND, SIR.

ULTRON-13 ESCAPED BEFORE HE COULD BE *IMPRISONED*, HOWEVER, AND STRUCK AT EMPIRE STATE UNIVERSITY --

-- IN A BID TO STEAL A *SYNTHETIC VIBRANIUM* CREATED BY ROXXON INDUSTRIES.

HE WAS OPPOSED BY SPIDER-MAN, IRON MAN, THE BLACK PANTHER AND SUNTURION -- *

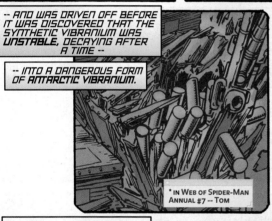

-- AND WAS DRIVEN OFF BEFORE IT WAS DISCOVERED THAT THE SYNTHETIC VIBRANIUM WAS *UNSTABLE*, DECAYING AFTER A TIME --

-- INTO A DANGEROUS FORM OF *ANTARCTIC VIBRANIUM*.

* IN *WEB OF SPIDER-MAN ANNUAL #7* -- TOM

VIBRANIUM. *HAD* TO BE VIBRANIUM, DIDN'T IT?

UNBIDDEN, THE YOUNG MUTANT'S MIND *FLASHES BACK* TO THE LAST TIME HE ENCOUNTERED THE EXTRATERRESTRIAL MYSTERY METAL --

-- A SECRET A.I.M. WAREHOUSE THE AVENGERS EXPOSED --*

-- WHICH WAS ALSO THE SITE OF THEIR BATTLE WITH THE *DOOMSDAY MAN* --**

YAAAAH!

-- THE BATTLE THAT SIDELINED HIM WITH A *BROKEN LEG*. THE MEMORY MAKES HIM FLUSH WITH SHAME. BUT HE PUTS IT ASIDE, AND FORGES ONWARD.

I'LL SET UP A CROSS-REFERENCED *SCAN* OF ALL THE FILES...SEE WHAT IT *LINKS* TO...

AND AT HIS SIDE, HIS TEA GROWS *COLD*...

* IN #13
** IN #17
-- TOM

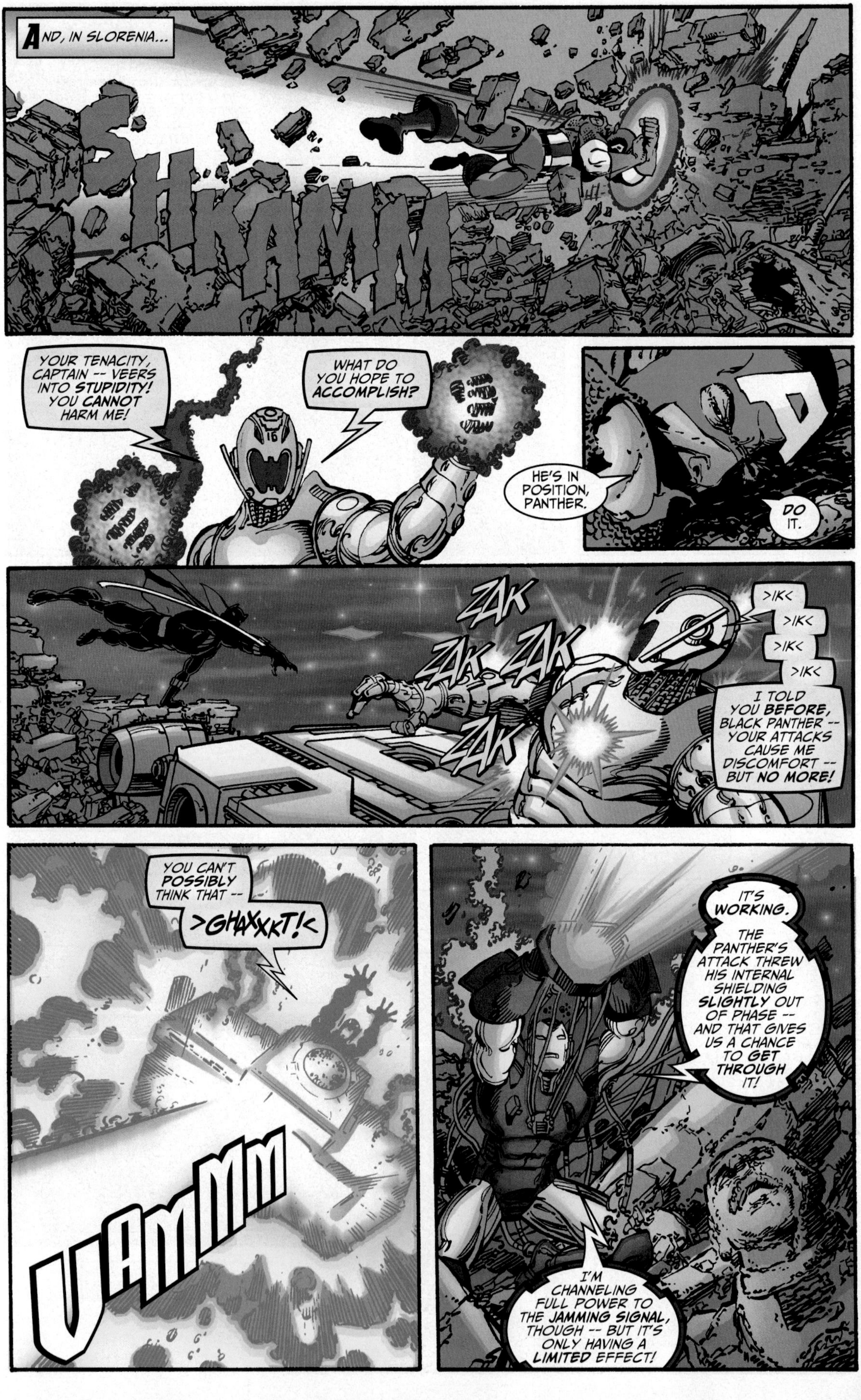
AND, IN SLORENIA...
SHKAMM
YOUR TENACITY, CAPTAIN -- VEERS INTO STUPIDITY! YOU CANNOT HARM ME!
WHAT DO YOU HOPE TO ACCOMPLISH?
HE'S IN POSITION, PANTHER.
DO IT.
ZAK
ZAK ZAK
ZAK
>IK<
>IK<
>IK<
>IK<
I TOLD YOU BEFORE, BLACK PANTHER -- YOUR ATTACKS CAUSE ME DISCOMFORT -- BUT NO MORE!
YOU CAN'T POSSIBLY THINK THAT --
>GHAXXKT!<
VAMMM
IT'S WORKING.
THE PANTHER'S ATTACK THREW HIS INTERNAL SHIELDING SLIGHTLY OUT OF PHASE -- AND THAT GIVES US A CHANCE TO GET THROUGH IT!
I'M CHANNELING FULL POWER TO THE JAMMING SIGNAL, THOUGH -- BUT IT'S ONLY HAVING A LIMITED EFFECT!

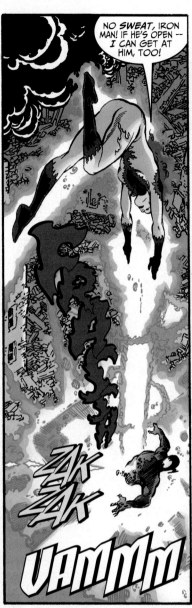

NO SWEAT, IRON MAN! IF HE'S OPEN -- I CAN GET AT HIM, TOO!

ZAK ZAK

VAMMM

I -- I TOLD YOU FLESH-BAGS --

SHRAMM

OH, MAN --

WHAT IS IT, SARGE? ARE THEY BEATIN' HIM?

CAN'T -- CAN'T TELL -- BUT I KNOW ONE THING --

-- I WOULDN'T WANNA BE IN THE MIDDLE OF THAT --!

YOU KEEP TELLING US WE CAN'T HURT YOU, ULTRON! AND I'VE GOT TO WONDER!

IS IT US YOU'RE TRYING TO CONVINCE?

EH?!

OR YOURSELF?!

SQUAWRKK!

CAPTAIN AMERICA'S PHOTONIC SHIELD, MORPHED INTO QUARTERSTAFF FORM, PENETRATES THROUGH ULTRON'S PRIMARY ION CHANNEL, BLOCKING IT --

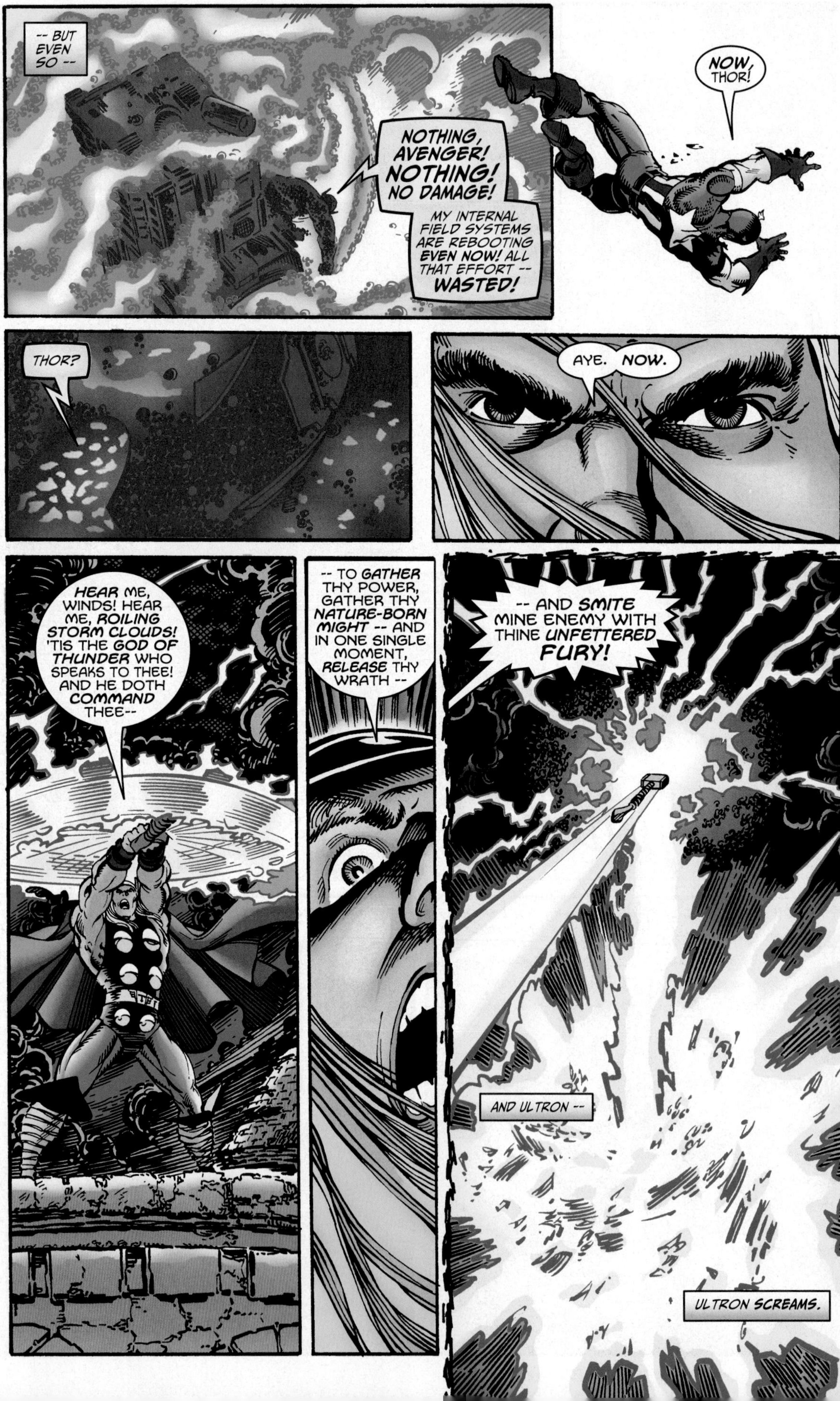
-- BUT EVEN SO --
NOTHING, AVENGER! NOTHING! NO DAMAGE!
MY INTERNAL FIELD SYSTEMS ARE REBOOTING EVEN NOW! ALL THAT EFFORT -- WASTED!
NOW, THOR!
THOR?
AYE.
NOW.
HEAR ME, WINDS! HEAR ME, ROILING STORM CLOUDS! 'TIS THE GOD OF THUNDER WHO SPEAKS TO THEE! AND HE DOTH COMMAND THEE--
-- TO GATHER THY POWER, GATHER THY NATURE-BORN MIGHT -- AND IN ONE SINGLE MOMENT, RELEASE THY WRATH --
-- AND SMITE MINE ENEMY WITH THINE UNFETTERED FURY!
AND ULTRON --
ULTRON SCREAMS.

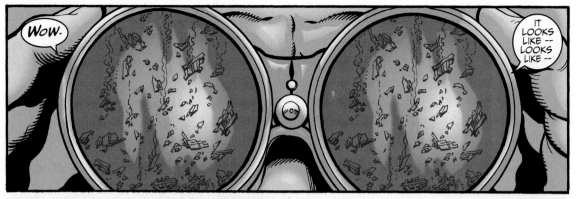

WOW.

IT LOOKS LIKE -- LOOKS LIKE --

WE... *DID* IT? WE *ACTUALLY BEAT* HIM?

WE... *SHOULDN'T HAVE,* FIRESTAR. EVEN UNDER A BARRAGE LIKE THAT, TRUE ADAMANTIUM SHOULDN'T EVEN *DENT,* MUCH LESS *SHATTER.*

THOU DOTH PUT TOO MUCH FAITH IN *SCIENCE,* OLD FRIEND.

THE AVENGERS DID GIVE THEIR *ALL,* AND MORE BESIDE. AGAINST SUCH AN ASSAULT --

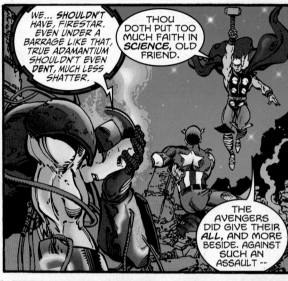

AGAINST SUCH AN ASSAULT, THOR, HE SHOULD HAVE HELD UP JUST FINE -- UNLESS HE'S TAKEN TO BUILDING HIMSELF OUT OF *SECONDARY ADAMANTIUM.*

I WAS HOPING TO *SHUT HIM DOWN,* NOT *BREAK* HIM.

WE CAN RUN TESTS *LATER,* IRON MAN -- SEE WHAT WE CAN *DISCOVER.* IN THE MEANTIME, I'VE PICKED UP A *SCENT* --

-- THERE ARE *PEOPLE* THIS WAY -- DEEP IN THESE TUNNELS.

*T*HE AVENGERS FOLLOW --

IS IT THE MISSING *AVENGERS,* PANTHER? CAN YOU *TELL?*

MY SENSES AREN'T *THAT* GOOD, FIRESTAR.

WE'RE AT LEAST A *MILE* AWAY, MAYBE MORE. BUT WE'LL KNOW SOON E --

GREETINGS, AVENGERS.

WHAT?!

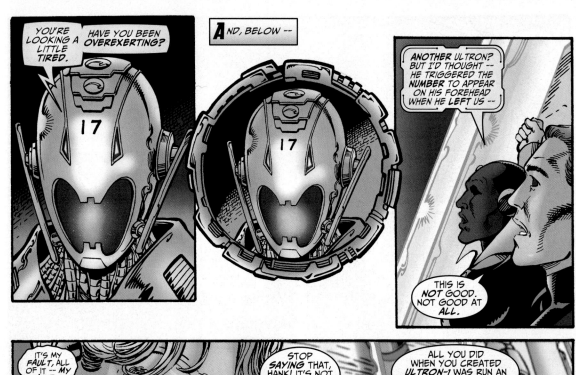

YOU'RE LOOKING A LITTLE TIRED. HAVE YOU BEEN OVEREXERTING?

AND, BELOW --

ANOTHER ULTRON? BUT I'D THOUGHT -- HE TRIGGERED THE *NUMBER* TO APPEAR ON HIS FOREHEAD WHEN HE *LEFT* US --

THIS IS *NOT GOOD.* NOT GOOD AT *ALL.*

IT'S MY *FAULT,* ALL OF IT -- *MY* FAULT --

STOP *SAYING* THAT, HANK! IT'S NOT TRUE, AND YOU *KNOW* IT!

ALL YOU DID WHEN YOU CREATED *ULTRON-1* WAS RUN AN *ARTIFICIAL-INTELLIGENCE* EXPERIMENT!

THE IDEA THAT IT WOULD TAKE ON A LIFE OF ITS *OWN* -- THAT IT WOULD EVOLVE INTO SOMETHING *HATEFUL,* SOMETHING *MURDEROUS* --

-- IT WAS A *FLUKE!* YOU COULDN'T HAVE *FORESEEN* IT! AND YOU CAN'T KEEP *BEATING YOURSELF UP* OVER IT!

NO -- YOU YOU DON'T KNOW THE *TRUTH* -- NOT THE *WHOLE* TRUTH. NO ONE DOES -- NO ONE BUT *ME.*

IT'S *WORSE* -- WORSE THAN ANYONE EVER *THOUGHT* --

SO, AVENGERS...

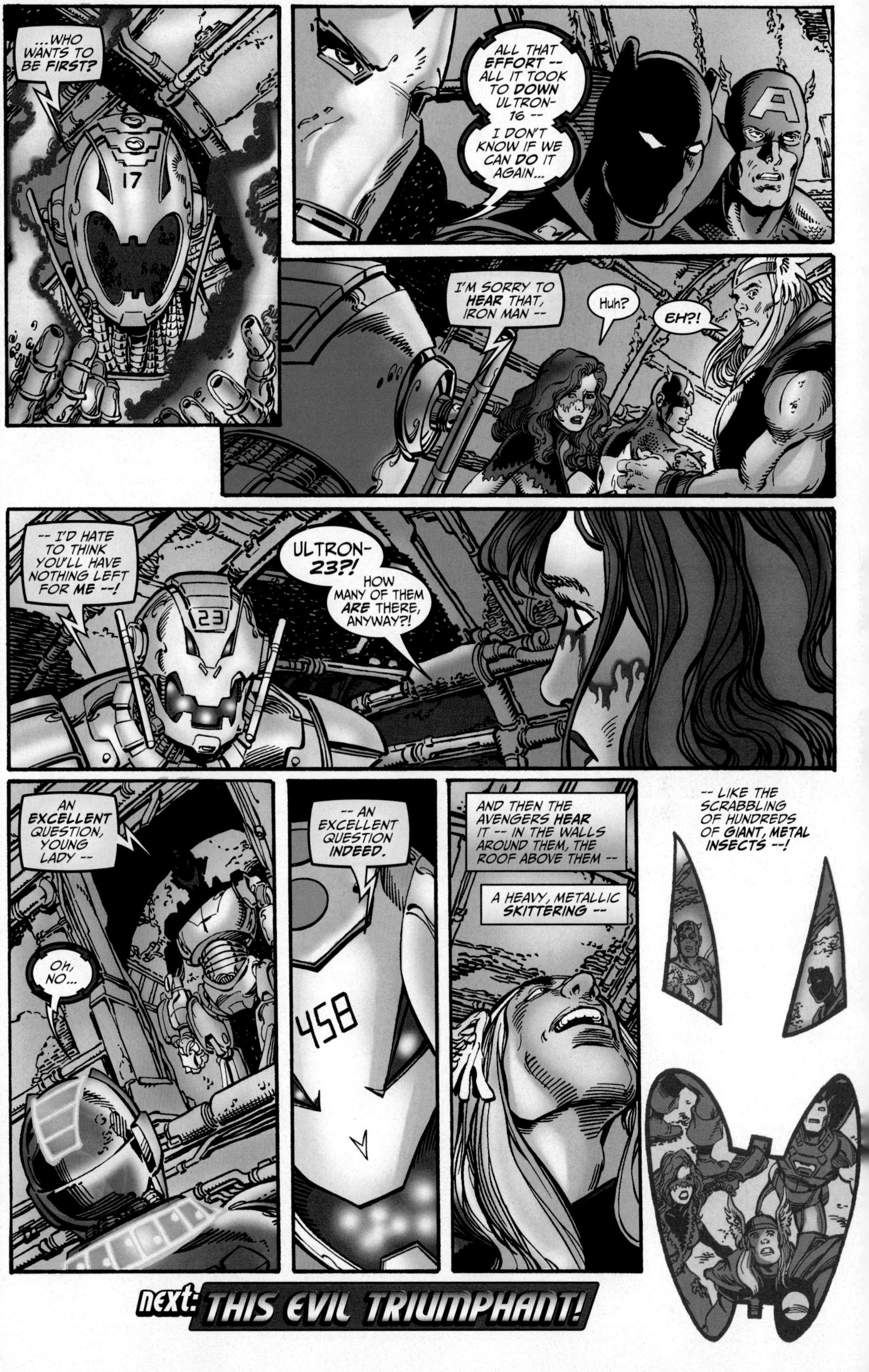
...WHO WANTS TO BE FIRST?
ALL THAT EFFORT -- ALL IT TOOK TO DOWN ULTRON-16 -- I DON'T KNOW IF WE CAN DO IT AGAIN...
I'M SORRY TO HEAR THAT, IRON MAN --
Huh?
EH?!
-- I'D HATE TO THINK YOU'LL HAVE NOTHING LEFT FOR ME --!
ULTRON-23?! HOW MANY OF THEM ARE THERE, ANYWAY?!
AN EXCELLENT QUESTION, YOUNG LADY --
Oh, NO...
-- AN EXCELLENT QUESTION INDEED.
AND THEN THE AVENGERS HEAR IT -- IN THE WALLS AROUND THEM, THE ROOF ABOVE THEM --
A HEAVY, METALLIC SKITTERING --
-- LIKE THE SCRABBLING OF HUNDREDS OF GIANT, METAL INSECTS --!
NEXT: THIS EVIL TRIUMPHANT!

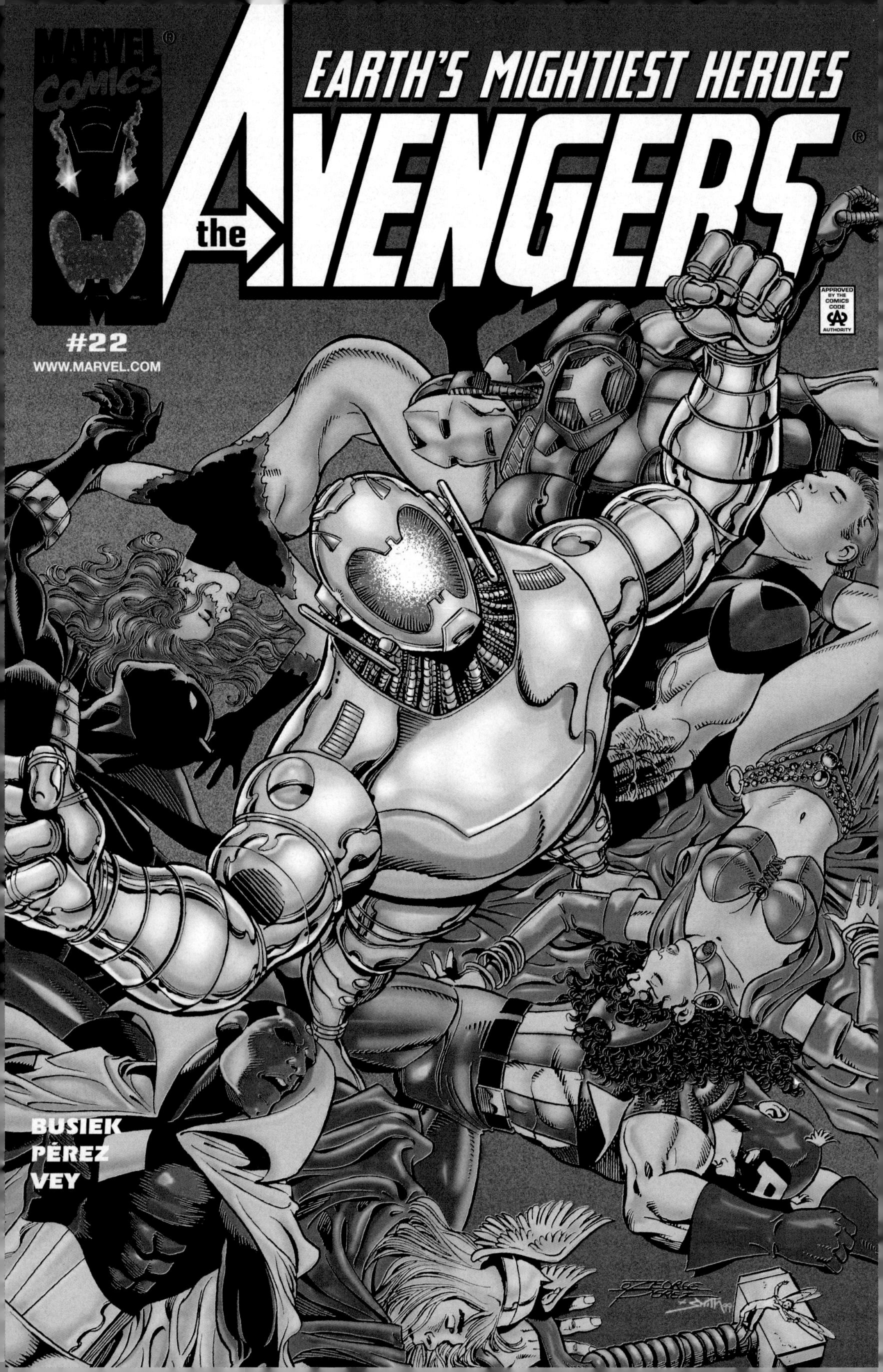
MARVEL COMICS
EARTH'S MIGHTIEST HEROES
the AVENGERS
APPROVED BY THE COMICS CODE AUTHORITY
#22
WWW.MARVEL.COM
BUSIEK
PÉREZ
VEY

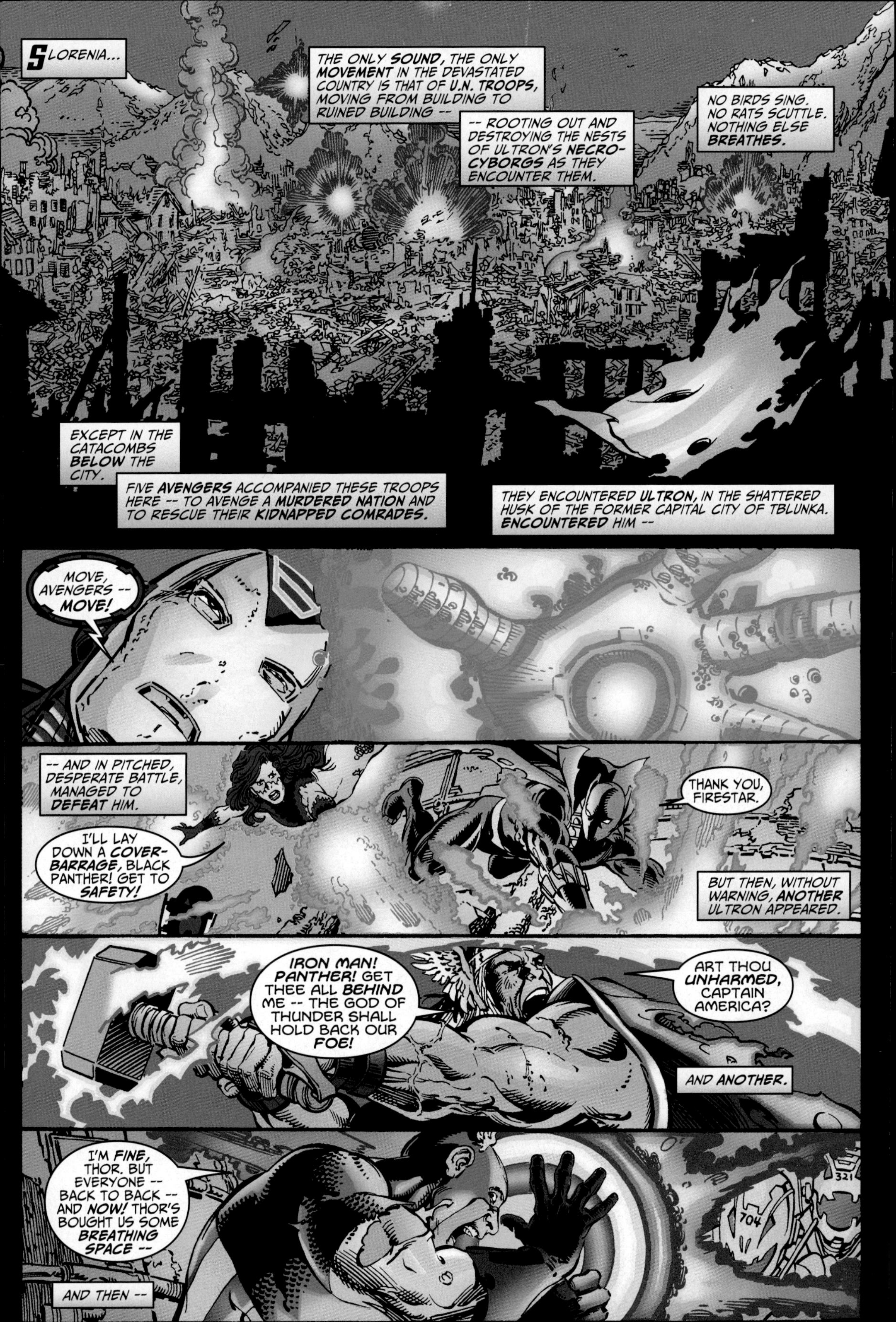
SLORENIA...
THE ONLY SOUND, THE ONLY MOVEMENT IN THE DEVASTATED COUNTRY IS THAT OF U.N. TROOPS, MOVING FROM BUILDING TO RUINED BUILDING --
-- ROOTING OUT AND DESTROYING THE NESTS OF ULTRON'S NECRO-CYBORGS AS THEY ENCOUNTER THEM.
NO BIRDS SING. NO RATS SCUTTLE. NOTHING ELSE BREATHES.
EXCEPT IN THE CATACOMBS BELOW THE CITY.
FIVE AVENGERS ACCOMPANIED THESE TROOPS HERE -- TO AVENGE A MURDERED NATION AND TO RESCUE THEIR KIDNAPPED COMRADES.
THEY ENCOUNTERED ULTRON, IN THE SHATTERED HUSK OF THE FORMER CAPITAL CITY OF TBLUNKA. ENCOUNTERED HIM --
MOVE, AVENGERS -- MOVE!
-- AND IN PITCHED, DESPERATE BATTLE, MANAGED TO DEFEAT HIM.
I'LL LAY DOWN A COVER-BARRAGE, BLACK PANTHER! GET TO SAFETY!
THANK YOU, FIRESTAR.
BUT THEN, WITHOUT WARNING, ANOTHER ULTRON APPEARED.
IRON MAN! PANTHER! GET THEE ALL BEHIND ME -- THE GOD OF THUNDER SHALL HOLD BACK OUR FOE!
ART THOU UNHARMED, CAPTAIN AMERICA?
AND ANOTHER.
I'M FINE, THOR. BUT EVERYONE -- BACK TO BACK -- AND NOW! THOR'S BOUGHT US SOME BREATHING SPACE --
AND THEN --
321
704

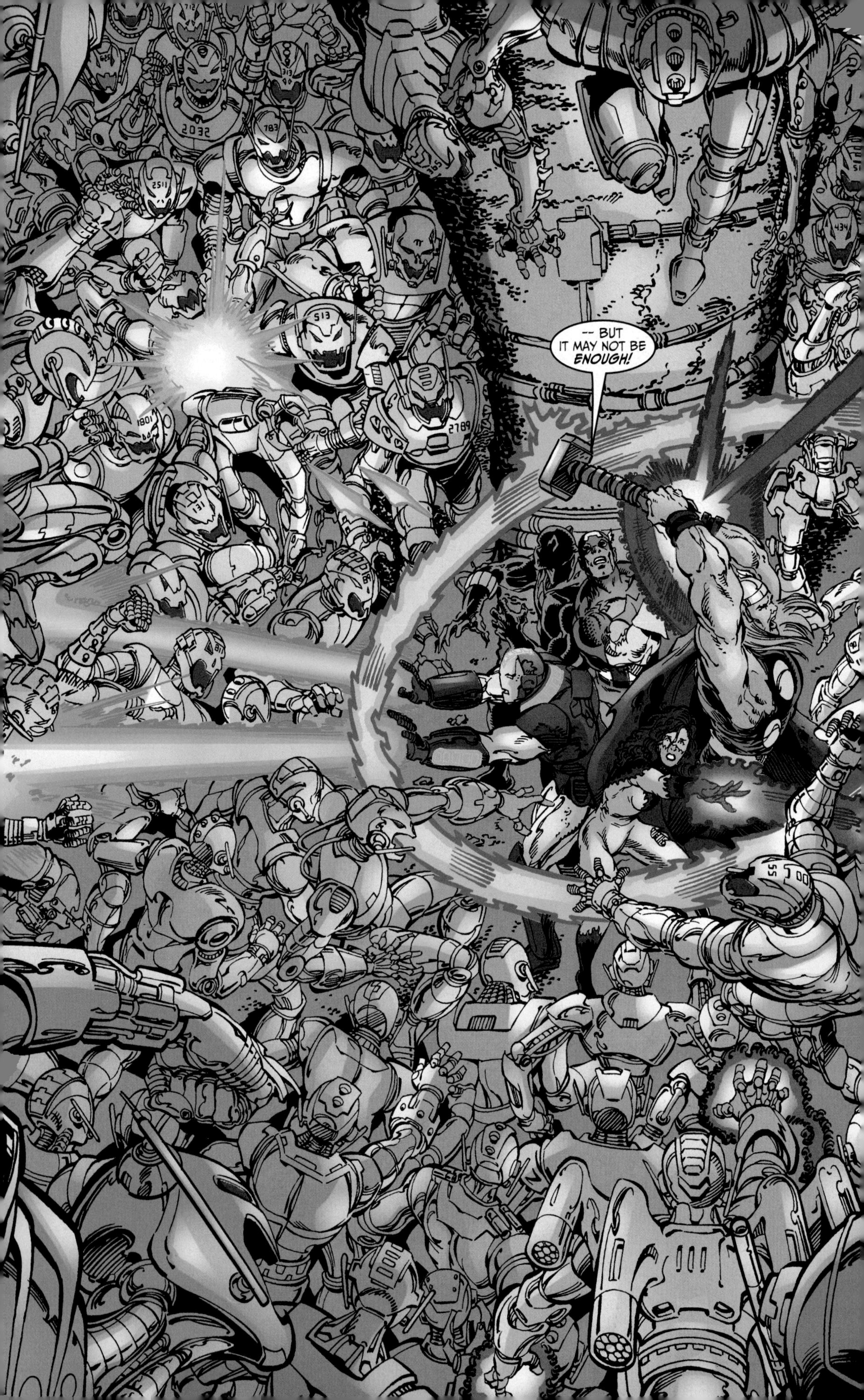
-- BUT IT MAY NOT BE ENOUGH!

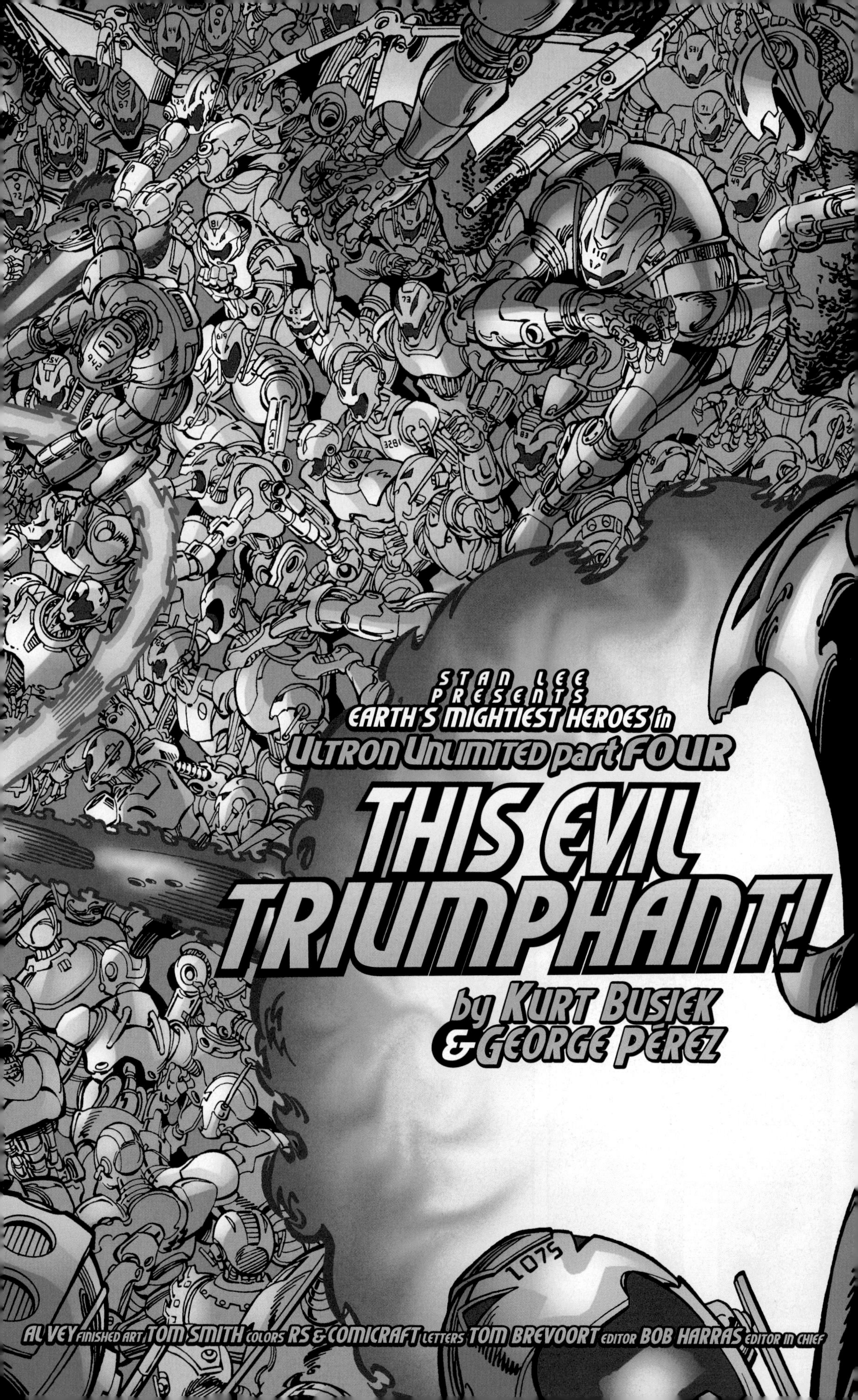
STAN LEE PRESENTS
EARTH'S MIGHTIEST HEROES in
ULTRON UNLIMITED part FOUR
THIS EVIL TRIUMPHANT!
by KURT BUSIEK & GEORGE PÉREZ
AL VEY finished art TOM SMITH colors RS & COMICRAFT letters TOM BREVOORT editor BOB HARRAS editor in chief

AVENGERS MANSION, IN NEW YORK. SEVEN TIME ZONES EARLIER, IT'S ONE IN THE MORNING --

-- AND IN THE BEDROOM RESERVED FOR THE AVENGERS' BUTLER, JARVIS --

BREET BREET

PRIORITY ALERT! PRIORITY ALERT! THREAT LEVEL A-16! ALKHEMA-2 HAS ESCAPED FROM FEDERAL INCARCERATION AT RAPHINE BASE --

-- WITH EXTREME LOSS OF LIFE! AVENGERS RESPONSE REQUESTED!

HMH? ULTRON'S TWISTED "BRIDE" -- THE AVENGERS CAPTURED HER* -- AND NOW SHE'S FREE AGAIN?

BUT -- THE COMPUTERS DON'T TRANSMIT INCOMING ALERTS TO MY ROOM, UNLESS THERE'S NO ONE ELSE IN THE MANSION --

*IN #19 -- TOM

-- AND THAT'S IMPOSSIBLE!

JUSTICE -- MASTER VANCE -- HAS BEEN CONFINED TO THE MANSION DUE TO HIS BROKEN LEG! HE'S BEEN SPENDING HIS TIME IN THE RECORDS ROOM --

-- RESEARCHING ULTRON! BUT --

JUSTICE? SIR?

GONE - AND HE HASN'T EVEN TOUCHED HIS TEA! WHEN I BROUGHT IT TO HIM, HE WAS LOOKING OVER RECORDS OF A RECENT BATTLE --

-- WHEN THE AVENGERS UNCOVERED AN A.I.M.* BASE BENEATH A WAREHOUSE IN THE BRONX.**

*ADVANCED IDEA MECHANICS.
**IN #13 -- TOM

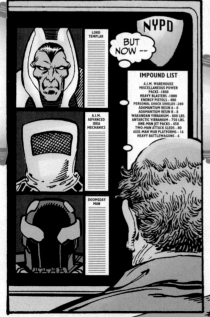

NYPD

LORD TEMPLAR

A.I.M. ADVANCED IDEA MECHANICS

DOOMSDAY MAN

BUT NOW --

IMPOUND LIST
A.I.M. WAREHOUSE
MISCELLANEOUS POWER
PACKS -1800
HEAVY BLASTERS -1800
ENERGY PISTOLS - 400
PERSONAL SHOCK SHIELDS -200
ADAMANTIUM RESIN A - 8
ADAMANTIUM RESIN B - 8
WAKANDAN VIBRANIUM - 800 LBS.
ANTARCTIC VIBRANIUM - 750 LBS.
ONE-MAN JET PACKS - 450
TWO-MAN ATTACK SLEDS - 80
6SIX-MAN WAR PLATFORMS - 16
HEAVY BATTLEWAGONS - 6

-- A POLICE IMPOUND LIST? WHY WOULD THAT MAKE HIM BOLT FROM THE MANSION LIKE THIS, AGAINST MEDICAL ADVICE? AND --

-- WHERE IS HE GOING --?

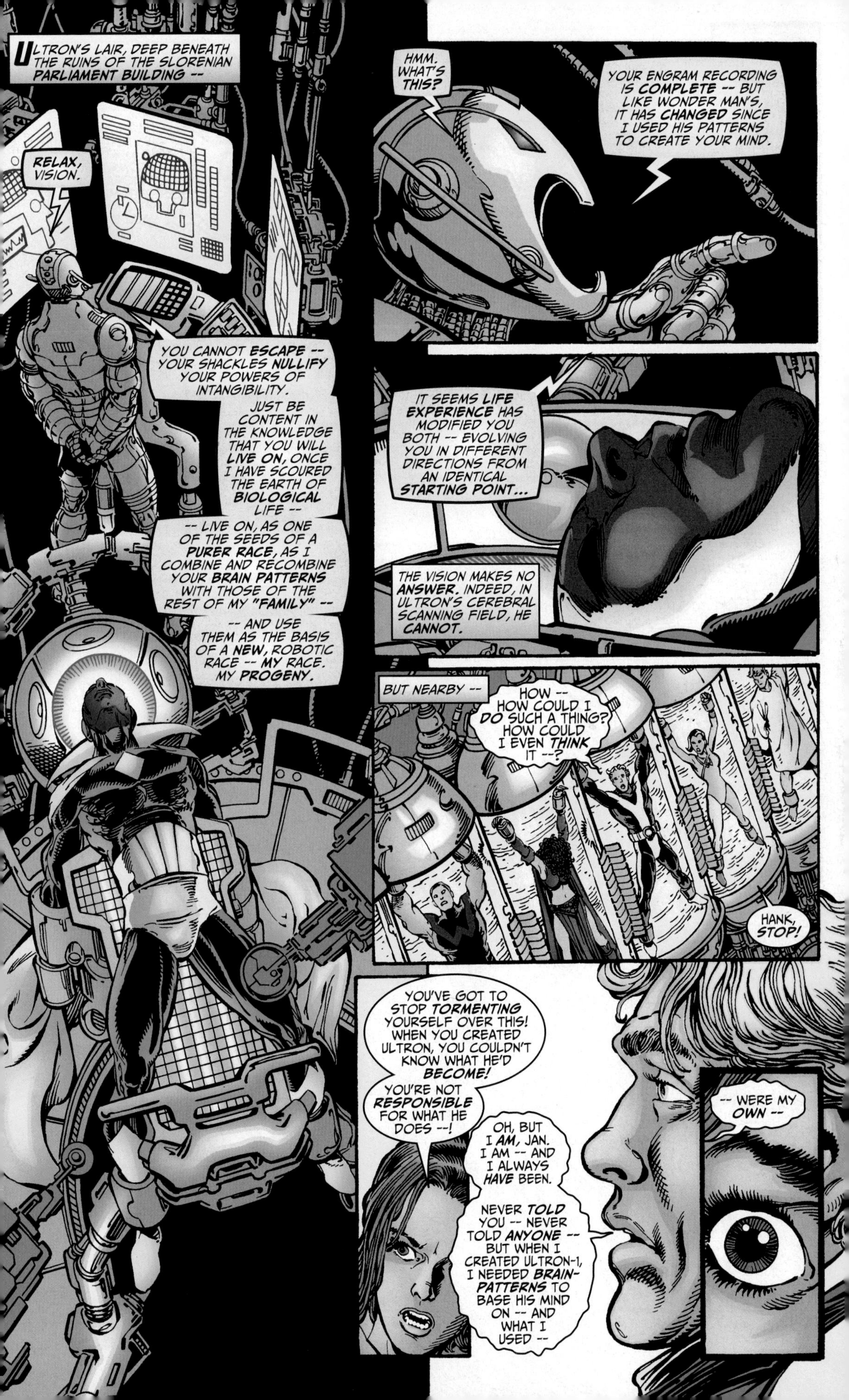
ULTRON'S LAIR, DEEP BENEATH THE RUINS OF THE SLORENIAN PARLIAMENT BUILDING --
RELAX, VISION.
YOU CANNOT ESCAPE -- YOUR SHACKLES NULLIFY YOUR POWERS OF INTANGIBILITY.
JUST BE CONTENT IN THE KNOWLEDGE THAT YOU WILL LIVE ON, ONCE I HAVE SCOURED THE EARTH OF BIOLOGICAL LIFE --
-- LIVE ON, AS ONE OF THE SEEDS OF A PURER RACE, AS I COMBINE AND RECOMBINE YOUR BRAIN PATTERNS WITH THOSE OF THE REST OF MY "FAMILY" --
-- AND USE THEM AS THE BASIS OF A NEW, ROBOTIC RACE -- MY RACE. MY PROGENY.
HMM. WHAT'S THIS?
YOUR ENGRAM RECORDING IS COMPLETE -- BUT LIKE WONDER MAN'S, IT HAS CHANGED SINCE I USED HIS PATTERNS TO CREATE YOUR MIND.
IT SEEMS LIFE EXPERIENCE HAS MODIFIED YOU BOTH -- EVOLVING YOU IN DIFFERENT DIRECTIONS FROM AN IDENTICAL STARTING POINT...
THE VISION MAKES NO ANSWER. INDEED, IN ULTRON'S CEREBRAL SCANNING FIELD, HE CANNOT.
BUT NEARBY --
HOW -- HOW COULD I DO SUCH A THING? HOW COULD I EVEN THINK IT --?
HANK, STOP!
YOU'VE GOT TO STOP TORMENTING YOURSELF OVER THIS! WHEN YOU CREATED ULTRON, YOU COULDN'T KNOW WHAT HE'D BECOME!
YOU'RE NOT RESPONSIBLE FOR WHAT HE DOES --!
OH, BUT I AM, JAN. I AM -- AND I ALWAYS HAVE BEEN.
NEVER TOLD YOU -- NEVER TOLD ANYONE -- BUT WHEN I CREATED ULTRON-1, I NEEDED BRAIN-PATTERNS TO BASE HIS MIND ON -- AND WHAT I USED --
-- WERE MY OWN --

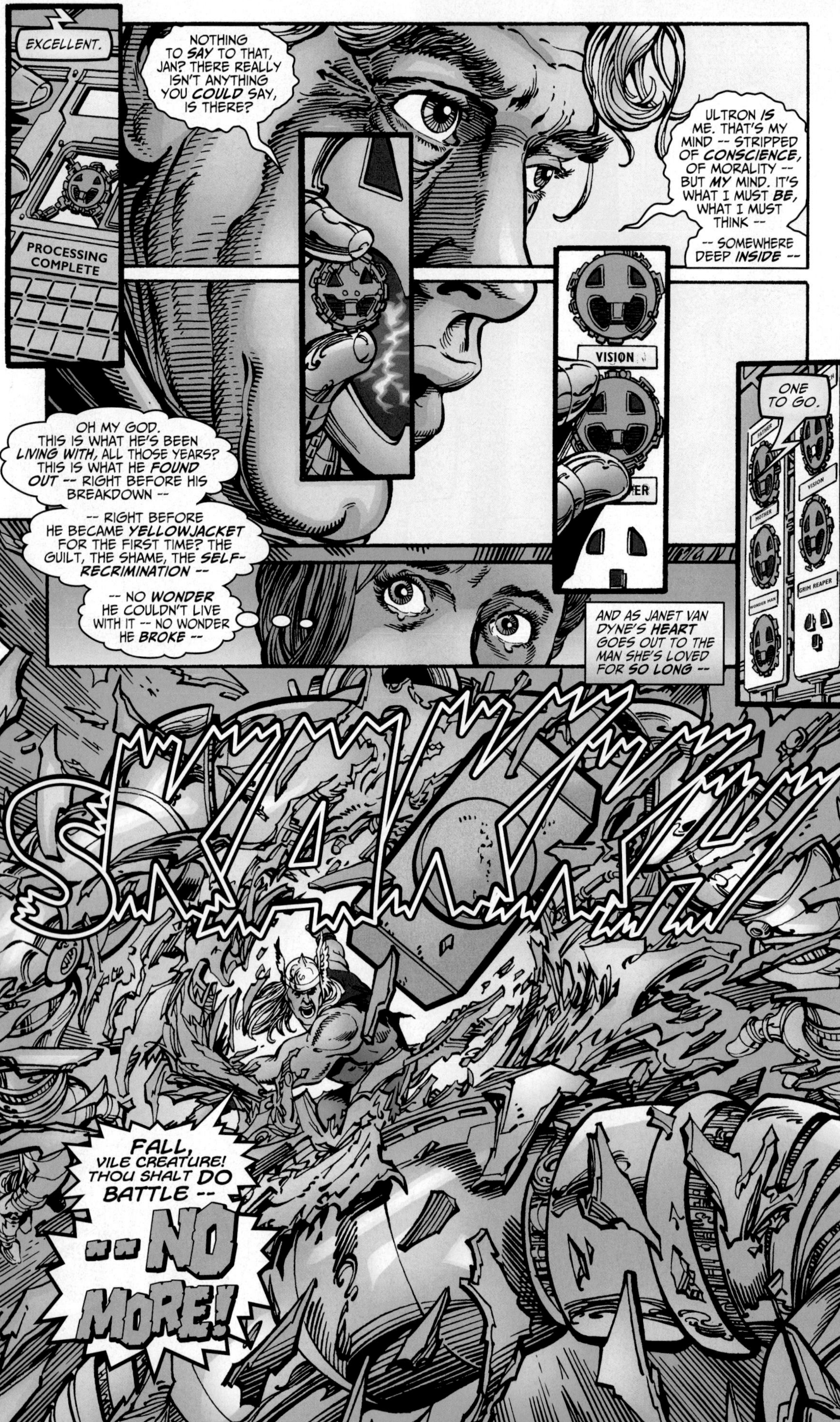
EXCELLENT.
PROCESSING COMPLETE
NOTHING TO SAY TO THAT, JAN? THERE REALLY ISN'T ANYTHING YOU COULD SAY, IS THERE?
ULTRON IS ME. THAT'S MY MIND -- STRIPPED OF CONSCIENCE, OF MORALITY -- BUT MY MIND. IT'S WHAT I MUST BE, WHAT I MUST THINK --
-- SOMEWHERE DEEP INSIDE --
VISION
ONE TO GO.
FATHER
MOTHER
WONDER MAN
VISION
GRIM REAPER
OH MY GOD. THIS IS WHAT HE'S BEEN LIVING WITH, ALL THOSE YEARS? THIS IS WHAT HE FOUND OUT -- RIGHT BEFORE HIS BREAKDOWN --
-- RIGHT BEFORE HE BECAME YELLOWJACKET FOR THE FIRST TIME? THE GUILT, THE SHAME, THE SELF-RECRIMINATION --
-- NO WONDER HE COULDN'T LIVE WITH IT -- NO WONDER HE BROKE --
AND AS JANET VAN DYNE'S HEART GOES OUT TO THE MAN SHE'S LOVED FOR SO LONG --
SKRAKKA
FALL, VILE CREATURE! THOU SHALT DO BATTLE --
-- NO MORE!

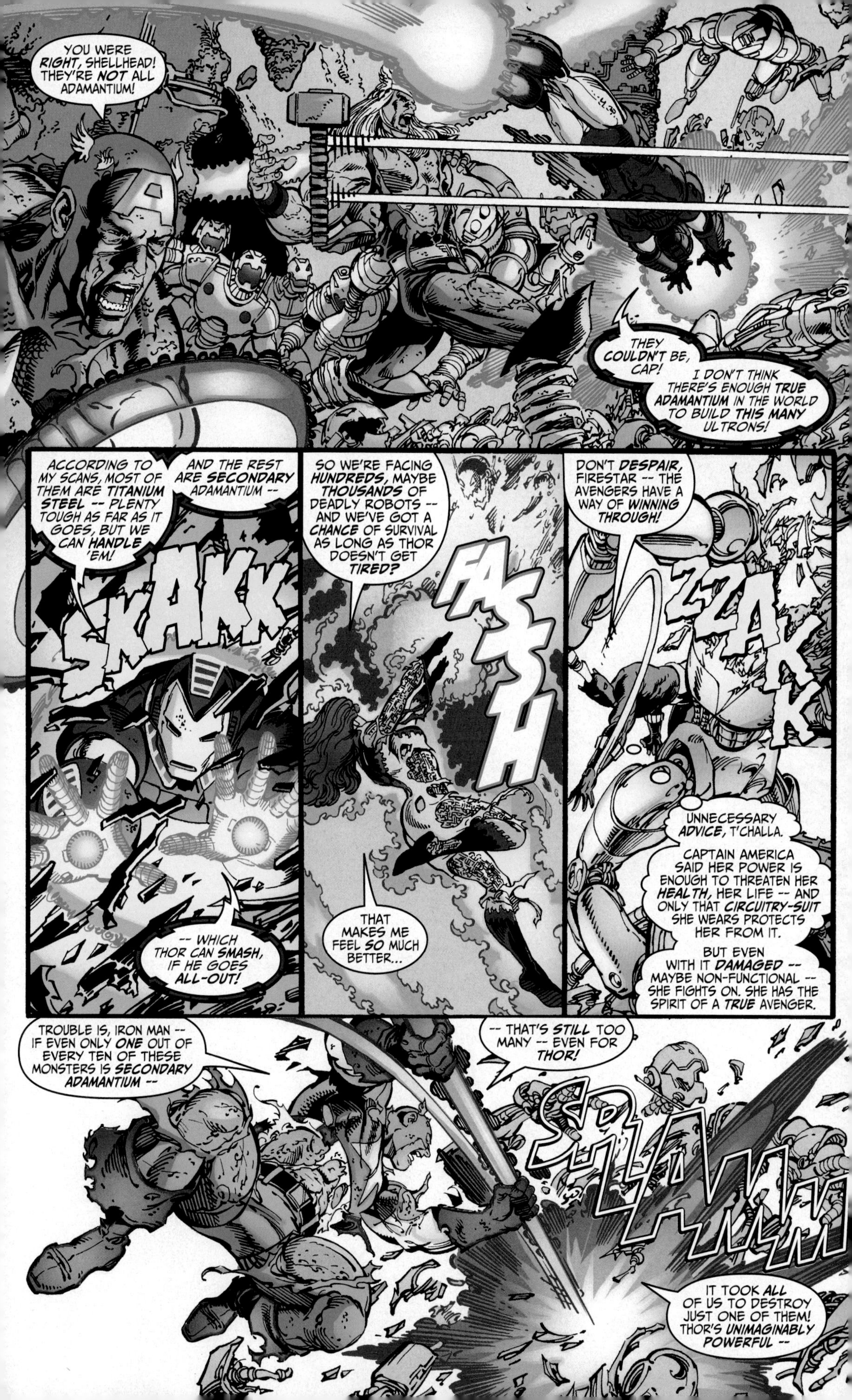
YOU WERE RIGHT, SHELLHEAD! THEY'RE NOT ALL ADAMANTIUM!
THEY COULDN'T BE, CAP!
I DON'T THINK THERE'S ENOUGH TRUE ADAMANTIUM IN THE WORLD TO BUILD THIS MANY ULTRONS!
ACCORDING TO MY SCANS, MOST OF THEM ARE TITANIUM STEEL -- PLENTY TOUGH AS FAR AS IT GOES, BUT WE CAN HANDLE 'EM!
AND THE REST ARE SECONDARY ADAMANTIUM --
SKAKK
-- WHICH THOR CAN SMASH, IF HE GOES ALL-OUT!
SO WE'RE FACING HUNDREDS, MAYBE THOUSANDS OF DEADLY ROBOTS -- AND WE'VE GOT A CHANCE OF SURVIVAL AS LONG AS THOR DOESN'T GET TIRED?
FASSH
THAT MAKES ME FEEL SO MUCH BETTER...
DON'T DESPAIR, FIRESTAR -- THE AVENGERS HAVE A WAY OF WINNING THROUGH!
ZZAKK
UNNECESSARY ADVICE, T'CHALLA.
CAPTAIN AMERICA SAID HER POWER IS ENOUGH TO THREATEN HER HEALTH, HER LIFE -- AND ONLY THAT CIRCUITRY-SUIT SHE WEARS PROTECTS HER FROM IT.
BUT EVEN WITH IT DAMAGED -- MAYBE NON-FUNCTIONAL -- SHE FIGHTS ON. SHE HAS THE SPIRIT OF A TRUE AVENGER.
TROUBLE IS, IRON MAN -- IF EVEN ONLY ONE OUT OF EVERY TEN OF THESE MONSTERS IS SECONDARY ADAMANTIUM --
-- THAT'S STILL TOO MANY -- EVEN FOR THOR!
IT TOOK ALL OF US TO DESTROY JUST ONE OF THEM! THOR'S UNIMAGINABLY POWERFUL --

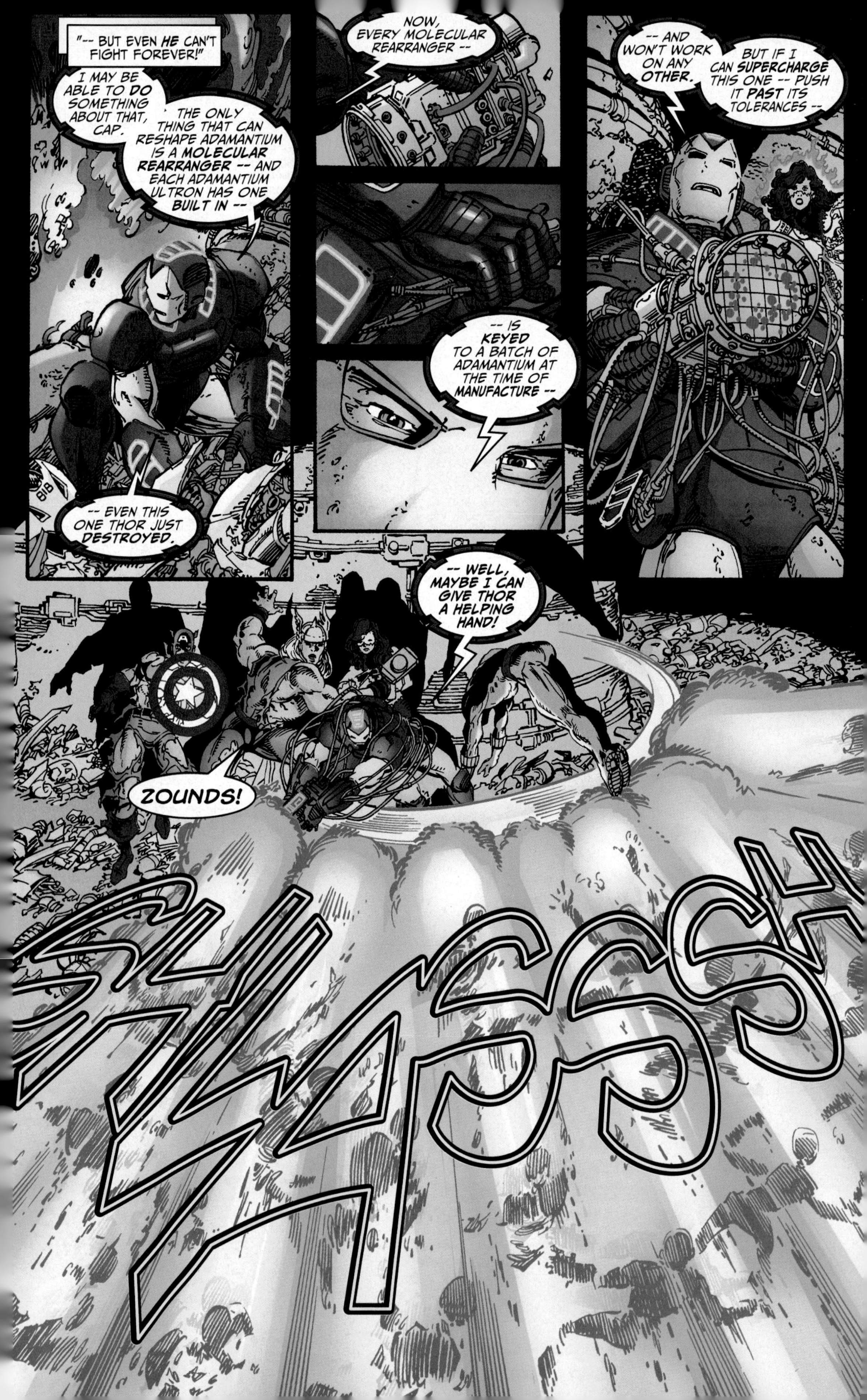
"-- BUT EVEN HE CAN'T FIGHT FOREVER!"
I MAY BE ABLE TO DO SOMETHING ABOUT THAT, CAP.
THE ONLY THING THAT CAN RESHAPE ADAMANTIUM IS A MOLECULAR REARRANGER -- AND EACH ADAMANTIUM ULTRON HAS ONE BUILT IN --
-- EVEN THIS ONE THOR JUST DESTROYED.
NOW, EVERY MOLECULAR REARRANGER --
-- IS KEYED TO A BATCH OF ADAMANTIUM AT THE TIME OF MANUFACTURE --
-- AND WON'T WORK ON ANY OTHER.
BUT IF I CAN SUPERCHARGE THIS ONE -- PUSH IT PAST ITS TOLERANCES --
-- WELL, MAYBE I CAN GIVE THOR A HELPING HAND!
ZOUNDS!

AND...

NNNH...

AND SO IT IS DONE.

THE GRIM REAPER DOES NOT SEEM TO HAVE *WEATHERED* THE PROCESS AS WELL AS THE REST OF YOU --

-- NOT THAT IT *MATTERS.* FOR I NO LONGER *NEED* --

THAT'S MY *BROTHER* YOU'RE HANGING BACK UP LIKE A PIECE OF MEAT, ULTRON! YOU'D BETTER NOT HAVE *HARMED* HIM, OR I'LL --

HE IS MY BROTHER TOO, WONDER MAN -- AFTER A *FASHION.*

BUT AT THE MOMENT, THAT IS NEITHER *HERE* NOR THERE. THIS IS *MADNESS,* ULTRON, AND I CANNOT ALLOW IT --

-- TO *CONTINUE.*

EH? THE VISION -- *FREE?* BUT THE DAMPING-UNITS SHOULD HAVE --

-- PREVENTED ME FROM ALTERING MY *DENSITY?* THEY DID -- UNTIL JUST NOW.

I HAVE *REDESIGNED* MYSELF SOMEWHAT SINCE WE LAST MET, ULTRON, AND I NOW HAVE THE ABILITY TO INTERFACE REMOTELY WITH *COMPUTER SYSTEMS.*

YOU HAVE VERY *TIGHT* SECURITY. BUT I SPENT MY TIME AS A PRISONER WORKING *THROUGH* IT -- GAINING ENOUGH *CONTROL* --

-- TO *DEACTIVATE* YOUR POWER-NULLIFYING *SHACKLES.*

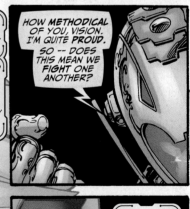

HOW *METHODICAL* OF YOU, VISION. I'M QUITE *PROUD.* SO -- DOES THIS MEAN WE FIGHT ONE ANOTHER?

NOT UNLESS YOU *WISH* IT, ULTRON. FOR MY PART --

-- I ONLY WANT TO *TALK.*

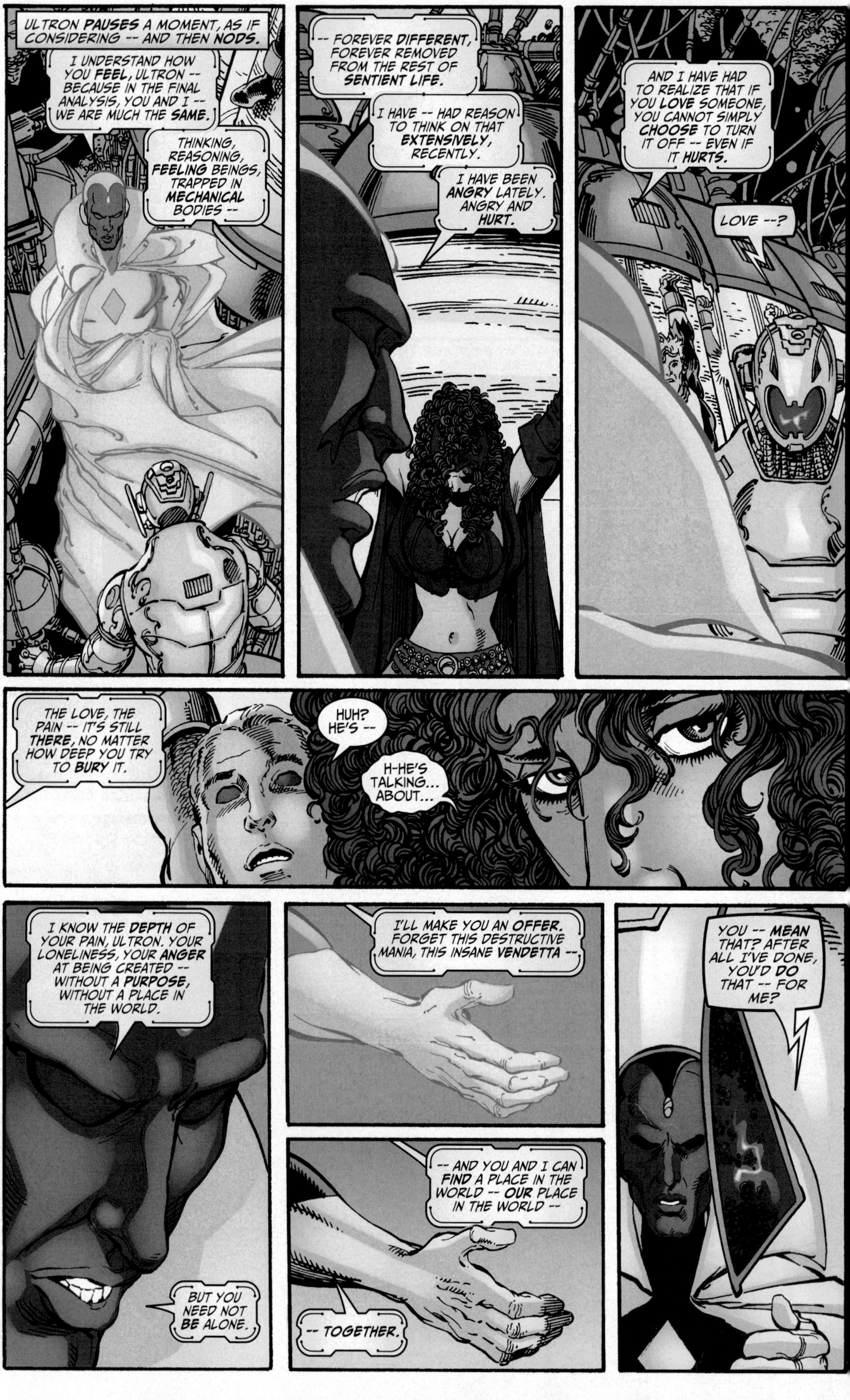
ULTRON PAUSES A MOMENT, AS IF CONSIDERING -- AND THEN NODS.
I UNDERSTAND HOW YOU FEEL, ULTRON -- BECAUSE IN THE FINAL ANALYSIS, YOU AND I -- WE ARE MUCH THE SAME.
THINKING, REASONING, FEELING BEINGS, TRAPPED IN MECHANICAL BODIES --
-- FOREVER DIFFERENT, FOREVER REMOVED FROM THE REST OF SENTIENT LIFE.
I HAVE -- HAD REASON TO THINK ON THAT EXTENSIVELY, RECENTLY.
I HAVE BEEN ANGRY LATELY. ANGRY AND HURT.
AND I HAVE HAD TO REALIZE THAT IF YOU LOVE SOMEONE, YOU CANNOT SIMPLY CHOOSE TO TURN IT OFF -- EVEN IF IT HURTS.
LOVE --?
THE LOVE, THE PAIN -- IT'S STILL THERE, NO MATTER HOW DEEP YOU TRY TO BURY IT.
HUH? HE'S --
H-HE'S TALKING... ABOUT...
I KNOW THE DEPTH OF YOUR PAIN, ULTRON. YOUR LONELINESS, YOUR ANGER AT BEING CREATED -- WITHOUT A PURPOSE, WITHOUT A PLACE IN THE WORLD.
BUT YOU NEED NOT BE ALONE.
I'LL MAKE YOU AN OFFER. FORGET THIS DESTRUCTIVE MANIA, THIS INSANE VENDETTA --
-- AND YOU AND I CAN FIND A PLACE IN THE WORLD -- OUR PLACE IN THE WORLD --
-- TOGETHER.
YOU -- MEAN THAT? AFTER ALL I'VE DONE, YOU'D DO THAT -- FOR ME?

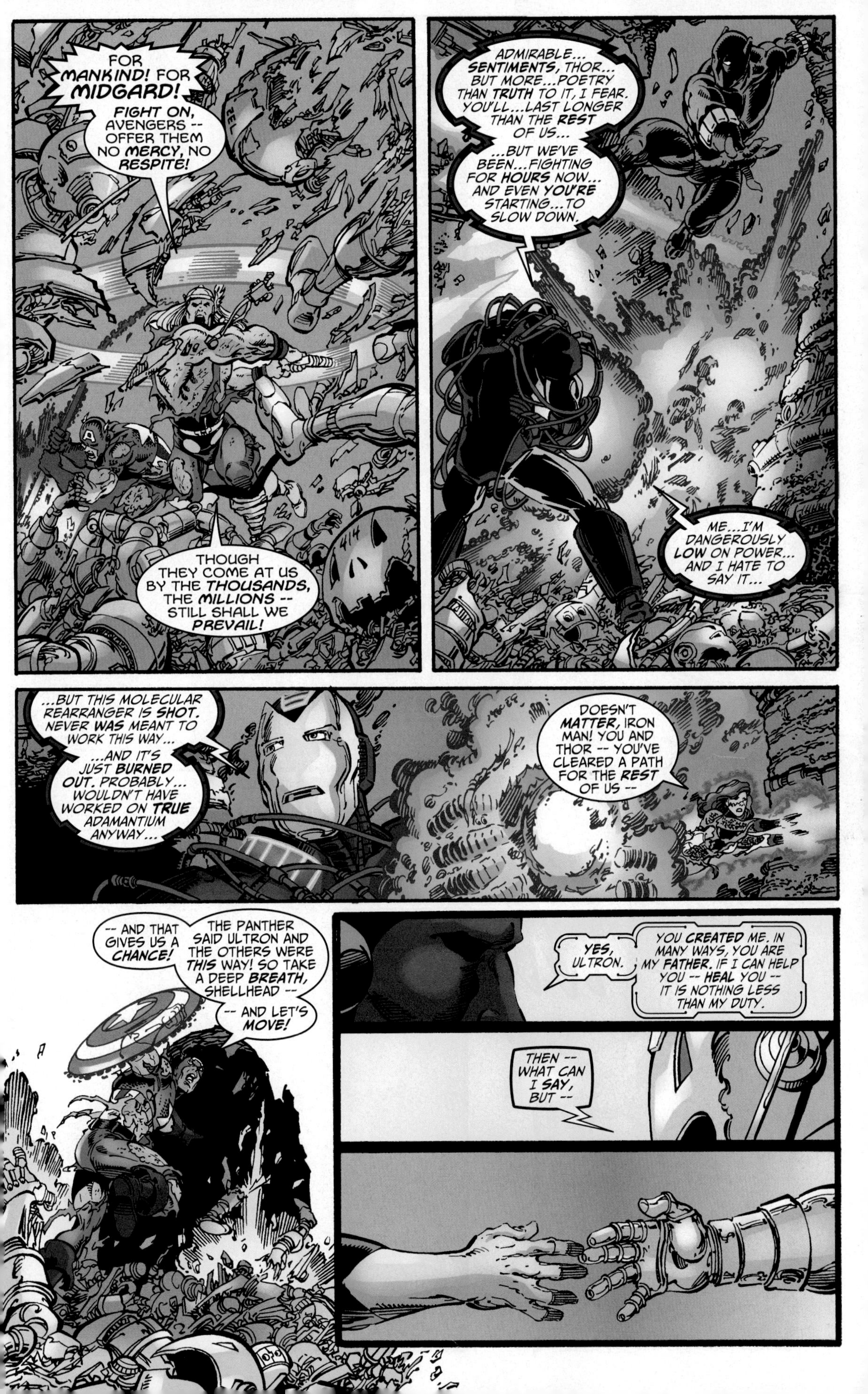
FOR MANKIND! FOR MIDGARD!
FIGHT ON, AVENGERS -- OFFER THEM NO MERCY, NO RESPITE!
THOUGH THEY COME AT US BY THE THOUSANDS, THE MILLIONS -- STILL SHALL WE PREVAIL!
ADMIRABLE... SENTIMENTS, THOR... BUT MORE...POETRY THAN TRUTH TO IT, I FEAR. YOU'LL...LAST LONGER THAN THE REST OF US...
...BUT WE'VE BEEN...FIGHTING FOR HOURS NOW... AND EVEN YOU'RE STARTING...TO SLOW DOWN.
ME...I'M DANGEROUSLY LOW ON POWER... AND I HATE TO SAY IT...
...BUT THIS MOLECULAR REARRANGER IS SHOT. NEVER WAS MEANT TO WORK THIS WAY...
...AND IT'S JUST BURNED OUT. PROBABLY... WOULDN'T HAVE WORKED ON TRUE ADAMANTIUM ANYWAY...
DOESN'T MATTER, IRON MAN! YOU AND THOR -- YOU'VE CLEARED A PATH FOR THE REST OF US --
-- AND THAT GIVES US A CHANCE!
THE PANTHER SAID ULTRON AND THE OTHERS WERE THIS WAY! SO TAKE A DEEP BREATH, SHELLHEAD --
-- AND LET'S MOVE!
YES, ULTRON.
YOU CREATED ME. IN MANY WAYS, YOU ARE MY FATHER. IF I CAN HELP YOU -- HEAL YOU -- IT IS NOTHING LESS THAN MY DUTY.
THEN -- WHAT CAN I SAY, BUT --

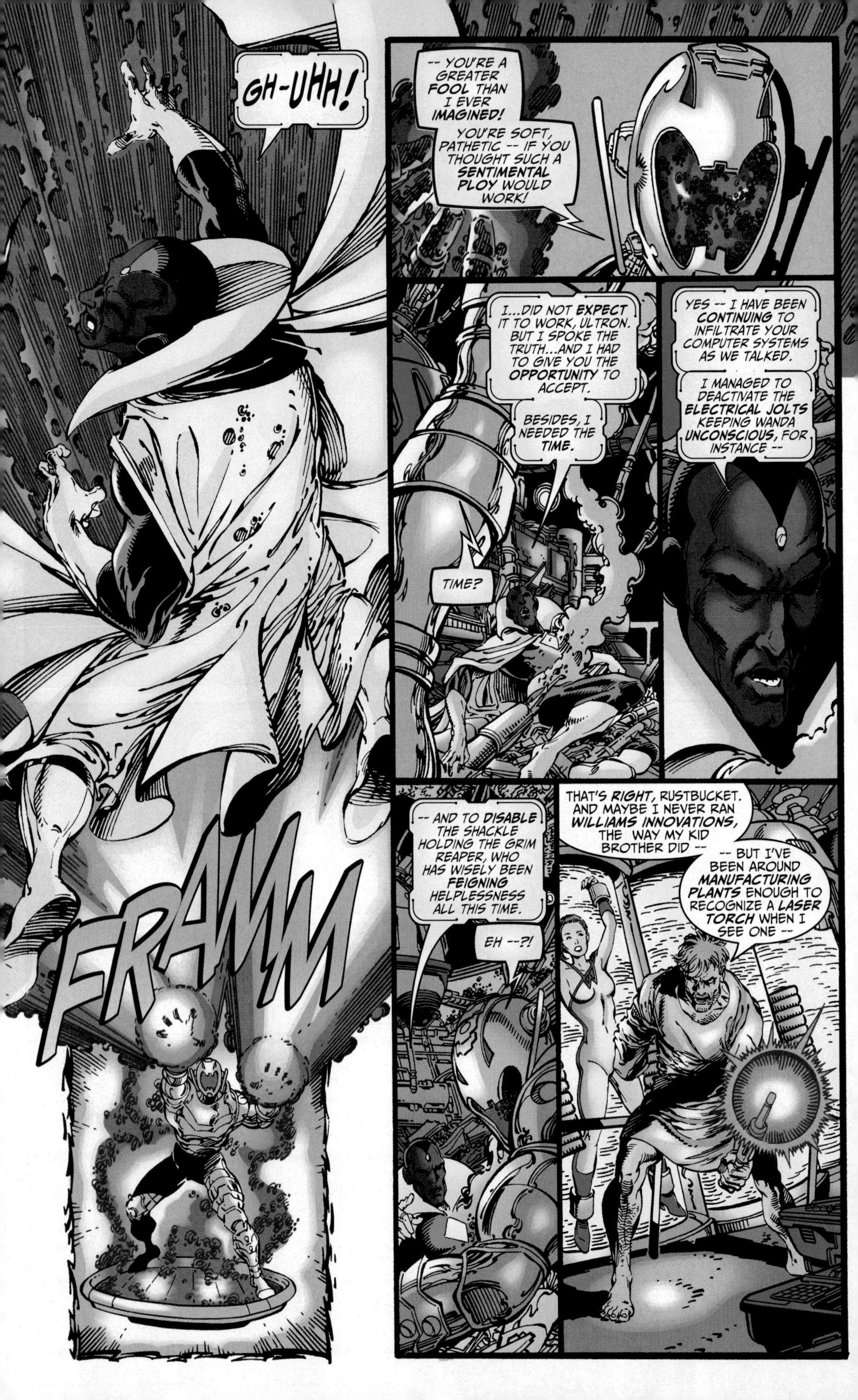
GH-UHH!
FRAMM
-- YOU'RE A GREATER FOOL THAN I EVER IMAGINED!
YOU'RE SOFT, PATHETIC -- IF YOU THOUGHT SUCH A SENTIMENTAL PLOY WOULD WORK!
I...DID NOT EXPECT IT TO WORK, ULTRON. BUT I SPOKE THE TRUTH...AND I HAD TO GIVE YOU THE OPPORTUNITY TO ACCEPT.
BESIDES, I NEEDED THE TIME.
TIME?
YES -- I HAVE BEEN CONTINUING TO INFILTRATE YOUR COMPUTER SYSTEMS AS WE TALKED.
I MANAGED TO DEACTIVATE THE ELECTRICAL JOLTS KEEPING WANDA UNCONSCIOUS, FOR INSTANCE --
-- AND TO DISABLE THE SHACKLE HOLDING THE GRIM REAPER, WHO HAS WISELY BEEN FEIGNING HELPLESSNESS ALL THIS TIME.
EH --?!
THAT'S RIGHT, RUSTBUCKET. AND MAYBE I NEVER RAN WILLIAMS INNOVATIONS, THE WAY MY KID BROTHER DID --
-- BUT I'VE BEEN AROUND MANUFACTURING PLANTS ENOUGH TO RECOGNIZE A LASER TORCH WHEN I SEE ONE --

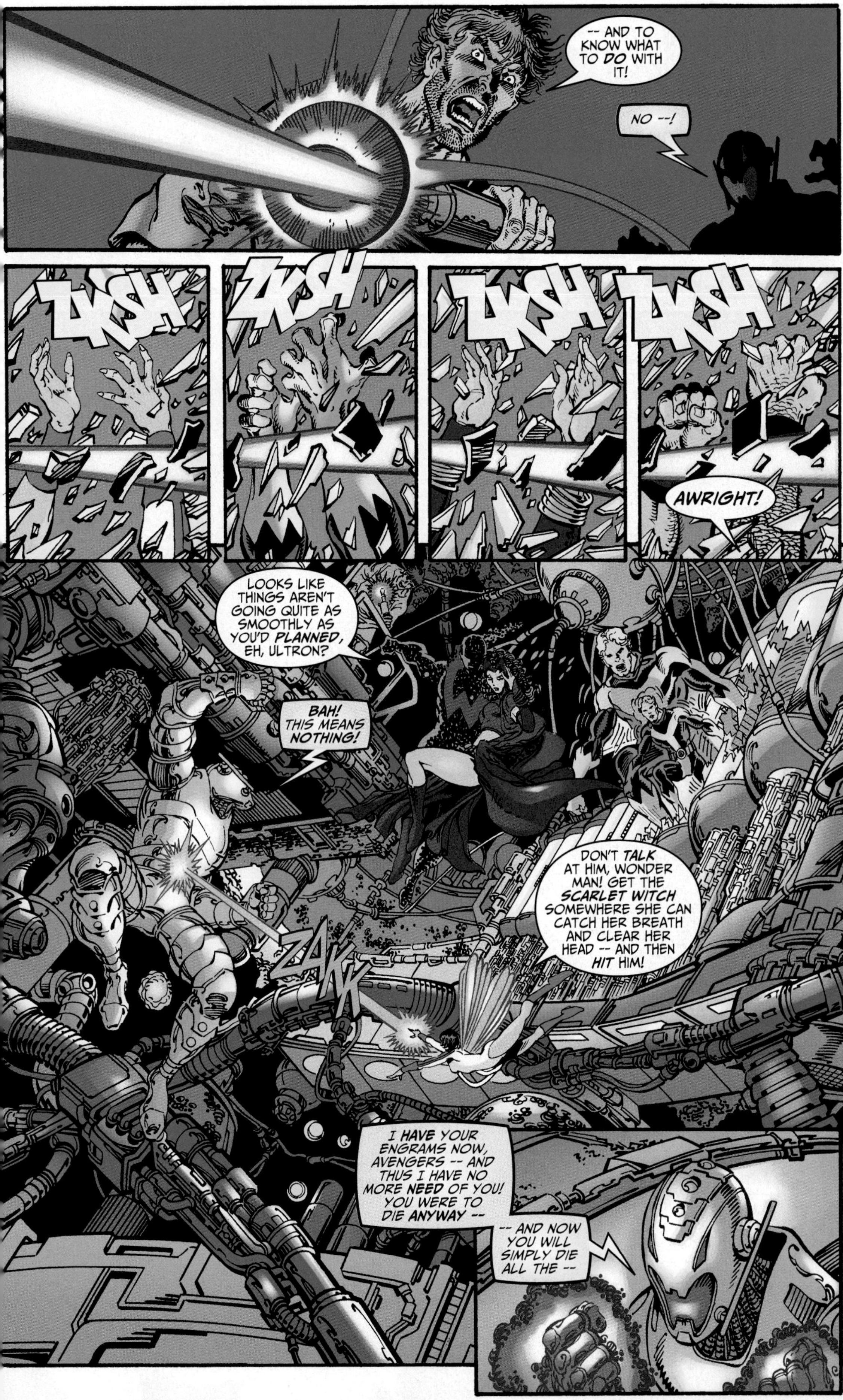
-- AND TO KNOW WHAT TO DO WITH IT!
NO --!
ZKSH
ZKSH
ZKSH
ZKSH
AWRIGHT!
LOOKS LIKE THINGS AREN'T GOING QUITE AS SMOOTHLY AS YOU'D PLANNED, EH, ULTRON?
BAH! THIS MEANS NOTHING!
DON'T TALK AT HIM, WONDER MAN! GET THE SCARLET WITCH SOMEWHERE SHE CAN CATCH HER BREATH AND CLEAR HER HEAD -- AND THEN HIT HIM!
ZAKK
I HAVE YOUR ENGRAMS NOW, AVENGERS -- AND THUS I HAVE NO MORE NEED OF YOU! YOU WERE TO DIE ANYWAY --
-- AND NOW YOU WILL SIMPLY DIE ALL THE --

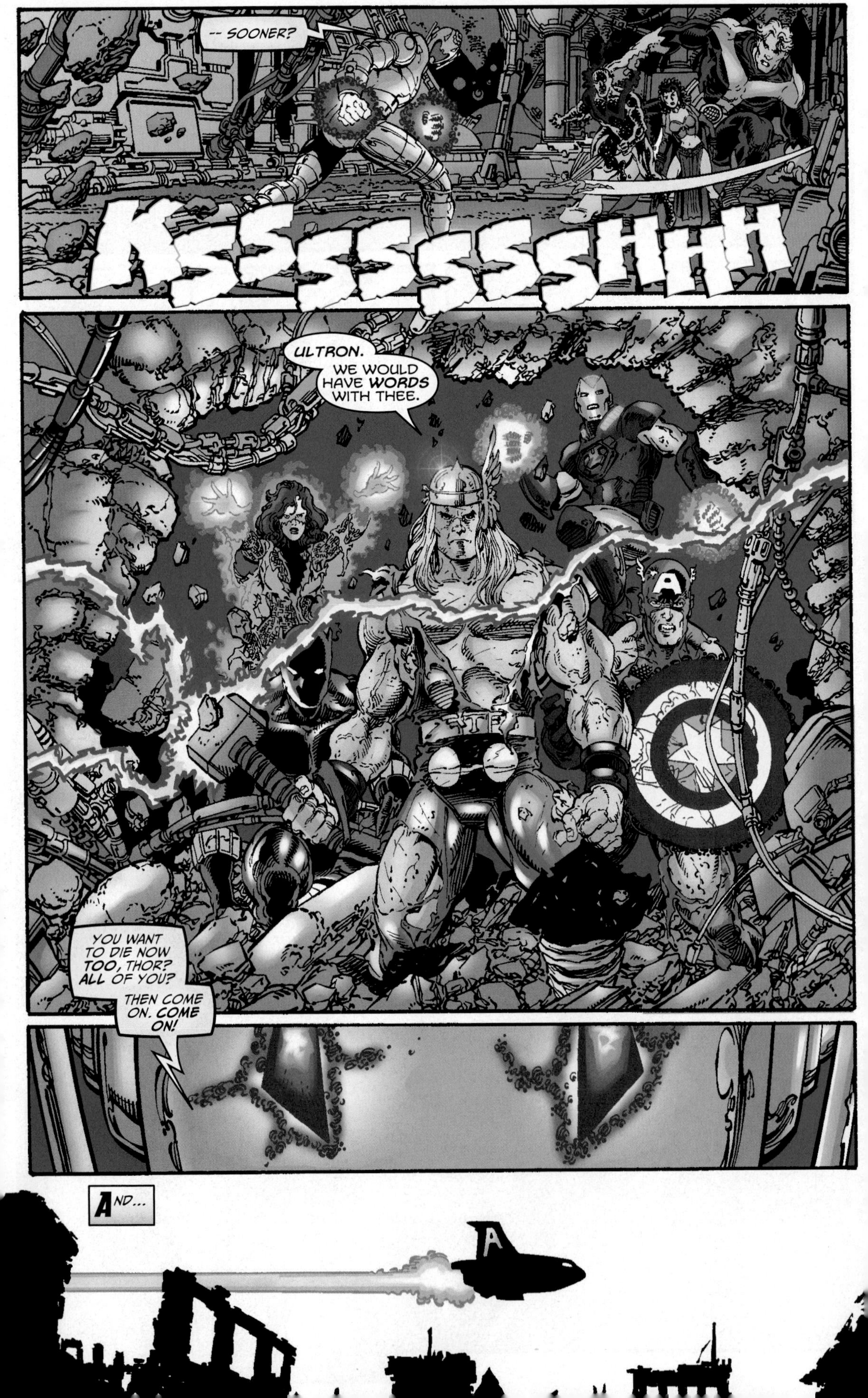
-- SOONER?
KSSSSSSHHH
ULTRON. WE WOULD HAVE WORDS WITH THEE.
YOU WANT TO DIE NOW TOO, THOR? ALL OF YOU?
THEN COME ON. COME ON!
AND...

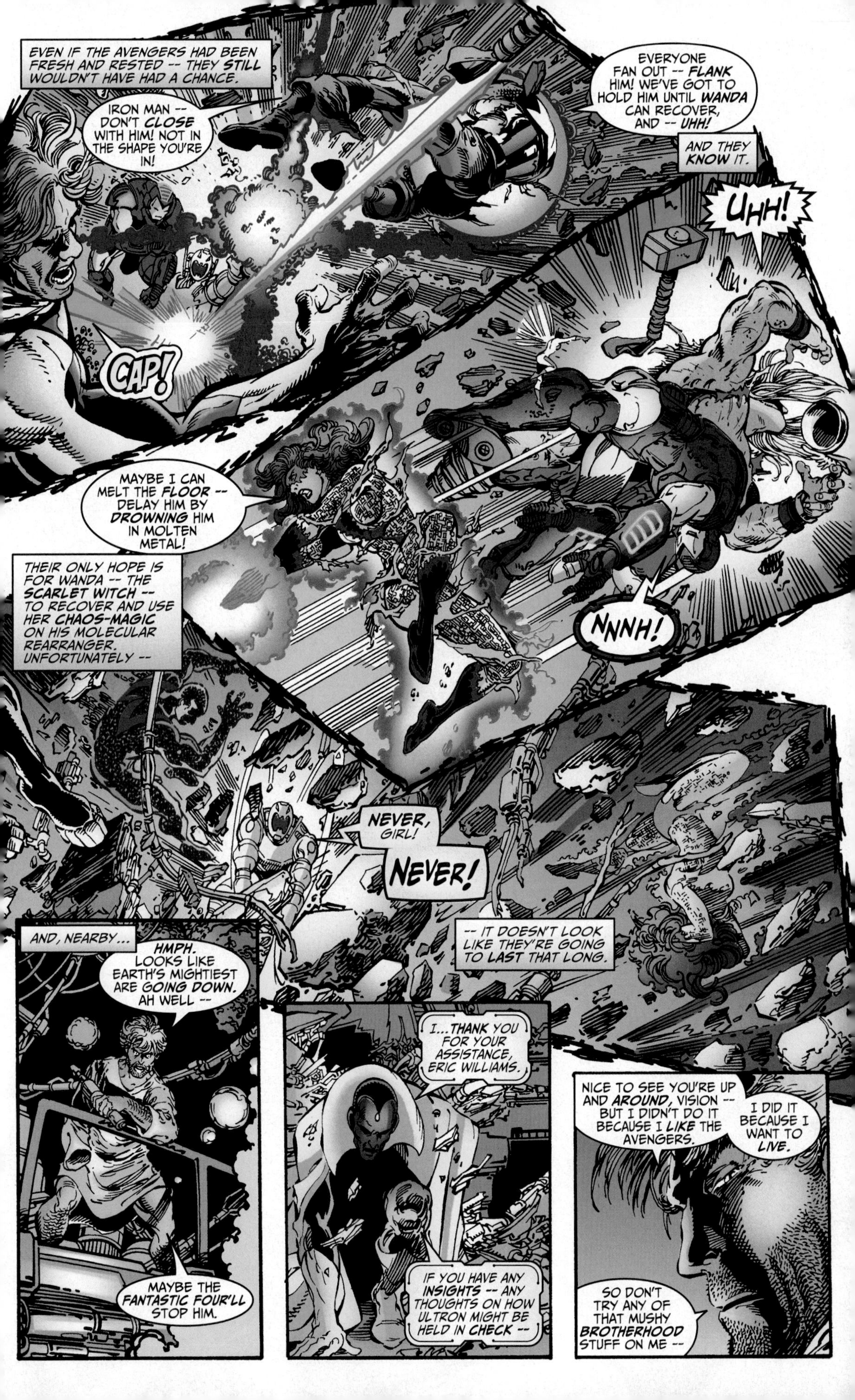
EVEN IF THE AVENGERS HAD BEEN FRESH AND RESTED -- THEY STILL WOULDN'T HAVE HAD A CHANCE.
IRON MAN -- DON'T CLOSE WITH HIM! NOT IN THE SHAPE YOU'RE IN!
CAP!
EVERYONE FAN OUT -- FLANK HIM! WE'VE GOT TO HOLD HIM UNTIL WANDA CAN RECOVER, AND -- UHH!
AND THEY KNOW IT.
UHH!
MAYBE I CAN MELT THE FLOOR -- DELAY HIM BY DROWNING HIM IN MOLTEN METAL!
THEIR ONLY HOPE IS FOR WANDA -- THE SCARLET WITCH -- TO RECOVER AND USE HER CHAOS-MAGIC ON HIS MOLECULAR REARRANGER. UNFORTUNATELY --
NNNH!
NEVER, GIRL!
NEVER!
-- IT DOESN'T LOOK LIKE THEY'RE GOING TO LAST THAT LONG.
AND, NEARBY...
HMPH. LOOKS LIKE EARTH'S MIGHTIEST ARE GOING DOWN. AH WELL --
MAYBE THE FANTASTIC FOUR'LL STOP HIM.
I...THANK YOU FOR YOUR ASSISTANCE, ERIC WILLIAMS.
IF YOU HAVE ANY INSIGHTS -- ANY THOUGHTS ON HOW ULTRON MIGHT BE HELD IN CHECK --
NICE TO SEE YOU'RE UP AND AROUND, VISION -- BUT I DIDN'T DO IT BECAUSE I LIKE THE AVENGERS.
I DID IT BECAUSE I WANT TO LIVE.
SO DON'T TRY ANY OF THAT MUSHY BROTHERHOOD STUFF ON ME --

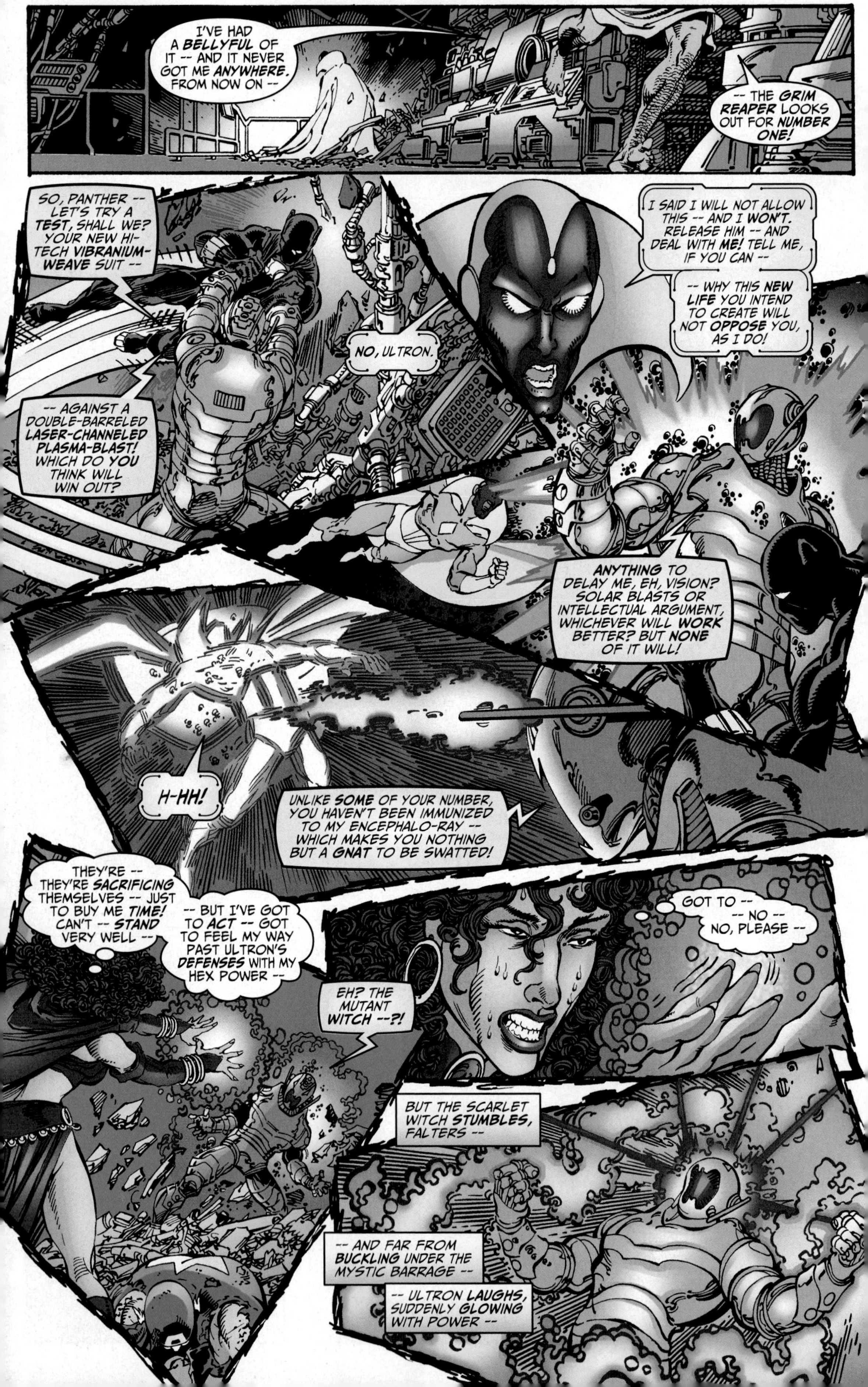
I'VE HAD A BELLYFUL OF IT -- AND IT NEVER GOT ME ANYWHERE. FROM NOW ON --
-- THE GRIM REAPER LOOKS OUT FOR NUMBER ONE!
SO, PANTHER -- LET'S TRY A TEST, SHALL WE? YOUR NEW HI-TECH VIBRANIUM-WEAVE SUIT --
-- AGAINST A DOUBLE-BARRELED LASER-CHANNELED PLASMA-BLAST! WHICH DO YOU THINK WILL WIN OUT?
NO, ULTRON.
I SAID I WILL NOT ALLOW THIS -- AND I WON'T. RELEASE HIM -- AND DEAL WITH ME! TELL ME, IF YOU CAN --
-- WHY THIS NEW LIFE YOU INTEND TO CREATE WILL NOT OPPOSE YOU, AS I DO!
ANYTHING TO DELAY ME, EH, VISION? SOLAR BLASTS OR INTELLECTUAL ARGUMENT, WHICHEVER WILL WORK BETTER? BUT NONE OF IT WILL!
H-HH!
UNLIKE SOME OF YOUR NUMBER, YOU HAVEN'T BEEN IMMUNIZED TO MY ENCEPHALO-RAY -- WHICH MAKES YOU NOTHING BUT A GNAT TO BE SWATTED!
THEY'RE -- THEY'RE SACRIFICING THEMSELVES -- JUST TO BUY ME TIME! CAN'T -- STAND VERY WELL --
-- BUT I'VE GOT TO ACT -- GOT TO FEEL MY WAY PAST ULTRON'S DEFENSES WITH MY HEX POWER --
GOT TO -- -- NO -- NO, PLEASE --
EH? THE MUTANT WITCH --?!
BUT THE SCARLET WITCH STUMBLES, FALTERS --
-- AND FAR FROM BUCKLING UNDER THE MYSTIC BARRAGE --
-- ULTRON LAUGHS, SUDDENLY GLOWING WITH POWER --

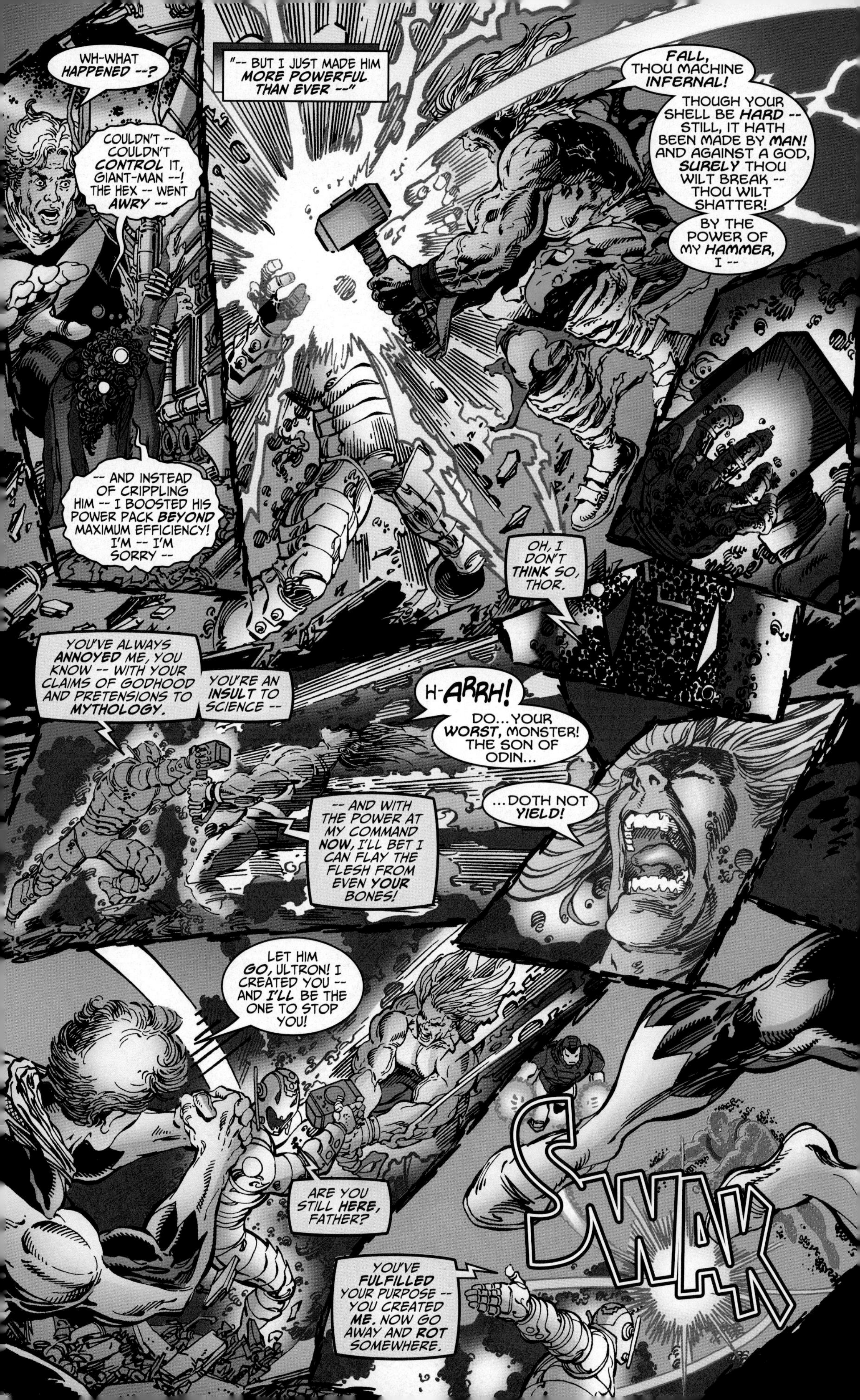
WH-WHAT HAPPENED --?
"-- BUT I JUST MADE HIM MORE POWERFUL THAN EVER --"
COULDN'T -- COULDN'T CONTROL IT, GIANT-MAN --! THE HEX -- WENT AWRY --
FALL, THOU MACHINE INFERNAL!
THOUGH YOUR SHELL BE HARD -- STILL, IT HATH BEEN MADE BY MAN! AND AGAINST A GOD, SURELY THOU WILT BREAK -- THOU WILT SHATTER!
BY THE POWER OF MY HAMMER, I --
-- AND INSTEAD OF CRIPPLING HIM -- I BOOSTED HIS POWER PACK BEYOND MAXIMUM EFFICIENCY! I'M -- I'M SORRY --
OH, I DON'T THINK SO, THOR.
YOU'VE ALWAYS ANNOYED ME, YOU KNOW -- WITH YOUR CLAIMS OF GODHOOD AND PRETENSIONS TO MYTHOLOGY.
YOU'RE AN INSULT TO SCIENCE --
H-ARRH!
DO...YOUR WORST, MONSTER! THE SON OF ODIN...
-- AND WITH THE POWER AT MY COMMAND NOW, I'LL BET I CAN FLAY THE FLESH FROM EVEN YOUR BONES!
...DOTH NOT YIELD!
LET HIM GO, ULTRON! I CREATED YOU -- AND I'LL BE THE ONE TO STOP YOU!
ARE YOU STILL HERE, FATHER?
SWAK
YOU'VE FULFILLED YOUR PURPOSE -- YOU CREATED ME. NOW GO AWAY AND ROT SOMEWHERE.

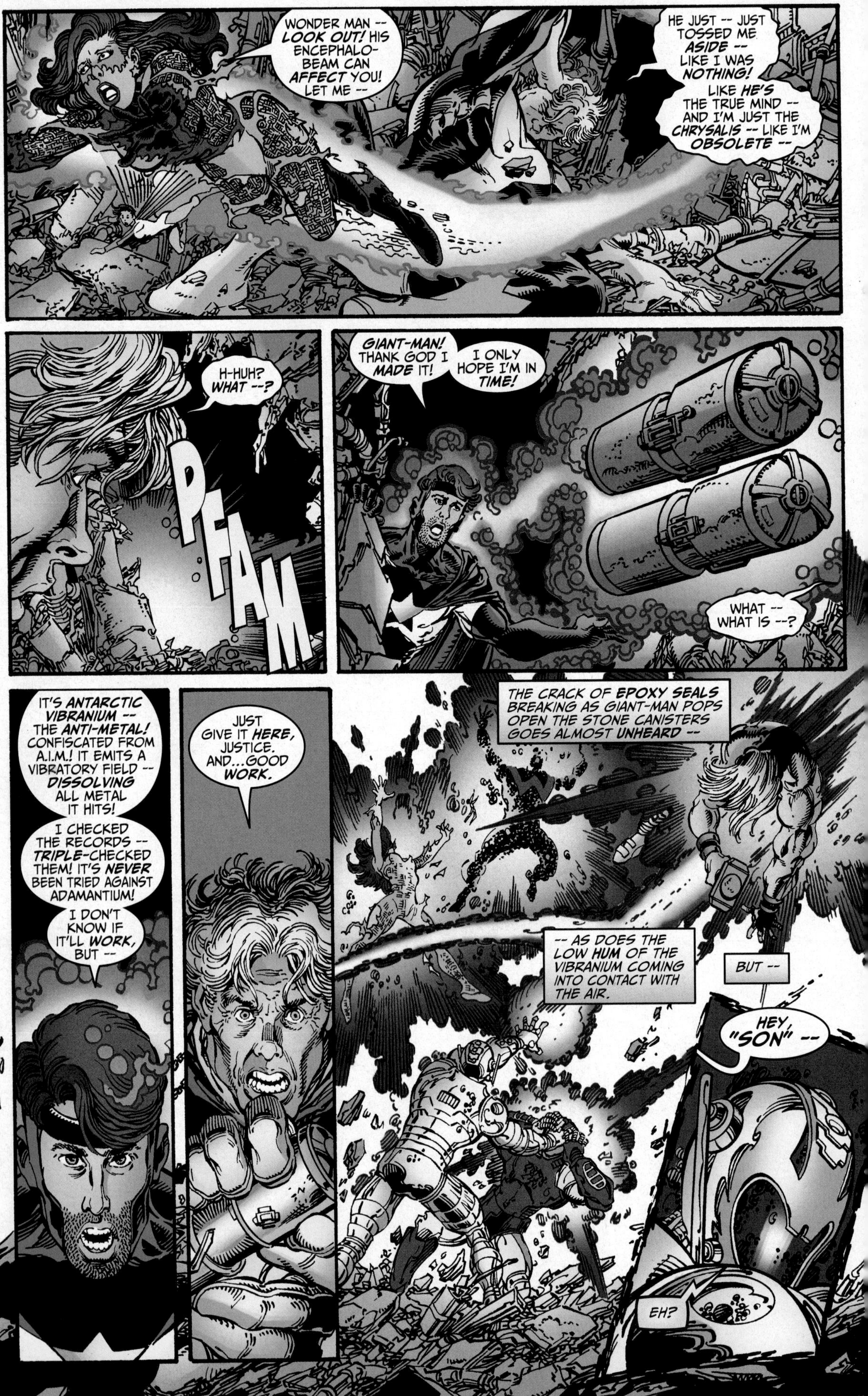
WONDER MAN -- LOOK OUT! HIS ENCEPHALO-BEAM CAN AFFECT YOU! LET ME --
HE JUST -- JUST TOSSED ME ASIDE -- LIKE I WAS NOTHING!
LIKE HE'S THE TRUE MIND -- AND I'M JUST THE CHRYSALIS -- LIKE I'M OBSOLETE --
H-HUH? WHAT --?
PFAM
GIANT-MAN! THANK GOD I MADE IT!
I ONLY HOPE I'M IN TIME!
WHAT -- WHAT IS --?
IT'S ANTARCTIC VIBRANIUM -- THE ANTI-METAL! CONFISCATED FROM A.I.M.! IT EMITS A VIBRATORY FIELD -- DISSOLVING ALL METAL IT HITS!
I CHECKED THE RECORDS -- TRIPLE-CHECKED THEM! IT'S NEVER BEEN TRIED AGAINST ADAMANTIUM!
I DON'T KNOW IF IT'LL WORK, BUT --
JUST GIVE IT HERE, JUSTICE. AND...GOOD WORK.
THE CRACK OF EPOXY SEALS BREAKING AS GIANT-MAN POPS OPEN THE STONE CANISTERS GOES ALMOST UNHEARD --
-- AS DOES THE LOW HUM OF THE VIBRANIUM COMING INTO CONTACT WITH THE AIR.
BUT --
HEY, "SON" --
EH?

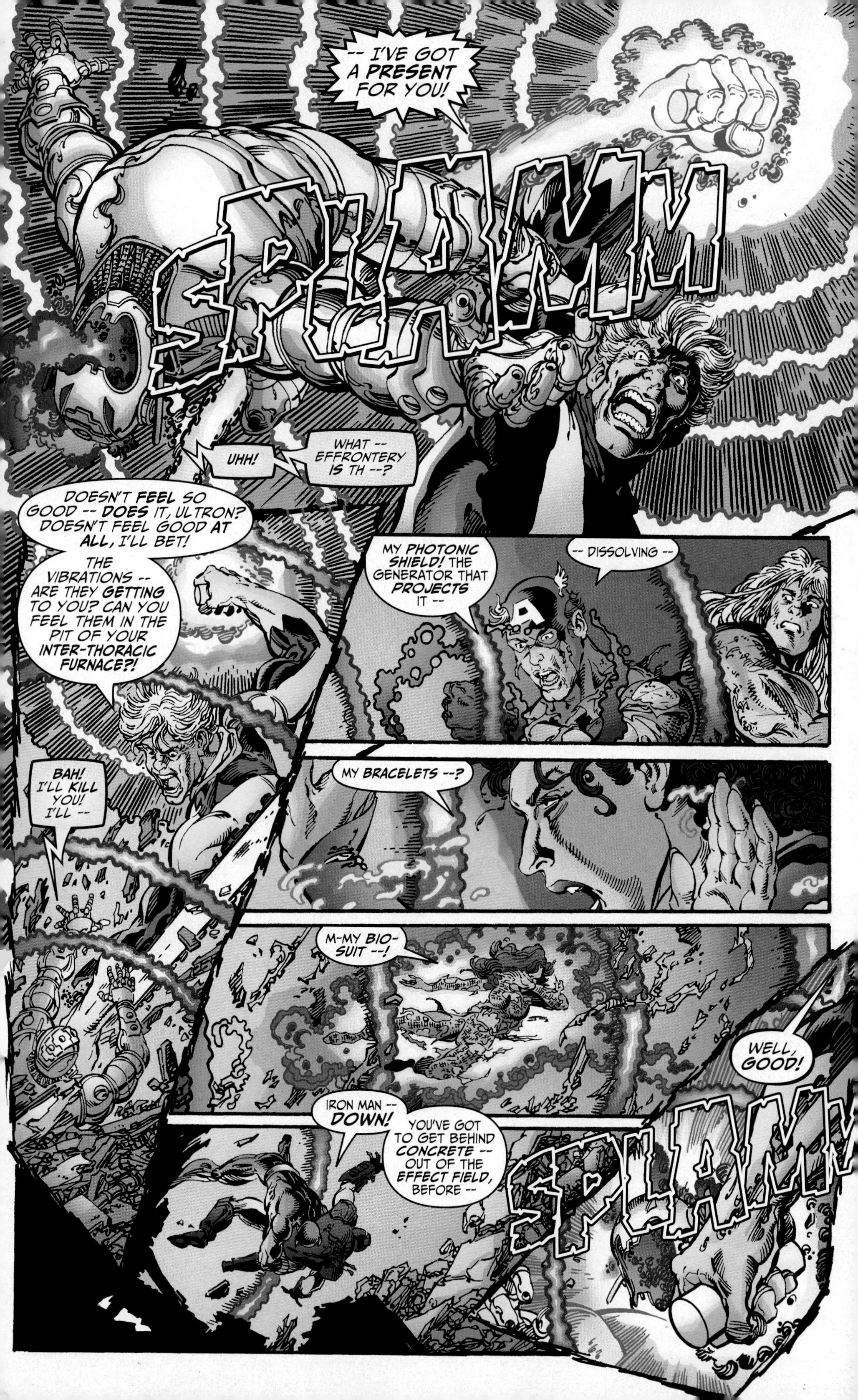
-- I'VE GOT A PRESENT FOR YOU!
SPLAMM
UHH!
WHAT -- EFFRONTERY IS TH --?
DOESN'T FEEL SO GOOD -- DOES IT, ULTRON? DOESN'T FEEL GOOD AT ALL, I'LL BET!
THE VIBRATIONS -- ARE THEY GETTING TO YOU? CAN YOU FEEL THEM IN THE PIT OF YOUR INTER-THORACIC FURNACE?!
BAH! I'LL KILL YOU! I'LL --
MY PHOTONIC SHIELD! THE GENERATOR THAT PROJECTS IT --
-- DISSOLVING --
MY BRACELETS --?
M-MY BIO-SUIT --!
WELL, GOOD!
IRON MAN -- DOWN!
YOU'VE GOT TO GET BEHIND CONCRETE -- OUT OF THE EFFECT FIELD, BEFORE --
SPLAM

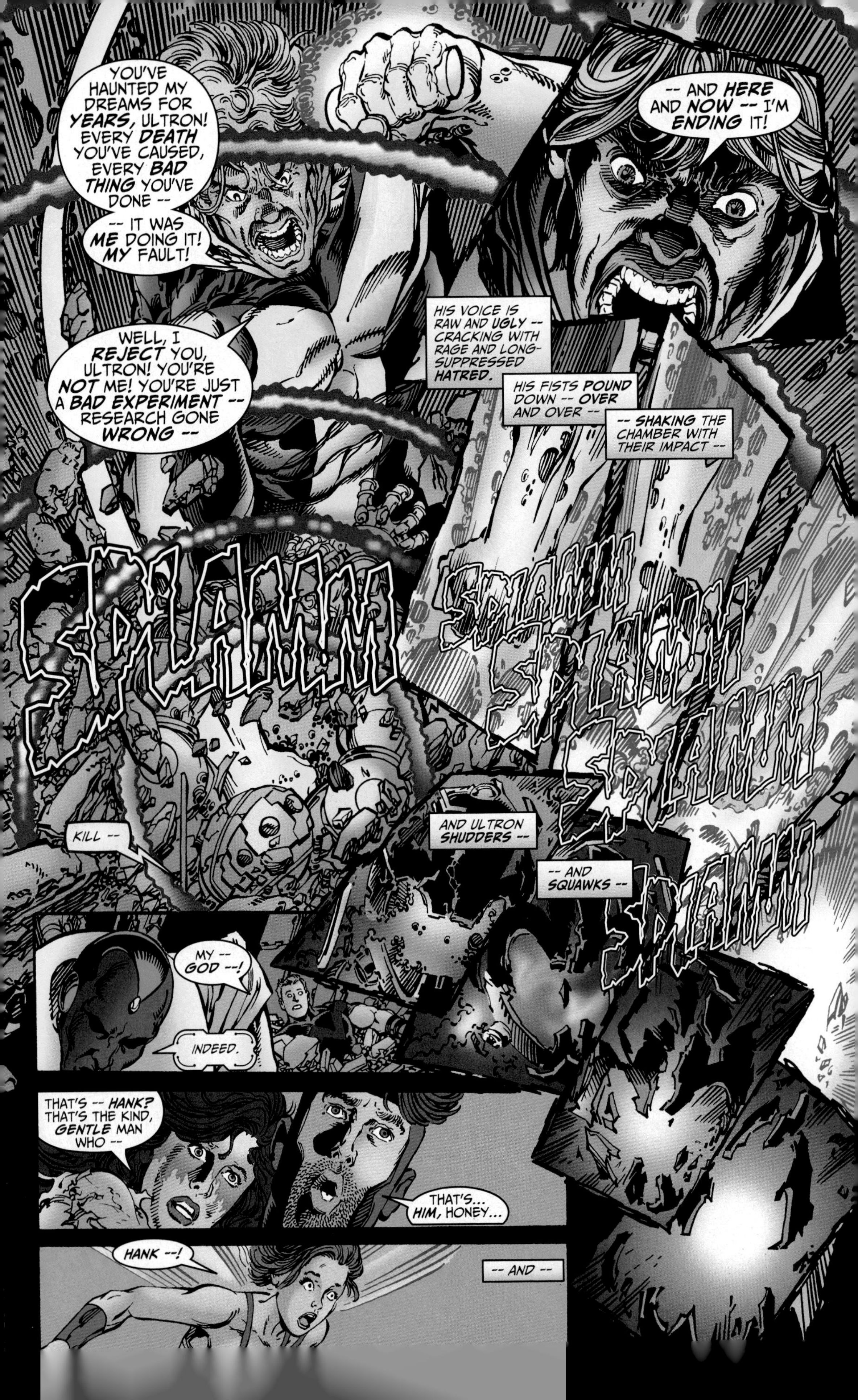
YOU'VE HAUNTED MY DREAMS FOR YEARS, ULTRON! EVERY DEATH YOU'VE CAUSED, EVERY BAD THING YOU'VE DONE --
-- IT WAS ME DOING IT! MY FAULT!
-- AND HERE AND NOW -- I'M ENDING IT!
WELL, I REJECT YOU, ULTRON! YOU'RE NOT ME! YOU'RE JUST A BAD EXPERIMENT -- RESEARCH GONE WRONG --
HIS VOICE IS RAW AND UGLY -- CRACKING WITH RAGE AND LONG-SUPPRESSED HATRED.
HIS FISTS POUND DOWN -- OVER AND OVER --
-- SHAKING THE CHAMBER WITH THEIR IMPACT --
KILL --
AND ULTRON SHUDDERS --
-- AND SQUAWKS --
MY -- GOD --!
INDEED.
THAT'S -- HANK? THAT'S THE KIND, GENTLE MAN WHO --
THAT'S... HIM, HONEY...
HANK --!
-- AND --

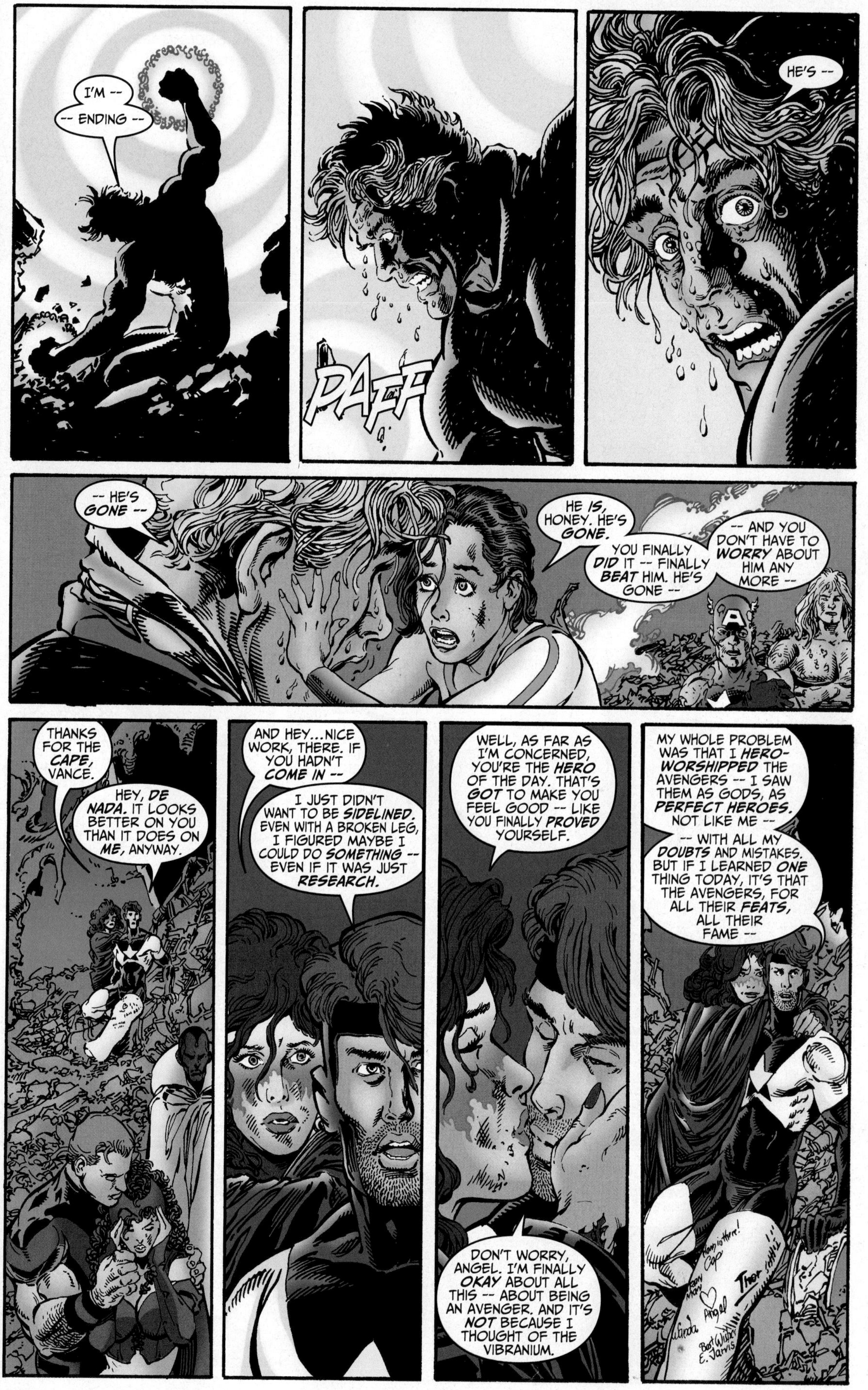
I'M --
-- ENDING --
PAFF
HE'S --
-- HE'S GONE --
HE IS, HONEY. HE'S GONE.
YOU FINALLY DID IT -- FINALLY BEAT HIM. HE'S GONE --
-- AND YOU DON'T HAVE TO WORRY ABOUT HIM ANY MORE --
THANKS FOR THE CAPE, VANCE.
HEY, DE NADA. IT LOOKS BETTER ON YOU THAN IT DOES ON ME, ANYWAY.
AND HEY...NICE WORK, THERE. IF YOU HADN'T COME IN --
I JUST DIDN'T WANT TO BE SIDELINED. EVEN WITH A BROKEN LEG, I FIGURED MAYBE I COULD DO SOMETHING -- EVEN IF IT WAS JUST RESEARCH.
WELL, AS FAR AS I'M CONCERNED, YOU'RE THE HERO OF THE DAY. THAT'S GOT TO MAKE YOU FEEL GOOD -- LIKE YOU FINALLY PROVED YOURSELF.
DON'T WORRY, ANGEL. I'M FINALLY OKAY ABOUT ALL THIS -- ABOUT BEING AN AVENGER. AND IT'S NOT BECAUSE I THOUGHT OF THE VIBRANIUM.
MY WHOLE PROBLEM WAS THAT I HERO-WORSHIPPED THE AVENGERS -- I SAW THEM AS GODS, AS PERFECT HEROES. NOT LIKE ME --
-- WITH ALL MY DOUBTS AND MISTAKES. BUT IF I LEARNED ONE THING TODAY, IT'S THAT THE AVENGERS, FOR ALL THEIR FEATS, ALL THEIR FAME --
Hang in there! Cap
Iron Man
Angel
Thor
Wanda
Best Wishes E. Jarvis

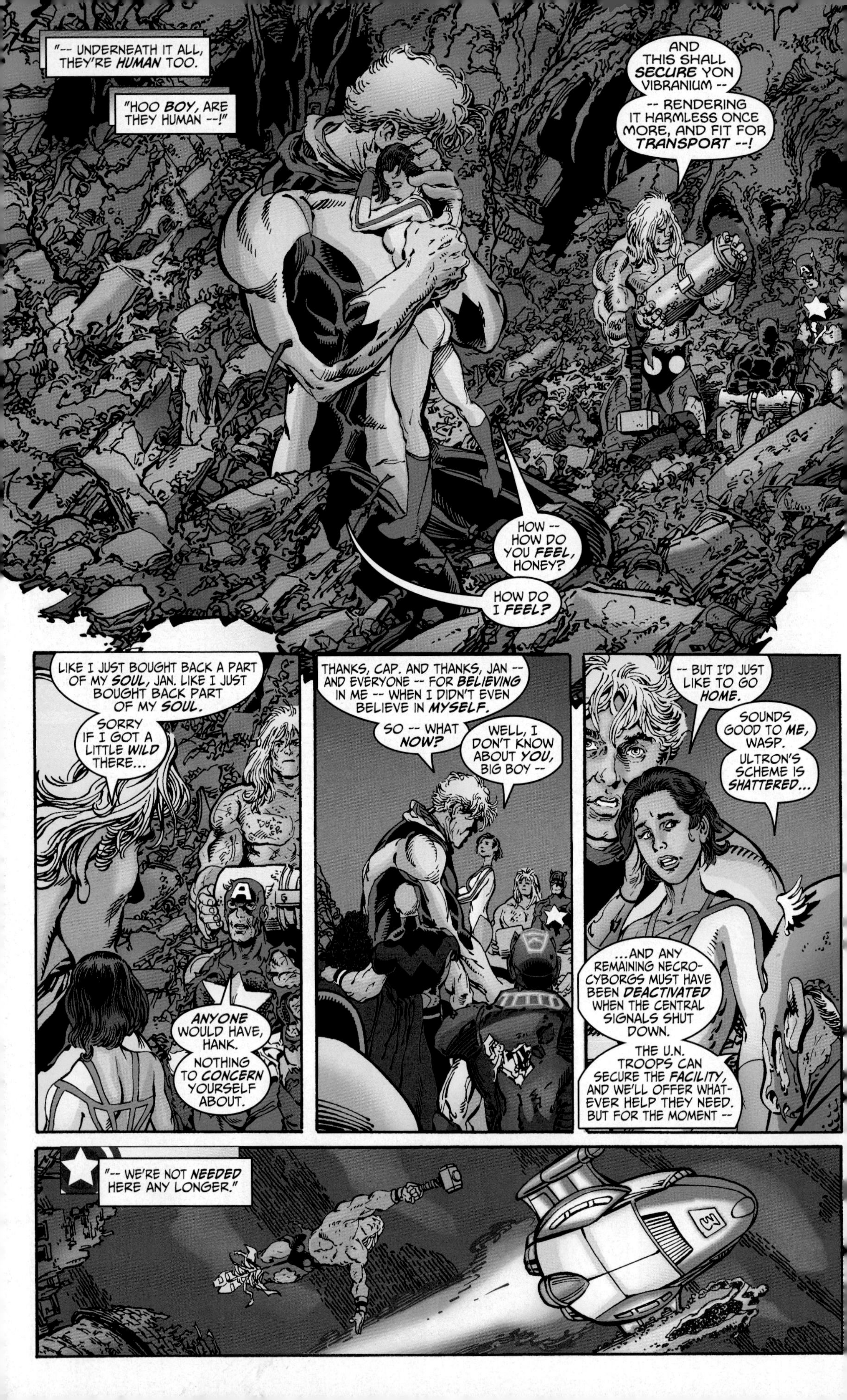
"-- UNDERNEATH IT ALL, THEY'RE *HUMAN* TOO.
"HOO *BOY*, ARE THEY HUMAN --!"
AND THIS SHALL *SECURE* YON VIBRANIUM --
-- RENDERING IT HARMLESS ONCE MORE, AND FIT FOR *TRANSPORT* --!
HOW -- HOW DO YOU *FEEL*, HONEY?
HOW DO I *FEEL?*
LIKE I JUST BOUGHT BACK A PART OF MY *SOUL*, JAN. LIKE I JUST BOUGHT BACK PART OF MY *SOUL*.
SORRY IF I GOT A LITTLE *WILD* THERE...
ANYONE WOULD HAVE, HANK.
NOTHING TO *CONCERN* YOURSELF ABOUT.
THANKS, CAP. AND THANKS, JAN -- AND EVERYONE -- FOR *BELIEVING* IN ME -- WHEN I DIDN'T EVEN BELIEVE IN *MYSELF*.
SO -- WHAT *NOW?*
WELL, I DON'T KNOW ABOUT *YOU*, BIG BOY --
-- BUT I'D JUST LIKE TO GO *HOME*.
SOUNDS GOOD TO *ME*, WASP.
ULTRON'S SCHEME IS *SHATTERED*...
...AND ANY REMAINING NECRO-CYBORGS MUST HAVE BEEN *DEACTIVATED* WHEN THE CENTRAL SIGNALS SHUT DOWN.
THE U.N. TROOPS CAN SECURE THE *FACILITY*, AND WE'LL OFFER WHAT-EVER HELP THEY NEED. BUT FOR THE MOMENT --
"-- WE'RE NOT *NEEDED* HERE ANY LONGER."

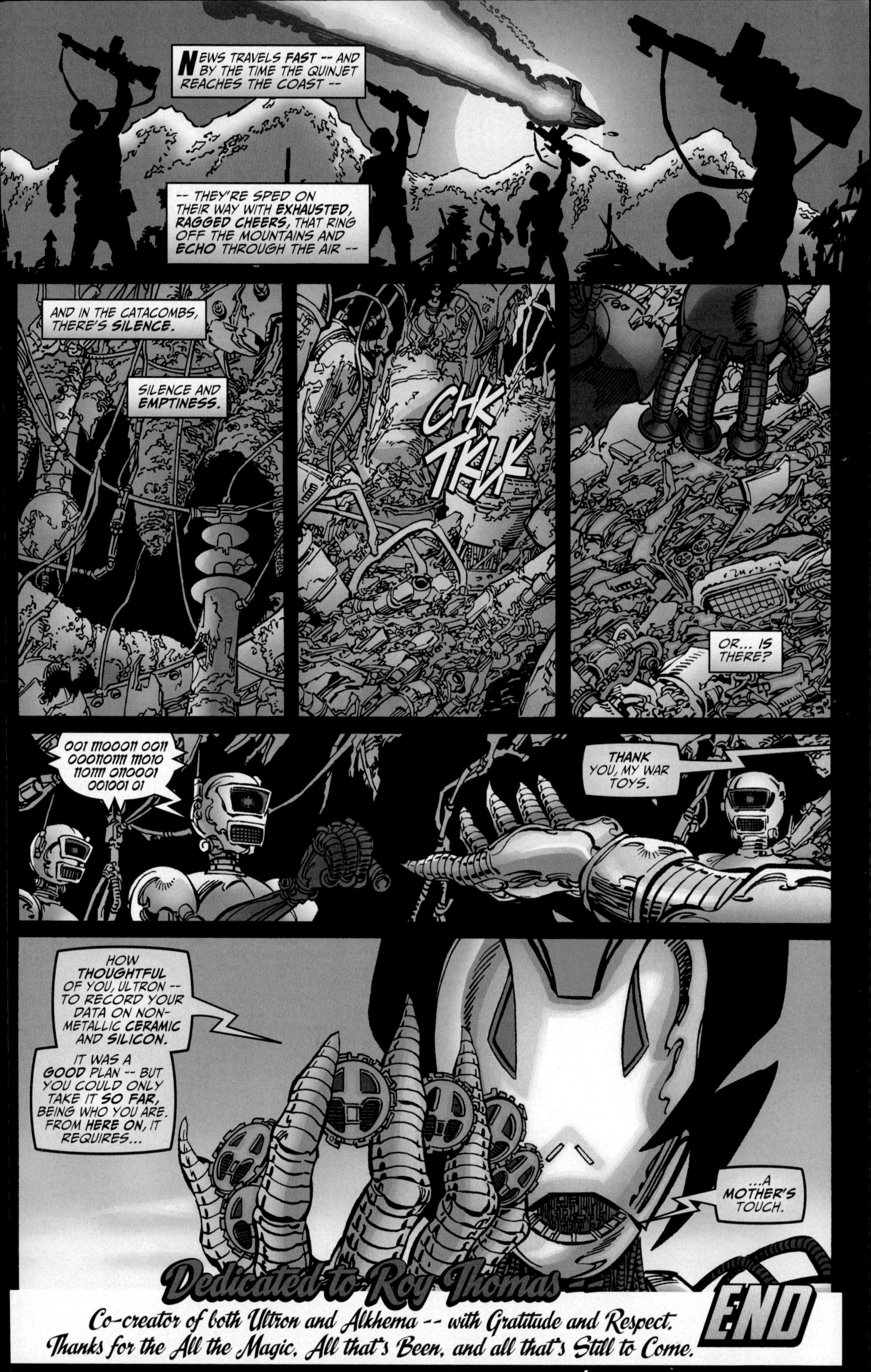
NEWS TRAVELS FAST -- AND BY THE TIME THE QUINJET REACHES THE COAST --
-- THEY'RE SPED ON THEIR WAY WITH EXHAUSTED, RAGGED CHEERS, THAT RING OFF THE MOUNTAINS AND ECHO THROUGH THE AIR --
AND IN THE CATACOMBS, THERE'S SILENCE.
SILENCE AND EMPTINESS.
CHK TKLK
OR... IS THERE?
001 M0001 0011 000101M M010 1011 010001 001001 01
THANK YOU, MY WAR TOYS.
HOW THOUGHTFUL OF YOU, ULTRON -- TO RECORD YOUR DATA ON NON-METALLIC CERAMIC AND SILICON.
IT WAS A GOOD PLAN -- BUT YOU COULD ONLY TAKE IT SO FAR, BEING WHO YOU ARE. FROM HERE ON, IT REQUIRES...
...A MOTHER'S TOUCH.
Dedicated to Roy Thomas
Co-creator of both Ultron and Alkhema -- with Gratitude and Respect.
Thanks for the All the Magic, All that's Been, and all that's Still to Come.
END

CONTINUED IN AVENGERS BY KURT BUSIEK & GEORGE PÉREZ OMNIBUS VOL. 1 HC

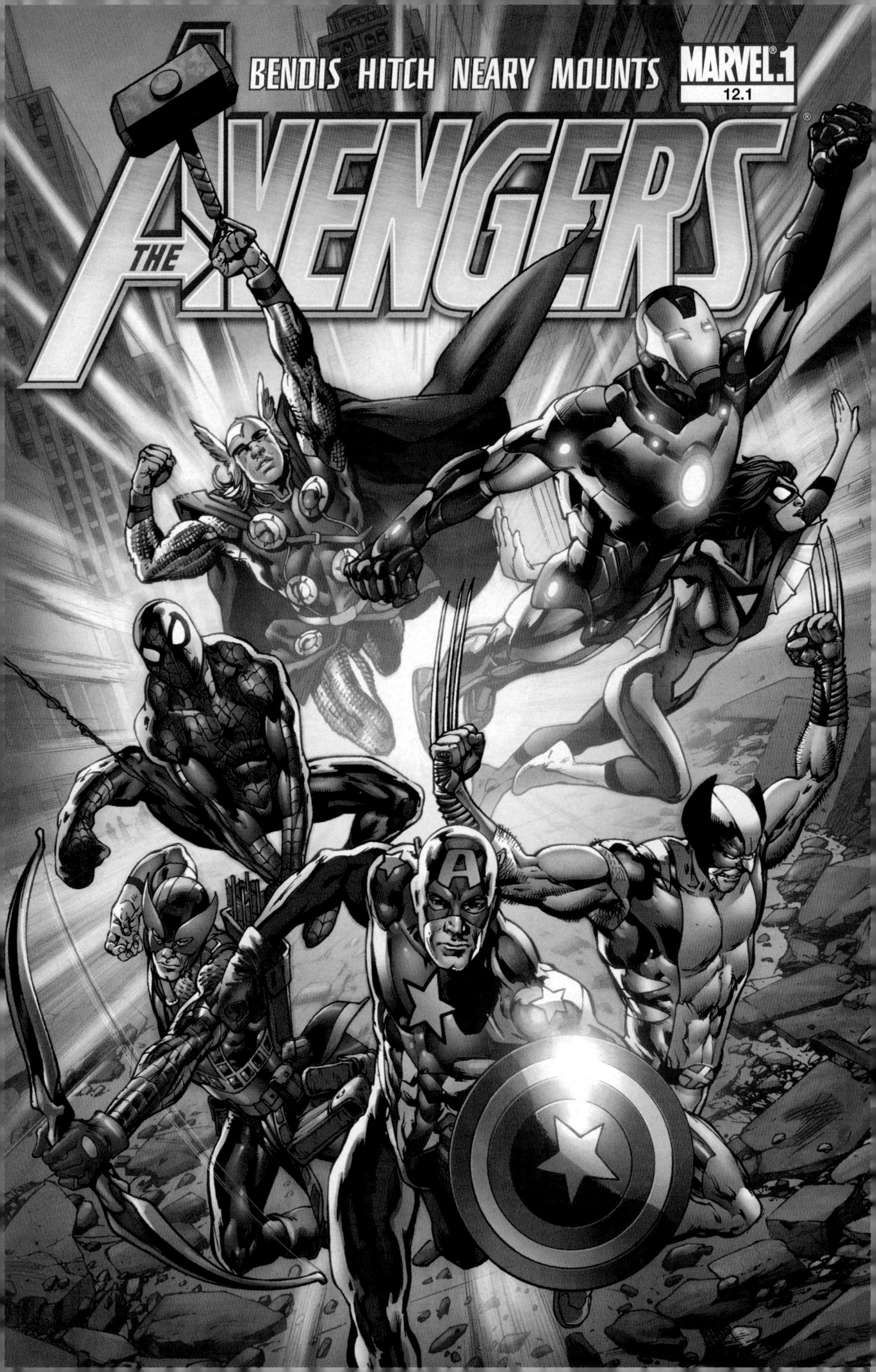
BENDIS HITCH NEARY MOUNTS
MARVEL.1
12.1
THE AVENGERS

EARTH'S MIGHTIEST HEROES, UNITED AGAINST A COMMON THREAT! ON THAT DAY THE AVENGERS WERE BORN, TO FIGHT FOES THAT NO SINGLE HERO COULD WITHSTAND!

THE AVENGERS

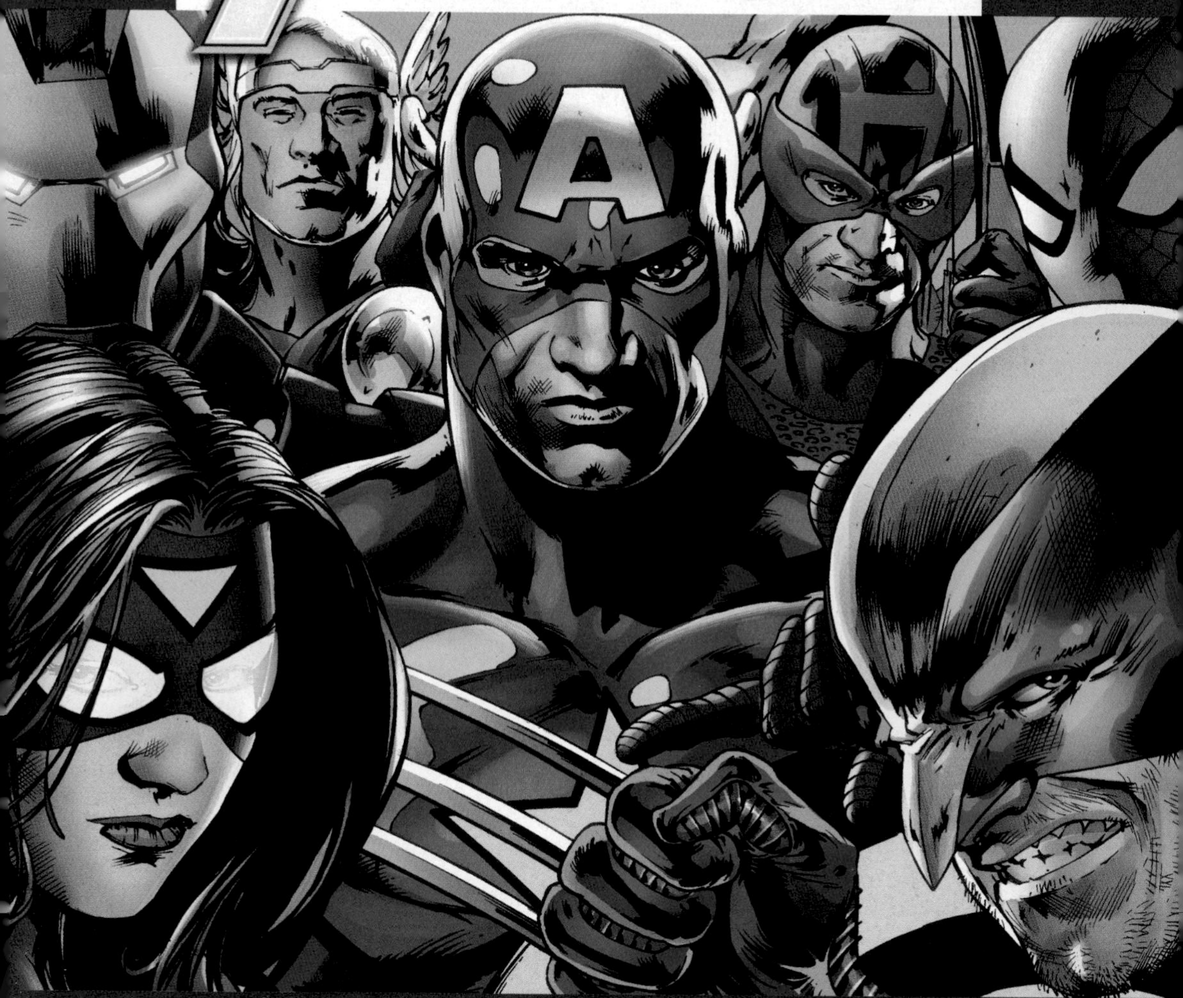

THE AVENGERS! WOLVERINE, IRON MAN, SPIDER-MAN, THOR, SPIDER-WOMAN, CAPTAIN AMERICA AND HAWKEYE ARE HANDPICKED BY STEVE ROGERS TO LEAD THE PREMIER AVENGERS TEAM!

BRIAN MICHAEL BENDIS WRITER
BRYAN HITCH PENCILER
PAUL NEARY INKER
PAUL MOUNTS COLORIST
VC'S CORY PETIT LETTERS

LAUREN SANKOVITCH ASSOCIATE EDITOR
TOM BREVOORT EDITOR
AXEL ALONSO EDITOR IN CHIEF
JOE QUESADA CHIEF CREATIVE OFFICER
DAN BUCKLEY PUBLISHER
ALAN FINE EXEC. PRODUCER

HITCH, NEARY & MOUNTS COVER ART

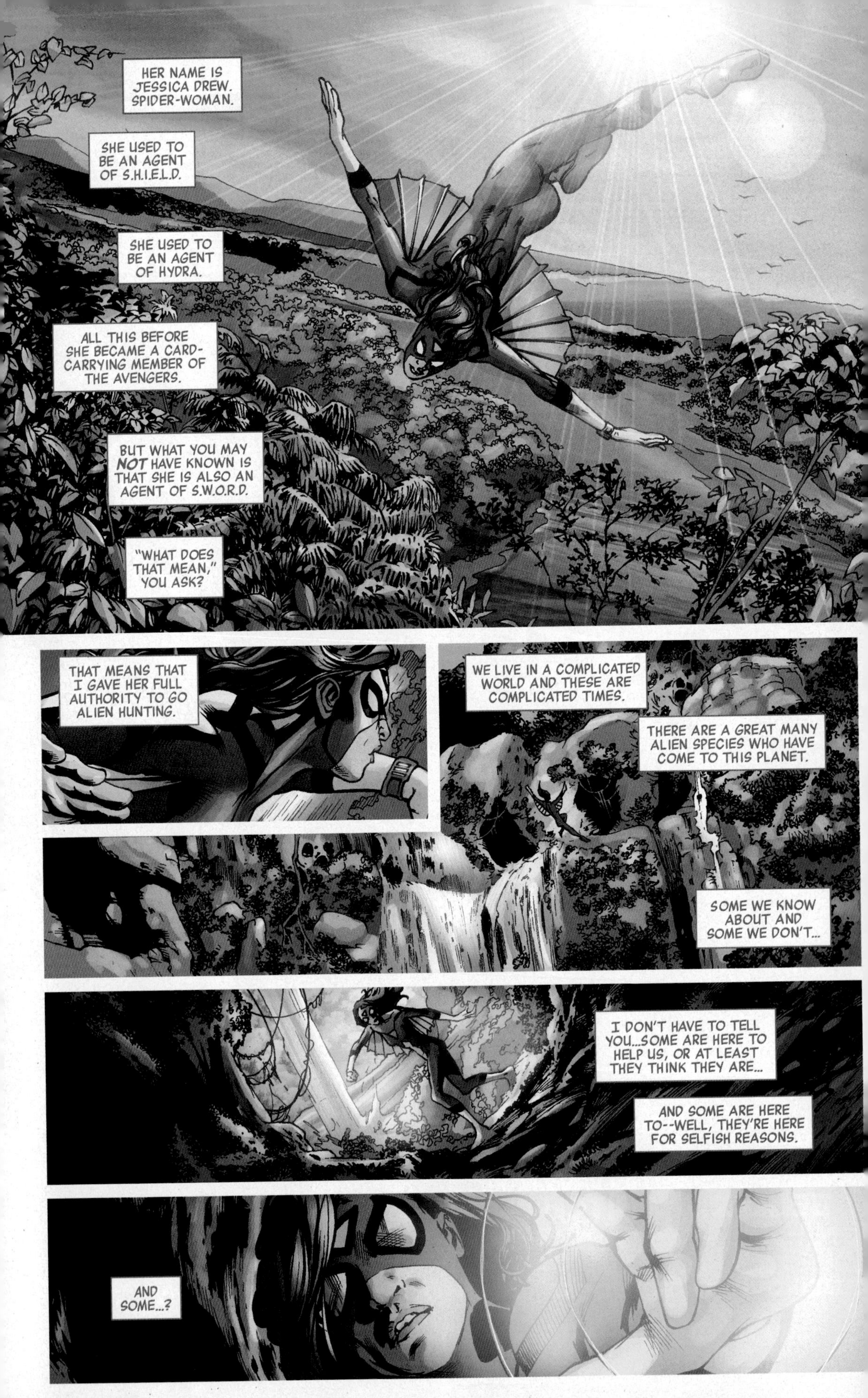
HER NAME IS JESSICA DREW. SPIDER-WOMAN.
SHE USED TO BE AN AGENT OF S.H.I.E.L.D.
SHE USED TO BE AN AGENT OF HYDRA.
ALL THIS BEFORE SHE BECAME A CARD-CARRYING MEMBER OF THE AVENGERS.
BUT WHAT YOU MAY **NOT** HAVE KNOWN IS THAT SHE IS ALSO AN AGENT OF S.W.O.R.D.
"WHAT DOES THAT MEAN," YOU ASK?
THAT MEANS THAT I GAVE HER FULL AUTHORITY TO GO ALIEN HUNTING.
WE LIVE IN A COMPLICATED WORLD AND THESE ARE COMPLICATED TIMES.
THERE ARE A GREAT MANY ALIEN SPECIES WHO HAVE COME TO THIS PLANET.
SOME WE KNOW ABOUT AND SOME WE DON'T...
I DON'T HAVE TO TELL YOU...SOME ARE HERE TO HELP US, OR AT LEAST THEY THINK THEY ARE...
AND SOME ARE HERE TO--WELL, THEY'RE HERE FOR SELFISH REASONS.
AND SOME...?

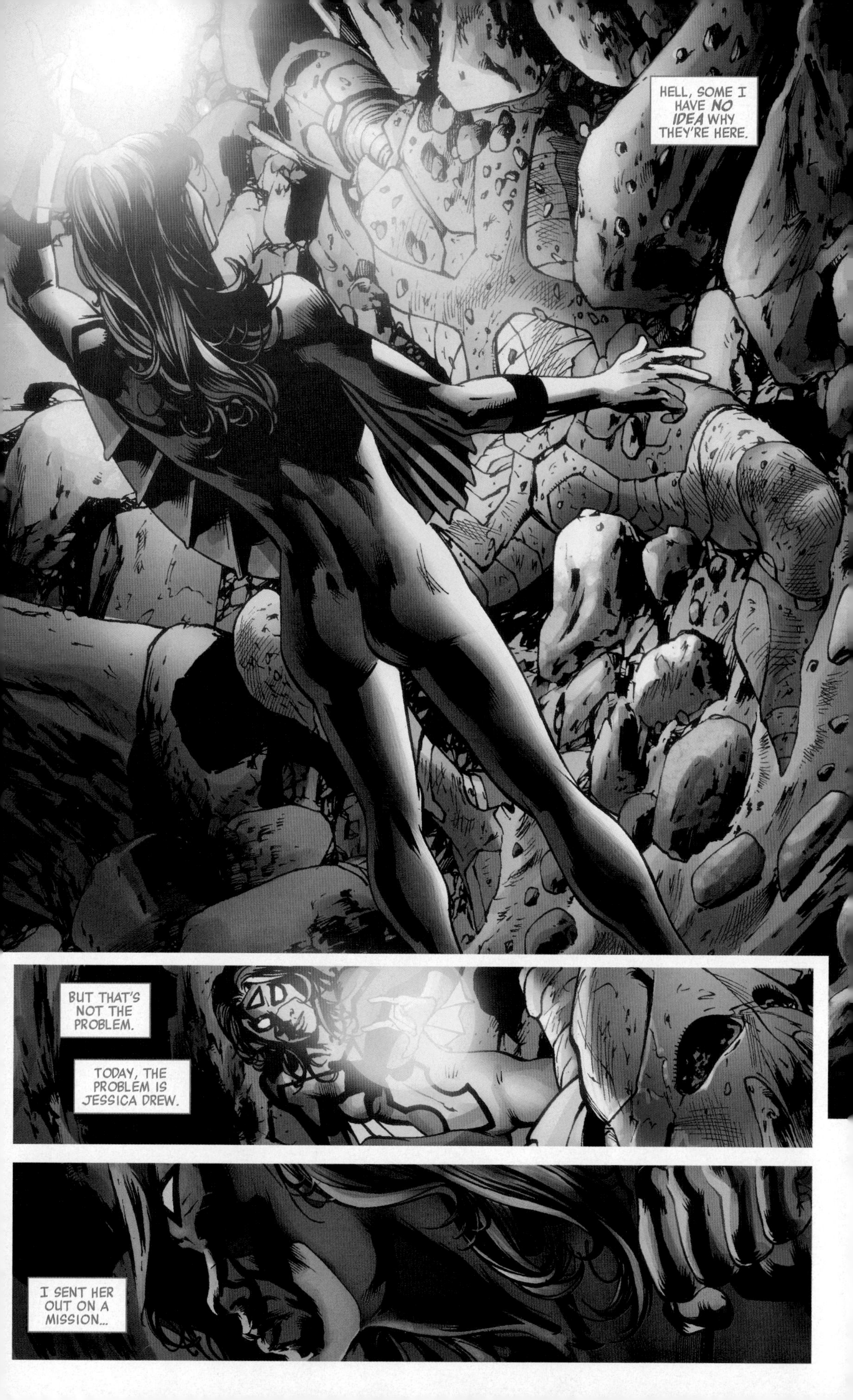
HELL, SOME I HAVE NO IDEA WHY THEY'RE HERE.
BUT THAT'S NOT THE PROBLEM.
TODAY, THE PROBLEM IS JESSICA DREW.
I SENT HER OUT ON A MISSION...

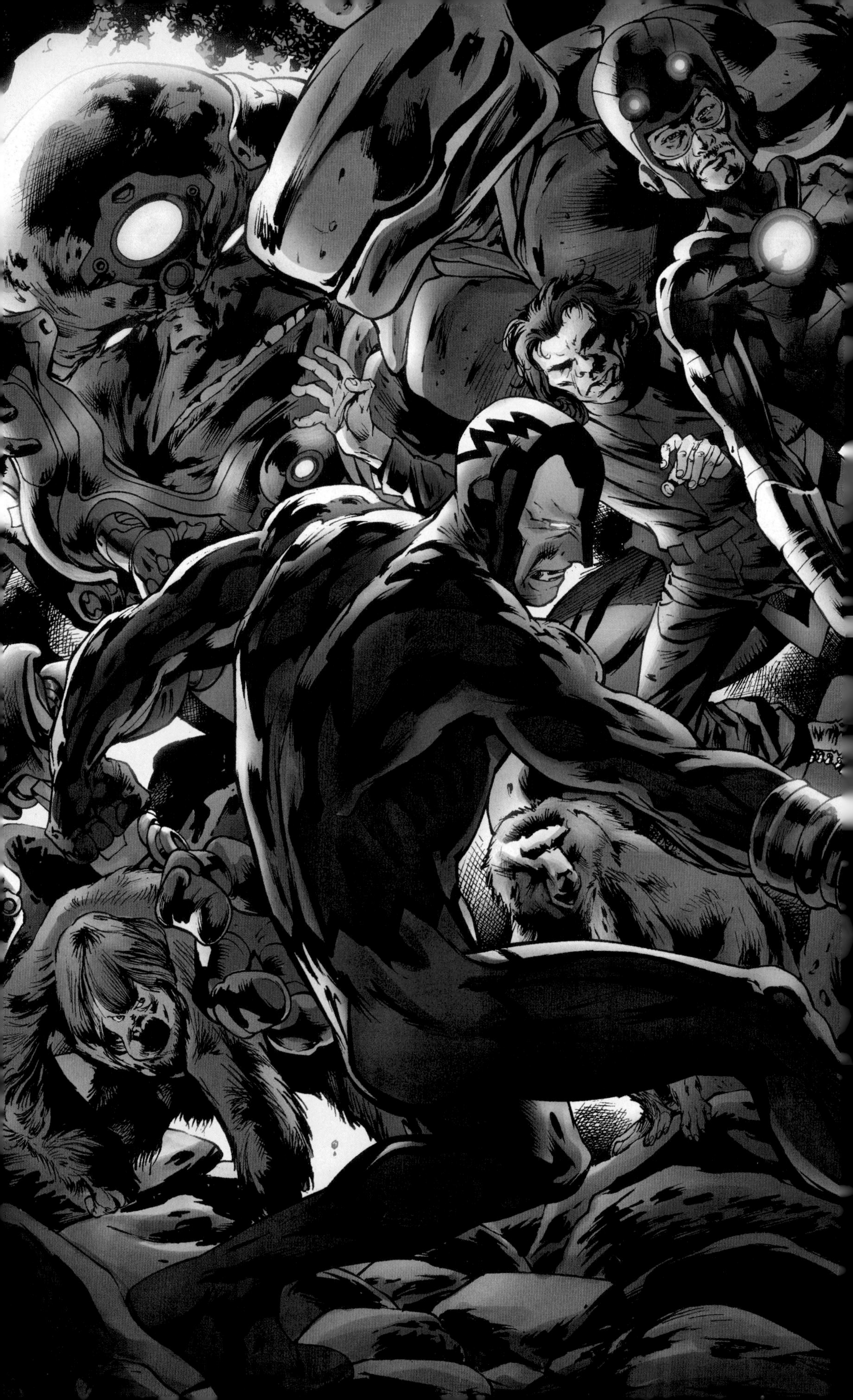

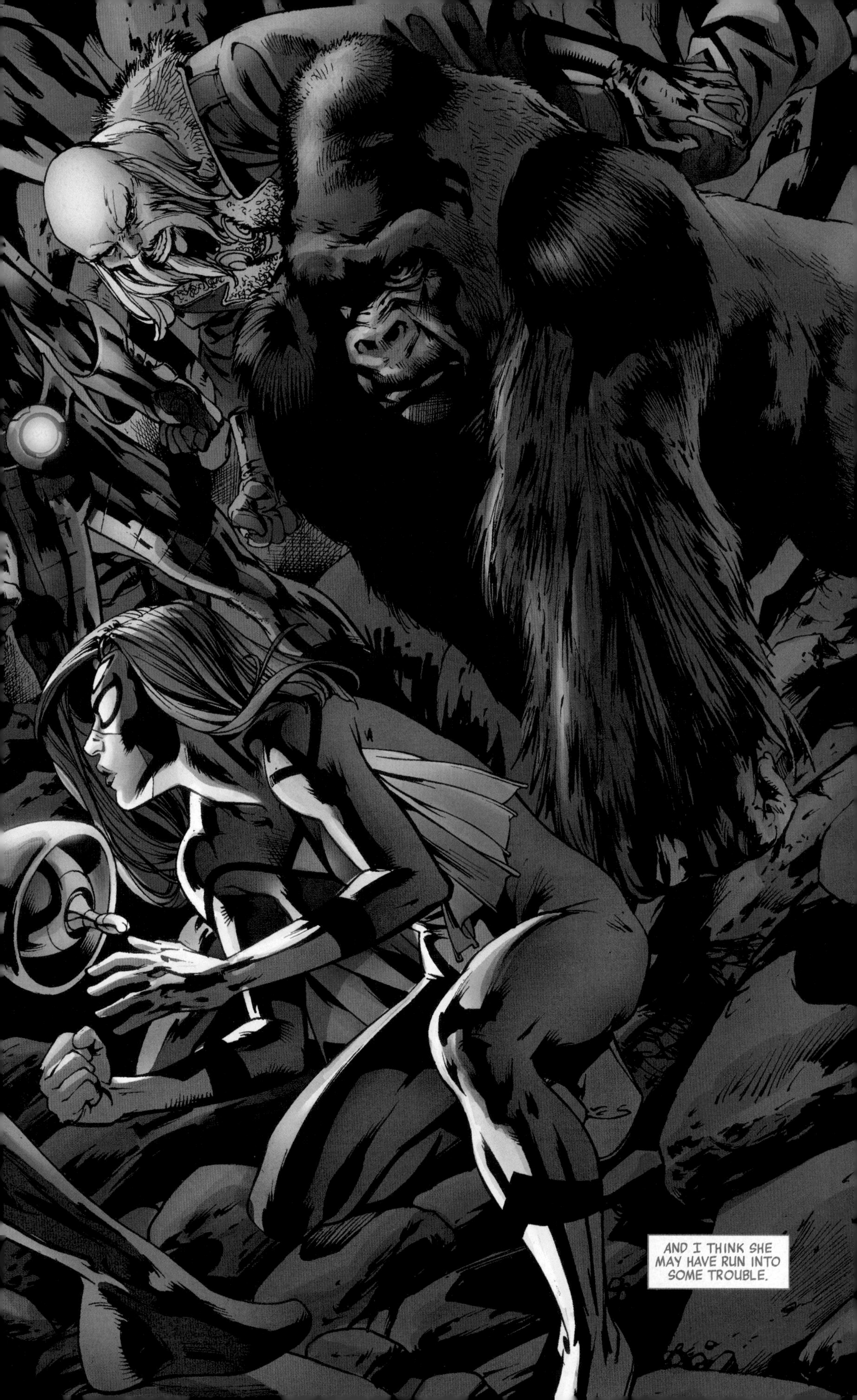
AND I THINK SHE MAY HAVE RUN INTO SOME TROUBLE.

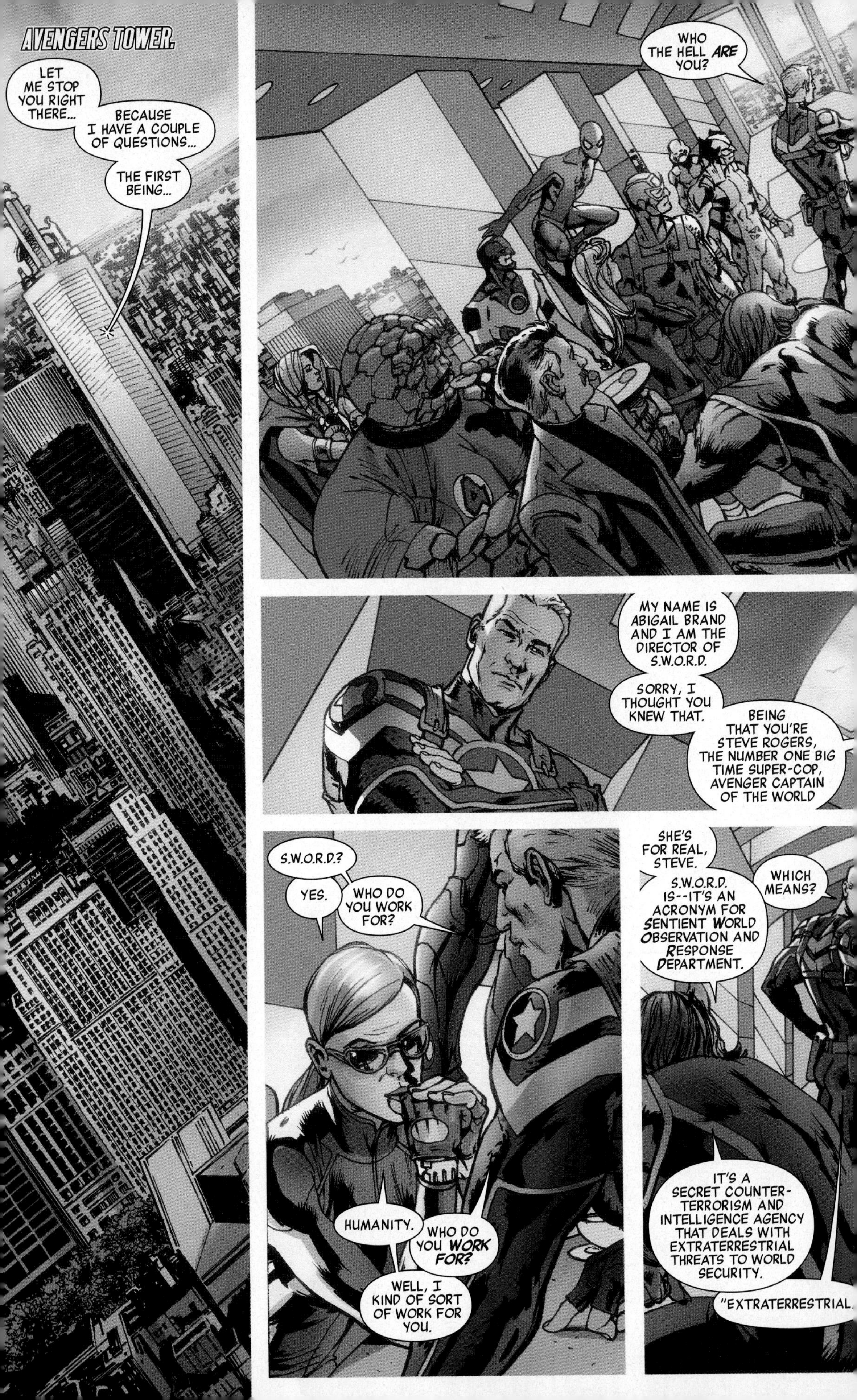
AVENGERS TOWER.
LET ME STOP YOU RIGHT THERE...
BECAUSE I HAVE A COUPLE OF QUESTIONS...
THE FIRST BEING...
WHO THE HELL ARE YOU?
MY NAME IS ABIGAIL BRAND AND I AM THE DIRECTOR OF S.W.O.R.D.
SORRY, I THOUGHT YOU KNEW THAT.
BEING THAT YOU'RE STEVE ROGERS, THE NUMBER ONE BIG TIME SUPER-COP, AVENGER CAPTAIN OF THE WORLD
S.W.O.R.D.?
YES.
WHO DO YOU WORK FOR?
HUMANITY.
WHO DO YOU WORK FOR?
WELL, I KIND OF SORT OF WORK FOR YOU.
SHE'S FOR REAL, STEVE.
S.W.O.R.D. IS--IT'S AN ACRONYM FOR SENTIENT WORLD OBSERVATION AND RESPONSE DEPARTMENT.
WHICH MEANS?
IT'S A SECRET COUNTER-TERRORISM AND INTELLIGENCE AGENCY THAT DEALS WITH EXTRATERRESTRIAL THREATS TO WORLD SECURITY.
"EXTRATERRESTRIAL.

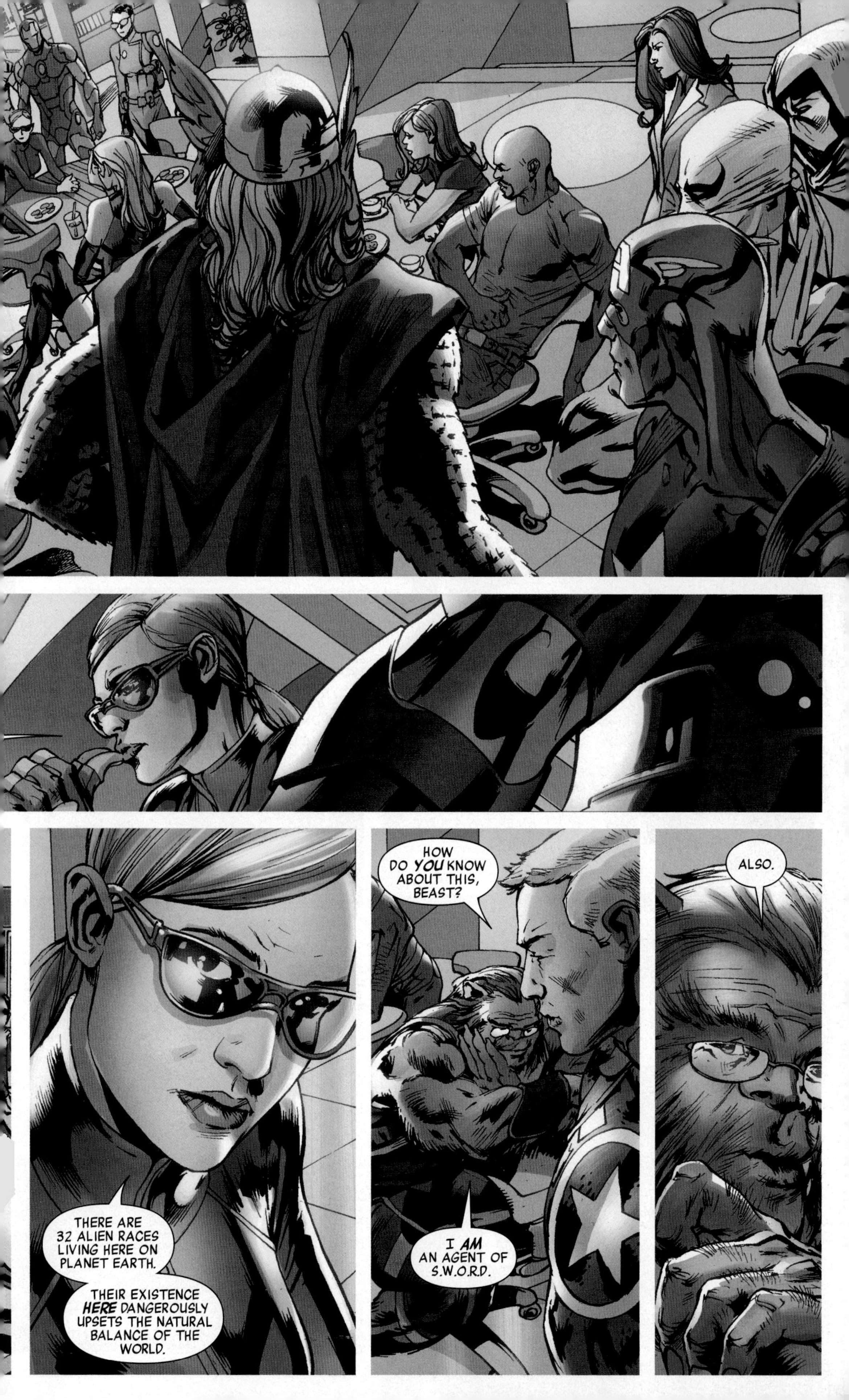
THERE ARE 32 ALIEN RACES LIVING HERE ON PLANET EARTH.
THEIR EXISTENCE HERE DANGEROUSLY UPSETS THE NATURAL BALANCE OF THE WORLD.
HOW DO YOU KNOW ABOUT THIS, BEAST?
I AM AN AGENT OF S.W.O.R.D.
ALSO.

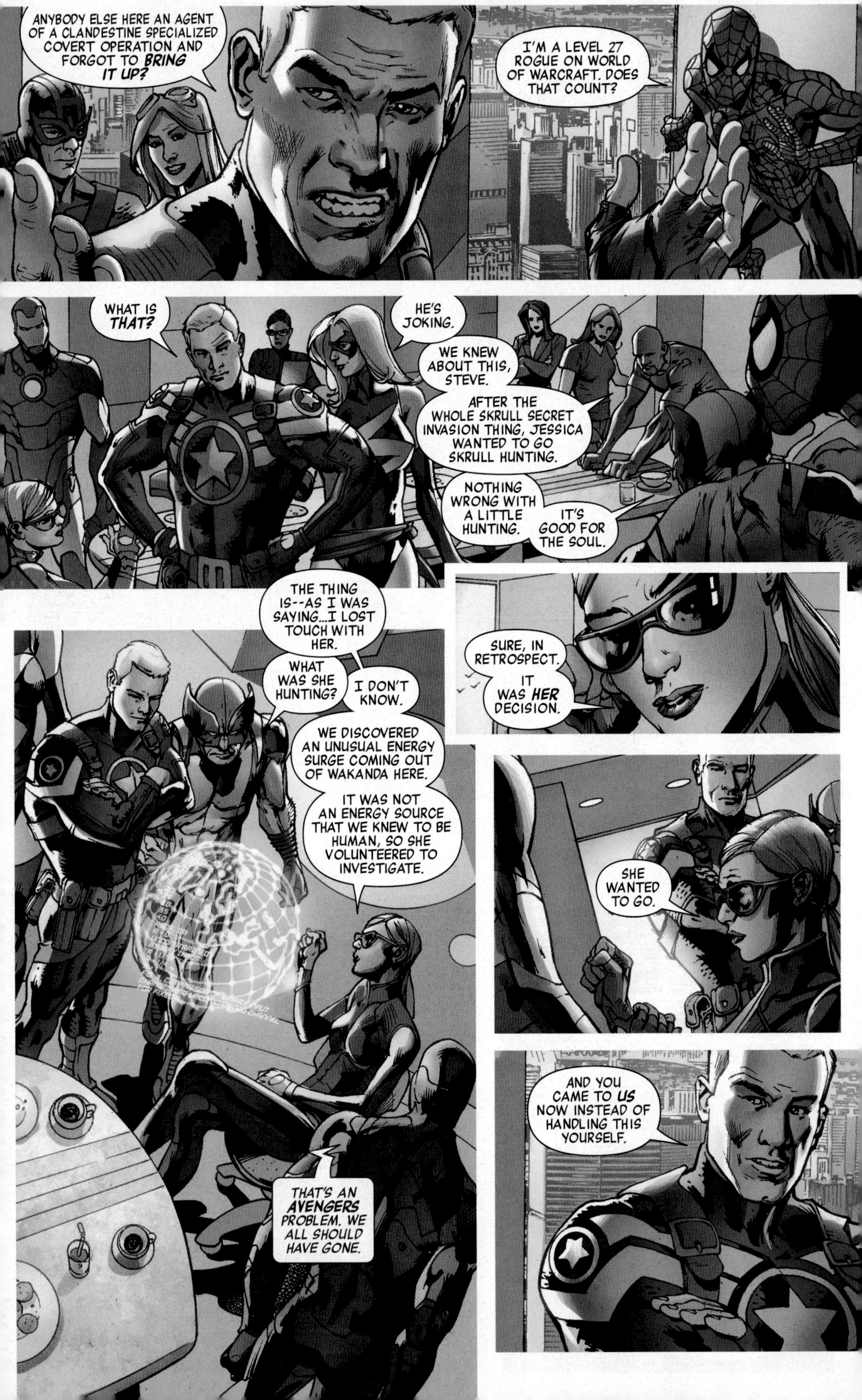
ANYBODY ELSE HERE AN AGENT OF A CLANDESTINE SPECIALIZED COVERT OPERATION AND FORGOT TO BRING IT UP?
I'M A LEVEL 27 ROGUE ON WORLD OF WARCRAFT. DOES THAT COUNT?
WHAT IS THAT?
HE'S JOKING.
WE KNEW ABOUT THIS, STEVE.
AFTER THE WHOLE SKRULL SECRET INVASION THING, JESSICA WANTED TO GO SKRULL HUNTING.
NOTHING WRONG WITH A LITTLE HUNTING.
IT'S GOOD FOR THE SOUL.
THE THING IS--AS I WAS SAYING...I LOST TOUCH WITH HER.
WHAT WAS SHE HUNTING?
I DON'T KNOW.
WE DISCOVERED AN UNUSUAL ENERGY SURGE COMING OUT OF WAKANDA HERE.
IT WAS NOT AN ENERGY SOURCE THAT WE KNEW TO BE HUMAN, SO SHE VOLUNTEERED TO INVESTIGATE.
THAT'S AN AVENGERS PROBLEM. WE ALL SHOULD HAVE GONE.
SURE, IN RETROSPECT.
IT WAS HER DECISION.
SHE WANTED TO GO.
AND YOU CAME TO US NOW INSTEAD OF HANDLING THIS YOURSELF.

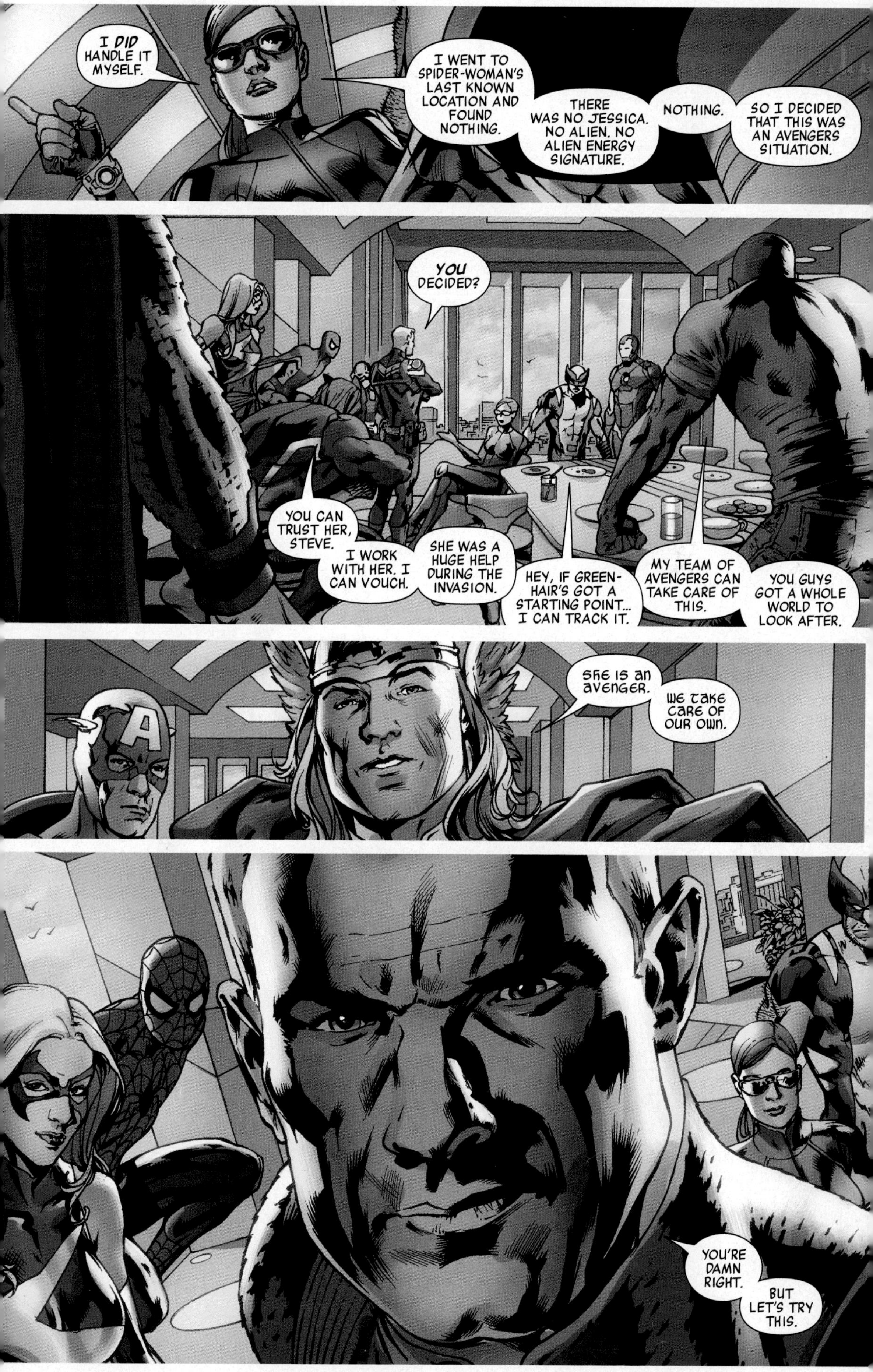

I DID HANDLE IT MYSELF.
I WENT TO SPIDER-WOMAN'S LAST KNOWN LOCATION AND FOUND NOTHING.
THERE WAS NO JESSICA. NO ALIEN. NO ALIEN ENERGY SIGNATURE.
NOTHING.
SO I DECIDED THAT THIS WAS AN AVENGERS SITUATION.
YOU DECIDED?
YOU CAN TRUST HER, STEVE.
I WORK WITH HER. I CAN VOUCH.
SHE WAS A HUGE HELP DURING THE INVASION.
HEY, IF GREEN-HAIR'S GOT A STARTING POINT... I CAN TRACK IT.
MY TEAM OF AVENGERS CAN TAKE CARE OF THIS.
YOU GUYS GOT A WHOLE WORLD TO LOOK AFTER.
SHE IS AN AVENGER.
WE TAKE CARE OF OUR OWN.
YOU'RE DAMN RIGHT.
BUT LET'S TRY THIS.

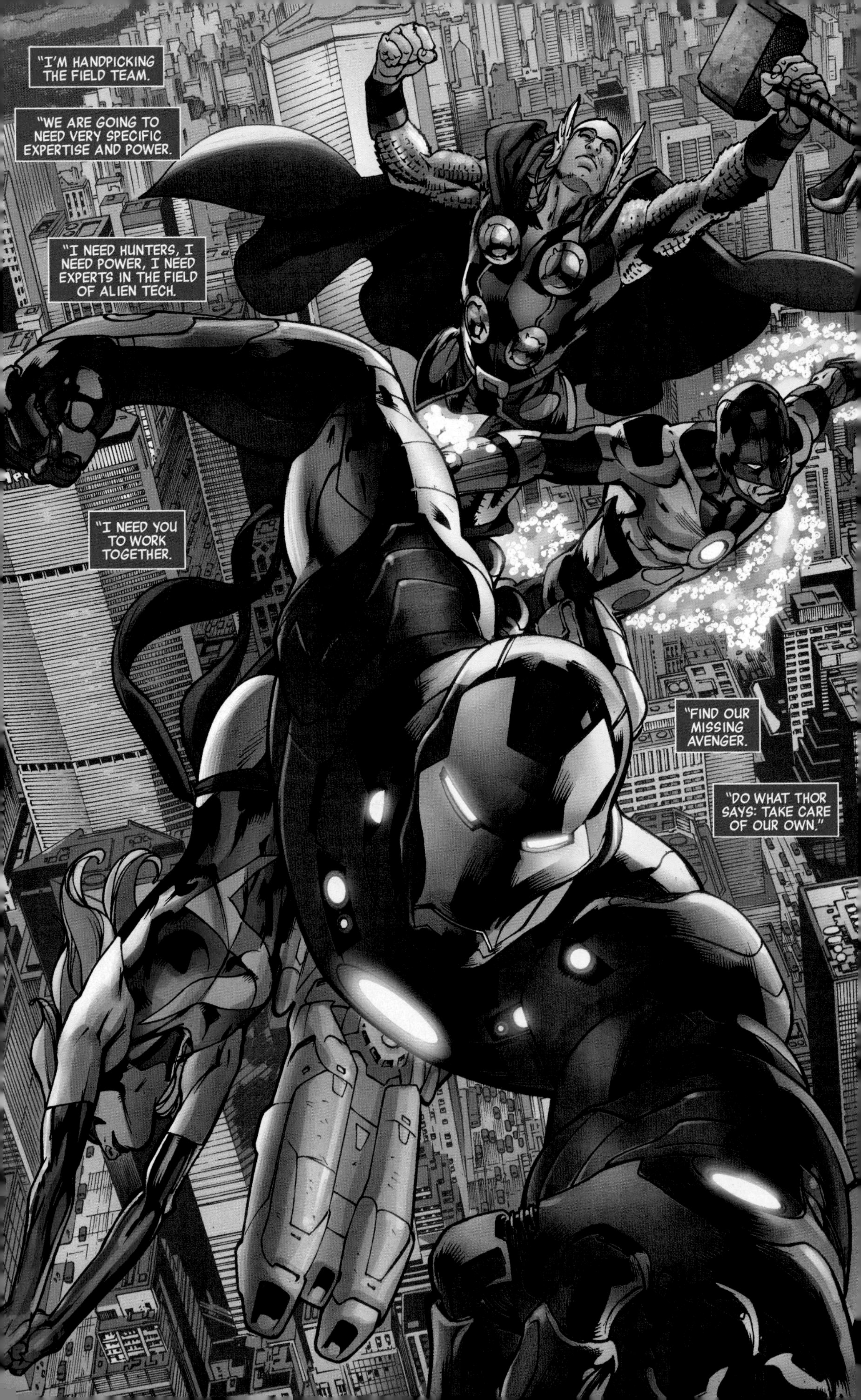
"I'M HANDPICKING THE FIELD TEAM.
"WE ARE GOING TO NEED VERY SPECIFIC EXPERTISE AND POWER.
"I NEED HUNTERS, I NEED POWER, I NEED EXPERTS IN THE FIELD OF ALIEN TECH.
"I NEED YOU TO WORK TOGETHER.
"FIND OUR MISSING AVENGER.
"DO WHAT THOR SAYS: TAKE CARE OF OUR OWN."

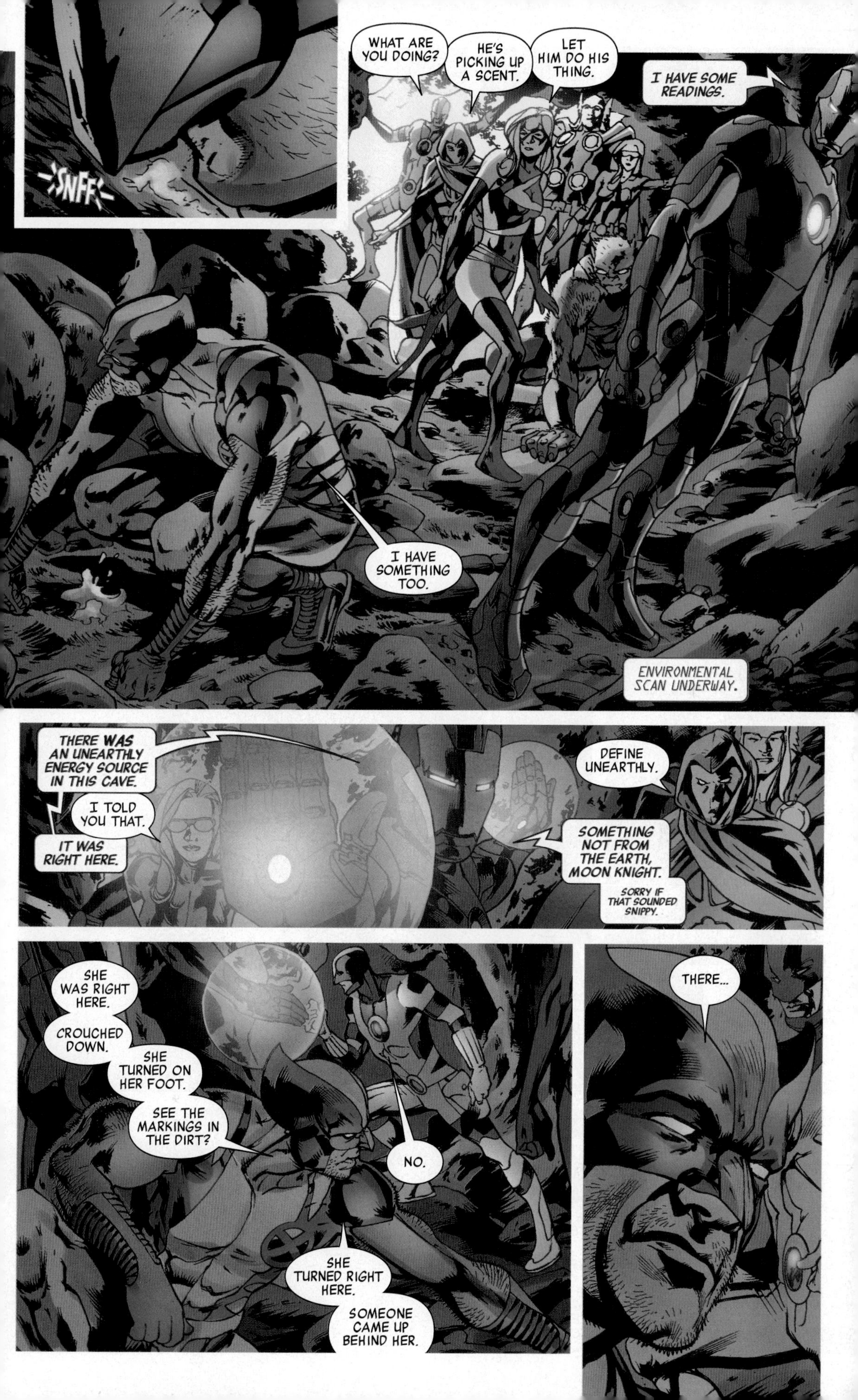

SNFF
WHAT ARE YOU DOING?
HE'S PICKING UP A SCENT.
LET HIM DO HIS THING.
I HAVE SOME READINGS.
I HAVE SOMETHING TOO.
ENVIRONMENTAL SCAN UNDERWAY.
THERE WAS AN UNEARTHLY ENERGY SOURCE IN THIS CAVE.
I TOLD YOU THAT.
IT WAS RIGHT HERE.
DEFINE UNEARTHLY.
SOMETHING NOT FROM THE EARTH, MOON KNIGHT.
SORRY IF THAT SOUNDED SNIPPY.
SHE WAS RIGHT HERE.
CROUCHED DOWN.
SHE TURNED ON HER FOOT.
SEE THE MARKINGS IN THE DIRT?
NO.
SHE TURNED RIGHT HERE.
SOMEONE CAME UP BEHIND HER.
THERE...

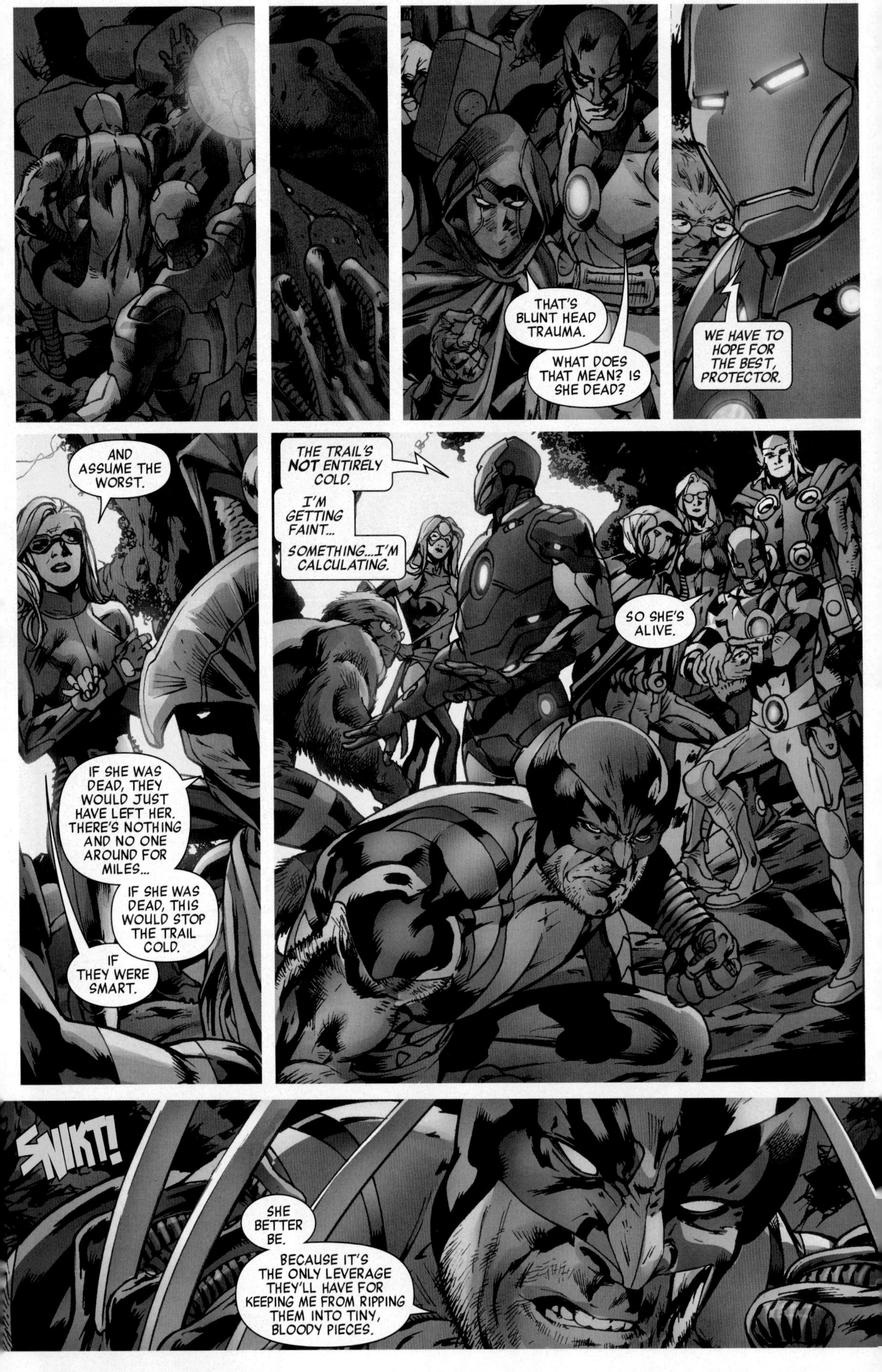
THAT'S BLUNT HEAD TRAUMA.
WHAT DOES THAT MEAN? IS SHE DEAD?
WE HAVE TO HOPE FOR THE BEST, PROTECTOR.
AND ASSUME THE WORST.
THE TRAIL'S NOT ENTIRELY COLD.
I'M GETTING FAINT...
SOMETHING...I'M CALCULATING.
SO SHE'S ALIVE.
IF SHE WAS DEAD, THEY WOULD JUST HAVE LEFT HER. THERE'S NOTHING AND NO ONE AROUND FOR MILES...
IF SHE WAS DEAD, THIS WOULD STOP THE TRAIL COLD.
IF THEY WERE SMART.
SNIKT!
SHE BETTER BE.
BECAUSE IT'S THE ONLY LEVERAGE THEY'LL HAVE FOR KEEPING ME FROM RIPPING THEM INTO TINY, BLOODY PIECES.

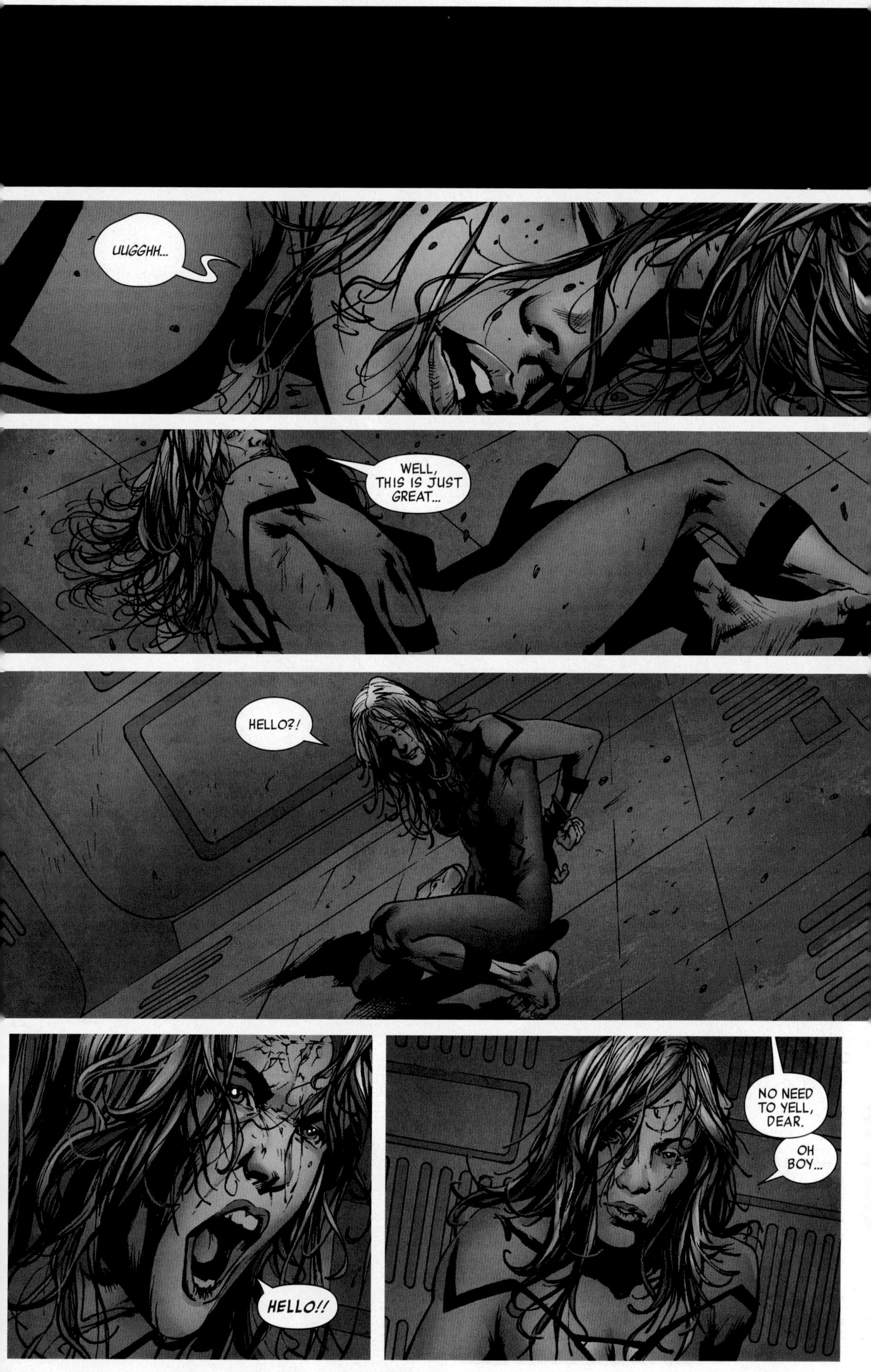

UUGGHH...
WELL, THIS IS JUST GREAT...
HELLO?!
HELLO!!
NO NEED TO YELL, DEAR.
OH BOY...

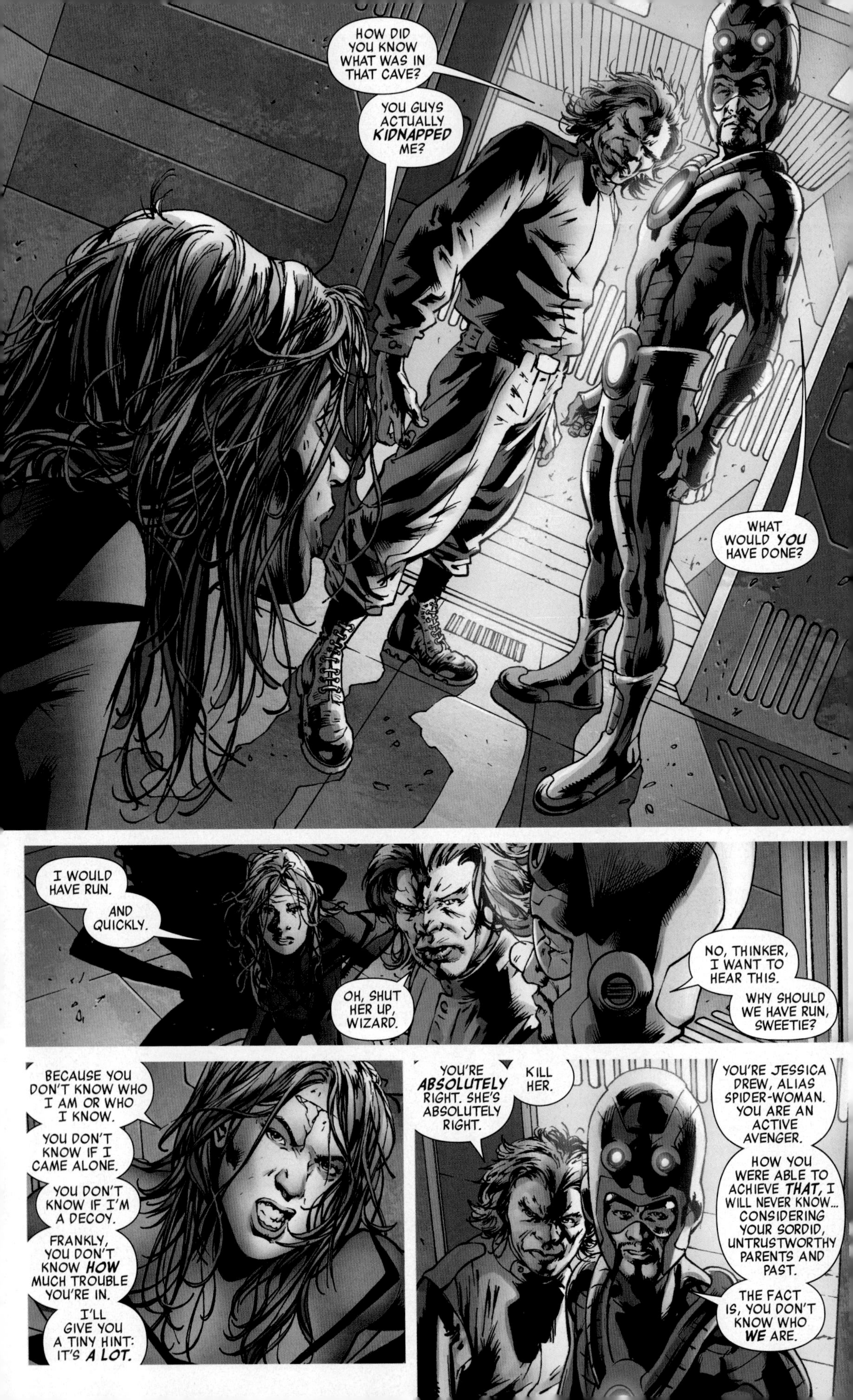
HOW DID YOU KNOW WHAT WAS IN THAT CAVE?
YOU GUYS ACTUALLY KIDNAPPED ME?
WHAT WOULD YOU HAVE DONE?
I WOULD HAVE RUN.
AND QUICKLY.
OH, SHUT HER UP, WIZARD.
NO, THINKER, I WANT TO HEAR THIS.
WHY SHOULD WE HAVE RUN, SWEETIE?
BECAUSE YOU DON'T KNOW WHO I AM OR WHO I KNOW.
YOU DON'T KNOW IF I CAME ALONE.
YOU DON'T KNOW IF I'M A DECOY.
FRANKLY, YOU DON'T KNOW HOW MUCH TROUBLE YOU'RE IN.
I'LL GIVE YOU A TINY HINT: IT'S A LOT.
YOU'RE ABSOLUTELY RIGHT. SHE'S ABSOLUTELY RIGHT.
KILL HER.
YOU'RE JESSICA DREW, ALIAS SPIDER-WOMAN. YOU ARE AN ACTIVE AVENGER.
HOW YOU WERE ABLE TO ACHIEVE THAT, I WILL NEVER KNOW... CONSIDERING YOUR SORDID, UNTRUSTWORTHY PARENTS AND PAST.
THE FACT IS, YOU DON'T KNOW WHO WE ARE.

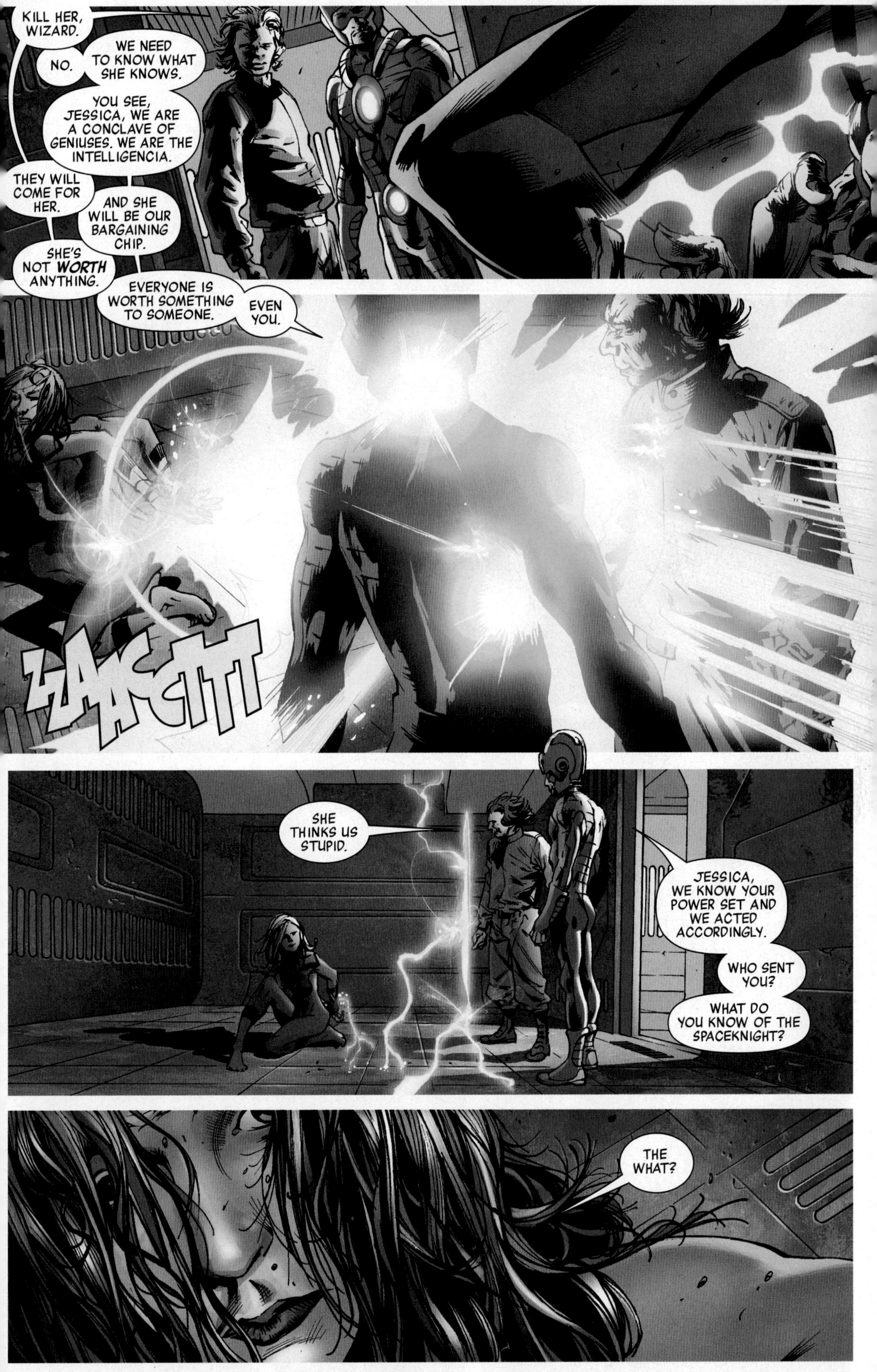
KILL HER, WIZARD.
NO.
WE NEED TO KNOW WHAT SHE KNOWS.
YOU SEE, JESSICA, WE ARE A CONCLAVE OF GENIUSES. WE ARE THE INTELLIGENCIA.
THEY WILL COME FOR HER.
AND SHE WILL BE OUR BARGAINING CHIP.
SHE'S NOT **WORTH** ANYTHING.
EVERYONE IS WORTH SOMETHING TO SOMEONE.
EVEN YOU.
ZZAACTTT
SHE THINKS US STUPID.
JESSICA, WE KNOW YOUR POWER SET AND WE ACTED ACCORDINGLY.
WHO SENT YOU?
WHAT DO YOU KNOW OF THE SPACEKNIGHT?
THE WHAT?

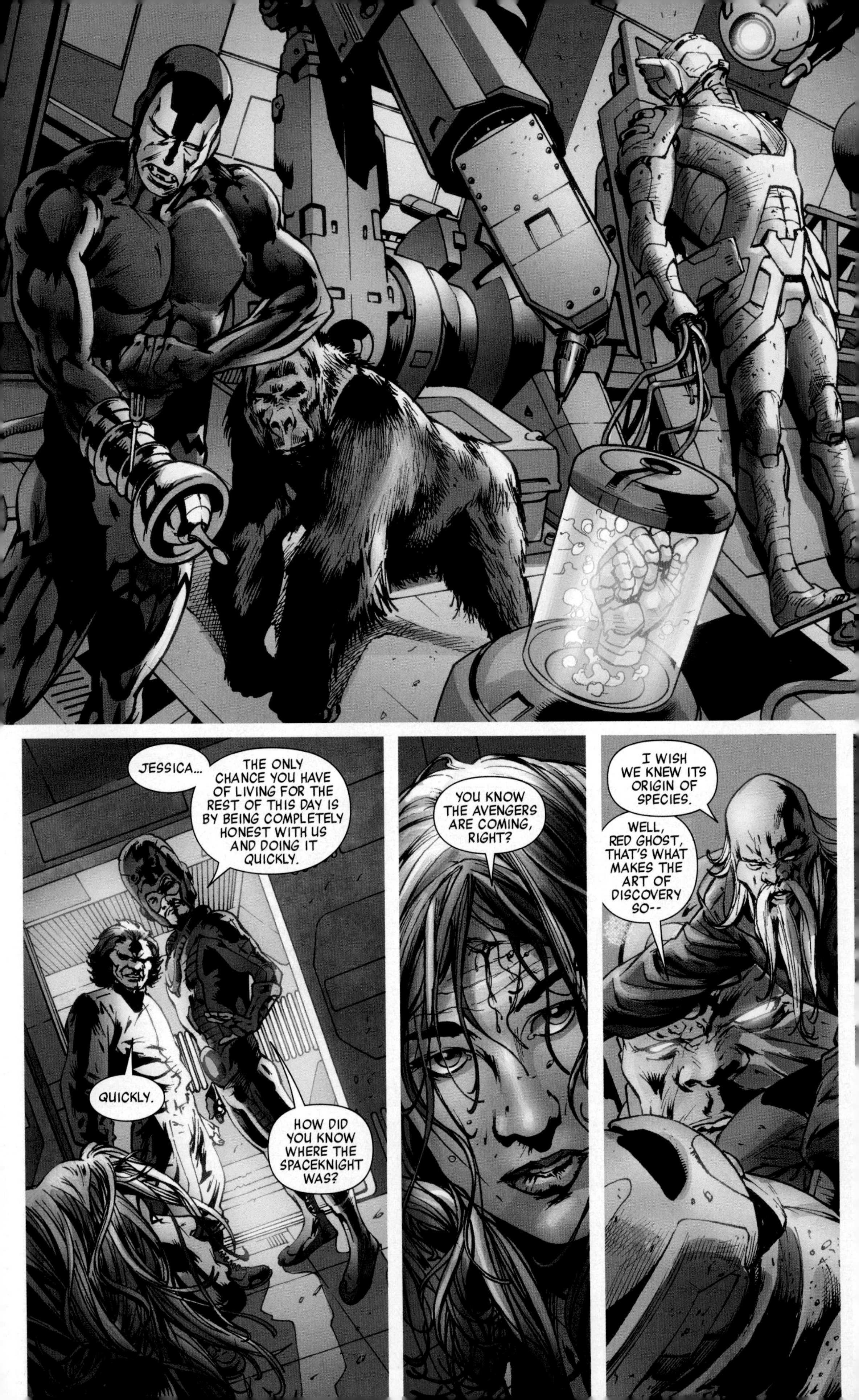
JESSICA...
THE ONLY CHANCE YOU HAVE OF LIVING FOR THE REST OF THIS DAY IS BY BEING COMPLETELY HONEST WITH US AND DOING IT QUICKLY.
QUICKLY.
HOW DID YOU KNOW WHERE THE SPACEKNIGHT WAS?
YOU KNOW THE AVENGERS ARE COMING, RIGHT?
I WISH WE KNEW ITS ORIGIN OF SPECIES.
WELL, RED GHOST, THAT'S WHAT MAKES THE ART OF DISCOVERY SO--

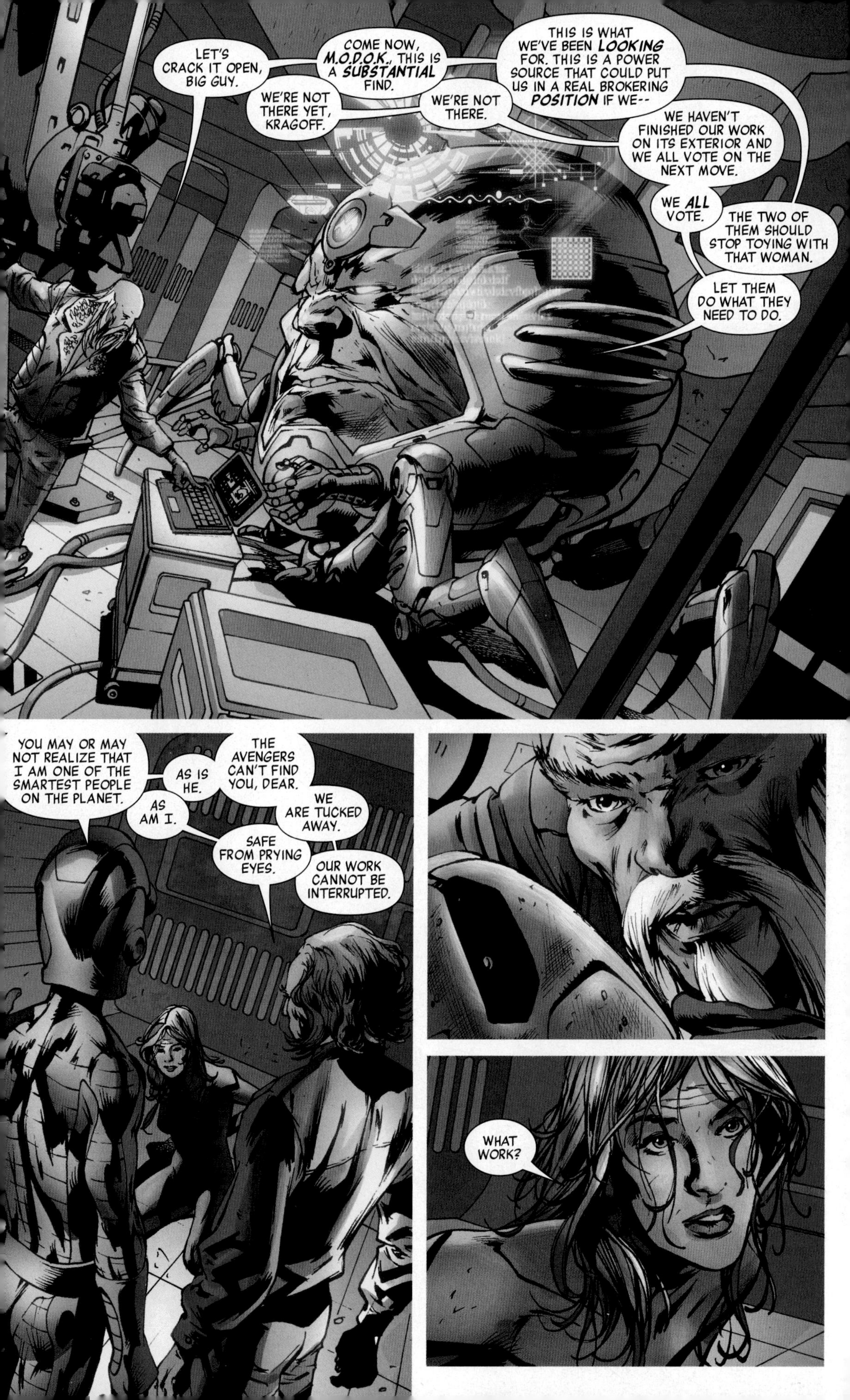
LET'S CRACK IT OPEN, BIG GUY.
COME NOW, M.O.D.O.K., THIS IS A SUBSTANTIAL FIND.
THIS IS WHAT WE'VE BEEN LOOKING FOR. THIS IS A POWER SOURCE THAT COULD PUT US IN A REAL BROKERING POSITION IF WE--
WE'RE NOT THERE YET, KRAGOFF.
WE'RE NOT THERE.
WE HAVEN'T FINISHED OUR WORK ON ITS EXTERIOR AND WE ALL VOTE ON THE NEXT MOVE.
WE ALL VOTE.
THE TWO OF THEM SHOULD STOP TOYING WITH THAT WOMAN.
LET THEM DO WHAT THEY NEED TO DO.
YOU MAY OR MAY NOT REALIZE THAT I AM ONE OF THE SMARTEST PEOPLE ON THE PLANET.
AS IS HE.
AS AM I.
THE AVENGERS CAN'T FIND YOU, DEAR.
WE ARE TUCKED AWAY.
SAFE FROM PRYING EYES.
OUR WORK CANNOT BE INTERRUPTED.
WHAT WORK?

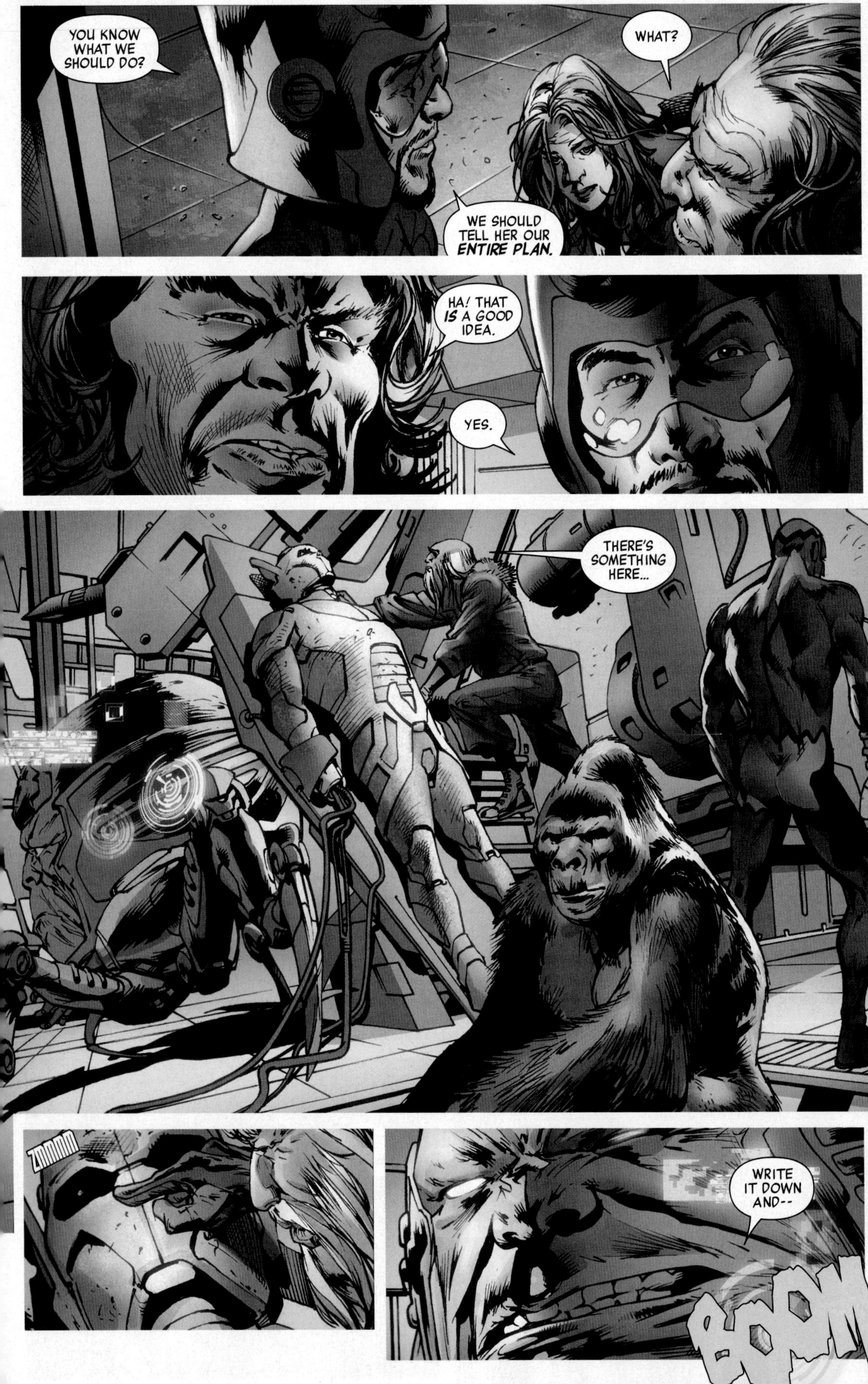
YOU KNOW WHAT WE SHOULD DO?
WHAT?
WE SHOULD TELL HER OUR ENTIRE PLAN.
HA! THAT IS A GOOD IDEA.
YES.
THERE'S SOMETHING HERE...
ZMMMM
WRITE IT DOWN AND--
BOOOM

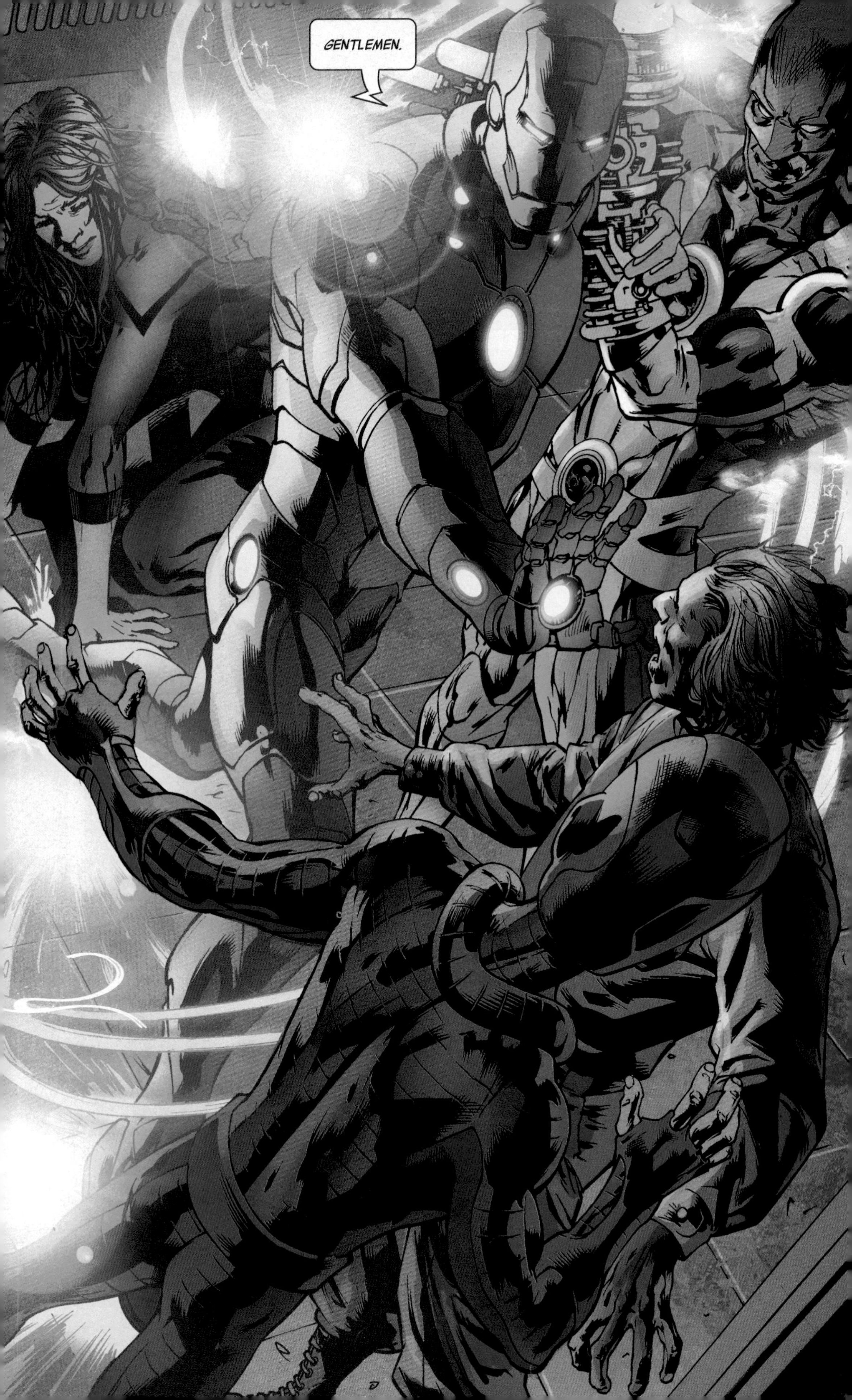
GENTLEMEN.

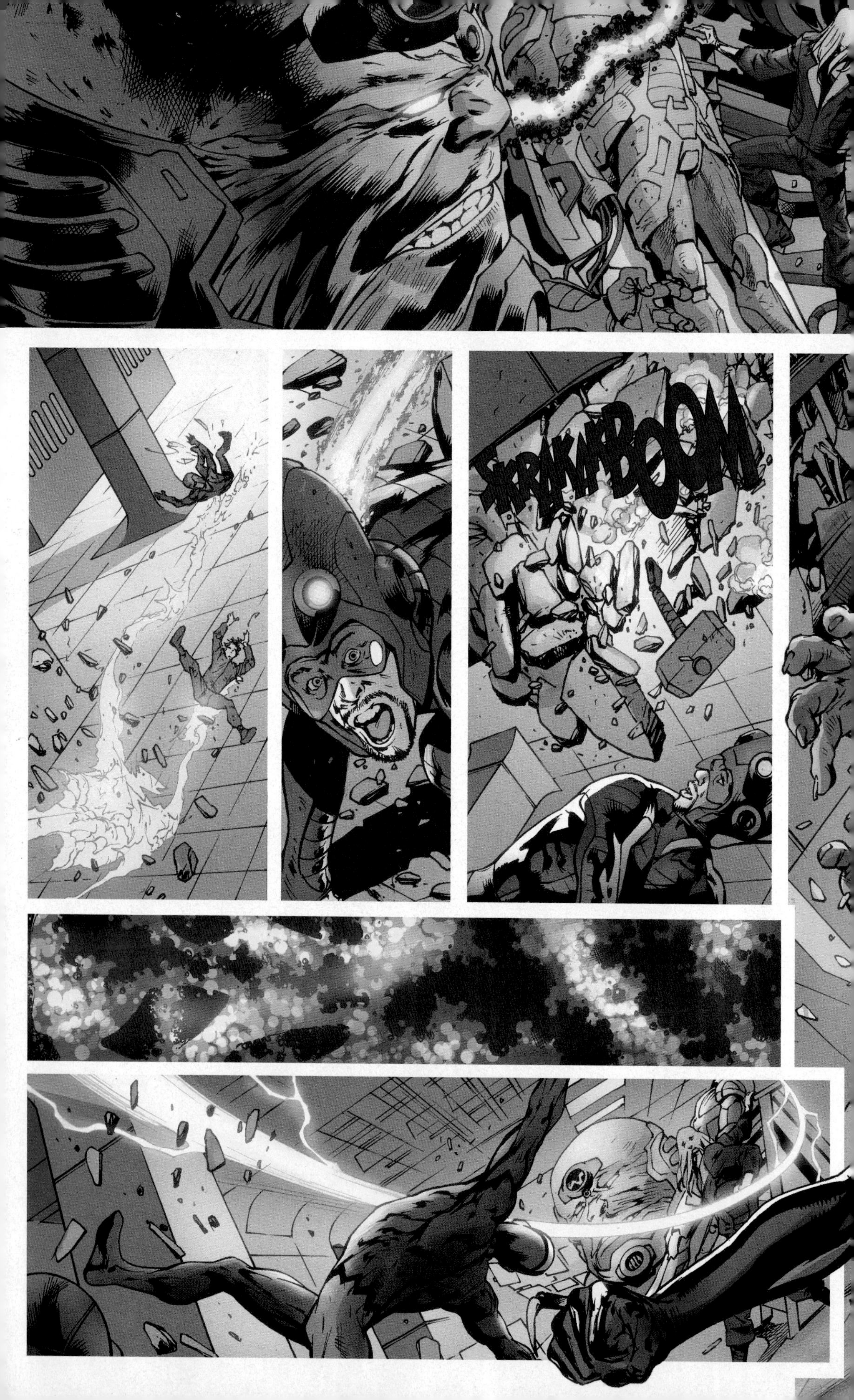
SKRAKAKBOOM

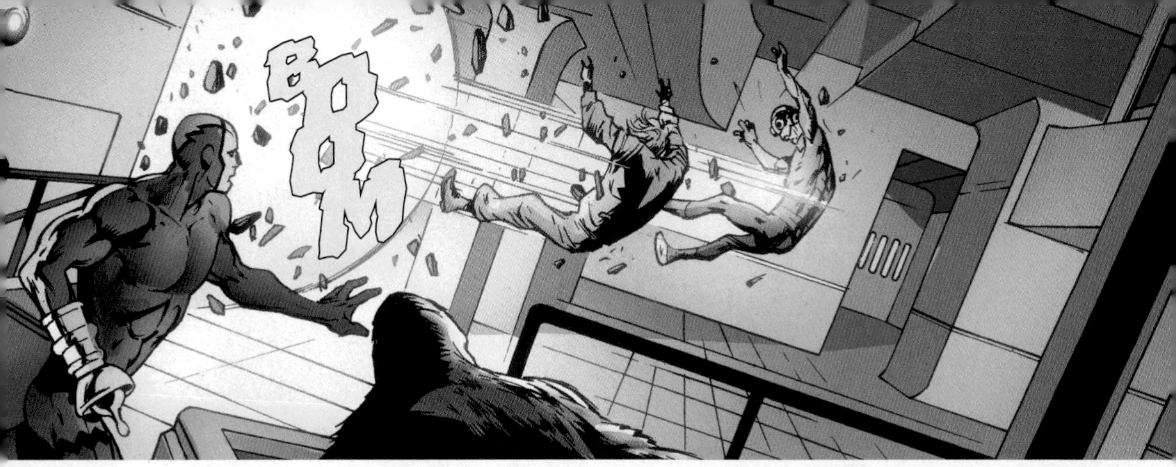
BOOM

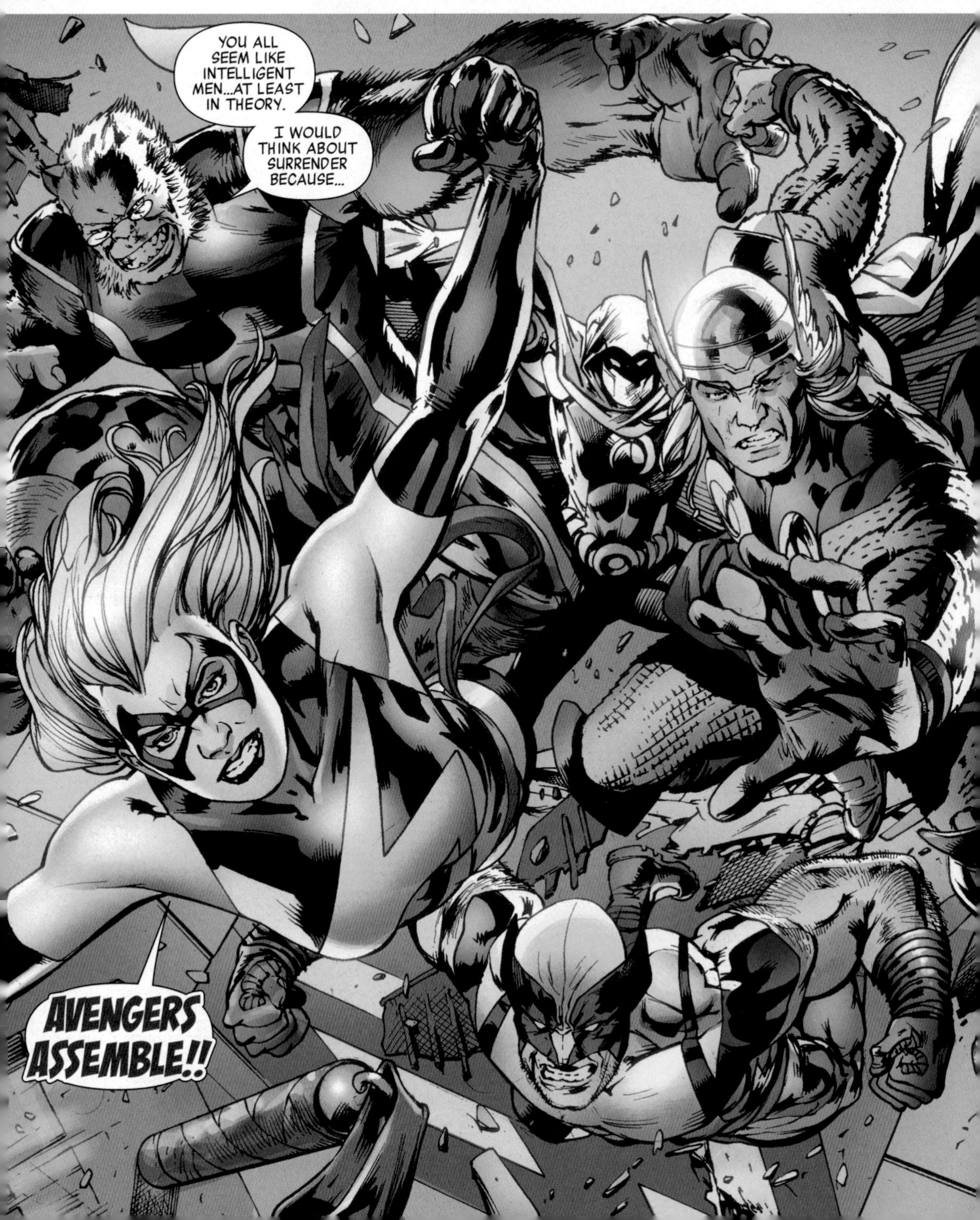
YOU ALL SEEM LIKE INTELLIGENT MEN...AT LEAST IN THEORY.
I WOULD THINK ABOUT SURRENDER BECAUSE...
AVENGERS ASSEMBLE!!

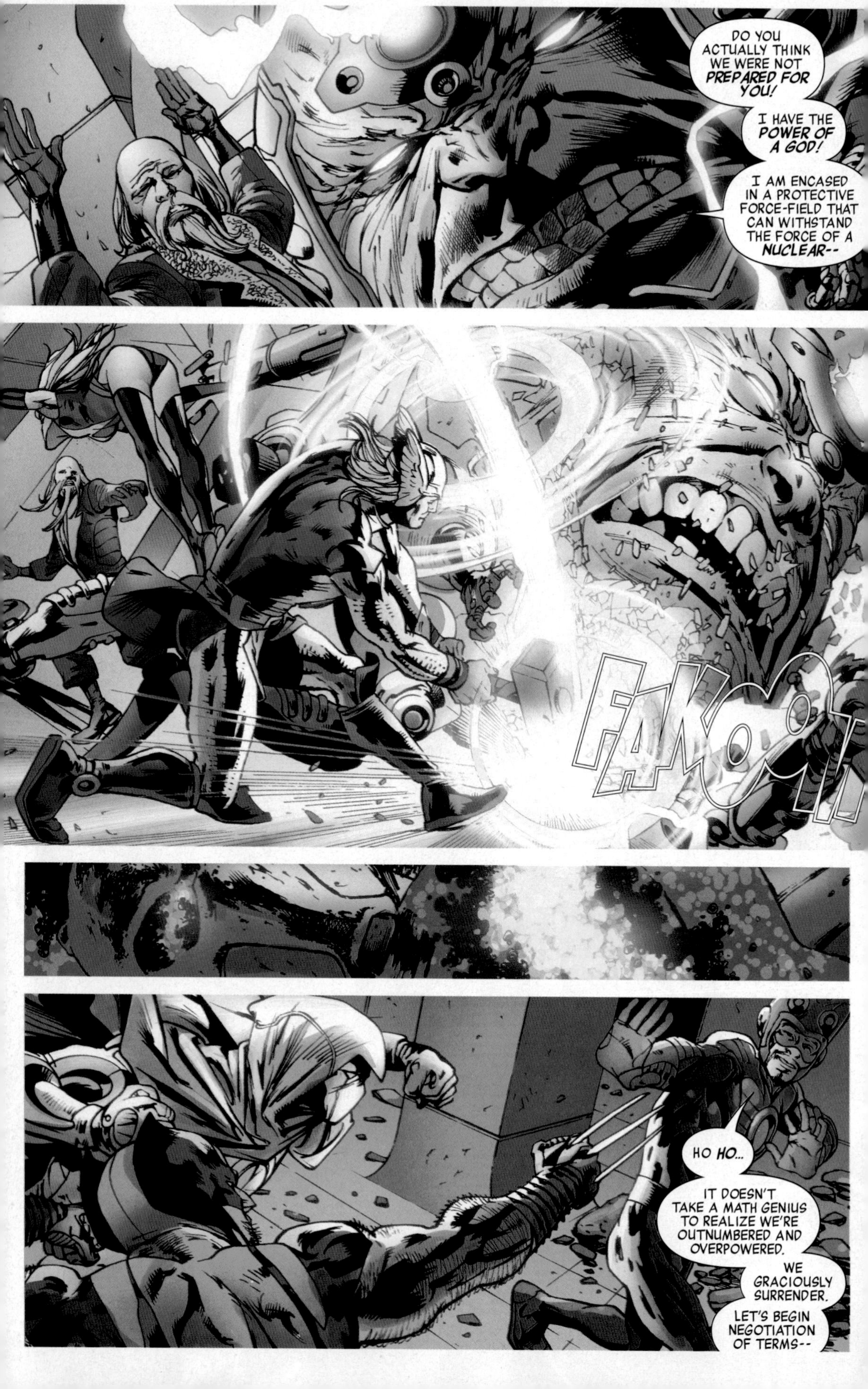
DO YOU ACTUALLY THINK WE WERE NOT PREPARED FOR YOU!
I HAVE THE POWER OF A GOD!
I AM ENCASED IN A PROTECTIVE FORCE-FIELD THAT CAN WITHSTAND THE FORCE OF A NUCLEAR--
FAKOOM
HO HO...
IT DOESN'T TAKE A MATH GENIUS TO REALIZE WE'RE OUTNUMBERED AND OVERPOWERED.
WE GRACIOUSLY SURRENDER.
LET'S BEGIN NEGOTIATION OF TERMS--

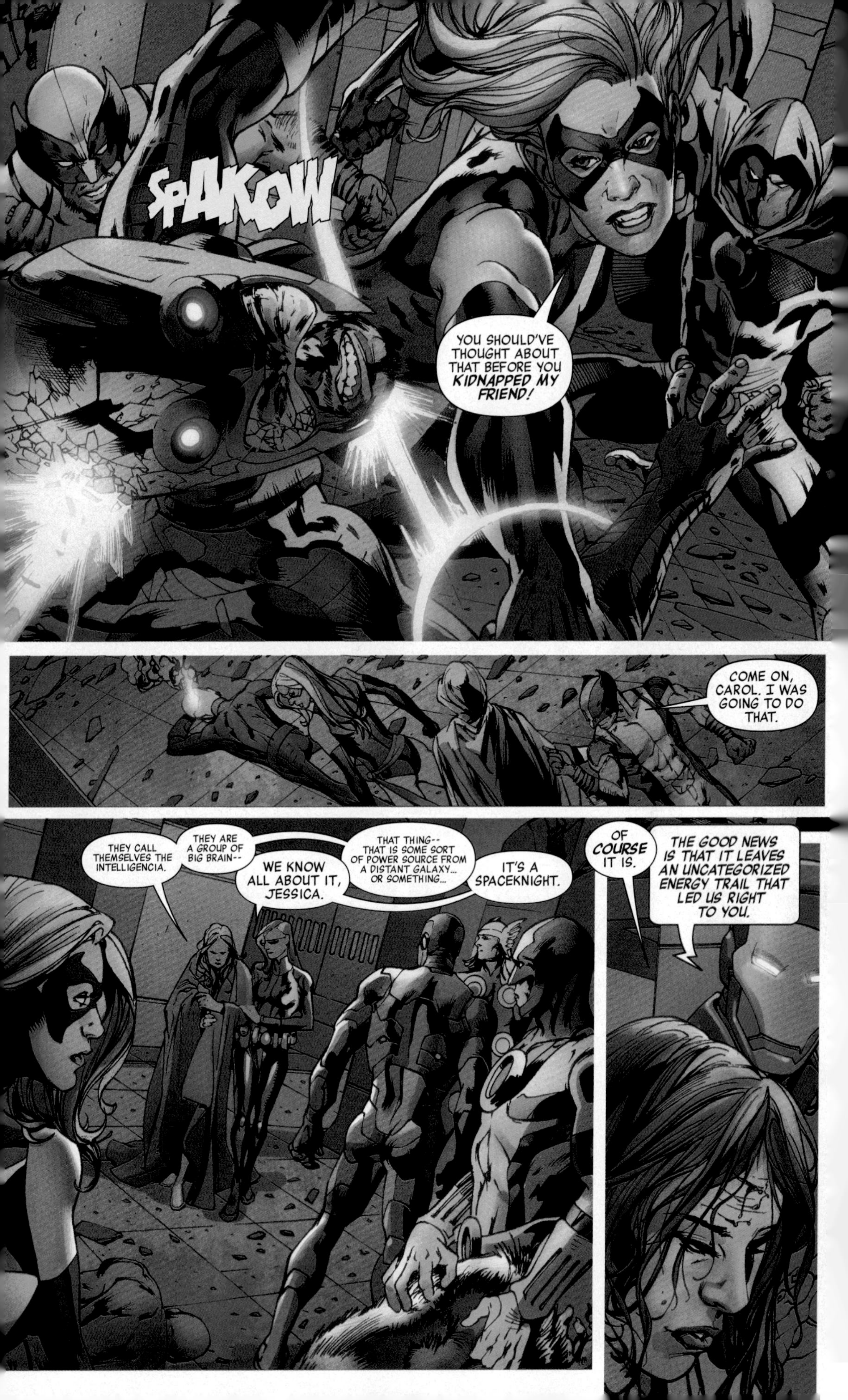
SPAKOW
YOU SHOULD'VE THOUGHT ABOUT THAT BEFORE YOU KIDNAPPED MY FRIEND!
COME ON, CAROL. I WAS GOING TO DO THAT.
THEY CALL THEMSELVES THE INTELLIGENCIA.
THEY ARE A GROUP OF BIG BRAIN--
WE KNOW ALL ABOUT IT, JESSICA.
THAT THING-- THAT IS SOME SORT OF POWER SOURCE FROM A DISTANT GALAXY... OR SOMETHING...
IT'S A SPACEKNIGHT.
OF COURSE IT IS.
THE GOOD NEWS IS THAT IT LEAVES AN UNCATEGORIZED ENERGY TRAIL THAT LED US RIGHT TO YOU.

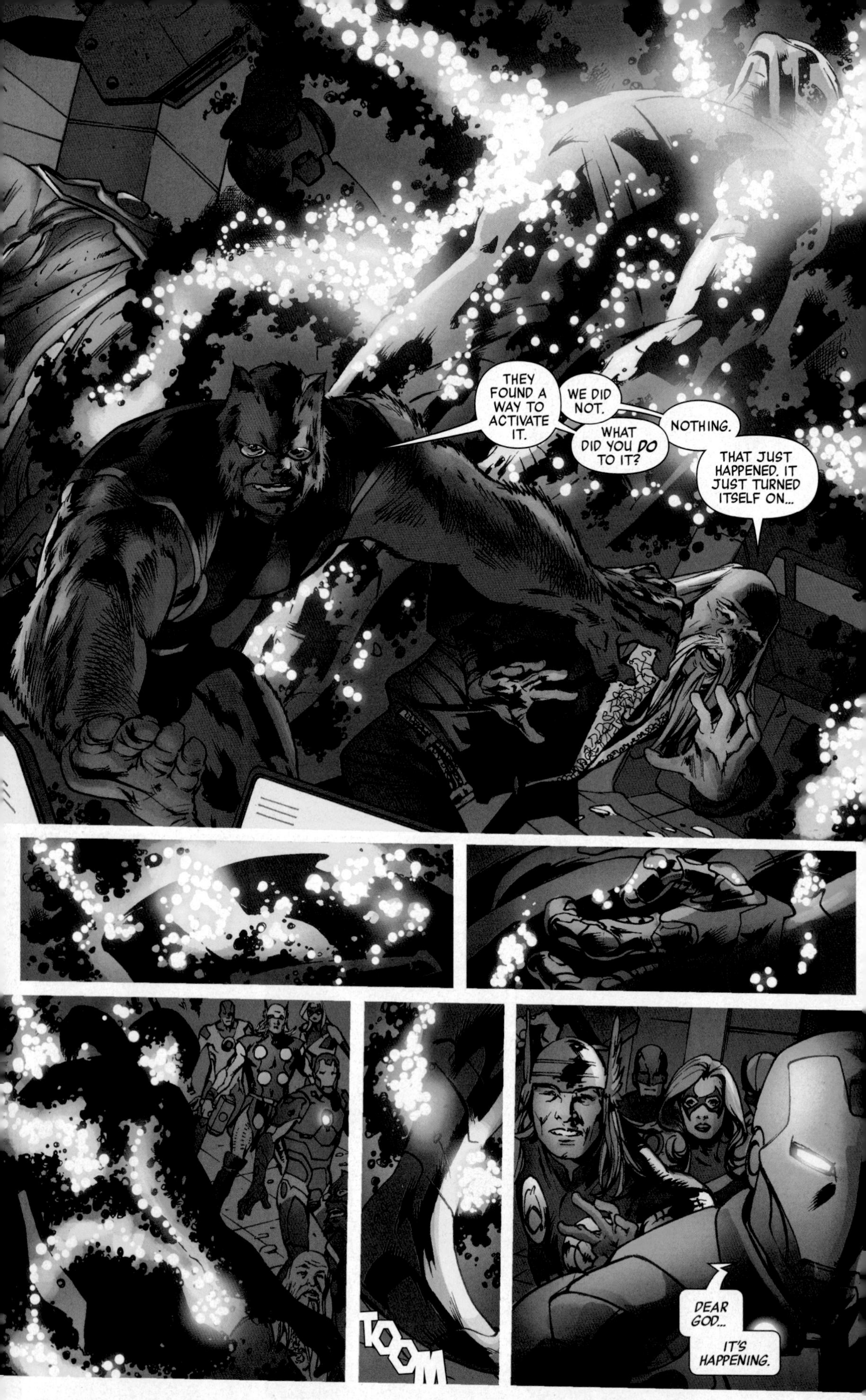
THEY FOUND A WAY TO ACTIVATE IT.
WE DID NOT.
WHAT DID YOU DO TO IT?
NOTHING.
THAT JUST HAPPENED. IT JUST TURNED ITSELF ON...
TOOM
DEAR GOD...
IT'S HAPPENING.

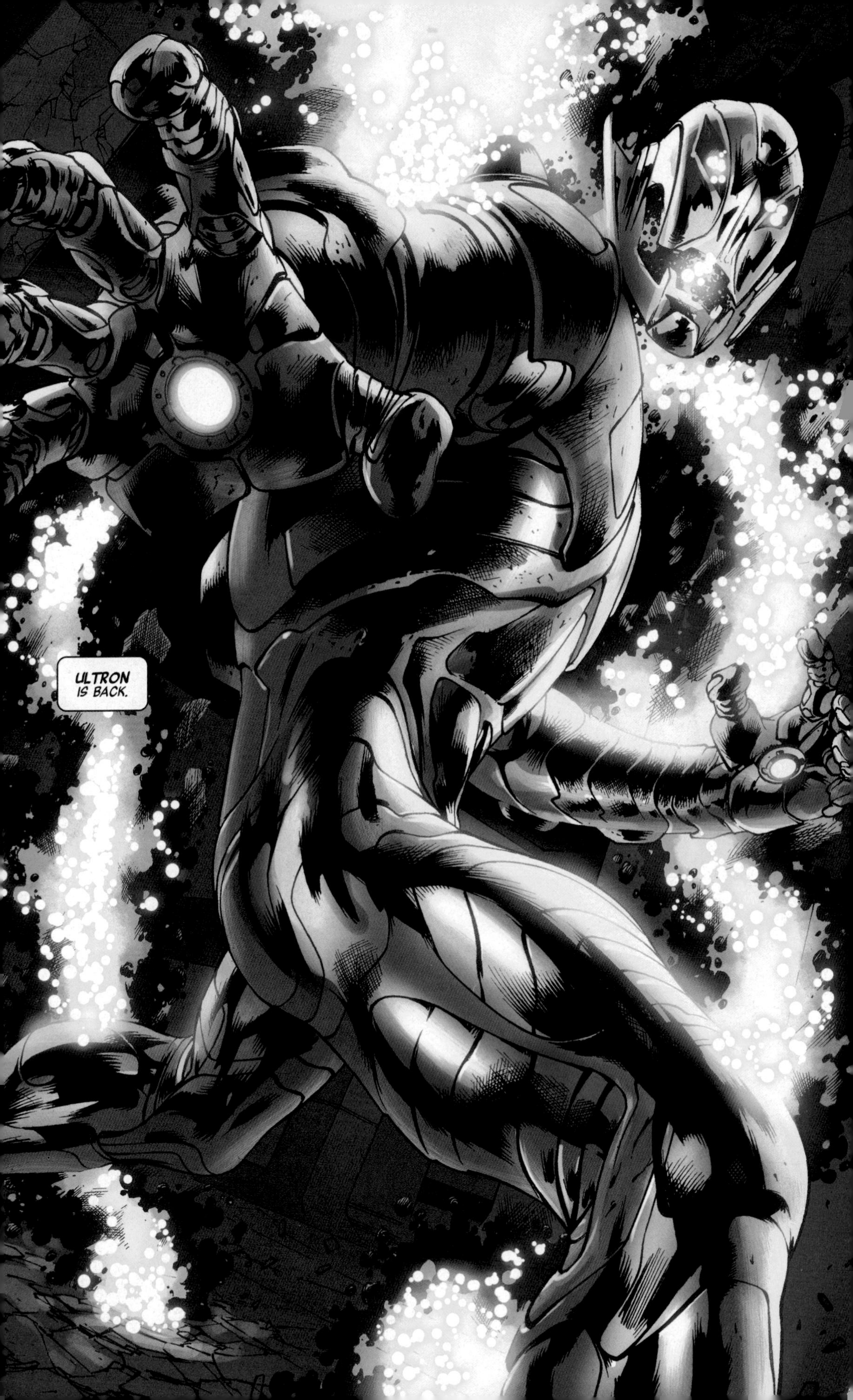
ULTRON IS BACK.

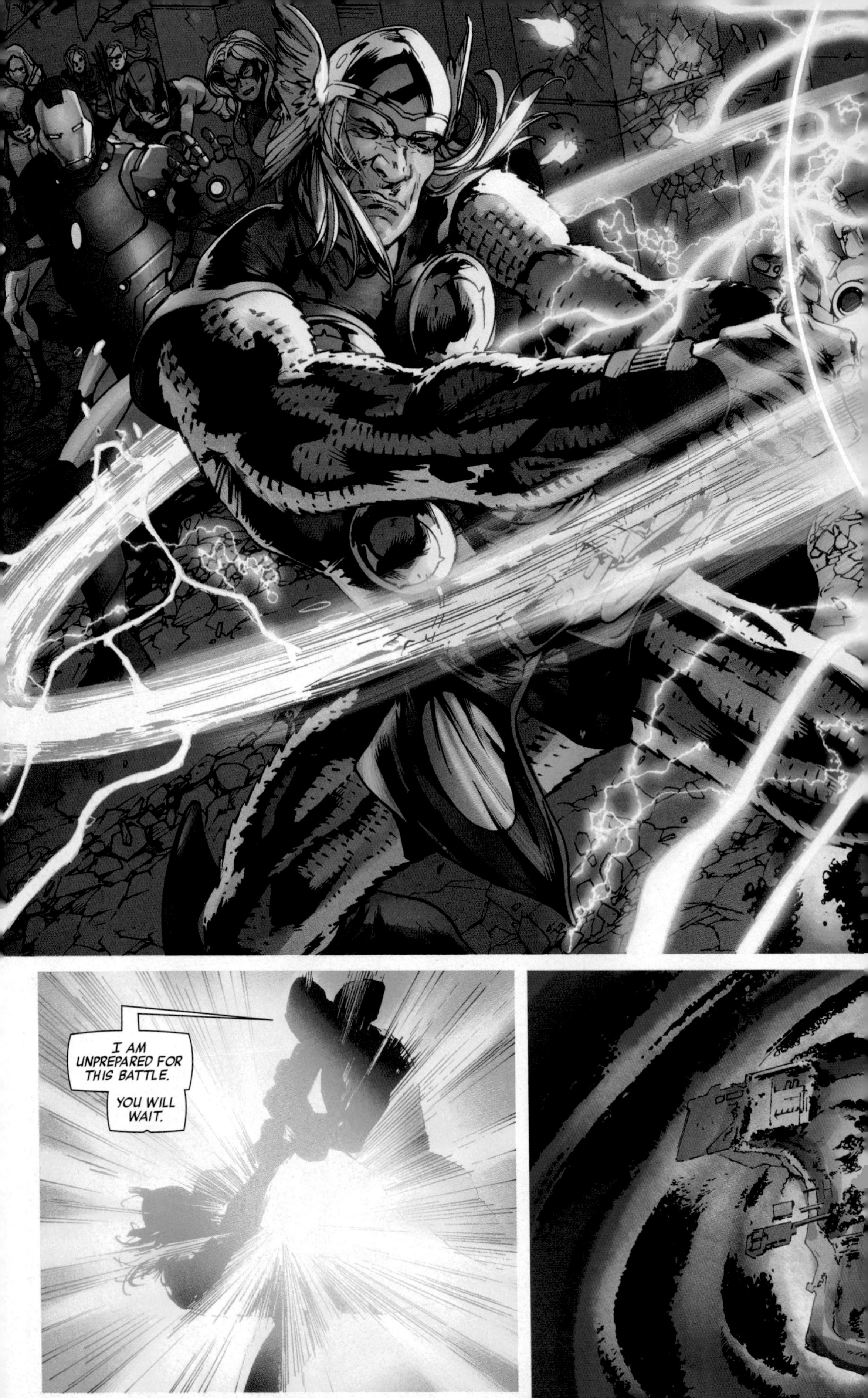
I AM UNPREPARED FOR THIS BATTLE.
YOU WILL WAIT.

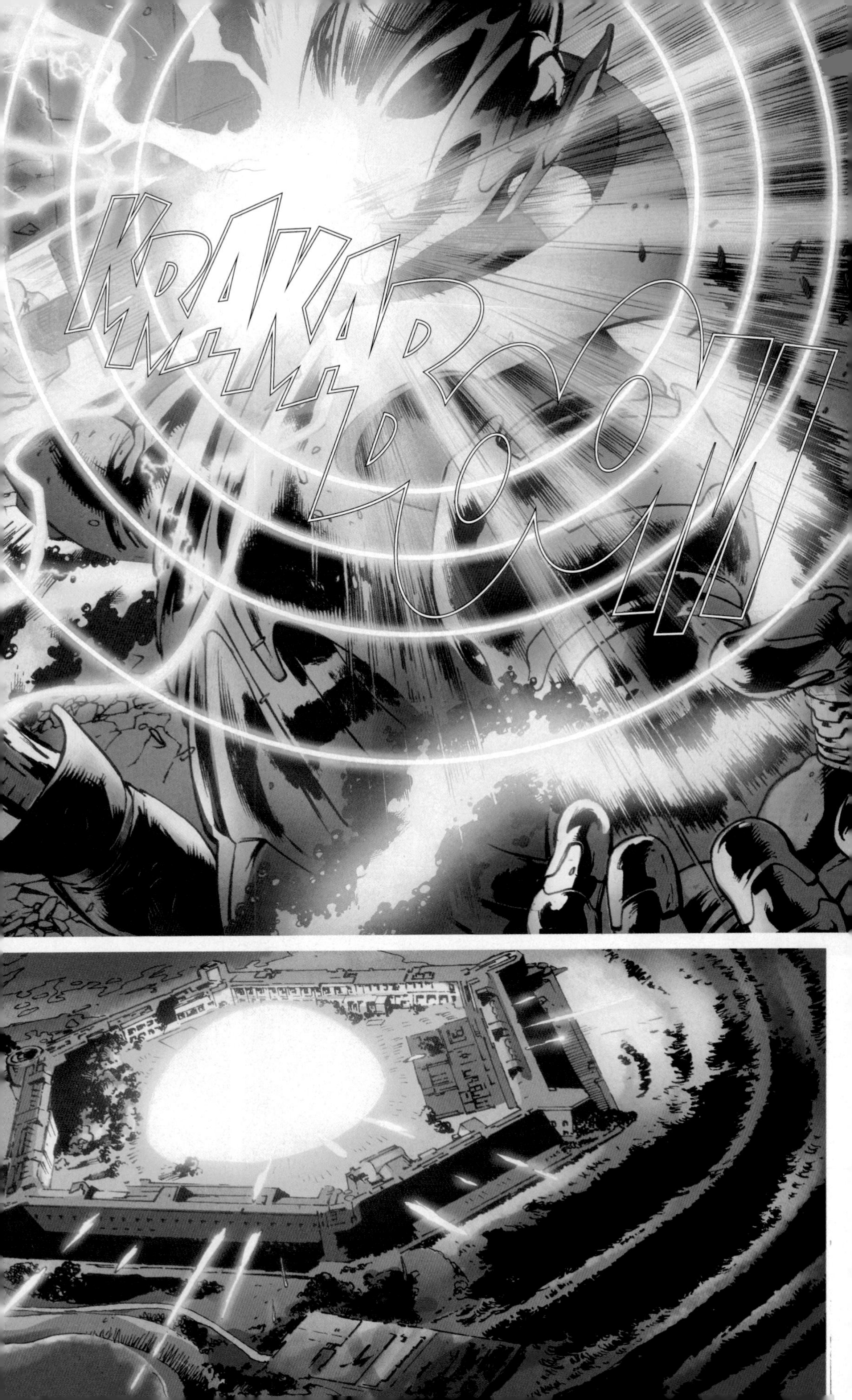
KRAKADOOOM!!

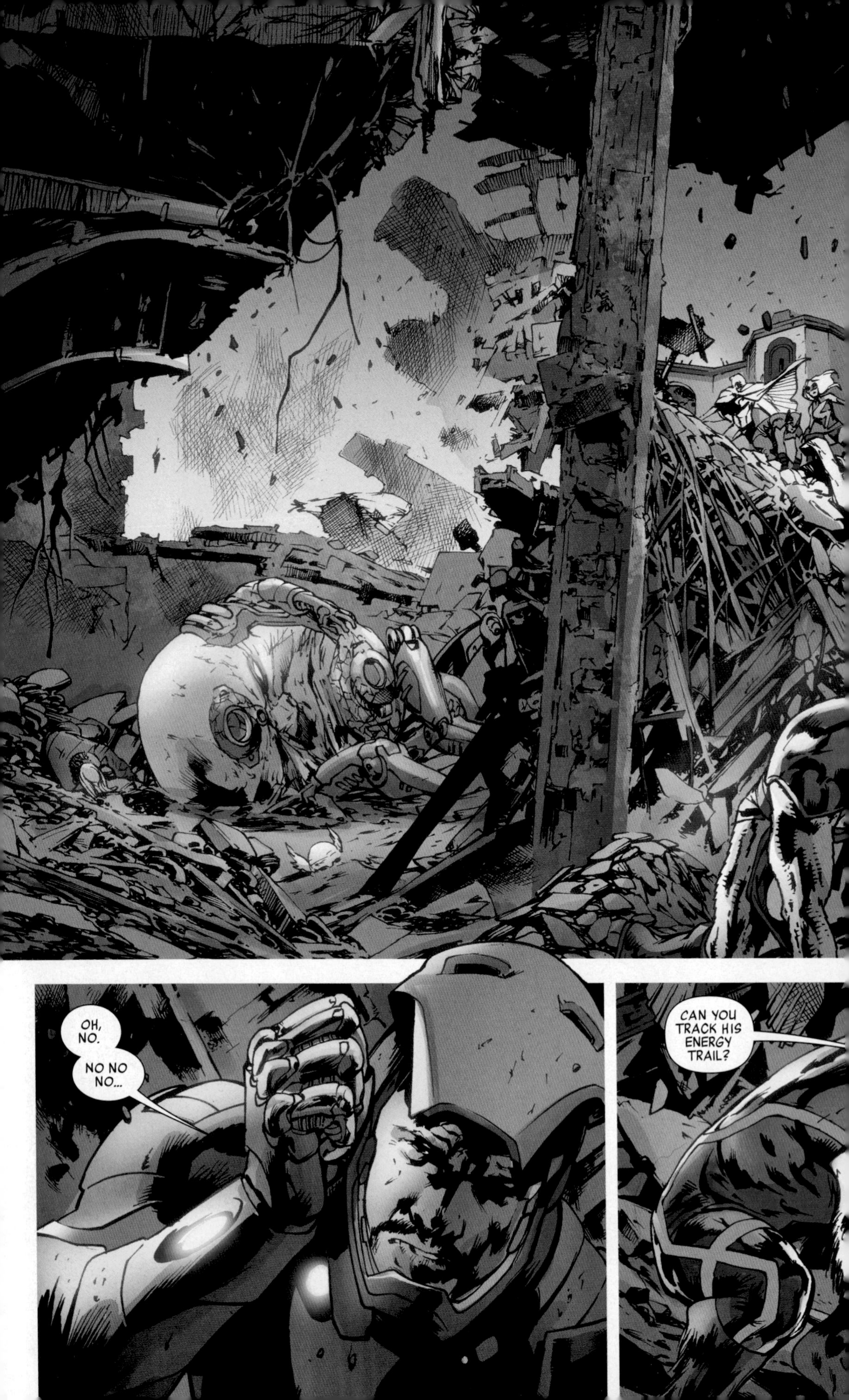
OH, NO.
NO NO NO...
CAN YOU TRACK HIS ENERGY TRAIL?

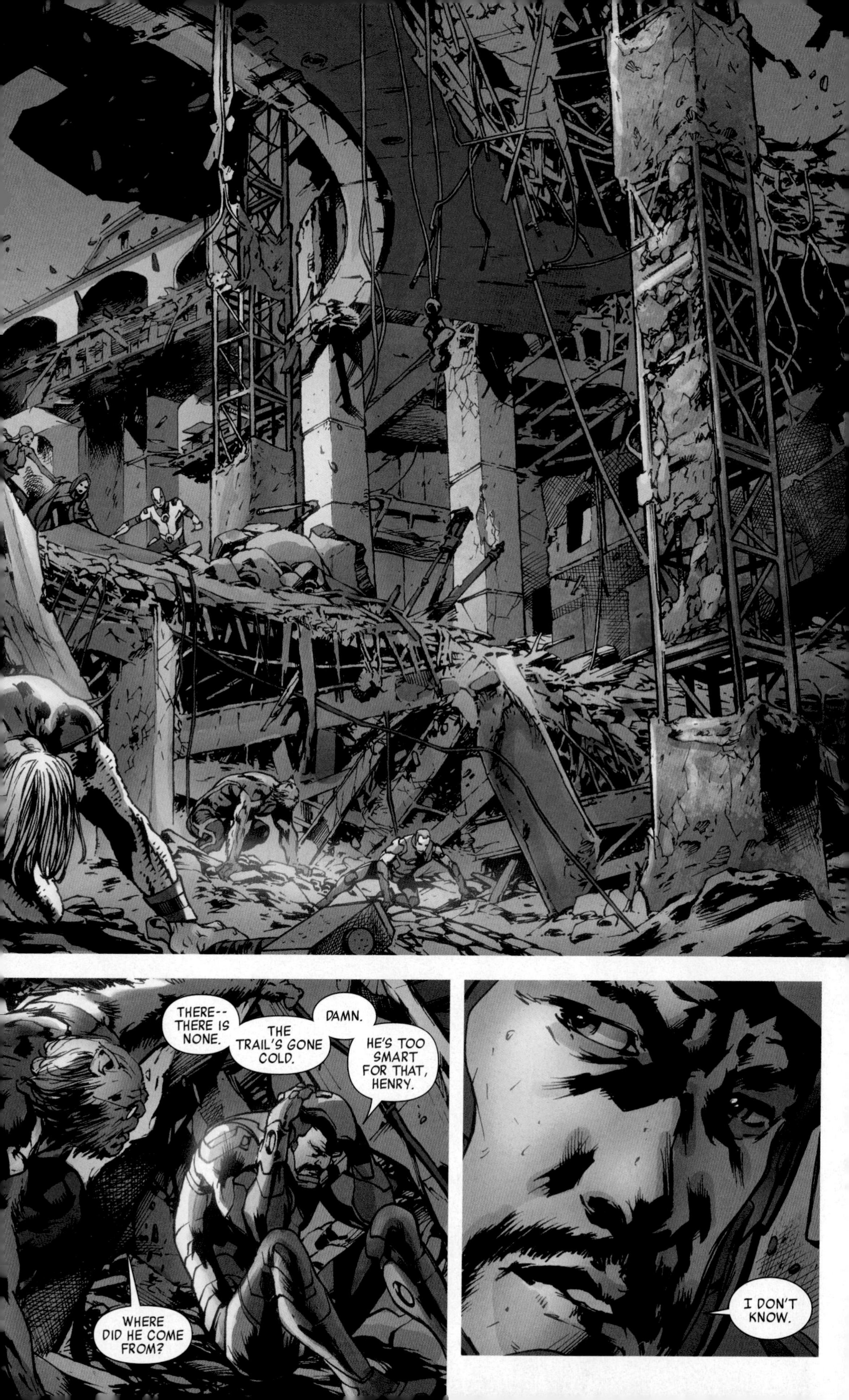
THERE-- THERE IS NONE.
THE TRAIL'S GONE COLD.
DAMN.
HE'S TOO SMART FOR THAT, HENRY.
WHERE DID HE COME FROM?
I DON'T KNOW.

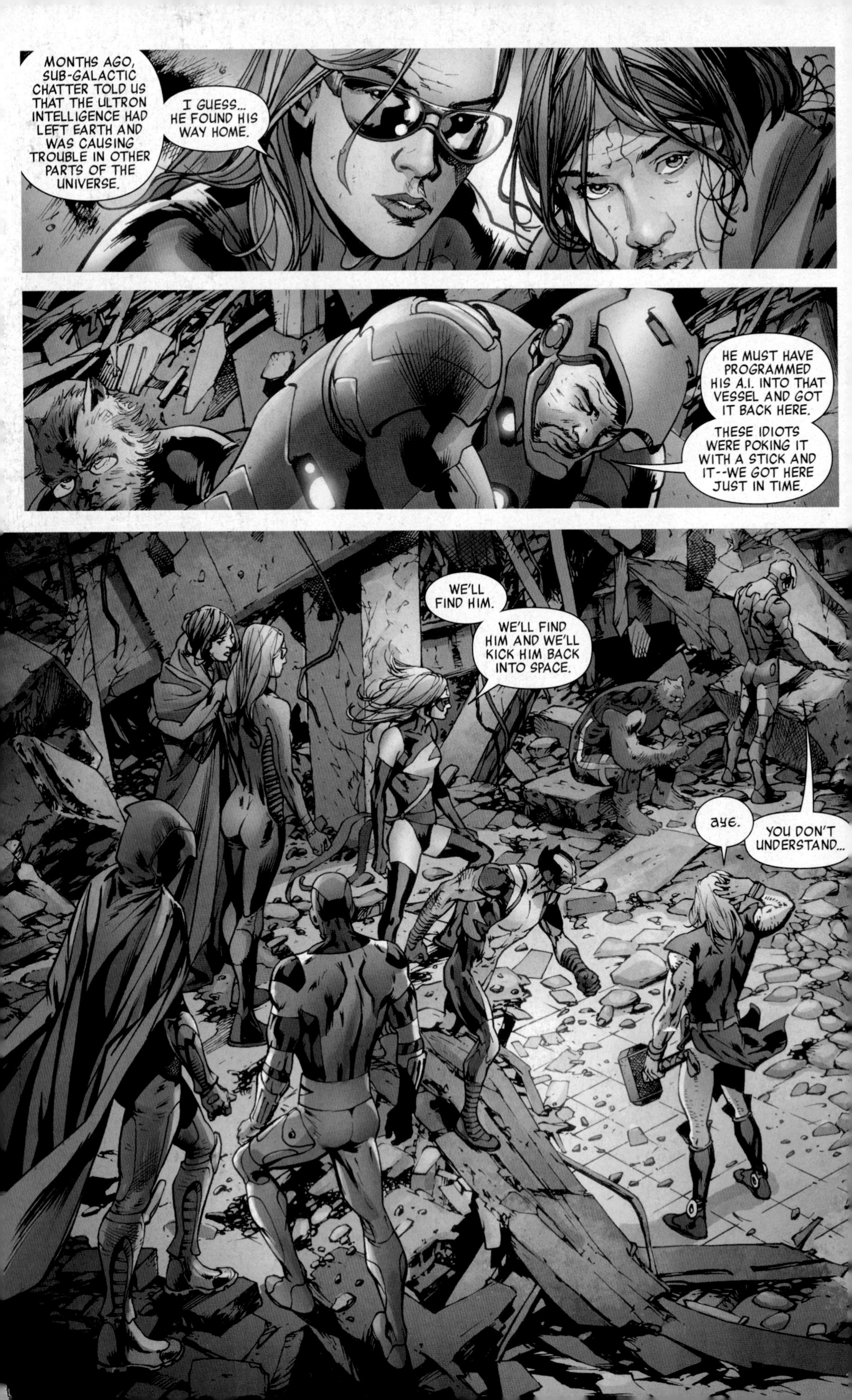
MONTHS AGO, SUB-GALACTIC CHATTER TOLD US THAT THE ULTRON INTELLIGENCE HAD LEFT EARTH AND WAS CAUSING TROUBLE IN OTHER PARTS OF THE UNIVERSE.
I GUESS... HE FOUND HIS WAY HOME.
HE MUST HAVE PROGRAMMED HIS A.I. INTO THAT VESSEL AND GOT IT BACK HERE.
THESE IDIOTS WERE POKING IT WITH A STICK AND IT--WE GOT HERE JUST IN TIME.
WE'LL FIND HIM.
WE'LL FIND HIM AND WE'LL KICK HIM BACK INTO SPACE.
aye.
YOU DON'T UNDERSTAND...

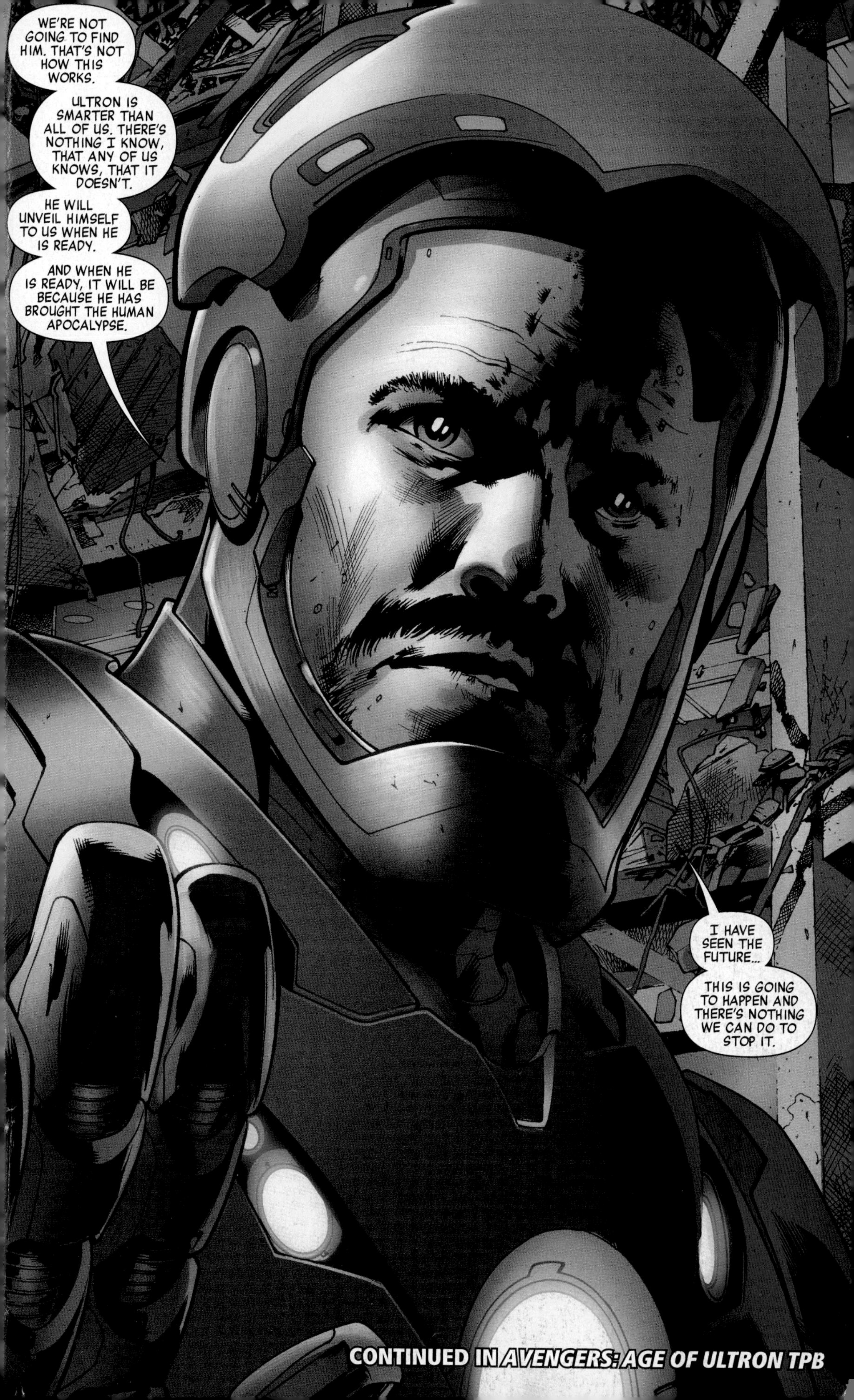
WE'RE NOT GOING TO FIND HIM. THAT'S NOT HOW THIS WORKS.
ULTRON IS SMARTER THAN ALL OF US. THERE'S NOTHING I KNOW, THAT ANY OF US KNOWS, THAT IT DOESN'T.
HE WILL UNVEIL HIMSELF TO US WHEN HE IS READY.
AND WHEN HE IS READY, IT WILL BE BECAUSE HE HAS BROUGHT THE HUMAN APOCALYPSE.
I HAVE SEEN THE FUTURE...
THIS IS GOING TO HAPPEN AND THERE'S NOTHING WE CAN DO TO STOP IT.

CONTINUED IN *AVENGERS: AGE OF ULTRON TPB*

STRATEGIC HOMELAND INTERVENTION ENFORCEMENT
LOGISTICS DIVISION